Forever Changed – Forever Loved

Jesus and His Intimate Love For You

A portion of the proceeds from each book will be sent to Central India to support a parachurch organization building spiritual unity among individuals and churches within their state and beyond.

Thank you to my dear friend and confidante Eric Olmstead from Peterborough Ontario Canada. A Holy Spirit led man used of God to encourage, pray, proof read and provide indispensable advice in completing this project. I thank God for the faithfulness he and Katherine have shared with our family since our inspiring days in bible college.
Much thanksgiving for the Heywood family, both Mike and Brenda who have a rare and blessed ability to see value beneath the surface and coax it out with love and kindness.

Forever Changed – Forever Loved

Jesus and His Intimate Love For You

A Devotional
by

ALEX G AUSTIN

ISBN-13: 9781475012989
ISBN-10: 1475012985

The Hebrew Greek Key Study Bible, 1984 AMG International Inc., compiled and edited by Spiros Zodhiates has been an invaluable resource. The study materials using original translations were invaluable in the study of intimacy with God.
Bible verses are taken from the New International Version with kind permission, as well as the King James Version.
High quality photo or canvas prints of the front and back cover pictures are available
alexgaustin@hotmail.com

Cover Design © 2012 David Austin, Rail Bend Studio

To Kathy my dear wife:
each and every day a joy and a privilege,
we have shared so many great times
David and Sarah
our greatest blessing

P R E F A C E

Welcome Dear Reader!

It is a privilege to join with you here on these pages!

Are you ready? As these pages unfold we are going on a journey together by the grace of God and the amazing Person of the Holy Spirit. He exists all the time everywhere - and therefore He is with you right now.
I hope for you to discover through Jesus Christ, how valuable you are. How precious you already are. What a treasure you are no matter where you are at in your life. No matter what you have done. No matter what you have failed to do. We all have these feelings.

You will find the book to be a 'whole' within itself. Each individual devotional follows as it should and they work together to help bring you a complete thought. An impression, if you will.
For this reason, even if there are challenges along the way, please continue reading. Some truths reach forward into other parts of the book and are more fully explained as you go along. It holds a unique quality in which the book knits itself together to uplift and encourage.

May I take a moment to explain how to get the most out of your reading time?

This devotional book has naturally occurring divisions. You may like to read one per day. You may feel encouraged to read many. It is really up to you and how you are feeling on that particular occasion. Write upon the pages if it inspires you. Here, there and everywhere. There are no rules!
Dates, impressions, observations, concerns and affirmations. All of these are extremely meaningful. That is because your life with your reactions, feelings and insights are extremely meaningful.

The contents of this book do not represent a new understanding of God and how to be a part of His loving plan in your life. As such, there is nothing remarkable about this book. As with similar writings, if you discover you are interested in spending time with Jesus, then this writing has served to point you to your greatest treasure.

You will find it encouraging to open these big pages, sit quietly and spend a little time getting to know God. It is published in this large format with your ease and comfort in mind.

Eternal love and joy and peace within your precious heart, Dear Reader.

Are you happy

in your love relationship
with God?

Saying, 'no' is okay
if that is how you feel.

Our Saviour says all those
who hunger and thirst after Him
shall be filled.

Being hungry and thirsty
is not a comfortable place to be.

But Jesus told us in the bible
if you hunger and thirst
after Him and His righteousness

then you shall be filled.

Jesus was able to make that statement as a fact
because He would offer Himself as the One
to fill your heart
with all the love you need.

Actually, He will fill your heart with Himself.

This occurs because He shares His life completely,
holding back nothing.

2

He is so vulnerable, so open and honest.

The bible word for the relationship He desires
is the same as a married couple share

in their deep

private
confidential relationship.

Intimacy shared by a couple
who love each other so much
they have to join together
in marriage.

Though this love is both unguarded and vulnerable,
its subtlety and nuance remains hidden
from all others.
No one else could know this secret love.
It is peculiar. They relate to no one else in this way.

It is a love held in highest esteem
by a Holy and trustworthy keeper.

3

He readily shares Himself with those who seek Him.

Jesus only asks for your willing surrender
equal to His own.

Jesus is very reliable in this regard,
but said if your commitment to Him
is not absolute
you are not worthy of Him.
You see,
He has high standards when it comes to surrender.
They are high but intentionally obtainable
by His own design.
He is an 'all or nothing' Person.

Jesus has put everything on the line for you
and He simply asks the same from you in return.

You experience the entire wealth of His saving and keeping love
but only if you are willing to forsake all other loves.

Living freely in wondrous joy,
He is completely true to you and responds lavishly
to your fidelity of heart.

What a kind and loving Saviour:
immediately seeing
your hunger and thirst;

rushing
to your aid;
more than willing
to answer your longing.
How wonderful Jesus is!
Jesus has the power and the will
to completely satisfy all those
who come unto Him.

4

Jesus said if you will ask Him to be your Lord and Saviour
then His Holy Spirit would be a spring of water inside of you.

He said after this you would never thirst again!

"Whoever believes in me, as Scripture has said, rivers of living water will flow from within them"
(John 7:38 New International Version).

Why would Jesus do this for you?

You have incredible value.

That is why He did this.

How much value? Well to start with you are created in His image.
So precious that there is no one else like you in all the world.
In fact, no one has ever lived on this earth that is like you.
No one else ever will.

God knew what He was doing when He made you
and He really liked what He did.
That is why He never made someone else like you.
It doesn't matter how you came to be –
there is only one of you.

'One'
of anything
makes it valuable beyond description.

God is thinking good thoughts about you all the time.

He thinks of you all day long.

He has more thoughts than the number of grains of sand
in all the beaches and all the deserts
found all over the earth.
So many thoughts. All the time thinking.
Each and every thought is a good one
about you.

With all of His kindness and good will
you would have to conclude
that this all-powerful God
would like to be your friend during the short time you inhabit this earth.

His plan for you very much includes a growing, dear and sweet friendship.

God made you so that you could be a friend unto Him
like no one else.

He is not taken up with all of creation.
All of that real estate, the houses, precious gems, gold, silver
and all the beauty found in nature
doesn't faze Him.

Imagine how special that makes you.

His focus is all about the here and now
and how the two of you are getting along.

I don't know if you noticed in an earlier statement,
but Jesus said he will come and fill you if you are hungry and thirsty.

He also said you would find him when you search for him with all our heart.

So if you are hungry and thirsty for his kingdom and his righteousness
and his Holy Spirit has come to live within
then why would you still be thirsty?
After all, He said you would never thirst again.

Your beloved Saviour speaks to you as to a sublime confidant.
You will love how He does that!

He is referring to your response in the total giving of Himself.
The stirring within your heart for someone choosing to love you absolutely –
even before you know they exist!
This makes you hungry and thirsty.
To experience this extraordinary love again and again.
To be conscious of His selfless vitality on your behalf and the longing
to have this love
more than anything else.

A few times in this life I have been in a place
where almost everything I valued was swept away.
A silly place where I could take hold of nothing
that would bring hope for a future
(except for my darling wife – always faithful,
always kind and always prayerful in my helpless estate).

Jesus Christ was so satisfying in that awkward time.
He would come to me and fill my inner being
completely and utterly.

He would love me,
accept me
and encourage my heart each day.

Through the tough times it slowly became apparent
that my ultimate need
was for His kindly friendship.
I could see it much more clearly when He freely lavished it
upon my aching heart in times of greatest need.

His kindness and faithfulness,
His gentleness and sincerity,
His power and perfection
provoked me to be alone with Him
more and more.

Jesus calls it 'hungry and thirsty.'

I think the greatest thing though, is how He inspires a love for ultimate truth
in the hearts of those who seek Him.

This is a good thing after all, for He says we are not able to be involved in a relationship with Him
through our own might or power.

"Not by might nor by power, but by my Spirit,' says the Lord Almighty" (Zechariah 4:6b).

Imagine being able to depend upon your beloved
for the ability to love Him
and to be susceptible to His love in return.

To know God,
to be devoted to this fellowship
you need so thoroughly,
to be 'ok' with helplessness.

The feeling of being a helpless person is not that great.
But having the grace to meet with God each day
on those terms is awesome.

In helplessness you have to depend upon Him for everything.
In time it is slowly illuminated within your heart
that your relationship is also
in His safe keeping.
You come to see
that no matter what happens
you are only growing closer.

"But when the kindness and love of God our Saviour appeared, he saved us, not because of
righteous things we had done, but because of his mercy. He saved us through the washing of
rebirth and renewal by the Holy Spirit, whom he poured out on us generously through Jesus Christ
our Saviour, so that, having been justified by his grace, we might become heirs having the hope of
eternal life" (Titus 3:4-7).

"for it is God who works in you to will and to act according to his good purpose."
(Philippians 2:13).

Once in a while when the dust settles and He enables you to perceive His plan is to sustain
this rapport with you indefinitely,

why,

there is no description for the mercy, security,
safety, honour, love,
support, power and astoundment
that gently materializes within one's grasp.
It is there for the taking.

Though it is Jesus who has taken hold of you
it almost appears that you have worked out an arrangement
and taken hold of Him in your time of need.
"The eternal God is your refuge, and underneath are the everlasting arms" (Deuteronomy 33:27a).

Jesus Christ will never leave nor forsake those sheep the Father has given Him.
The loving tie that binds Him to each sheep will be assailed
but always He prevails.

He is the faithful One. Never failing.
When you are aware that He has been looking after you . . .

He is pleased

with the delight you feel.

Jesus is the Word.

Jesus is the Truth.

Nothing gets by Him. He is the last say on everything.

Unfortunately there will be times when people
will beset themselves against you.

Accuse
accuse
accuse.

But one day
if they have not gotten right with God
and asked you to forgive them,

God will listen to their complaint and allow Himself
to be subjected to their accusations on your behalf –

but only one time.

"If the world hates you, keep in mind that it hated me first" (John 15:18).

They won't be able to go on and on for years and years like they do now.
Once.
Only once will God in His justice give them their say.

Then,
He will speak the truth.
Immediately
their whole world
and all its falsehood will vanish and likely be forgotten for all eternity.
As will they.

Forgotten.

The loving Holy Spirit will have you alert to pray at times
on behalf of your accusers
should they ever indicate a desire to make things right.

You will hope some day they will
for every person must one day make an answer to the Truth.
He loves His sheep and has given His life for them.

When you are in His care He sorts things out.

For some it will be now, for others it will be later but a day of reckoning awaits.

"Make every effort to enter through the narrow door, because many, I tell you, will try to enter and will not be able to. Once the owner of the house gets up and closes the door, you will stand outside knocking and pleading, 'Sir, open the door for us.' "But he will answer, 'I don't know you or where you come from.' "Then you will say, 'We ate and drank with you, and you taught in our streets.' "But he will reply, 'I don't know you or where you come from. Away from me, all you evildoers!' "There will be weeping there, and gnashing of teeth, when you see Abraham, Isaac and Jacob and all the prophets in the kingdom of God, but you yourselves thrown out. People will come from the east and west and north and south, and will take their places at the feast in the kingdom of God. Indeed there are those who are last who will be first, and first who will be last" (Lk. 13:24-30).

I love to spend time with Someone like this.

Jesus tells it like it is, and I find this so very helpful and refreshing because I am self-centered as a human being.

I want to see things from my own perspective.
I can't help but perceive events based upon the sensory awareness
wired into my earthly body.
I always need His help to see past my physical limitations.
He is the Truth, you see.

When we spend time together I have to wait awhile at first.
I am submerged in my own perceptions
about what is going on around my beloved family and me.

After a bit
His Holy Spirit has His way
and brings me around to His way of thinking.

The bible calls this 'having the mind of Christ'.
You can't have this mind
unless you spend time alone
with Jesus Christ Himself.

Spending time alone with Jesus really changes you.

This heritage for the followers of Jesus
goes way back to the original disciples.

When the highly intelligent, religious men could not figure out
what made these followers so supernatural and influential in their society
they could only observe,

"they have been with Jesus."

Have you . . . you know . . . have you been with Jesus?

His passion is all about being with you for all eternity!

Eternity is where no one needs to be saved.

Heaven is a place where people will see their Father's will
being done all the time.
Everyone will be acting the way they should.
No one will hurt another person accidently or on purpose.

For those spending eternity where Jesus is
there won't be a need for ministry to the poor.
Nor outreach to the sick or visitation to the grief stricken.
There will be no more death. No more sorrow and no more lies.
No one will have the desire to take advantage of you.
No one will have autonomy to decide how to treat you.
No one will want to take advantage of you
and no one will take advantage of you.

Everyone will live in the manner Jesus asks us to live here on earth – preferring one another.

Can you handle living forever in an atmosphere like that?

12

Some people don't want to help their fellow man.

They are content to choose their own way and decide right from wrong using their own standards
and values.

Freedom in the mind of others might mean,
'I don't answer to a higher power.'

Some folks set out on their journey and figure,
'As long as I don't hurt anybody'.
That was me when I rejected God at an early age
and chose to do my own thing.

How are you planning to live, without God? Write it in the space below if you desire.

" _____ "

Can you see that you have to make a decision
to enable God to prepare you for an eternity with Him?

Similarly Dear Reader,
are you aware that it is a conscious decision on your part
that prevents God from saving you
and blessing you in the afterlife?

When your journey with Jesus begins He changes you from the inside.

For me it felt like I had had a shower – only it was inside of me and I had become clean.

Pure, even.

"wash me, and I will be whiter than snow" (Psalm 51:7).

I walked around immediately feeling like a weight had been lifted off.
That weight that had a physical sense of heaviness

was my own sinful condition.

The weight of my own sin
even though I had set out to not hurt others and live in a good way.

My sinful past and all its effects. Things done by me
and things done to me.
Bad things that still bring sorrow, anger and sadness to this day.
I am so glad the Holy Spirit enables me to bring every single matter
to my heavenly Father. Though I have to return to Him over and over again,
each time He welcomes me. He knows I am helpless with these memories
without the power of His love and forgiveness.
Because of His mercy
I am a new creation! Old things have passed away!

"Therefore, if anyone is in Christ, he is a new creation; the old has gone, the new has come!"
(2 Corinthians 5:17).
"as far as the east is from the west, so far has he removed our transgressions from us"
(Psalm 103:12).
"For I will forgive their wickedness and will remember their sins no more" (Hebrews 8:12).

These issues, some grievous, are best left with God.
God is always in the business of sorting them out.
He always does what is right.
He always does it in the right timing.

He can be trusted with your past.

14

Do you have a friend?

Do you have a friend who is always there for you?

A friend who wants to be available when you feel like talking?
There are many times when a friend comforts you without saying a word.
Your friend is there . . . with you.

God places a premium on the relationship that brings people together.
While together they can talk, sit, listen, cry, laugh, or just be still.
If they are both listening . . . how are they communicating?
When alone with Jesus Christ,

being there with Him,

it all starts with listening.

He is there whenever you set aside time for Him.
His Holy Spirit will quiet your heart.
He will help you as you struggle with stillness.
He will faithfully guide, direct and acquaint you
with your Divine, supernatural Father.

"I will bring him near and he will come close to me - for who is he who will devote himself to be close to me?' declares the Lord" (Jeremiah 30:21a).

With God, it is important to want to listen to Him while alone together.
To begin with, He has to be respected.
The bible calls this 'reverence' and 'awe'.

He wants you to stand in awe of Him.

Therefore, since we are receiving a kingdom that cannot be shaken, let us be thankful, and so worship God acceptably with reverence and awe, for our "God is a consuming fire" (Hebrews 12:28-29).

15

If you were fortunate enough to have the personal attention of the creator and ruler of the whole universe . . . wouldn't you be sort of speechless at first?

Wouldn't there be a lot of respect?

Here is an example to help you grasp the magnitude of what it is like
when you get to spend time with Jesus Christ.

Let's say you received word . . . that the ruler of your country had gotten your name somehow.
You have been invited to go and meet with him or her. You are to be picked up by special
motorcade at your house and taken directly to a secure airport facility. You would then be escorted
onto a government jet and taken directly to the capital. Special vehicles and personnel would then
take you past security and onto the property of the capital building. Through the doors you follow.
Up the stairs and along the hallways you are taken until you are outside the door of the ruler's
office. You hear the muffled sound of his or her voice inside the office. Then you are told by the
personal assistant, 'go ahead, you may enter.'

Think.

How would that make you feel?
Would you be overwhelmed?
I mean, no one you know will ever get to do this.
No member of your family has ever done this.
For some reason, you were chosen to pay a visit with the ruler of your entire country.

What will you do?

Pay attention.
Show respect.
Be thankful and listen to this person who sits before you
carrying the responsibility of the entire country upon their shoulders.
And here you sit because they have set aside time in their day
to focus upon you.

I have amazing news for you.
A human Ruler or Politian is unable to save your soul.
Only Jesus the Son of God can do that.

Jesus wants you to spend time with Him.
Right now,
today.
Because today is the day of your salvation.

"For he says, "In the time of my favour I heard you, and in the day of salvation I helped you." I tell
you, now is the time of God's favour, now is the day of salvation" (2 Corinthians 6:2).

16

Is it worth it to take time for an audience with your own personal creator?

The things He could tell you!

I'll let you in on a great mystery,
He wants more than anything
for you to get to know Him personally - and . . .

He is very much in love with you.

You are number one on His list.
And He can't love you more than He does!

That is why Jesus Christ came to earth.
To make your relationship with Him possible.

The whole thing was because of His timeless love for you.

17

As the Truth He already has the final word on everything.

So it is very helpful to be still in His presence.
He is a wise and loving Shepherd.

He is ready for you to put your full trust in Him.

He has gone to much trouble
to invite you to a personal time with Him.
More than any world leader would ever have to.

It simply means a lot to Him for you to know:
He is going to be with you to the end of your days and all eternity.
Jesus is going to be with you now and for all eternity.

Fear not.
Do not be anxious.
God is with you.

Did I say 'God'?

Yes, that's right! _God_ is with you.

There is so much your merciful God shares with you.

It has been 30 years now since I came back to the Lord.

Turning away from Him early in life is another story altogether.
I truly regret the years I lived apart from Him. But He brought me back.
The time I lived away from His care was only about 8 years.
When I think of it now though, it seems so much longer.
It was unredeemed time. Time spent doing what I thought was right.
Funny how that is. It seemed right to me at the time but now I see it as dead time.
Lost years. They still remain in my memory - not yet swallowed up
by the 30 years since. I can remember those years.
The Lord has been careful to take away a sense of regret. He has shown me His perspective on this
and we have moved on together.

I still remember however,
the wonderful people that I have met. Talented, gifted people.
People that I pray for to this day.
People that I cherish.

I think I turned from God partly because I was unable to meet other people my own age
who knew Jesus. It was a mistake on my part to tell Him to leave my life. The truth is it goes back
to my own decision to leave God. It was my own responsibility and the sinfulness of my heart.
I am one of those lost sheep Jesus goes out to search for.

When Jesus reached out to me the second time I was on my own and far from where I grew up.
I was a sheep that had wandered.

When I was ready, He knew. He sent a wonderful lady tremendously in love with Him.
It's like He took the most special, best person He could and set her right there in my path.
She also was set in the path of many other young people too.
The lost sheep she reached were in local coffee shops, the swimming pool, the mall
and the place she taught school.
Jesus pursued me the day she came to the booth in the mall where I was selling cablevision
subscriptions. This peculiar lady had a walk with Jesus. She knew Jesus and Jesus would say He
knows her too. She asked me to a house prayer meeting and I couldn't refuse. Everything in me
wanted to find out what made her so different.
It was there, looking into those radiant faces that I decided I had to have what they had.
They were from many different churches in town but they had something in common.
Their faces glowed! These were clearly not ordinary people. They were different.
I discovered they had been saved. Born again. They had asked Jesus to forgive them
and had started on a journey of relationship with Him.

This was decidedly different than following do's and don'ts and showing up
on time in the correct attire.
They shared God's love with me in a home meeting.

I spent some time with them and because of this it changed my life forever.
I have not seen one of these dear people for decades for they live far away.

But Jesus has been with me every step since then.

19

When Jesus was on earth you could observe and get to meet Him in public places.

Markets, highways and byways.

The church leaders were busy in church.
Outside of church they were on the look out for transgressors
and condemned other church people for not obeying the law as they saw fit.

They weren't walking with God
so it is sad they missed out on how much He loved them.
They were unable to communicate true love to their fellow man.
They thought up a job description.
They were experts in the law.

Jesus love and miracles turned things upside down wherever He went.
He met people where they were at.
He welcomed them and was able to love them in their weakness, shortcomings and sinfulness.

He was moved by how much they needed Him.

20

The whole idea of a relationship with God is about being influenced by Him.

It is called obedience.

He is the potter. You are the clay in His hand.
You see, He calls 'you' the church now.
A 'building' is lifeless in and of itself. It is useful but it is no longer the church
because Jesus set up a new place for His Spirit to dwell.

He said His goal was to do away with a physical building as the place to come and meet with Him.
This 'Holy Spirit in you' means His kingdom is inside all people who believe and follow Jesus.

I love the Lord.

The Holy Spirit lives inside of me.

Do you love the Lord?
Isn't it great to consider and then give thanks
if His Holy Spirit resides inside of you too?
That means the kingdom of God is within you.
God no longer lives in a temple of canvas, brick or stone.

He lives inside His people.

21

People won't be led to find God in a building.

Even if it is really big, the right colour of carpet, high on a hill has the correct architecture
and has been there for centuries. He doesn't occupy an inanimate object any longer.
That practice ended when Jesus was raised from the dead.

People can encounter His kingdom through the wonder of His Holy Spirit dwelling in you.

"For where two or three gather in my name, there am I with them" (Matthew 18:20).

This verse is helpful because it says God in all His fullness meets with even a few people at a time.

People can't find buildings devoted to God where it is against the law to be a Christian.
But they can find out about a meeting held in secret.
Then they may choose to attend a gathering of the followers of Jesus wherever that may be.

In some parts of the world it is still possible for a building to be identified freely as a church.
Otherwise the gathering may take place
in a cave.
The cave is not the big thing.

Can you see it is the people inside that cave -
God's mercy and grace in individual hearts and lives gloriously shining forth His love?

Those who are forced to worship their God and find fellowship in a cave
don't at all
fall in love with that cave.

They sure look forward to seeing their brothers and sisters in the Lord again though
wherever that will take place.

I love my wife and family.

They love me right back.

Just now when I called them with video conferencing,
my son was on the screen large as life and my little daughter
would whip back and forth through the air behind him.

It was the first time we had used the video.

Why was she doing that?
I am so glad she did. I think she was letting me know that she was there,
celebrating life and glad we were in touch.

God is also glad, so glad when we set aside time to meet with Him face to face.
I am certain the degree of His joy is commensurate with the degree of His sacrifice
to bring us together with Him.

In this case it cost Him His Son.
The precious Son of God, Jesus Christ.
It means that much to our Father in heaven when we reach out to Him.
To see and to be seen. To listen and to be listened to.
To understand and to be understood.
If it would take a living sacrifice then He would do it.
Yes, His own Son.

Our heavenly Father would hear those words,
"Father why have you forsaken me?"
He would live with it.
He was willing to learn
to live with it.

I wonder if our heavenly Father has ever gotten over it.
Like the wounds in the hands of His Son from the nails that held Him to the cross,
our heavenly Father must have an unseen evidence of excruciating pain
when the sins of the world were placed upon His Son.

To this day He loves His Son so much.

"He is the atoning sacrifice for our sins, and not only for ours but also for the sins of the whole world" (1 John 2:2).

On the other side of those words people would be drawn to God
and introduced to His love forever.
People who would do anything to spend time with Him.

Jesus loves you too
even though it cost Him His life.
No, He didn't love you too much. That is because you were worth every drop of blood,
the crown of thorns, the whipping and scourging.

He only went through it once because that was all that was needed.
But He would do it again
just for you.
Would you like to be taken into His arms right now?
He is right there with you. Full of joy

waiting.

23

There is an assurance God creates in your heart while spending time right there with Him.

Often it does not come right away.

You have to wait 5, 10, 20 minutes sometimes.
It is like being on the phone with someone you are close to.
You communicate together (listening - talking - listening - talking) for an extended period of time.
Do you notice toward the end of the call you get into the more serious topics.
Heart topics.
Things you may only share with this one person.
Like you have to sort through a host of mundane things
to re-establish rapport,
the sense of safety and familiarity
and then
you easily slide into topics that are more personal,
deeper.

I have had the privilege certainly less then a handful of times
to communicate with a friend who says,
'I am telling you things I've never shared with anyone else.'
Astonishing.

Breathtaking.

My friend.

That is what I find anyway.
It is also like that in God's presence. Neat eh?

Often while sitting quietly in His presence
much time will pass and it feels like the whole idea
of spending time with God
is not going to happen.
In the mean time,
people come to mind who are in need.
Situations are brought into your understanding and the Holy Spirit
has you observe and agree with Him in what He wants to do.
Things move along

and there it is

that sudden feeling of peace, love and joy in the Holy Ghost.
God has been there all along.
He is the creator, the Higher Power.
He had a plan for your time together after all!

Oh my!
It is good to reverence God and stand in awe of Him!
What wisdom to be still,
to wait upon the Lord
while spending time with Him.

Oh the confidence you can have in Him that He will always do the right thing
when you are with Him.
He loves
you
so.
Trust Him.
Wait there in His presence. He will always do the right thing when you are together.
Be thankful.

"Enter his gates with thanksgiving and his courts with praise; give thanks to him and praise his
name" (Psalm 100:4).

24

There is nothing you need to do to get God to love you.

That is an astonishing reality.

Even more so if you are in God's care.

He will mercifully remind you

from time to time

throughout your life.

The same Jesus who taught people in person
will select times and places to teach you
about this and other things
to help you.

Stop.

Stop right there.

Stop doing good as if God will love you more for doing it.
Doesn't God love people who do good?

Dear friend, God loves people before they even know Him!

Great mercy and love make it possible for any person to receive Him.
Young and old. Child or adult.
Male or female. Educated or uneducated.
Successful or not. Healthy or infirm.
Rich or poor. Popular or not.
Fashionable or not.
Everyone.

Everybody that believes in Jesus and accepts Him does so when they are sinners
and have no relationship with Him.

He instantaneously forgives and transforms the human heart.
It is a free gift given directly from God.

25

There is no such thing as a favourite.

We are all His favourites - once we receive forgiveness and salvation from Jesus Christ who is God.
Can you imagine how hard the devil and his angels are working to prevent this from happening?

But nothing can stop Love. Oh Hallelujah!

Light is not hidden by darkness. Light always overcomes darkness.
There is no power that can prevent the Light from shining
and the Love from invading a human heart.
You accept Jesus Christ; you believe in Him, you ask Him to come into your heart and life
and you will be born again.
No longer sitting alone in darkness.
In the very next second if you were to tragically die
you would be in heaven!
This is how God's miraculous saving power changed the life
of one of the criminals
who hung on a cross alongside Jesus.

"One of the criminals who hung there hurled insults at him: "Aren't you the Christ? Save yourself and us!" But the other criminal rebuked him. "Don't you fear God," he said, "since you are under the same sentence? We are punished justly, for we are getting what our deeds deserve. But this man has done nothing wrong." Then he said, "Jesus, remember me when you come into your kingdom." Jesus answered him, "I tell you the truth, today you will be with me in paradise" (Luke 23:39-43).

This is the power of God's love.

No good deed you have done has given you this new birth.
You believed in Jesus Christ and asked Him into your heart and life
and you received a free gift right away without having to do any good thing.

He is so into forgiveness. You can't miss with Jesus Christ.
If you sincerely ask,
He immediately forgives.

"At one time we too were foolish, disobedient, deceived and enslaved by all kinds of passions and pleasures. We lived in malice and envy, being hated and hating one another. But when the kindness and love of God our Saviour appeared, he saved us, not because of righteous things we had done, but because of his mercy. He saved us through the washing of rebirth and renewal by the Holy Spirit, whom he poured out on us generously through Jesus Christ our Saviour, so that, having been justified by his grace, we might become heirs having the hope of eternal life" (Titus 3:3-7).

26

There are people who are so wounded

so broken
so damaged
so disenfranchised
so abused so hurt

so

without hope

so alone.

For a moment
can you see if the Lord would have you pray on behalf of these precious lives?
You don't have to know their names.
Lift them up to Jesus.

If you feel so in need yourself
and you can't barely stand it . . .
you need to know
people are praying for you
as you read this.
Neat eh?
Let Jesus bring His healing and love into your life.
He is the Way, the Truth and the Life.
He is waiting for you to invite Him into your heart.

It is a short devotional today.

There is a lot of time left for you to be loved and to love in return as you see fit.

27

God has a 'camera' pointed in your direction.

That is to say, He keeps track of you dear one.
His eye is upon you and He looks to and fro throughout the land
for those who would seek Him and know Him.

"The eyes of the Lord range throughout the earth to strengthen those whose hearts are fully
committed to him" (2 Chronicles 16:9a).

That is because there is only one of you in all the world.

You are special.

If you want to belong to Him
then He is taking care of you around the clock.
When you don't think He cares
oh yes He is there.

He is with you right now.
But this isn't like a surveillance camera.
It is more like a baby monitor.
Like the interest a mother or father has in the welfare of their new child.
Only, God's interest never wanes. All the time He is there with you.
He knows all about you but only because He cares.
He never fails
and will always work things out for your good.

"And we know that in all things God works for the good of those who love him, who have been called according to his purpose" (Romans 8:28).

These things we have talked about so far
are somewhat general understandings about our great God.
Do you hunger for deeper truth?

I haven't got any for you.

After 30 years only one truth has become more dear
than any other.
I can only tell you that God loves you.

He does not save a person according to their accomplishments.
His salvation (saving love) is a gift you never need to earn.
He thinks good thoughts about you all the time.

He only asks for obedience and His purpose is within your grasp so that you are able
to do what He has planned for you.

I just looked over what we have so far in today's devotion and imagined how easy
it would be to completely write off this information!
It sounds too extreme. It is so general.

It sounds removed from reality to say that God can love everyone
and is able to forgive any sin no matter how big it looks to us.
It sounds fanciful and unrealistic to declare that God desires a deep walk of intimacy
with all of His children.

"Now what I am commanding you today is not too difficult for you or beyond your reach"
(Deuteronomy 30:11).

It will only get better from here on Dear Reader.
You are destined to walk with God in a deep, intimate love.

May you find comfort and rest this day in Jesus.

That is how great your God is.

There is room for everyone.

You are really asking in your heart how a love like this can exist.
You are desperate to know if you might somehow fit into this great love
and still retain your individuality.

Today you can just ask Him to enable you
to fulfil His purpose for your life.
Ask God to enable you
to be obedient to all that He has called you to.

Now to finish off for today,

the reason we do not need to earn this love from God
is because Jesus has already satisfied God's righteous demands
in regard to your sin condition.

That is why He is so important to you though you may not be aware of it.

When you walk with Jesus He faithfully brings you back to the reality
that your calling is fulfilled
through your friendship with Him.

"I want to know Christ and the power of his resurrection and the fellowship of sharing in his sufferings, becoming like him in his death," (Philippians 3:10).

Over and over again He has comforted my heart
in the midst of circumstances that are out of my control.

Situations go sideways and it seems I have failed the Lord
when my expectations are unmet.
My fears give way to the reality that He has become my salvation all over again.
I am free as He reminds me that He has become my salvation.
I am saved not by anything I do but because Jesus lives
and what He has done for me.
I am safe in His care.

He just loves me.

"I sought the Lord, and he answered me; he delivered me from all my fears" (Psalm 34:4).

"I will give you thanks, for you answered me; you have become my salvation" (Psalm 118:21).
"The Lord is my strength and my song; he has become my salvation. He is my God, and I will praise him, my father's God, and I will exalt him" (Exodus 15:2).

29

He already took care of the price of your eternal salvation in the short time He was on the earth.

Specifically when He died on the cross and was raised from the dead.

It was at that precise time Someone loved you enough to give their life for you.
Now is the time to receive that freedom and walk in that love.

I wonder sometimes if I can be loved enough by God.
Is there something that somehow makes me not entirely loved by God?

Once when I was feeling this way, He broke in on my thoughts.
Quietly I heard these words inside.
Methodically, with subtlety and passion, "I have loved you with an everlasting love."
He then helped me understand He was communicating to me the quality of His love.
Who could say their love for you is everlasting
                                        but God.

Remember the people who are meeting in a cave somewhere in the world right now to fellowship and worship God? They are ordinary people like you and me.
But they have been saved and now live in a new reality based upon the love God has for them.
They are desperately poor and some have even lost all of their possessions, family and loved ones.
After counting the cost they have chosen to follow Jesus. The only One with an everlasting love.
It is worth even the loss of all things to have Jesus love.

Since it is unsafe to meet out in the open they gather together to meet with God
where it is safe to do so. It is not safe in their country because it is against the law
but they meet together anyway.
That is because God's love is more important to them than their own life.

His loving kindness is better than life.

"Because your love is better than life, my lips will glorify you" (Psalm 63:3).

30

Today I want to convey to you how glad I am that we have worked through the daily devotions up to this point!
We are becoming acquainted to some degree.

I am glad if you and I have invited the Lord Jesus to join our times together.
If you are not ready to ask Jesus to come into your heart and save you,
would you please still continue
with each daily devotional?

How are you doing so far?
What we are discussing together
is moving us into an understanding
of what you do after being saved by Jesus Christ.
It is written,

"Salvation is found in no one else, for there is no other name under heaven given to men by which
we must be saved" (Acts 4:12).

Pretty straight forward eh?
If you do not know you are saved
(believe in Jesus Christ and received forgiveness of your sins through Him)
then you are not saved.
But once you are saved,
how do you live for God?
How do you even begin to be a holy person
and please God and keep from legitimately offending others
because you are, 'a new creature in Christ Jesus'?

"Therefore, if anyone is in Christ, he is a new creation; the old has gone, the new has come!"
(2 Corinthians 5:17).

It is not complicated.
There are no hoops to jump through.

And this long preamble is not meant to scare you off.
It isn't setting you up for this big, huge answer.
Truth be told, it is not a new insight either.

You can get this same information from any person on earth that is walking in a love relationship
with Jesus.

31

With the freedoms we enjoy here in North America it has given opportunity for many to identify
themselves as a person who follows after the Lord.

It doesn't normally cost anything to walk right down Main Street and be seen with a bible in hand.
In many countries you would be thrown in jail or disappear without explanation.

Some countries empower their citizens to take the life of a suspected Christian right on the spot. A brother from a country such as this told me if you are seen with a bible the common practice is to set upon the individual with a sword hacking them to bits - before carrying on with the day's business. Their national religion encourages this practice. In North America this is not something for which we take precautions.

Myself, I am very thankful to serve the God of love. The God of forgiveness. My God's name is Jesus Christ. He is the Spirit of God made manifest in the flesh.

In North America it is no big deal if your car is observed in a church parking lot. We seldom have a church meeting disrupted by gun wielding individuals who take people out and shoot them without any recrimination like I've heard it told.
Telling someone you are a Christian or being seen with people who are known Christians is a wonderful blessing for which we are thankful. It is a normal part of life to have the privilege to meet with a brother or sister in the Lord whenever we want to.

Still, there are few who know Jesus on a one to one basis.

I believe the ratio is one in ten identifying themselves as believing in Jesus who actually know Him. This is called a remnant.

The other nine know about Him just as we know our National Ruler.
We know who the Ruler is.
We know where they live and what they look like.
What they do, what they say
and we can legitimately claim to live under their rule.

Ah,
but because we don't spend time alone with our national ruler

we don't
know
them.

If we said to the Ruler, "Greetings, I know you!"
They would have to say without any malice whatsoever,
"I'm sorry, I don't know you. We have never had the opportunity to meet and spend some time together."

One can answer in this manner and still be a loving person.

I don't want Jesus to say that to me one day.
After all, there is no other Saviour given among men
whereby we must be saved.

"Jesus. I know you. Sure I do! I have done many wonderful things in your name! I have gone to church all my life! "

Jesus who cannot lie responds, "I don't know you."

32

The main content we shall explore together concerns how surely you can count on God to take care of you if you choose to surrender everything to Him.

The way He skilfully nurtures and guides the desire in your heart to find your rest in Him.

'Man' will always add on to your simple need for friendship with Jesus.
You will be told you must do this, and that.
Pray this way or that way.
But Jesus is pleased
when you receive Him

and spend the rest of our life getting to know Him.

"One thing I ask of the Lord, this is what I seek; that I may dwell in the house of the Lord all the days of my life, to gaze upon the beauty of the Lord and to seek him in his temple." (Psalm 27:4).

"One thing I ask of the Lord and seek...
all the days of my life...
to gaze upon the beauty of the Lord
and to seek Him in His temple."

David, who wrote this Psalm, was simple and resolute.

There really isn't anything else to do as a lover of God.
A relationship with God is the only measure of your spirituality.
A relationship with God is the measure of your faith.
A relationship with God is the measure of your love for mankind.
A relationship fulfills the heart of God.

It is all to do with His love that sets you free from the law of sin and death.
One other thing.
Notice this passionate arrangement
is lived out only between

David

and God.

That will bode well for David because the only Person
he answers to at the end of his life will be God.

His life will remain fruitful because the only Person He is pleasing . . . is God.

"But now a righteousness from God, apart from law, has been made known, to which the Law and
the Prophets testify. This righteousness from God comes through faith in Jesus Christ to all who
believe. There is no difference, for all have sinned and fall short of the glory of God, and are
justified freely by his grace through the redemption that came by Christ Jesus" (Romans 3:21-24).

33

Out of this relationship He leads you in the pursuits you were created for.

Little or large, the consequence of your labours will be pleasing to Him and they shall abide
forever.

You will be doing what you were created for
and fulfilling the works He prepared in advance for you to do.
That makes you very special.
It means He can count on you.

"but those who hope [wait] in the Lord will renew their strength. They will soar on wings like
eagles; they will run and not grow weary, they will walk and not be faint" (Isaiah 40:31).

Waiting upon the Lord must come before the work of the Lord.

Don't just do things for God and hope He will bless it.
Don't assume He is pleased because it is done in a building set aside for His use -
even if the building

is really, really big.

Even if you ask Him to bless it in prayer and in Jesus name,
if it is not out of obedience to God you are praying in vain.
Your labour will be in vain and your work will count for nothing.

34

He comes alongside and enables you to be a worshiper.

It is God that enables you to be an obedient servant of His.

To love others. To love yourself.

To accept others who are different,
to accept the things you don't understand,
to forgive others
and to forgive yourself.
To be patient while He sorts out evil people,
situations
and those who have wronged you or a loved one.
It is God that will always remain with you as your very best friend.

All the days of your life.

Isn't this a lot more meaningful than working at getting better
at keeping the law?
The law being the things we do because we think it makes us more acceptable to God.

He will be there when you are poorly treated
and turn those experiences around for your good every time.

"and we know that all things work together for good to them that love God, to them who are the called according to his purpose" (Romans 8:28).

35

He will open doors and sometimes close doors.

This refers to opportunities or new circumstances.

Each one is called a 'door'.
Through difficulties and mysteries you will have an all-knowing Friend.

You are in a great adventure of faith.
It is all possible because God already loves you.

"You, dear children, are from God and have overcome them, because the one who is in you is greater than the one who is in the world" (1 John 4:4).

This verse will be a comfort to those with a religious leader who has been
making uncomfortable demands of you.
Deep inside you can admit that something isn't right
but haven't been able to put your finger on why.
You have been challenged by other people to fulfil conditions and terms
in order for God to love you
when God already does love you
right now.

All the love He will ever have for you -
He wants to give unto you each and every day!

Jesus went through enough for you. He only had to do it once.
The death and resurrection fulfilled your debt of sin to God.
You are on the other side of obligation - you are in the realm of forgiveness.

Get alone with Jesus.
Let Him sort things out with you. Let Him sort things out for you.

"Let all ye that labour and are heavy laden come unto Me and I will give you rest" (Matthew 11:28).

Jesus Christ said that.

Praise His Holy name! Even your family members and friends can see through
the bondage of 'religion' you have been put in.
Now is the time to get free.

"So if the Son sets you free, you will be free indeed" (John 8:36).

36

I can't take your hand today.

Though I love you in the Lord.

But God can take you into His loving arms.

"The eternal God is thy refuge, and underneath are the everlasting arms" (Deuteronomy 33:27a).

This verse is always new.
Always fresh.

In the arrival of each new day
His arms are gathered round about you.

"The eternal God is your refuge, and underneath are the everlasting arms" (Deuteronomy 33:27a).

He is committed to you.
Because He is Almighty power, He is also committed to your success.

For most of the time I have been given the grace and mercy to be a follower of Jesus,
I never gave thought to the second part of this verse in Deuteronomy.
I plain didn't know there was a second part.

"For the eternal God is thy refuge, and underneath are the everlasting arms,"
I would recall with a great sense of comfort.
The Lord would send His word to my heart and He would comfort me.

One day I looked up the verse.
It turned out there is more after that first part.
It says,

"and he shall thrust out the enemy from before thee;
and shall say, Destroy them" (Deuteronomy 33:27b).

Ouch.

"Everlasting arms",
"your refuge".
I used to love those words
and I still do.

All those years I would wonder aloud in conversation with my dear wife,
'why is the Holy Spirit making me aware of uncomfortable and dark insights
about people and the world around us? I am not looking for this kind of information.
I am coming to God to learn of Him and love Him.'
My wife is a good listener.

Oh how my dear wife loves me.

From the very start of our relationship people would attack our marriage or my reputation.
Gut wrenching insights in the lives of others would rock my sensibilities. Around every corner
there was adultery, uncleanness, idolatry, gossip, the spirit of Jezebel at work in the church.
People torn apart, addictions and broken hearts, broken families and folks with no hope or help.

I was just seeking a love relationship with God!
Why am I seemingly confronted with so much darkness at the same time?

The quiet place of seeking God
is precisely where these unseemly insights
were being thrust out before me.

As a follower of Jesus
you are held in those arms of God at all times.
He is your refuge.
That's because your good works can never be a refuge.
Counting upon your ability to do good -
that's not a refuge either.

Ever had a health set-back? A time when you are unable to do any normal activity you used to do? You will know what I am talking about here.

Good health is not a refuge.
On two different occasions
I was flat on my back for months and sidelined for five plus years in total.
I could not take comfort in my works.
I had no works.

My darling wife who looked after me -
she had all the works! I would not be here without her.

"I thank you God for my dear wife."

Those who follow Jesus are in need of His protection. They are an offense to the enemies of God.

So, while you are continuously being held safely there,
"He shall thrust out the enemy from before thee."
He does this because it is His nature.
He will protect you, deliver you from evil and defeat it.

Exodus 14:14 says, "The Lord will fight for you." The second part says, "you need only to be still" (New International Version).

37

How are you today?

It matters to God.

It matters very much.

Won't you please
take time to be still before Him - even if things rage around you?

"When thou passest through the waters, I will be with thee; and through the rivers, they shall not overflow thee; when thou walkest through the fire, thou shalt not be burned; neither shall the flame kindle itself upon thee" (Isaiah 43:2 King James Version).

If you are in the arms of God you shall have tribulation.

But there is comfort, fellowship and intimacy with your God
when you spend time alone with Him.

Some people who go to church feel they are exactly what God wants them to be because:
they go to church,
don't make waves,
do what they are told
and they are not aware of any tribulation or persecution in their life.

The religious thinking is that you have problems
if you need to get right with God.
Once you figure out how to do the 'Christian thing'
then everything will work out the way it should.

"Many are the afflictions of the righteous: but the Lord delivereth him out of them all."
(Psalm 34:19).

When God is making you aware of those who are against you,
when God is showing you the hidden needs of those around you,
when God thrusts out the evil before you -
keep on setting aside time to be with your faithful friend Jesus every day.
Let His loving arms bring comfort to you.

Don't stay away from Jesus because you have troubles.
Trouble comes
but not because you have done something wrong
or because something has changed between you and God.
This is most certain if you have kept up your daily fellowship with Him.
God has not changed.
He is looking after you through the tribulation.

He is looking after you in the tribulation.

"In fact, everyone who wants to live a godly life in Christ Jesus will be persecuted,"
(2 Timothy 3:12 New International Version).
"These things I have spoken unto you, that in me ye might have peace. In the world ye shall have
tribulation: but be of good cheer; I have overcome the world" (John 16:33 KJV).

Because Jesus has overcome the world we are to be of good cheer.

38

To bring an encouragement to your heart. This is really the purpose of this writing.

It is meant to be an encouragement for you to get alone with God every day.

This one thing is the very heart of the plan Jesus has for your life.

"The name of the Lord is a strong tower; the righteous runneth into it, and is safe" (Proverbs 18:10).

Folks who seek a god of convenience would interpret this verse to say,
'some of the righteous run into it and are safe',
or 'it is for some but I don't need to go in all the time,'
or 'I will decide when it is time to run in.'

For some it is time to seek God when there is serious trouble.

We have invited our children to become a friend of God.
Each day we come to God together. They also spend time alone with God each day.
They find it helpful overall and have become familiar with His presence,
companionship and kindness.

Inevitably there are times in life when there is trouble.
How comforting it is for their little souls to run to someone they are familiar with!
They already know they are welcomed.
They don't have to invest their time convincing God how much they love Him.
They don't have to seek forgiveness for not seeking out His fellowship
for days and weeks prior.
There is a knowing, one of another.
It is a blessed place. Their very own refuge.
A safe place to run and hide.

I don't know the number of times they have sought the Lord, safely tucked in alone at night
just before going to sleep. The precious and blessed times when they have poured out their little
hearts to the One always there to listen.

The God with no favourites.
The God who freely and generously gives them the fullness of His wisdom.

At one time the bible says Jesus prayed for His Holy Ghost to be with them and in them.
Making them strong,
mighty,
full of faith,
vanquishing fear and laying waste to their enemies.

Yah! Go Jesus! Dear God look after my little ones, you terrible, awesome, Almighty, All powerful,
Glorious Saviour of the WORLD! What about that Jesus!

"You are my hiding place; you will protect me from trouble and surround me with songs of
deliverance" (Psalm 32:7 New International Version).

A friend seeks companionship at all times.

There are those who never spend time with the Lord,
or do so only on special days,
or do so when they are in big trouble.

Meanwhile their life is passing by

day by day

and all the while
there is a host of people passionately in love with God
who would not think to let a day pass without getting alone with God.

"For you have been my refuge, a strong tower against the foe" (Psalm 61:3).
"The name of the Lord is a strong tower; the righteous run to it and are safe" (Proverbs 18:10).

It is important to note that the only opportunity to exercise your free will
and make the choice to be alone with God is in the life you are living
right now.
It is your ultimate expression of love toward God.

After this life,
after this one short window of time has passed,
this expression of your love is no longer available
nor will it be relevant.

Only now can you prioritize,
make the choice,
and go aside.

If you are going to draw near to God this is the time.

Jesus often spent time alone with His Father while He was here on earth.
You can do it! You can make the choice!
Jesus is waiting for you.

There are many people all over the world
right now
enjoying His fellowship.

What a thrill to join with them.

A refuge is a safe place.

It is only useful if you leave where you are and make your way into it.
You move from one place to another.

If you stay right where you are
you will miss out on the safety of your refuge.
In a disaster people run for safety.
Running to God enables Him to quickly become the refuge you need.

"God is with me all the time." some will say,
consciously choosing not to avail themselves
of the intimacy they were born to inhabit.
They would be offended at the notion that God is not constantly following them around
and influencing their life when they snap their religious finger because they believe He will.
Just like that! 'In Jesus name.'

Remember when it mentioned there are many people to whom Jesus will say,
'I don't know you.'
This kind of thinking mistakenly feels that intimacy with God
is the product of what they have learned about faith.
They are offended by the notion that they are not in step with God.
A God they never spend time with.
A God they don't know,
but seem to know a lot about.

Their sacrifice for Him is most pleasing in their own sight.

Why should we have to spend time with God when He wants us to anyway?!
Martha was all about this notion.
Jesus loved Martha
but Jesus had to step in
when Martha started to verbally abuse her sister.
Mary was sitting right there at the time.
She could hear what Martha was saying about her. How rude and hurtful of Martha.
All the while thinking she was actually helping Jesus
while her stinging words were tearing apart her own sister.

It wasn't Martha; it was Mary who was doing the right thing.
Who said so? Jesus said so.
Jesus - said - so.
We'll talk about that later on, okay?

The story of Mary and Martha helps us understand what Jesus thinks
about spending time with Him.

A relationship with God though, means you seek fellowship with Him.
That is different than trying to convince Jesus
you are doing what you are supposed to do
and believing for what you are supposed to believe for.
I've been there too.

It was early on in my adventure of faith. I moved on from telling Jesus what He was going to do
for me after my best efforts to get Him to keep me from wearing glasses. Later on my wife agreed
it was a good idea to get Laser surgery when I was involved in film work for a few years.

If you are going to be intimate with the Lord Jesus Christ
you have to put yourself in a position of trust.

A time and place where you are able to be still.
An unguarded place where the two of you can communicate
in an unstructured manner.
In this blessed experience, when you present yourself to a Holy God -

you are humbling yourself.

Part of that experience of humbling yourself is to wait upon Him according to His timetable.
Drawing near to Him where you are able to listen to Him
just like you want Him to listen to you.

This is a huge act of trust.
Being willing to listen to what the Master wants to say to you
about anything He wants to.
Going to God daily no matter what,
means you consider Him to be trustworthy. A safe refuge.

That is why you 'run' to Him consistently.

41

Here is a truth: no one who has experienced a lifestyle of daily fellowship with God
has any problem with it.

No one.

You will never find anyone who says it is unnecessary to spend time alone with Jesus
once they have entrusted themselves to their loving Saviour in this way.

You will never hear them say,
'go do your own thing and ask Jesus to bless it.'

That is what King Saul did.

He figured the leading and blessing of God in the past meant he no longer
needed to get alone with God to hear from Him. Didn't need to receive
the instruction he needed for himself and the nation that very moment.
Right after that God was done with him.

Nobody serves God adequately
who is not devoted to Him first
in the place of intimate fellowship.
Sorry you busy Martha's out there...

At some point Jesus will need to step in and have a word with you just like He did
on behalf of Mary. Right now I invite you to stop trusting in your works.
Start spending intimate time with Jesus and enjoy the favour that Mary had.

42

God has prepared for your salvation.

His Son the Lord Jesus Christ has taken the initiative to reach out and save you because He first
loved you. You are encouraged afterward to trust Him.

"And it shall be said in that day, Lo, this is our God; we have waited for him, and he will save us:
this is the Lord; we have waited for him, we will be glad and rejoice in his salvation" (Isaiah 25:9).

All followers of Jesus are saved but not because there is a special secret
or ability to get through the trials of life.
It is because of
His so great
salvation.
"The Lord is my strength and song, and is become my salvation" (Psalm 118:14).

"But the salvation of the righteous is of the Lord; he is their strength in the time of trouble"
(Psalm 37:39).

In difficulties you find Him to be your only refuge.
How wonderful to have a Person to turn to
no matter what befalls you.

There is a solution that lifts you above your circumstances.

There is a remedy that lifts you up above your own human nature
and transforms you beyond all other means.

When trying to decide what made the disciples of Jesus so different the overseers of the day
could point to only one dynamic they all had in common.
"Now when they saw the boldness of Peter and John, and perceived that they were unlearned and
ignorant men, they marvelled; and they took knowledge of them,

that they had been with Jesus" (Acts 4:13).

The same Jesus is able to spend time with you right now
if you want to.

43

It is hard to understand why God would go to all this trouble just to have a relationship
with you, me and every other person on the planet.

Why would God care about the pedophile?

Why would God care about the lover of money?
Why would God care about the poor,
the hungry, the insane, the depressed,
the manic, the religious, the hypocrites,
the murderers, the kind, the nurturing,
the loving, the abortionist, the aborted,
the drunk driver, the incontinent,
the victim, the less intelligent
and the philosopher.

When you look at humanity
and what we are generally capable of,
one would wonder why He cares about any of us at all?

When you follow Jesus
His Holy Spirit will work within
to ever broaden your understanding
of this love.
To grow in the knowledge
of His love is to be involved
in the very center of His plan
for your life.
It is God's work in you
that you may know this love.

Each day the power of God
more fully acquaints you
with your own phenomenal value
and the unsearchable value
of those around you.
Can you handle that?
What a great relief that the Lord has become your salvation!

He is waiting to spend time with you today. Let me step aside.

We can meet again tomorrow.

44

How difficult would it be if we had to measure the degree we love others?

Our nature has us look around and perhaps think how great someone else is at loving people
or doing God's will.

When we hear or see
what others do in Jesus name
we may rejoice or maybe
feel our own expression of love
is somewhat paltry in comparison.

Broken hearted people easily assume they could 'love' better,
or they are not able to love
as well as another.

Whew.

Thank God. The measure of true love
rests in the intimate times alone with your loving Saviour Himself!
That is because you have no control over how others will respond to your walk with God.
And you are unable to control everything that happens in your world.

His loving welcome and embrace
becomes the ultimate reflection of your self worth.
His unconditional acceptance lifts the human heart with gentleness and truth.

It is an all encompassing approval that registers deep within the human heart and it can't be found
anywhere else. Jesus sets you free from trying to work hard enough to please Him.

It is God's grace - not our ability - that enables us to abide in His love.

45

He nurtures His supernatural love for the people in your life and provides timely wisdom
in what to do about it.
It is never about 'how much' we can do.

His death and resurrection
has given you a free gift
and you are forever free from being justified by your works.

"For by grace are ye saved through faith; and that not of yourselves: it is the gift of God: Not of
works, lest any man should boast" (Ephesians 2:8-9 King James Version).

'Jesus. I am free through your Holy Name and through your precious blood shed on the cross for
me. Let me look unto you for love's sake. I need not concern myself with how to please you. You
love me already, loving me before I believed. Now that I am yours, use me as you have planned
before you made the earth. I will find this purpose because I am seeking you. Growing clearer and
brighter to me in Your mercy and this sweet fellowship with You each day.'

46

It is about Jesus Christ, His love for you and the wisdom in Him that guides you to live as a born
again, supernatural, Spirit-led child of His - now forever in His care.

You have received His heart when you received Jesus as Saviour of your soul.

"The man (person) without the Spirit does not accept the things that come from the Spirit of God,
for they are foolishness to him, and he cannot understand them, because they are spiritually
discerned. The spiritual man makes judgments about all things, but he himself is not subject to any
man's judgment: "For who has known the mind of the Lord that he may instruct him?" But we have
the mind of Christ" (1 Corinthians 2:14 - 16 New International Version).

Your love for Him compels you to be obedient and available - as He leads you.
This becomes His manifestation of love through you
to the world around you.

He builds His kingdom with the greatest power in the universe -
the awesome power of His love.
And love abides forever.
The kingdom of God is within you.
The gates of Hell cannot prevail against you.

"Neither shall they say, Lo here! or, lo there! for, behold, the kingdom of God is within you"
(Luke 17:21).

"And I tell you that you are Peter, and on this rock I will build my church, and the gates of Hades will not overcome it" (Matthew 16:18).

47

Let's look at what the bible says about the role of wisdom and understanding.

Because of their importance in your walk with Jesus Christ, here are all nine verses of Proverbs 4.

"Listen, my sons, to a father's instruction; pay attention and gain understanding. I give you sound learning, so do not forsake my teaching. For I too was a son to my father, still tender, and cherished by my mother. Then he taught me, and he said to me, "Take hold of my words with all your heart; keep my commands, and you will live. Get wisdom, get understanding; do not forget my words or turn away from them. Do not forsake wisdom, and she will protect you; love her, and she will watch over you. The beginning of wisdom is this: Get wisdom. Though it cost all you have, get understanding. Cherish her, and she will exalt you; embrace her, and she will honour you. She will give you a garland to grace your head and present you with a glorious crown" (Proverbs 4:1-9).

Wow.

Wisdom and understanding.

In Jesus wisdom ever flows on your behalf.

Seeking wisdom
is a joyful part of faith in God.
I praise God for His wisdom.
His wisdom is always with you.
How hard is it
to get this wisdom dear reader?

"If any of you lacks wisdom, he should ask God, who gives generously to all without finding fault, and it will be given to him" (James 1:5).

There is a 'place' always available to you. The place of wisdom.
It is your own personal refuge where wisdom abounds unto you.

All you have to do is ask for it.

Wisdom will define you
if you devote yourself to spending time with Jesus.
That is wisdom.

In all ways and in all things Jesus is your life.

"Jesus answered, 'I am the way and the truth and the life. No man comes to the Father except through me" (John 14:6).
"It is because of him (your Heavenly Father) that you are in Christ Jesus, who has become for us wisdom from God - that is, our righteousness, holiness and redemption" (1 Corinthians 1:30).

Where is wisdom?
Jesus has become your salvation:
wisdom; righteousness; sanctification; and redemption.
At the same time Jesus also became unto you wisdom.
Oh great is His holy name!

Where is . . . your life itself?
The answer is astonishing,
for Jesus Christ really is your everything.

"Salvation is found in no one else, for there is no other name under heaven given to men by which we must be saved" (Acts 4:12).

48

"For you died, and your life is now hidden with Christ in God" (Colossians 3:3).

Friend, if your life is hidden you will never be able to find it.

If you look for something that is hidden you search everywhere but in vain.

Humble yourself,

set your priorities around your time alone with God.
You will find your life where it is hidden - with Christ in God.
Oh dear reader how He loves you!
You are the apple of His eye.

So precious are you right there in that prison cell,
in that comfy chair of yours,
that cold dirt floor,
in front of your computer,
looking at your smart phone,
in the coffee shop,
on that airplane flight,
all alone and crying,
in that car
or in that waiting room.
Jesus loves you.

Be still for He is already pleased with you.

"Be still and know that I am God: I will be exalted among the heathen, I will be exalted in the earth." (Psalm 46:10).

You know, He will be exalted.

Let's be still for He already is exalted and desires your listening ear more than anything else you will give Him.

49

"For I know the plans I have for you," declares the Lord, "plans to prosper you and not to harm you, plans to give you hope and a future" (Jer. 29:11).

How merciful and revealing about the heart of God - already having plans to make you a success.

In His eyes you are a success already!

Imagine telling someone they have already won their race
when they are positioned at the starting blocks!

"To him who is able to keep you from falling and to present you before his glorious presence without fault and with great joy - to the only God our Saviour be glory, majesty, power and authority, through Jesus Christ our Lord, before all ages, now and forevermore! Amen." (Jude 1:24-25).

He comes right out
and tells you - 'find your life in me.'
It is true that your life is hidden there.
When you look where something is,
you find it - right?

Oh Hallelujah and Amen!

50

"For we are God's workmanship, created in Christ Jesus to do good works, which God prepared in advance for us to do" (Eph. 2:10).

God has already established your works.

Where are they?
They are prepared in advance by Jesus so that you can walk in them.

Among the followers of Jesus we are working together,
encouraging one another in the works prepared in advance by Jesus.

How great are these works?

Oh my God!
Don't you just love this Son of God right now?
Friend, have you ever felt less than adequate in your service to God?
We are a people called to learn of His love! That is our mandate.
We are not indentured servants heaped with duties.
Yours is a daily quest revealed in your own heart.

Deeper.
Higher.
Longer.
Wider.
This love of God
has no end.
Indeed it surpasses knowledge.

"Jesus sat down opposite the place where the offerings were put and watched the crowd putting
their money into the temple treasury. Many rich people threw in large amounts. But a poor widow
came and put in two very small copper coins, worth only a fraction of a penny. Calling his disciples
to him, Jesus said, "I tell you the truth, this poor widow has put more into the treasury than all the
others. They all gave out of their wealth; but she, out of her poverty, put in everything - all she has
to live on" " (Mark 12:41-44).

How could Jesus be pleased with the widow's offering?
How could the widow herself be pleased with this offering - if indeed she was measuring it
with all the other offerings that had gone before her.
It was miniscule in comparison with the offerings of the other devotees.

Everyone was showing up at church. Now it was offering time.
Even Jesus was there.
He arranged His busy schedule around the time the widow was to arrive
and make her offering. Jesus Christ came to church that day because she would be there.
He did so because of the pleasure it would be unto Him.

Jesus Christ, the Spirit of God made manifest in the flesh, was there waiting for her to arrive.
If Jesus Christ shows up at church

it is a big deal!

For the most part, on that day it appears not much was happening.

We are seeing that you cannot outwardly scrutinize your works, activities or purpose in life as the measure of your eternal value in the eyes of God.
Else, the widow would really be the least important person at church that day.

When you see your entire purpose in life as God's workmanship
to bring you into daily communion with Him,
then it is a whole new perspective.

This widow,
so highly valued in the eyes of God,
brought a loving, devoted heart to church that day
and was met by her dear Love in return.
Her joy would be meeting with Him.
Her offering was a pure and devoted heart unto her Master, Jesus.

"The sacrifices of God are a broken spirit; a broken and contrite heart," (Psalm 51:17a,b).

God as a 'Person' had become her salvation. His name is Jesus.

She offered what she could,
and loved Jesus Christ with all she had.

51

Many who love God can't give a lot of finance.

The wisdom to serve God with next to nothing can't be found in a book.

It can't be found listening to excellent teaching.
It can't be found on TV or in meetings.
In your relationship with God you will find your own personal leading.
A sheep cared for by One Shepherd.
It will fit nicely within the historical principals of great biblical teaching.

Lots of people apply prudent and timely financial principals - both believers and non-believers.
Few people are led by the Holy Spirit as they apply the principals found in the bible.

You can know about the Lord, allow yourself to be identified with Him and do the things
that successfully manage money but still miss His heart for the people in your life
and His plan for yours.

The widow did not miss the plan of God for her life. Out of the abundance of her heart she gave
already knowing God would be pleased. Out of the abundance of her heart she gave what she had.
The overflow from her heart did not look like much. God was pleased anyway.

It is a terrible temptation to honour and show favour to church members when they heap cash
on the collection plate week after week. It is so tempting to want to make them a leader, a deacon,
a teacher, an elder or whatever they want to be
just to keep them happy - and contributing.

Please pray for God to be able to appoint the people of His choice for positions of responsibility
in the Christian church. Do the wealthy not know they might be ascending in their responsibilities
due to evil thoughts on their behalf?

It is sad when evil thoughts are directed toward any human being.

When a leader appoints a rich person to a position of leadership and trust because of their money
than that leader has judged with evil thoughts toward that generous giver!

"My brothers, as believers in our glorious Lord Jesus Christ, don't show favouritism. Suppose a man
comes into your meeting wearing a gold ring and fine clothes, and a poor man in shabby clothes
also comes in. If you show special attention to the man wearing fine clothes and say, "Here's a good
seat for you," but say to the poor man, "You stand there" or "Sit on the floor by my feet," have you
not discriminated among yourselves and become judges with evil thoughts?" (James 2:1 - 4).

52

His loving purpose is available to all who would seek Him.

He will gladly share His heart with anyone.
Remember the list of people we had earlier on when we asked
if God would love the vast number of people bound and blinded in their sin?

If you spend time alone with Him you will cross over into an experience
of personal, intimate fellowship.
This experience is available right now,
for everyone.

You see, Jesus wants to meet with you and it is not based on how good you are
or whether you deserve His kindness or not!

"But because of his great love for us, God, who is rich in mercy, made us alive with Christ even
when we were dead in transgressions - it is by grace you have been saved. And God raised us up
with Christ and seated us with him in the heavenly realms in Christ Jesus, in order that in the
coming ages he might show the incomparable riches of his grace, expressed in his kindness to us in
Christ Jesus. For it is by grace you have been saved, through faith - and this not from yourselves, it
is the gift of God - not by works, so that no one can boast" (Ephesians 2:4-9).

You will know the Lord but in a different way than just knowing 'about' Him.

Do you see the difference?

In the wondrous experience of fellowship (alone with Him) He somehow enables you
to grasp a little more how wide, long, high and deep His love is for you -
and for others.

His love is multi dimensional, multi faceted.
A reality no one could ever study enough or sort out using the faculty of the human mind
or with any amount of human effort. If a person could arrive at this based upon his or her own
efforts, it would greatly limit the number of people who could walk with God and share His love.

God reveals Himself as a loving Friend in His own way and in His own timing
to everyone who seeks Him.

"You will seek me and find me when you seek me with all your heart" (Jeremiah 29:13).

Remember, it is your daily fellowship that He came to earth to establish.

He is not here to measure your love for Him as if it were a sporting event.

53

Let's look at the fantastic prayer in Ephesians!

Contained in here is the statement that His love 'surpasses knowledge.'

That is like saying,
don't even try to find it in books or with your own power.
It is not that kind of love. A love we measure and therefore compare with others.
Don't even 'compare' it to what you read about Jesus and what He did.
Just love Him.
Spend time with Him.
He created you

for that reason.
To become your friend in deed.
Someone you choose above all others as your refuge
and your gentle companion who is also able to forgive your sins.

"I pray that out of his glorious riches he may strengthen you with power through his Spirit in your
inner being, so that Christ may dwell in your hearts through faith. And I pray that you, being
rooted and established in love, may have power, together with all the saints, to grasp how wide and
long and high and deep is the love of Christ, and to know this love that surpasses knowledge - that
you may be filled to the measure of all the fullness of God" (Ephesians 3:16-19).

The person who wrote this letter to the Ephesians was praying for God's power
to be working inside of the followers of Jesus. Wouldn't that be something?
To have the power of God
working inside your heart!
Like, are we talking about something miraculous?

Jesus is a supernatural God. To this day He raises the dead back to life again.

In His holy name demons are cast out, bound and repelled.

"And these signs will accompany those who believe: In my name they will drive out demons;"
(Mark 16:17a).
"I have given you authority to trample on snakes and scorpions and to overcome all the power of
the enemy; nothing will harm you" (Luke 10:19).

54

There is a desire in the heart of God to bless you.

It is a blessing no other person on earth can have.

God your heavenly Father
wants to bless you with a healthy,
supernatural,

exclusive,

love-relationship with Him. He will share Himself with you.
It will be unlike any other relationship He has.
It is intimate
because it takes place when the two of you are alone.
When you are alone with your spouse and you love each other,
you speak to one another uniquely.

Consider being at a gathering with other people. The time passes; you might eat a little, have
something to drink, move from room to room and visit with this person or that. Then you leave
and are on your way walking or whatever, and begin to speak to your beloved
without anyone else on hand to hear you.
It is an entirely different kind of conversation.
Unguarded.
Without pretence.
The topics are different. You will probably talk about your feelings.
You might share concerns about individuals at the gathering you just left.
You might confer about an observation you share for someone or something.

You socialize in gatherings just like this when you are at church, a 'home meeting' or with Christian friends. God is there it is true. But so are other people and you are not alone with Jesus Christ your best friend. The idea that you and God will communicate like a loving couple in the midst of a crowd of people is not reasonable nor is it possible.

God is always with you it is true.
God is able to speak to you in any circumstance it is also true.
But consider in all practicality, we would become embarrassed if a couple began to share intimate information in the midst of a crowd where others would clearly hear them. We might even be tempted to strain our ear to try and pick up what they are saying. Something would twinge in us and we would automatically know this kind of conversation is strictly private.

I am referring here
to being as close as possible to Jesus Christ the only Son of God.
An intimate relationship
and how to nurture and maintain it.

It is based upon communication
just as with a natural husband and wife.

"Husbands, love your wives, just as Christ loved the church and gave himself up for her to make her holy, cleansing her by washing with water through the word, and to present her to himself as a radiant church, without stain or wrinkle or any other blemish, but holy and blameless. In this same way, husbands ought to love their wives as their own bodies. He who loves his wife loves himself. After all, no one ever hated his own body, but he feeds and cares for it, just as Christ does the church - for we are members of his body. "For this reason a man will leave his father and mother and be united to his wife, and the two will become one flesh." This is a profound mystery - but I am talking about Christ and the church. However, each one of you also must love his wife as he loves himself and the wife must respect her husband." (Ephesians 5:25-32).

55

Getting alone with the One you love brings the privacy and honesty of heart that is central to intimacy.

In an unguarded and safe place with your true love you feast in the absence of appearances and pretence.
Each participant in the relationship can just be themselves.
You can luxuriate in the freedom of sitting quietly together
because it brings such joy.
You each feel so very fortunate to have found each other and you are filled with exhilaration over what you share with one another.
You intuitively know that no one else knows what it is like when the two of you are together!

Would anything quite please a girl's heart except for her fiancé to make time just for her? To listen to her about any topic of her choice . . . for any length of time she desires to dwell upon it? Or a groom-to-be who's beloved says, 'you and I are going to get together tonight. I miss you all day long. There is no one I love more than you. I am finding it so difficult to wait until we are married. Let's get together tonight just you and me.'

This is a portrait of a happily engaged couple on their way to getting married.

People in love spend time alone talking with one another.
They will choose to be with each other ahead of any other friend,
any other family member,
any other obligation.

All of it comes second place to the love of their life.

56

God can speak to you like He did to the multitudes that loved to follow Him and listened to His teaching.

But Jesus was very candid and admitted that He was openly enticing them, wanting to draw them into fellowship.

He said to truly follow Him it was more than an outward observance or following rules.
Showing up at His meetings wasn't good enough.
Think of it.

They left their jobs. 'Sorry boss, even if it means my job, this may be my only opportunity to hear the teachings of my Master. I will risk you firing me, but I must follow Jesus while I can over the next few days. Who knows when He will be back in the area?'
So said the wife or husband willing to risk a backlash.
The officials, students and their teachers, tradesmen and shopkeepers.
Each who followed Jesus left without food and the money to buy some on the way. It must have been a spontaneous expression of devotion. They risked being rejected for their faith, persecuted for being identified with Jesus Christ and were willing to suffer the consequences.
They up and left - some with their ears ringing at the sound of criticism,
rejection and misunderstanding.
Their hearts may have longed for loved ones to join them.

Some may have known they would have no home, job, family or friends to return to.
They would leave; risk it, just to be near Jesus Christ and to hear Him teach first hand.

"Jesus answered, "Very truly I tell you, you are looking for me, not because you saw the signs I performed but because you ate the loaves and had your fill" (John 6:26).

How could people be willing to give up so much to identify with Jesus Christ,
yet still be deprived of a personal fellowship with Him? He was not able to identify these devoted
listeners as members of His family. He bluntly said, 'you follow Me because I give you food to eat.'
Jesus came to give us life. There is no Life except in the Son of God.

Church attendance is excellent, but it is not the same as coming to Jesus personally.

57

Jesus invites you to come to Him that He would be the very bread of heaven you need to have
eternal life.

There is no life in what you do in our own strength.
Ah, but there is Life in Him. Life eternal.

"Then Jesus declared, "I am the bread of life. Whoever comes to me will never go hungry, and
whoever believes in me will never be thirsty" (John 6:35).
"All those the Father gives me will come to me and whoever comes to me I will never drive away"
(John 6:37).

Do not fear the consequences of coming to Jesus.
Those who come will find the comfort, forgiveness, help,
understanding and intimacy they are starved for.

Remember earlier on, when we said that no one who has ever devoted themselves to daily,
intimate fellowship with God would consider it optional?

Jesus keeps those who seek Him.

Jesus' favour rests upon those who seek Him.

Power and purpose and life eternal belong to those who seek Him.
Those who seek Him each day will be delivered from fear as often as is needed. Oh glory!
The helpless will find their refuge and the forsaken will be received.

And dear one, you will find your resting place when you feast each day on the Bread of Life.

58

Who is able to remain alive if they eat the bread they need only once or twice
or every once in a while?

How can you be alive if you never prioritise and return to eat that bread and satisfy your daily,
hourly, normal hunger?

You will become skinny, malnourished, and sickly and eventually die.
Jesus talks about the basic human need for food to alert you to how integral intimate fellowship is for spiritual life. For some, it can mean the difference between physical life and death.

"The thief [Satan and his demons] comes only to steal and kill and destroy; I have come that they may have life, and have it to the full" (John 10:10).

Jesus is the Bread of Life. Those who come to Him have been given to Him by the Father.
Just as with the bread or natural food that sustains us on earth,
Jesus is not talking about 'coming to Him' as an infrequent arrangement of convenience.
Coming to God and believing on Him is a daily, life-altering experience.
It is as necessary as consuming the bread you need to keep you alive on a daily basis.
Only, Jesus is the heavenly bread sent by God the Father. Bread you need every day.
He even compares Himself with the manna God sent from heaven to sustain His people
in the Old Testament. He said that bread was important because it kept them alive
and was given by the very hand of God.
Jesus Christ piped up and said it was only keeping their natural body alive for one more day!
He boldly told them He was offered to them as a gift from God.
They may once again receive their daily Bread and by Him have Life eternal.
Coming to Him daily to be kept alive just as they did with the natural manna.

"And this is the will of him who sent me, that I shall lose none of all those he has given me, but raise them up at the last day. For my Father's will is that everyone who looks to the Son and believes in him shall have eternal life, and I will raise them up at the last day" (John 6:39-40).

Jesus Christ will be able to raise you up if you are alive in Him!
Those who are alive in Him have availed themselves of the gift of Bread God sent from heaven.
The precious, wonderful, magnificent Son of God.
His name is Jesus. He is God.

He has come for you Dear Reader.

59

Jesus did not come to introduce humanity to a lifestyle choice.
There are many people in the world right now with no freedom to make a lifestyle choice.
Remember Jesus Christ said He is the Way the Truth and the Life?
The people whom the Father has given come to Him?

The people who left everything to see Jesus, hear Him teach and enjoy free picnic meals
were revelling in the here and now.
They had adjusted their lifestyle in a religious manner.
They did what they needed to do to be near Jesus.
To outwardly follow Jesus.

But in His everlasting love and mercy Jesus said they could 'see' their redemption
but they were not entering in.
They were hearing about redemption but declining an invitation offered by Jesus Christ Himself.
They believed Jesus was the Bread of Life but avoided the intimacy with Him.
He was Bread but they were leaving Him on the shelf.

He began to teach once more and open up about the 'true' followers and worshipers.

The true followers are intimately involved with the One they had believed,
received as Saviour chose to spend time with
and listen to.
The One as relevant as the food they eat.

The understanding is like going into your refuge, sitting down and taking the time needed
to consume an entire meal. Do you see the wisdom of your loving Saviour
comparing Himself to a commodity that must be eaten?
He made this reference to food on purpose.

"I love Jesus. I am a follower of Jesus," one might proclaim.
But do you spend time with Him that you may know Him?
Has He become the Bread of Life to you, or do you follow Him outwardly with great crowds
of people? Never getting to know Him, never taking time to be alone with Him,
never finding out what He wants to tell you personally.

Now is your opportunity!
Come to Jesus. Be with Him. Delight Him by giving Him time alone with you.

"Therefore, there is now no condemnation for those who are in Christ Jesus, because through
Christ Jesus the law of the Spirit of life set me free from the law of sin and death" (Romans 8:1).

You have your freedom.

Exercise it
by having a passionate, overflowing personal relationship with the Son of God.

Be known by others because of the love of Jesus in your life,
not because you use the name of Jesus in your life.
Be known by others because you love as Jesus loves,
not because you have strong beliefs and talk lots about Jesus.
Most of us conclude that Jesus is with someone when they are able to talk or preach about Him
in a very loud continuous voice. Actually, it all goes back to Jesus being the Bread of Life.

Loud people are just . . . loud.

If Jesus only needed religious, outwardly capable followers then what of the cripple, the poor, the children and the elderly?
The infirm in mind and body?
Those forbidden through political means or withheld by circumstances beyond their control - like the flesh and blood family they are born into or where they live.

People with limitations of this sort would have been deprived of the privilege of leaving town to hear Jesus teach when He passed through.
They would be totally out of luck.

They don't have the power
nor influence
nor pedigree
nor offerings
to keep up with those who 'truly love the Lord'?

No friend!
These abilities and opportunities are not needed to be a follower of Jesus Christ!

The message is for all who would receive Him!
Here is a mystery. It is still that way today.
Jesus is still not looking for greatness.

Jesus is looking for love.

He is looking to give love,
and receive your love.

His lovers are fed in the quiet, alone place. Where deep friends are open and honest.
They are keen to listen to one another.

Don't you love Jesus and love to be with Him? Just you and Him.

He is waiting for that time with you today.

He loves you.

He loves you with an everlasting love.

You are His precious one.

Who starts a day and considers which meal they will leave out?

Is supper optional tonight?

For some, 3 meals a day is a given.
For some, it will be 2 meals.
For others, just one.
Others hope to have something but can't be sure.

But when it comes to food, if it is there we eat it.

Jesus said
His followers come to Him as their Bread and their drink.
The fundamentals needed to sustain . . . Life!
People the heavenly Father gives to Jesus
come to Jesus.

They do it without questioning because they discover on their own that they need to.
They go aside,
spending time with their bible, a personal writing journal and all the time Jesus requires of them.

They do so because in Him is the Way and the Truth and the Life.
Salvation is found in no other name.
Not in what you wear,
the day you worship or how you worship,
your hairstyle,
your financial status,
who you know
or
how long you have been going to church.

D o   y o u   k n o w   H i m ?
If you have not spent time with Him can you really say you know Him?
You are in need of the only Bread God has given among men whereby we must be saved.

Whoa! What of the countless thousands and thousands
that do meet with Him each day?
Join along with them.
Join with your Saviour.

He longs to become your food and drink, your Bread and Wine.

As Jesus and his disciples were on their way, he came to a village where a woman named Martha opened her home to him. She had a sister called Mary, who sat at the Lord's feet listening to what he said. But Martha was distracted by all the preparations that had to be made. She came to him and asked, "Lord, don't you care that my sister has left me to do the work by myself? Tell her to help me!" "Martha, Martha," the Lord answered, "you are worried and upset about many things, but only one thing is needed. Mary has chosen what is better, and it will not be taken away from her" (Luke 10:38-42).

1. ONLY ONE THING IS NEEDED.
To be with Jesus on your own, listening to what He says to you.
Mary sat quiet and alone with Jesus.
Martha was busy with the preparations.

2. MARY HAS CHOSEN WHAT IS BETTER.
There were many things to do. Mary took it upon herself to simply sit at the feet of her Master.
She made a choice. She chose not to do other things in exchange for alone time with Jesus.
She had intimate fellowship with Jesus as a result of her own choice.

3. IT WILL NEVER BE TAKEN AWAY FROM HER.
Have you ever lost someone or something most precious to you?
When you had it, it was everything to you. Necessary in your life.
Dear Reader, every minute you spend with Jesus will remain with you forever.
You will not ever lose the times you have been together. Imagine how wonderful that is.

It is possible to be in the perfect will of God and lose your health, your wealth, your loved ones, your reputation, your fame, your career, your investments, your house or lands, your possessions.
You can possibly lose anything in this life.
All of this has happened to me. All of it.

It happens all the time to Christians who live in a country where there is open persecution.

The times you spend with Jesus
you
will
never
lose.

This time you are about to spend with Jesus after your reading today.
You will never lose that time. What a comfort. What a comfort that is.

It is apparent from this story of Mary and Martha, that the Lord Jesus did not want his followers to consider their own personal efforts as equivalent to intimacy with Him.

Doing things for Jesus or in Jesus name is not the same as intimacy with Jesus.

The people who left all to walk with Jesus when He was in town and enjoy His teaching were technically, 'followers'.

They were passionate and happy.
They were sustained.
They were fellowshipping with one another - apparently in agreement and getting along fine.
They were sitting in a group listening to the Saviour of the world.
Nobody was stirring up any trouble.
Could it get any better than this?
Jesus says emphatically, "yes".
He shows mankind that we can get closer yet.
He compares this kind of closeness to the unique role of motherhood in nature.

"O Jerusalem, Jerusalem, you who kill the prophets and stone those sent to you, how often I have longed to gather your children together, as a hen gathers her chicks under her wings, but you were not willing" (Matthew 23:37).

"I have longed . . . as a hen gathers her chicks under her wings."

A first impression of this verse is how close Jesus wanted everyone to be with Him.
The chicks are not supposed to be running around showing their mother how much they love her! Those little chicks naturally go to the safest place they know. They go to Momma! They run to her and she hides every one of them. They leave it up to her to take care of them and in they go. Straight away!

The heart of God for you dear one is so poured-out with compassion.
Jesus said He longs to love His people exactly like the example of a mother hen.

Which of the chicks needs to offer an explanation or seek permission to take refuge with their mother hen? Are they not all allowed to run in under those feathers, allowed to come in as close as is possible? What kind of love is this that your heavenly Father has for you?

"See what great love the Father has lavished on us, that we should be called children of God! And that is what we are! The reason the world does not know us is that it did not know him"
(1 John 3:1).

In the Old Testament, before the death and resurrection of Jesus Christ, offerings and sacrifices were crucial works of obedience. There were specific acts of obedience to be made by the High Priest. Only the High Priest could make that offering and only the High Priest could be in direct contact with God in the section of the temple called the Holy of Holies.

When Jesus Christ - the Spirit of God made manifest in the flesh - obeyed His Father to offer Himself unto death the need for outward religious sacrifices ended.
This sacred obedience of God's Son unto death on a cross only needed to be offered one time.

Now, the invitation of God to all mankind is, "whosoever will may come" with the compassion and fervency of a mother hen to her little chicks.

64

"As a hen gathers her chicks under her wings."

There is room for every last one of those chicks to be safe with mother!

The invitation given by Jesus Christ to receive refuge and intimacy is offered
out of His vast heart of love.
That is all a mother hen has for her chicks!
This is all Jesus is looking for in His followers.

Like the mother hen, all the chicks need to do is respond to the call and refuge is freely given.
Those little chicks had nothing to offer their mother; neither did she require anything from them.
Neither does our loving Jesus.

"Whosoever will may come."
"Come unto Me all ye that labour and are heavy laden."
He is the gate, or door of access to the eternal love of God.
Jesus is your salvation now and an eternity of intimacy with God.
Do you want this?
Some people are proud they belong to the devil. They think nothing of their own value.
They don't have a care about being in heaven.
They are deceived into thinking the devil and his demons have regard for them.
But Jesus wept. He wept when He spoke of His heart for all people living in the city of Jerusalem.

In the midst of all the excitement heaped on his arrival, all He desired
was for people
to come to Him
as
they
are.
Coming close to Him
so that He could lavish His awesome power and love upon them.

To give people shelter in a cruel world where they would be misunderstood.

A place with Him where they would be treasured and their every need understood.

69

People who have no time for God have all the shelter they want.

Riches, fame, accomplishments, addictions, real estate, investments, retirement, reputation, alcohol, drugs, friends, health - there is no prohibition when it comes to things to put your confidence in!

People who live in daily surrender to Jesus freely receive all the shelter God can give.
At the end of life, they go to an eternity where their Father's love awaits them
with approval, affirmation and acceptance.
Those who were happy with the offerings of the world, the flesh, and the devil will sink into
an eternity in the fires of hell where the true nature of their father is revealed.
Of those who reject the Lord it says,

"You belong to your father, the devil, and you want to carry out your father's desire. He was a murderer from the beginning, not holding to the truth, for there is no truth in him. When he lies, he speaks his native language, for he is a liar and the father of lies" (John 8:44).

That's right. Jesus Christ knows the devil.
 Jesus has no qualms in revealing the existence of the devil.
In His compassion for all people Jesus freely exposes the purpose of Satan to bring people to hell.
Jesus Christ is Lord of all.
Jesus Christ is also the Word made flesh so He has the truth about all things.
Would you want to have anything to do with the devil
after hearing what Jesus Christ the Righteous says about him?

Do you want to know the Lord? Are you longing to be sheltered by someone who already gave His life to prove His love for you?
Be still and know that He is Lord.

Be still, for He is right here with you because you seek Him!

"Very truly I tell you Pharisees, anyone who does not enter the sheep pen by the gate, but climbs in by some other way, is a thief and a robber" (John 10:1).

The blind church leaders who are robbers and thieves get the people climbing.
Doing things to get to God. Doing things to be good enough because they say God requires it.
Oh yes, they may even say to have to 'believe' in Jesus.

But: "you have to be in this church only or you will be damned;
you have to observe this day or that;

you must wear only these fashions;
you can't associate with those kinds of people;
you have to prove your love with the size of your offering;
you have not served God long enough for Him to speak to you about these matters;
you are female so you are not entitled to respond to your calling from God.

Be very careful of this one. You can't understand the bible without this extra, special, incredible revelation received by our great founder. In fact our founder's super secret special revelation is so incredible that no one else has ever had this same revelation and only we get to go to heaven because only our church has it."

Do you see all the intricate climbing going on here?
What happened to the invitation of Jesus?

"Come to me, all you who are weary and burdened, and I will give you rest" (Matthew 11:28).

Dear friend, just go to Jesus as you are.
Just like Jesus said.
Like a little chick goes naturally to the mother hen.

67

"The one who enters by the gate is the shepherd of the sheep. The gatekeeper opens the gate for Him, and the sheep listen to his voice. He calls his own sheep by name and leads them out" (John 10:2-3).

Jesus knows your name already.
He is the shepherd of the sheep.

But not all sheep follow Him. Isn't it obvious that some of the sheep are not interested in following Jesus? Think of the many that left home to hear Jesus teach (and enjoy free picnic meals).
Jesus said they were not interested in Him as a little chick needs the mother hen.
They were enthusiastic followers who enjoyed the benefits of having Jesus come to town.

Those who are mighty in God - young and old alike, male and female -
live daily in the shelter of their God. They savour their refuge like a chick that runs unquestioned to their mother hen.

God is not a hen.
Jesus Christ was a man and not a woman.
Those who respond to the heart's cry of God need not stumble at their profound helplessness.
They can run to God with the abandon
of a little chick.
They realise trying to get 'good' enough is not necessary.

They disregard the voices of thieves and robbers who cry out that we are not worthy of God's shelter and love unless we first obey their instruction.
Here is a picture of the faithfulness of God.
The little chicks just pass right by the leaders who crow aloud with their religious spectacle.
'Do this, do that. Sign this, sign that. Give this, give that,' they say. The little chick runs safely past.
They hear the voice of the True Shepherd. They are happy to be loved and valued just as they are.

Oh, you have great value Dear Reader.

68

Is there a future for a little chick in this world?

There is a future in the world for all of God's little chicks.

The little chick belonging to Jesus has no future in the world of the 'religious' however.
Once they determine that the chick is not a climber, that this precious heart does not revel in the many shelters apart from the unconditional love of Jesus (their mother hen) - then the religious employ an uncanny ability to exclude the little chicks of God. To sideline them.
This is especially true of the plethora of church leaders
who do not spend time alone with Jesus.
They are intimidated.
By a little, bitty chick.
Imagine. If religious church goers are this shook-up by people who are intimate with Jesus, then just imagine how terrified the devil and his demons are! Undone by the men, women and children who will not let their flesh keep them from the presence of God every day.
The little ones who need the Bread of Life. That small band of believers worldwide who allow God to unleash His Holy, Mighty power because they have paid the price to run . . .
and hide . . .
with Christ in God.

Jesus answered, "It is written: 'Man does not live by bread alone, but on every word that comes from the mouth of God" (Matthew 4:4).

Won't you spend time alone with Jesus?

Wait on Him.

Honour Him.

Extol Him.

Allow Him to live within you as your Lord and Saviour.

It's the helpless little chicks who bring the fragrance of Christ out into the community and wherever they go. The gates of hell are unable to stand against those who, like Mary, have chosen what is better.

Church leaders with no fellowship with Jesus are only a threat to the faithful. They fear man and honour the flesh and you will find it impossible to support them for very long in prayer. That is because they have already made their decision. Once they let the Lord know how far they are willing to go with their surrender to Him then He must leave them with their decision. He can't force them to submit. He can't force them to obey. They are deceived though, because Jesus wants a complete surrender or nothing at all.

He wants people who are red hot on fire for Him, or cold as ice toward Him.

"I know your deeds, that you are neither cold nor hot. I wish you were either one or the other!" (Revelation 3:15).

69

Jesus won't force an individual.

All he can do with lukewarm, prayer-less church leadership is to one day spew them out of His mouth. When this life is done it will be too late - for many.

"So, because you are lukewarm - neither hot nor cold - I am about to spit you out of my mouth. You say, 'I am rich; I have acquired wealth and do not need a thing.' But you do not realize that you are wretched, pitiful, poor, blind and naked. I counsel you to buy from me gold refined in the fire, so you can become rich; and white clothes to wear, so you can cover your shameful nakedness; and salve to put on your eyes, to you can see. Those whom I love I rebuke and discipline. So be earnest and repent. Here I am! I stand at the door and knock. If anyone hears my voice and opens the door, I will come in and eat with that person, and they with me" (Revelation 3:16-20).

The only thing God will continue to do in this life is to beckon them. Jesus will knock at the door of their heart and beseech them to allow a relationship to start.

The obstinate and lukewarm make it look so difficult to be in the kingdom of God. Fear not Dear Reader! Your Lord is the comfort, the refuge and is unto you as a mother hen to her needy chicks!

"Fear not, little flock; for it is your Father's good pleasure to give you the kingdom" (Luke 12:32).

Do you want God to give you the kingdom? Remember what Jesus said. Jesus said He will give us the kingdom and He leaves it up to us. There is no mention that another message of redemption would be sent. Jesus is God, sent here to bring salvation to all. He succeeded.

Who is God, except Jesus Christ the Lord, along with the Father and the Holy Spirit.
1) Only one thing is needed.
Getting alone with God for intimate fellowship.

2) Mary (the sister of Martha) has chosen the better part.
Prioritize your time so that you make time with Him each day.

3) It cannot be taken from you.
His fellowship is true, unchanging. Though everything in your life is subject to change you will always retain those sacred times with your Lord.

Getting to know the Lord in this life is mankind's one objective.

One day when you stand before God,
you don't want to hear Jesus say, "I never knew you."
He leaves it up to you to open that door of our heart so that He can come in.
Whatever you do, don't get caught following a blind guide.
Someone who never takes time to enter in and hear from God for themselves. Someone without the love to enable you to enter in with God on your own.
Someone who will waste your precious life dancing around the subject of intimacy with God, talking about God but never an instrument of God that you might
experience His fellowship for yourself.

Someone who's idea of discipleship
is that you end up looking, acting, sounding
and believing just like them.

A blind guide may be difficult to spot at first. They appear as a guide because their deeds give the illusion of having a relationship with God. If you are listening to the Lord though, He will be faithful to tell you if your spiritual leader has an intimate relationship or not.

God the heavenly Father has already sent the Bread of Heaven.
Are you steadily getting to know Jesus?

It is your heavenly Father' good pleasure to give you the kingdom!

70

Those who respond to Jesus with complete surrender know that all good needs are freely provided for in His perfect timing.

It becomes their joy in life - being aware that they are in the perfect timing of God.
Being alone with God, resting in Jesus, being nourished through the anointing of the Holy Spirit is the very Life of the follower of Jesus.

Their heart then, naturally seeks a fellowship with believers who also desire above all things to hear from the Lord.
People who can't help but just let God be God.

"How good and pleasant it is when brothers live together in unity! It is like precious oil poured on the head, running down on the beard, running down on Aaron's beard, down upon the collar of his robes. It is as it the dew of Hermon were falling on Mount Zion. For there the Lord bestows his blessing, even life forevermore" (Psalm 133).

Please don't give up your fellowship with Jesus if you are not able to find others who love Him as you do. He knows what is best for you. He will take care of your needs. He will absolutely redeem this time that may seem such a waste.

You will see His wisdom along the way as you continue to be faithful and minister to Him.

Love the Lord. He is faithful to you.

"To the faithful you show yourself faithful, to the blameless you show yourself blameless, to the pure you show yourself pure, but to the crooked you show yourself shrewd. You save the humble but bring low those whose eyes are haughty. You, O Lord, keep my lamp burning; my God turns my darkness into light. With your help I can advance against a troop; with my God I can scale a wall. As for God, his way is perfect; the word of the Lord is flawless. He is a shield for all who take refuge in him" (Psalm 18:25-30).

71

"these I will bring to my holy mountain and give them joy in my house of prayer. Their burnt offerings and sacrifices will be accepted on my altar; for my house will be called a house of prayer for all nations" (Isaiah 56:7).
"It is written," he said to them, "My house will be called a house of prayer, but you are making it 'a den of robbers'" (Matt 21:13).
Dearest praying brother or sister, your Lord assures you of His fellowship.

Don't feel down if you don't feel 'spiritual'.
Don't consider yourself less qualified than anyone else even if they appear to possess a great flourish and even rampage around in Jesus name!
Instead of having to rely on some unusual spiritual resolve within you,
God says He will bring you to that place of meeting with Him face to face!
Isn't this mystery magnificent! It is stupendous! To God be all the glory.
There is a place for you and God brings you there in His presence!

Jesus is the Shepherd and all of His sheep are meant to follow Him.
Remember, your purpose in church is to be following Jesus.
Isn't that where sheep are supposed to be? With the Good Shepherd?

Carnal and lukewarm leadership are deceiving their people with religious thinking
but there is no talent or unique quality needed
to be a faithful servant of God.
You see, Jesus obliterated the notion of 'levels' of privilege, honour and access attached to serving
Him. That is an Old Testament model. A model that allowed for only one of the tribes to attend to
the duties of a high priest. Those in ministry today are not defined by their pedigree but by their
servant's heart. A leader sent by God is assigned to be a servant to God's people.
They esteem the flock above themselves.

"But you are not to be like that. Instead, the greatest among you should be like the youngest, and
one who rules like the one who serves" (Luke 22:26).

Church people served by a leader led by the Spirit of God
conclude afterwards how wonderful Jesus is!
Their spiritual leader is pleased that they run to the strong tower of their Lord!
He or she knows that there is a Shepherd who is jealous for the love of each one of His sheep.
True leadership sees the measure of church growth as the abundance of the fruit of the Spirit
and unity in the leading of the Holy Spirit.
The people under the care manifest by the Holy Spirit gather to seek God
and not to talk about the greatness of their leader.
People who continually dwell upon the greatness of their leader
are actually kept from finding solace, comfort and purpose
in God alone.
They are stuck with a leader who has chosen to serve God in their own strength.
Or worse yet, a leader who gathers purpose and strength from the praise of man.

If you realize that you have been sidetracked by a leader like this, show kindness and love.
Do not criticise or say negative things. Just seek God for a new place to go to church.
If the Lord leads, then follow Jesus to pray as He directs on behalf of the situation.
Do not stay one minute longer in that church than the Lord directs. Do what Jesus says.
You have permission to find a new place to fellowship if the Lord directs you to do so.

72

How can you tell one sheep from another?

Ah, the Shepherd and only the Shepherd of that flock can tell one sheep from another.
Can you catch this simple truth?
The strength of a sheep is in 'following' the Good Shepherd.
That is all there is to being an on-fire, sold out Holy Ghost man, woman or little child of God!
Follow! Anyone can follow!
That is because the entire responsibility for you rests upon the shoulders of the shepherd!
The sheep bear no responsibility with purpose or plan -
only the shepherd.

When you get right down to it, a sheep and a man are not even the same species. Yet with this vast difference between them, all the sheep need is a commitment to follow their Shepherd.
When they stay close by following their Shepherd they are kept in His brilliant design, His plan and His all encompassing love. All they need to do is follow Him!

That is how God made this essential experience possible for all people. The only thing needed is to 'follow' Him. Can anyone follow Him? Yes. It doesn't take profound intellect because the Shepherd has already prepared the way.
You don't have to take careful pains to please man because you are only asked to follow God.
You are not following 'man'. It doesn't take money because God owns it all.
The bible says His sheep hear His voice and follow Him.
They don't cook up amazing plans, they don't study and study and somehow become imbued with spiritual super hearing.

The journey in life is the result of one step after another.
Each step takes place as you follow Jesus.
Bless God! Am I a follower of Jesus? Oh yes, and thank God I am.
I realise I may not be able to do a lot of things, but I can follow!
I will rely on His strength,
His wisdom,
His resources,
His opinion of me,
His timing,
His anointing,
His opportunities,
His favour,
His open or closed door,
His zeal,
His strength,
His plans,
His appointment with death,
His sweet and Holy fellowship every day of my life.

He is faithful and He is a friend like no other!

73

"**these I will bring** to my holy mountain and give them joy in my house of prayer. Their burnt offerings and sacrifices will be accepted on my altar; for my house will be called a house of prayer for all nations" (Isaiah 56:7).

His 'holy mountain' is another way of saying a personal meeting with Him, just as he had with Moses when asked by God to climb up the mountain where they could meet face to face.

We do not need to find joy, He will give us joy. It is given to us by God.
We find joy and all good things hidden with Christ in God.

Now, what of the mention of His house being 'a house of prayer?'

Jesus said that His house is meant to be an unusual place. Unlike another other building it was set apart for but one purpose - to meet with God.
Jesus wailed, 'My house is a house of prayer.' As such, one expects a reverence, awe and anticipation just to approach and gather with others in such a profound setting.
Prayer is a complete surrender to communication
with an omnipotent, loving Creator.
You surrender to the process
of both speaking and listening.
Your emphasis is to present yourself before God to listen, to be still
and accept that God is Almighty.
It is wisdom to assign Him complete control of your time together.
It is a place of reverence and awe just as it would be with earthly Royalty.
If you are blessed to be able to assemble with other believers why not aim to draw near to God together to get to know Him? Let's consider Jesus words spoken while He wept. Should we not be 'like chicks as they run to their mother hen?'
Why not?
Worship Him. Thank Him. Praise Him.
Let His Holy Spirit direct a gathering of His people.
His Holy Spirit has only one purpose on this earth.
To lift up Jesus.
Why shouldn't the Holy Spirit do this?

For there is no other way for mankind to be saved and escape the endless, ever scalding, eternal, flaming fires of hell.

74

To be excluded by religious people is not the end for the follower of Jesus.

Going to a church where it is clear your leadership is too busy to find refuge in Jesus
is a sad thing though.

It means they are busy like Old Testament followers with Jesus weeping all the while.
'Why don't you just come to me like little chicks,' He says.

Man makes the decision to invite only certain people to sit around a table and talk and feel like much is being accomplished. It seems like such high level stuff. Doesn't it suddenly seem like it is important to God
if you get on a board or be on some committee?

Man wants to keep from 'rocking the boat' whatever that means.
It is too comfortable the way things are without turning the church into a house of prayer!
It is too complicated to allow the Holy Spirit to move and use whomever He chooses.
The only thing that gets complicated when there is prayer is the devil's plans. That is because the
Light of the world takes His rightful place and He shuts those plans down!
God's people need His Holy Spirit to overcome through prayer.
The precious Holy Spirit was so important that Jesus said His death would now enable
the Spirit's arrival upon the earth.

"But I tell you the truth: It is for your good that I am going away. Unless I go away, the Counsellor
will not come to you; but if I go, I will send him to you" (John 16:7).

Jesus said He will send the Holy Spirit to those who are His (true) followers.
The Holy Spirit is important.
Jesus sent Him.
Sadly, there are many church goers, who believe the Holy Spirit is irrelevant,
a myth, an unknowable entity and unnecessary.

Here is the truth.
The Holy Spirit is sent by Jesus to all who would follow in obedience.
If the Holy Spirit is rejected or written off then the only agency from God to bring us
into intimate fellowship has been pushed aside.

Jesus said this was the will of His Father. Jesus would pray and God the Father would send the
Holy Spirit into the world. This is very important.

The Holy Spirit is the Person God uses in our day and age to direct His work on earth.
So let us talk about the Holy Spirit.
Today, when you are still and waiting before the Lord, the Holy Spirit is there to guide you.

75

Today we look at a critical component of our sharing together in these pages.

Romans 8:37-39.

This will be very important in your relationship with God. Here it is.

"No, in all these things we are more than conquerors through him who loved us. For I am
convinced that neither death nor life, neither angels nor demons, neither the present nor the
future, nor any powers, neither height nor depth, nor anything else in all creation, will be able to
separate us from the love of God that is in Christ Jesus our Lord."

The love of God is in Christ Jesus our Lord. Your life is hidden there as well.

Jesus said we will come to Him because the Father has given us to Him.

It would be like chicks that freely come to their mother hen. Those little chicks' one aim is to get under those wings - and they make it every time! The mother hen is waiting and when she sees them running she instinctively brings them in closely to her where they will be safe.

None are excluded.

There is no special reserved spot for any particular one.

"Come to me, all you who are weary and burdened, and I will give you rest" (Matthew 11:28).

This is important for us.

Jesus gives rest to all of His people.

It is not earned. It is not better for some and not for others.

All who desire to come to Him are welcomed.

Received.

Enfolded in His loving arms.

76

Consider, while weeping over Jerusalem Jesus called the inhabitants 'children'.

He was ready and willing to receive them but He says, "they would not".

Every single person in that city could have known the Lord.

Romans 8:37-39 describes everything
that could possibly come between you and God.

"No, in all these things we are more than conquerors through him who loved us. For I am convinced that neither death nor life, neither angels nor demons, neither the present nor the future, nor any powers, neither height nor depth, nor anything else in all creation, will be able to separate us from the love of God that is in Christ Jesus our Lord."

This scripture is important because it shines a light upon the many elements in conflict with God's plan to save you and keep you as His friend.

He wants you to know that He has taken care of every obstacle and hindrance.

He successfully defeated all that opposes His plan for you.

Through Christ, at no time will you be denied His loving-kindness
nor the overwhelming resources of heaven.

Your destiny is to walk with God in utmost intimacy.

He has gone before you. He will be there always, for you.

He said clearly that He freely shared with Mary,

because <u>she</u> had chosen.

He considers all of mankind to be children.
But His loving relationship is only given to those who humble themselves

and come aside to spend time with Him.

77

How frightful for a chick deceived into thinking they will find life apart from their mother hen.

How sad to live a life of discipline, outward observance and sacrifice and have nothing to show for it in the end because it was done without intimacy with Jesus.

How horrifying it will be for those who would not come to Jesus in this life.

What will their end be?

"Whoever believes in the Son has eternal life, but whoever rejects the Son will not see life, for God's wrath remains on him" (John 3:36).

They are alive but shall not see life.
Dear Reader, that is only while they yet remain in this body.
Our earthly body is ours for only a short period of time.

We are free to live with the nurture, care and plan of the Master and we are equally free to never come to Jesus. Lots of church people never come to Jesus.
Yet they say prayers, give money, gather with others in church, give sermons, write books, dress nicely and some tell others about Jesus. What of the little chick who 'chooses never' or 'chooses seldom' to be near Jesus?
Choosing not to abide in the only place intimate relationship for two betrothed people is realized?

Once, I was in a church service in the early days of spending time with Jesus. One Sunday morning there was a wondrous sense of God's presence.
Out in the foyer, numerous individuals scurried out with great excitement. Some commented, 'what a great service', as they raced out. There was great rejoicing of heart. Right there, the Holy Spirit framed that moment in my thinking and spoke to me. To my shock He said, "they missed it."
He said the wondrous presence of God was not the blessing. Thinking His presence was all the blessing - folks were rightly thrilled and were caught up in the majesty, the glory, the thrilling sense of our God.
But the Holy Spirit yearned for something real.
A connection. An openness of heart.

"It was only the invitation. It was a peek at who I am. It was meant to entreat a response from My people to get to know Me."

The Lord was wooing the people in church. His presence was meant to provoke intimacy in the hearts of His people.

It wasn't the blessing! It was an invitation to His blessing. 'Here! Look here! How beautiful I am, how glorious, how majestic, let us love one another! Look at how much I love you', as the congregation was caught up and enthralled at the power and splendour of the presence of God.

I did not think those thoughts of my own accord. It was God who spoke to me. He was sad. God was not asking us to commit to attending more church services, saying we believe certain things about the bible, and give more money. As they raced out that Sunday morning, they left without the blessing Jesus Christ offered to them. That's what God told me.

Can you see the tie-in with the story about the mother hen and the chicks?
Jesus has never wanted more of anything we can do for Him.

He weeps because we withhold ourselves from His intimate love.
Imagine how deeply it must hurt to love someone so much that their indifference makes you cry.
It is a truly pathetic picture of mankind's indifference toward God.

Jesus stood out there in a public place overlooking the city of Jerusalem and cried.
He said,
'you don't want my love

but I
love you still.'

For the lukewarm after awhile it is about what God is doing instead of who He is.
They are shockingly complicit with an unbiblical model of relationship that says we are intimate with God because 'we know all about Him.'

"Oh, the depth of the riches of the wisdom and knowledge of God! How unsearchable his judgments, and his paths beyond tracing out!" (Romans 11:33).
"As the heavens are higher than the earth, so are my ways higher than your ways and my thoughts than your thoughts" (Isaiah 55:9).

Getting to know Jesus is the blessing. He is wonderful to observe, it is true.
But He demonstrates His power because He loves all people and wants to bring them to Himself.

Just let Him love you.
Come to Jesus.
He will be so pleased that someone has taken up His invitation.
It will make His heart glad that you have taken up His invitation.
All that He has belongs to those who surrender all to know Him
and grow in the knowledge of His love.

78

On this earth Jesus was the Spirit of God made manifest in the flesh.

When Jesus rose from the dead and ascended into heaven the Holy Spirit began a ministry on earth to attract people and bring them to Jesus.

The Holy Spirit does this in part by convicting people of their sinfulness.
Being 'convicted' of sin means you become acutely aware of your need of forgiveness and cleansing.
The precious blood of Jesus has power throughout all time to wash away any manner of sin.
It takes the blood of Jesus to make a person completely whole and forgiven.
I mean, supernaturally whole!
This is not the wholeness offered on a talk show. No, I mean 'acceptable in the sight of God' whole. There is no need to go to man and the newest self-help book to do something Jesus did for you on the cross. He awaits your request. Don't turn on the TV, go directly to God and receive all that you need from Someone who really loves you.
'Dear Jesus. Oh Jesus. Forgive me of my sins. Set me free. I surrender my life to You. Come and live in my heart and enable me to serve you, belong to You and live forever in heaven with you."

If you already know the Lord and you know someone who is hurting and has no where to turn, if you feel led to do so by the Holy Spirit, please lift them up in prayer to our merciful and loving Saviour.

79

Do you feel dirty inside?

Deep down inside in a place you seldom think about?
Maybe you have pushed it aside successfully for years but you know it still exists inside of you.
'I've dealt with that,' you figure. Did someone do something to you or do something with you to make you feel dirty inside? Have you treated others in a way that makes you feel dirty or feel you have wronged them? Or do you feel as if you haven't sinned but readily acknowledge you are not exactly perfect?

Do you feel church people are hypocrites and conclude that God has nothing that you need?
By the way, the people in church who did not know Jesus kept me from turning to Jesus for many years. I was wrong.
Jesus is ok. He saves to the uttermost. He lifts the burden of sin and sorrow and sets the captive heart free! That is what I personally experienced.

Most church people here in North America don't know Jesus personally.
I don't know why, all they have to do is spend time with Him each day.

That is all.

In my youth a church person railed on me one day at school because I was hopelessly lost and in sin. A problem drinker making mistakes. He had no idea how broken up I was inside. I am so sorry he verbally abused me. The more he spoke the more he pushed me away from the idea of God. I pray one day he gets to know this Jesus he is zealously proclaiming.

Oh man, he was busy for Jesus. Not afraid for others to know about his faith. Jesus wept that day when he piously chastised me. Jesus wept but not for me. It was for the young man who was doing so much in the name of God. My heart was cold. Jesus doesn't have a problem with people who are cold. Jesus says He would rather have people cold or hot.
But not lukewarm. Running around in the name of someone they don't even know.
Lukewarm people talk about Jesus but don't spend time with Jesus and certainly don't know Him. They know Jesus like they know the ruler of their country (whom they have never spent time with). How sad. It makes our Jesus cry.
Remember, "O Jerusalem, Jerusalem . . ." when Jesus prayed over the city?

His heart was broken because nobody wanted to get to know Him.
What I am getting at is every human being on the earth needs Jesus Christ - Church people who say they believe in Him and all the rest who have never considered the horrors of eternity without God.

It includes the people who try to get good enough on their own. I was one of those. I figured as long as I didn't hurt others I should 'be ok'. I didn't understand what 'being ok' was. Even though I didn't know it, it was the Spirit of God at work with me. I was compelled to answer for my existence even though I couldn't acknowledge the existence of God.
What a great God eh?

"He has made everything beautiful in its time. He has also set eternity in the human heart; yet no one can fathom what God has done from the beginning to the end" (Ecclesiastes 3:11).

But God will reveal many deep things to you once you repent of your sin,
and receive His Holy Spirit? This next bible verse is written about sin in the lives of church people who don't spend time with Jesus.

"if my people, who are called by my name, will humble themselves and pray and seek my face and turn from their wicked ways, then will I hear from heaven and will forgive their sin and will heal their land" (2 Chronicles 7:14).
"However, as it is written: 'No eye has seen, no ear has heard, no mind has conceived what God has prepared for those who love him - but God has revealed it to us by his Spirit. The Spirit searches all things, even the deep things of God" (1 Corinthians 2:9-10).

Let us thank God for His Holy Spirit who takes the deep things of God and reveals them unto us!

Praise God.

Praise God for ever and ever.

84

Jesus weeps for all people. Even though He is all powerful, He would never force anyone to be in an intimate relationship with Him.

I really hope you have a friend, or at one time had a great one.

Imagine if your best friend one day said, 'I am with you because I was forced to do so. I never volunteered or offered my friendship. I did not choose to be with you.'

This is why God allows mankind to run around and do whatever they want to do.
Even if it is to hurt others or themselves -
it is about having a free will.
Not being forced to do something one doesn't choose to do.
The right to bear arms.
To wear a motorcycle helmet or not.
To wear a seatbelt while in an automobile.
People feel very strongly about having a free will.

The freedom to come to God and enjoy His friendship or reject Him to follow another path.
This is the essence of what it means to be created in His image.
You have the power to tell the creator of the world to leave you alone.
You and I have the power of free will so much so that we can reject Almighty God.
At the same time Jesus is reaching out to us in mercy to become a member of His family.
All of mankind are invited by Jesus to come into relationship with Him.

81

"Just as people are destined to die once, and after that to face judgment" (Hebrews 9:27).

Where do people go to after they die?

In this verse it says we will all die and afterward we will all face judgement. That is a clear word describing every person's initial experience in the afterlife.

It is not like scheduling a hair style or an oil change.
Even planning ahead does not guarantee you will get your hair styled or oil changed. Another more important need may suddenly arise. In that case, you would cancel your appointment and reschedule for a more convenient time. These are far less serious appointments.

When it comes to your time to die it may not be according to your schedule.
It may be sudden. It may be unexpected.
It will be tragic.
You do not have to be alone though. You can take care of that now!

It is important not to wait for the appointment. Here is the verse we just looked at including the other verses around it. We are looking at it in context.

"Nor did he enter heaven to offer himself again and again, the way the high priest enters the Most Holy Place every year with the blood that is not his own. Otherwise Christ would have had to suffer many times since the creation of the world. But he has appeared once for all at the culmination of the ages to do away with sin by the sacrifice of himself. Just as people are destined to die once, and after that to face judgement, so Christ was sacrificed once to take away the sins of many; and he will appear a second time, not to bear sin, but to bring salvation to those who are waiting for him" (Hebrews 9:25-28).

Friend, it is certain you will die.

This is an appointment you can't get out of.
It is also certain that Jesus will be there waiting for you and take you with Him to heaven - if you choose Him before you die.

"We are confident, I say, and would prefer to be away from the body and at home with the Lord" (2 Corinthians 5:8).

You won't have to face death alone.
The choice is offered to you by Jesus. Please consider making it now.

The only thing preventing you from truly experiencing Jesus is your decision to reject Him.

82

Jesus prayed for you while He was on earth.

"Father, I want those you have given me to be with me where I am, and to see my glory, the glory you have given me because you loved me before the creation of the world. "Righteous Father, though the world does not know you, I know you and they know that you have sent me. I have made you known to them and will continue to make you known **in order that the love you have for me may be in them** and that I myself may be in them" (John 17:24-26).

Jesus is God.

While in prayer with His Father, His prayers would be answered
because the Father and the Son are One.
These times of prayer when they were alone together sustained their timeless love for one another.

Time together in prayer was actually a sacred time of love.
Jesus speaks of how much His Father loves Him.
He fondly recollects the great love they shared before they created the world.

When He was on earth Jesus and His Father spent time alone together
and it was everything to Him.
This activity enabled Jesus to remain in His Father's love.

He could express His love there.
He could be with the One who loved Him so -
the One who wanted only what was best for Him.

Jesus Christ.

The Good Son.

83

Though He was doing phenomenal supernatural miracles there is no record that He kept
reminding His Father of this fact - except to affirm that He was always obedient.

Yet it was a big deal to do miracles and Jesus was being spoken of far and wide.

Raising the dead,
casting out devils,
healing the sick,
fulfilling prophecy!

Yet here is your tender hearted Jesus going on about how much His Father's love means to Him.
This is important to Jesus.

This love for one another was more important to Him than anything.
It compelled Him to do exactly what His Father planned.

It was His Father's will to make this love known to all mankind.
Jesus says He is making His Father known and this same love will be in all who receive Him.
It meant everything to Jesus that people would know His Father's love
because Jesus only lived to please His Father.

To know your heavenly Father is to be eternally changed because of His love for you.

84

Jesus wants you to be filled with the Holy Spirit.

The Spirit personally brings you the knowledge and experience of God's love.
It is this love that changes you.
The experience of God's love transforms you.

Jesus said [John 17:24-27] He is making the Father known to you and will fill you
with the Father's love.

Here is the incredible truth.
Jesus came to earth
to bring <u>you</u> into the fellowship of love shared together with the Father, Son and Holy Spirit.

This present life is only the beginning.

You have an endless eternity ahead of you.
An endless eternity in which He will treasure you.
He already treasures you just as He treasures His Son Jesus.
Jesus described it like this,
"that the love you have for Me may be in them."

"Father, I want those you have given me to be with me where I am, and to see my glory, the glory
you have given me because you loved me before the creation of the world. "Righteous Father,
though the world does not know you, I know you, and they know that you have sent me. I have
made you known to them, and will continue to make you known in order that the love you have
for me may be in them and that I myself may be in them" (John 17:24-27).

Go aside to spend your own time with Jesus.
Let Him fulfill your destiny
by bringing to you the love you have always longed for.

"for it is God who works in you to will and to act according to his good purpose"
(Philippians 2:13).

85

Right in the middle of His prayer in John 17:24-26 Jesus is mentioning you!

Jesus is so candid.

He is so transparent.
This is of utmost importance to Him - to keep making the Father known to you.
He wants His heavenly Father's love to be in you. It is apparently God's perfect will that you are
filled with the Father's love just as this great love was shared with Jesus.

Do you wonder if you qualify?
Jesus says, "in order that the love you have for Me may be in them."
He went on to say, "and that I myself may be in them."
This is accomplished by the Holy Spirit, the person who fills you when you believe in Jesus
and receive Him as your Saviour.

This is why God assigns such a premium to your time together with Him.
He already has an everlasting love for you.
There is nothing for you to prove.
You don't need to get better.
You don't need to be more mature in the faith.
You don't need to memorize more and more doctrine.
He wants you to experience the love He has for Jesus
not the love you feel you deserve.

You would not be able to imagine in your mind how much God the Father loves His Son
the Lord Jesus Christ. You are destined to be loved as Jesus is loved by His Father.
This is your destiny. That is the love prepared for you.
It is already there and Jesus wants you to receive it.
Go aside like Jesus did.
He is your great example of the faith.
When you are alone with God and not in a crowd,
you will be spending time with your heavenly Father just as Jesus did.

Today's sensational news headline seen around the world:

"GOD LOVES YOU THE SAME AS HE LOVES HIS OWN SON!"

86

Love was the number one thing between Jesus and His Father.

He had to spend time alone a lot. Love was their bond.
They could share this intimate love when they were alone.
As often as He could, Jesus would go off to a solitary place. This was not an onerous task.
Love was all that mattered to the heart of Jesus.
Love is why He came.

No one could love Jesus like His Father could.
No one can love you like your God will.

He has done all that is necessary to reach your heart as soon as you ask. He died and rose again.
Now it is vitally important that you enable Him to show you how much He loves you.
You are valuable. You are worth it.
When He suffered He thought of you - and this brought joy to His heart in His darkest hour.

"Looking unto Jesus the author and finisher of our faith; who for the joy that was set before him
endured the cross, despising the shame and is set down at the right hand of the throne of God"
(Hebrews 12:2).

Our precious Jesus endured sacrifice, death and resurrection knowing it would fulfill His Father's purpose to redeem mankind.

Attaining fellowship with those who would receive Him was a 'joy set before' Him. He knew a 'joy' along with His heroic suffering.

He knew with each drop of blood His Father's love would prevail and set mankind free.
To die was the plan.
Jesus was meant to die.
He did so much to get this privilege of redemption for you.
It cost Him so much. It all came down to His Father's love.
In love He was free to yield in trust and complete selflessness.
He really wanted to obey in everything asked of Him by His Father.

Who will receive
the blood of this loving,
holy Son of God
to cleanse from sin?

Who will enter into this joyful, costly sacrifice?

Who will bow before Him and be lavished with His extravagant forgiveness?

What relief must come to the heart of Jesus Christ when a desperate soul says,

'let your blood wash away my sins.
Cleanse me.
I want to be in heaven one day with You.'

An unavoidable appointment with death and an eternity in hell - this is a dilemma both desperate and diabolical. This explains the great cost to God for just one soul. Eternal life and eternal death. Those lost to Him in death forfeit His redemption for all eternity. They will be lost forever.
In God's eyes you are valued beyond measure.

When you live in His plan you belong to Him.
You are forever His child to be watched over day and night.
In the plan of Satan and his demons you are a despised prey to rob, kill, steal and destroy.

"The thief comes only to steal and kill and destroy; I have come that they may have life, and have it to the full" (John 10:10).

He would pay whatever price was needed to pay the ransom for any person desiring to live with Him forever. It matters not how sinful.

"This righteousness is given through faith in Jesus Christ to all who believe. There is no difference between Jew and Gentile, for all have sinned and fall short of the glory of God, and all are justified freely by his grace through the redemption that came by Christ Jesus" (Romans 3:22-24).

He will hear your cry for forgiveness, mercy and eternal redemption.

89

"I have made you known to them, and will continue to make you known..." (John 17:26).

Jesus explains that He will enable us to know our Father in heaven so that the love He has for His Son Jesus will also be in us.

This is God's will for your life.
That the love God the Father has for Jesus will also be in you.

It is the daily project of the Holy Spirit. He is here in the earth to make your Father's love known to you. His love brings salvation, joy, forgiveness, protection, grace, understanding, comfort, discipline, chastening, guidance, instruction, healing, deliverance and the list continues on!

In your personal encounter with the Divine,
Jesus says that He will make the Father known to you.
Could you have a better teacher?
One who never slumbers nor sleeps.

He keeps watch over you with every breath you take.

"For the Lord God is a sun and shield: the Lord will give grace and glory: no good thing will he withhold from them that walk uprightly" (Psalm 84:11).
"indeed, he who watches over Israel will neither slumber nor sleep" (Psalm 121:4).

90

"He will cover you with his feathers, and under his wings you will find refuge; his faithfulness will be your shield and rampart" (Psalm 91:4).

Remember how Jesus said His desire for the people of Jerusalem was to be as a mother hen providing shelter to her little chicks?

This invitation was also given in Psalm 91.

Here, your Father God says the same thing. He covers His children with His feathers.
Under His wings they find refuge. Not that God has wings that appear when we are in trouble.
Our Father says 'He' is our place of refuge. He says He is as present and dependable as nature's
example of a hen with her chicks.

The answer for little chicks is not complicated.
That is exactly why Jesus used these little animals for an example.
They just need to avail themselves of the offer to run and hide.
The mother hen takes responsibility for everything else.
Today is a new day but God is still the same. Once again, go to Him.
He is the refuge you need. He has begun a good work in you for this very reason.
The mother hen is all those little chicks need.

BE SAFE

He is always available.

91

"He who dwells in the shelter of the Most High will rest in the shadow of the Almighty"
(Psalm 91:1).

How pleasant to have a place to call home!

How fortunate to have a place to go where one can rest.
For many in this world, it may never be possible to live in such privilege.

For many others, home is a simple covering of tin, cardboard or leaves over ones head.
For others 'home' is unpleasant beyond description, a place to shun or avoid at all costs.

But God has bankrupted all of heaven to provide shelter and rest to those who will receive.
In offering His Son to be the sacrifice for the sin of mankind, you are given shelter.
You have a place to rest. There is no money you need to pay, it is all about who you know!

If you have accepted Jesus Christ and are born again you have chosen Him to be your shelter.
He becomes a place to rest.
This is very handy if one should end up in prison.
The physical surroundings are not the shelter. The care of the guards does not bring the rest.

It is extremely necessary for the innocent accused of wrongdoing by family members.
The sick or infirm, the investor whose portfolio is sliding downward without remedy,
the wealthy or connected that have no cares.

All are in need of shelter given freely by God to those who would receive.

God has shelter for all people.

There is enough love and grace and mercy for every person who will ever live.

Will you enter into this mercy today?

"The Lord is not slow in keeping his promise, as some understand slowness. Instead he is patient with you, not wanting anyone to perish, but everyone to come to repentance" (2 Peter 3:9).
To repent of sin and receive forgiveness from Jesus Christ begins a journey.
It is a journey between you and God!
It is entirely possible to have a relationship with the creator of the universe
if you decide to spend time alone with Him.
These times create a bond with a loving God.
It is like having a safe place, a refuge or hiding place you can run to any time you want!

"The name of the Lord is a fortified tower; the righteous run to it and are safe" (Proverbs 18:10).

Not only will you find the shelter that brings total fulfillment, but it says,
"He who dwells in the shelter of the Most High will rest in the shadow of the Almighty."

To be in intimate fellowship with Jesus Christ is the ultimate place of rest.

So be with your God.

He will reveal His love to you.
Let Him take care of your needs of the day. A rest will come.

First He is your shelter, and then He is your rest.

Psalm 91 says, "he who dwells in the shelter of the Most High."

This helps us understand the mind of the Lord in the matter of fellowship.

It is like the place you call home.
It is your home because you live there.
There may be many people who live there with you.
They do not have a certain talent, gifting or ability that makes it home for these individuals.
A house is lived in by people because it is their home.

There are other homes and certain people belong there too.

But their home is not your home. In other homes we 'visit'.
In order for it to be our own home we have to 'dwell' there, or 'live' there.

"This is my home," you will say, "because I dwell here."

If you were only stopping by once in a while it would not be a dwelling.

The place where you find shelter, where you are able to rest, where you identify as your
place of refuge - that is where you dwell.

94

Thank God it doesn't take skill to have a relationship with God.

It is on account of what Jesus did that enables you to choose a relationship with Him.
To know the Lord is to understand that fellowship with Him is an exceedingly precious
result of His grace.
Years and years of fellowship will shape and fashion the follower of Jesus.
Inwardly you will see His mercy and unconditional love.

In spite of this caring and sharing intimacy there remains a thorny question in the human heart.

"But there is a place where someone has testified: "What is man that you are mindful of him, the
son of man that you care for him?" " (Hebrews 2:6).

That is the honest expression, 'why do you bother with any one of us?'

When Jesus takes you into His care you understand it is a privilege that you have not earned!
It is Jesus after all, who has become your refuge.
The answer to your every need.

He is so supreme and complete that He is there for you no matter what happens to be your need.
He never fails to care - but you have not earned His good favour. You need not earn the love
of a Saviour who willingly went to the cross before you even knew Him.

He went to the cross for everyone.
Only a small few shall choose Him.

"We love him, because he first loved us" (1 John 4:19).

It will be His good pleasure to lavish all manner of mercy, love and grace upon you
all the days of your life.

It was His idea to obediently surrender all to redeem you in the first place.

When you receive Jesus Christ as your Saviour the Holy Spirit takes up residence inside of you.

The precious Holy Spirit works to fulfil God's passion for fellowship.

He will communicate the desire that you become more than a visitor.
His only mission is to establish your rapport with God
so that He can be your dwelling.
The powerful love of the Holy Ghost working inside you
will enable you to acquire your own personal dwelling -
just because you spend time with Him.

"When they saw the courage of Peter and John and realized that they were unschooled, ordinary men, they were astonished and they took note that these men had been with Jesus" (Acts 4:13)
For many in the world this is great news! They don't have the privilege of living in a physical shelter. In exchange they are freely invited to experience a supernatural shelter in this life
and an eternal one in the life to come!
"There was a rich man who was dressed in purple and fine linen and lived in luxury every day. At his gate was laid a beggar name Lazarus, covered with sores and longing to eat what fell from the rich man's table. Even the dogs came and licked his sores. The time came when the beggar died and the angels carried him to Abraham's side. The rich man also died and was buried. In hell, where he was in torment, he looked up and saw Abraham far away, with Lazarus by his side. So he called to him, 'Father Abraham, have pity on me and send Lazarus to dip the tip of his finger in water and cool my tongue, because I am in agony in this fire.' But Abraham replied, 'Son, remember that in your lifetime you receive your good things, while Lazarus receive bad things, but now he is comforted here and you are in agony" (Luke 16:19-25).

In this 'shelter experience' you also gain a friend!
Jesus will rejoice and be glad when your journey is over and you finally get to stand before Him.
In the hardships the two of you will have shared so much together.

I think God put the story of the Rich Man and Lazarus in the bible to throw a monkey wrench into the whole religious mindset that there are levels in Christianity.

Clearly Lazarus would fit in somewhere in the minus level. Polished he was not. Some might say he had no faith to even get his healing. Some might add that he couldn't have paid a tithe or else he could have at least afforded to buy some badly needed medicine for himself - and donate some to the needy. Others might say he must have had issues and needed inner healing because not one person would help him out of the street. Some might say Lazarus had a sin problem and definitely had problems with unforgiveness - the obvious reason he had things going against him.

But God chose Lazarus of all people to illustrate what is important and what is not.
Lazarus benefited in life from the love God had for him. God loved Lazarus.

He had nothing to earn according to his own deeds and his own strength.

There can be any number of legitimate reasons that Lazarus was in the sad state he was in!
It is not said why he suffered so much. If it were important . . . I imagine the bible would have included this information. What we do see however, is that one man ended up with God forever and the other didn't.

Many people who go to church will trust that their wealth and well being are the evidence that God has favour upon them. They have concluded that they are doing the Christian thing the right way.
They can't for the life of themselves figure out why other church goers have such a rough time.
In the context of this paragraph why do you think the other church goers are suffering so much?

True bible intimacy is not about doing things for God or in God's Holy name.
It is about communicating.
All those times of listening and being listened to.
'Seeing' and being 'seen.'
Understanding and being understood!

What a relief it will be for the faithful to finally meet Jesus face to face!
Their suffering in this life will finally be over.
Remember earlier on when we mentioned the religious doctrine,
'if there is something wrong with your life, what's wrong with you?'
Does the story of the rich man and Lazarus make things a little bit clearer?

God loves.

Even in hell the rich man was addressed as, 'son'.

Love abides forever. The rich man made his choice in life and went to hell.
It was not for any lack of love on God's part.

Being together with Jesus in heaven after getting to know one another will be exquisite.

Sublime.

A joy beyond description.
No one, no one has loved you throughout your lifetime more than Jesus.

"His Lord said unto him, Well done, good and faithful servant; thou hast been faithful over a few things, I will make thee ruler over many things: enter thou into the joy of the Lord"
(Matthew 25:23).

Oh what joy, to finally actually see your greatest of all friends face to face. You will never part!
You will be able to be together for all eternity.

Jesus is kind and thoughtful, wanting to freely and immediately become shelter to all who come to Him.

Jesus said 'anyone who comes to Me, I will not drive away.'
How welcoming He is.
Do you feel unworthy to come to Jesus?
Or do you figure you may meet with Him because there are things about your life that He will be happy with? Jesus says even if you are convinced your sin would cause Him to drive you away when you bring it into the Light - He won't.
Jesus Christ can handle your sin. That's right.
He is able to handle you and He is able to love you.
He wants to be there alongside you in your need.
He will forgive you.
Make you new inside.
He is able to give you the experience of being born again!

He doesn't want to just make you better.
      He will recreate you
from the inside out.

He can save, forgive, heal, deliver, protect, provide and is ready right now
to be your very best friend. He loves you.

Let Him lift your burden of sin.

Jesus can handle your needs.

Jesus will enable you to have the rest you need.

God invites each one who receives Him to make His fellowship a dwelling.

You will never need some special secret or teaching. People for centuries have enjoyed spending time with God. Remember the faithful fishermen Jesus first called to be His followers?
It says they were unlearned and ignorant. Jesus has come to the earth to redeem any person who will believe in Him and take up their own cross and follow Him.

"And he said to them all, If any man will come after me, let him deny himself, and take up his cross daily, and follow me" (Luke 9:23).

Even with all that you will read here, it remains for you to spend time alone with Jesus.

He becomes a shelter and place of rest for those who seek Him.

Seeking Him means you are open to Him, you spend time with Him.
Seeking Him sounds active but in the spiritual context it is not outwardly active.
People who wait quietly upon the Lord are active.

If you wait for a bus by running all over town learning about busses - you will miss the bus.
This is actually heart-breaking and sad when it comes to Jesus.
It is not funny.
When people are helped by God's precious Holy Spirit to become still
while alone in His presence
they are 'active'.
Be still.
Wait upon the Lord.
It is alright.

The Holy Spirit knows you and He knows you need His help.
Give Him a chance to change your life, your heart and your world.

Psalm 46:10 "Be still, and know that I am God: I will be exalted among the heathen, I will be exalted in the earth."

What happens when you are still?

God says He is exalted when you are still.

98

"But they that wait upon the Lord shall renew their strength; they shall mount up with wings as eagles; they shall run, and not be weary; and they shall walk, and not faint" (Isaiah 40:31).

He will prove Himself from the very first time you meet with Him.

This means He wants you to choose a time alone with Him every day or as often as you are able.
It is there that you wait upon the Lord.

"His faithfulness will be your shield and rampart" (Psalm 91:4).

He is faithful. He is your caregiver.
Live as His 'care-taker', receive all the 'care' He wants to give you and be filled with the Holy Spirit!

Life is hard.
As life's challenges overwhelm,
you will find His shelter more and more pleasant as a dwelling place.

How splendid He becomes as your daily shelter.
You bring such pleasure to His heart when you move into an intimate walk
and seek more than a just a place to visit.

He will renew your strength!
You will mount up with wings like an eagle!
You will not be weary as you run, and you shall walk and not faint.
You will be supernaturally enabled.
You will rise up from being still with God.
You will move forward from waiting upon God.
You will find wisdom and words to speak -
from being quiet before God.

99

When you go to the doctor or make an appointment for something special you usually arrive in
time to wait.

At the doctor's office you let the receptionist know you have arrived.

Then you go to a room where you wait. You sit and remain in one place. It is actually called,
'the waiting room.' It is understood that you remain there.
You wait in that room until you are called. The dentist is the same.

It is also true in line-ups where you take a little piece of paper with a number. When your number
is called it is your turn, so you wait there with everyone else who also has a number of their own.
Sometimes they call the number but no one answers. That is because the person is no longer
waiting. They still have the number but they went somewhere else.
At the doctor or dentist waiting room it is the same. If you leave the waiting room you will miss
your opportunity for help. The receptionist simply calls for the person with the next appointment.

This manner of 'waiting upon God' is just like this.
It is being available before God in a specific way.

The joy for all concerned is that it is not more challenging to wait upon God
than to wait for your Dr. appointment!
'Christ in you' is your hope.
He is doing the work within you like a Master Potter
as soon as you go aside to wait upon Him.

Where is boasting then? When all you have to do is sit there with God -
where is the boasting in this?
The boasting is in God. Boasting in the Lord.
Take no credit for the wondrous work He does in your heart.

You are formed from dust and to dust your body will return.

Do not dare boast.
You are a created vessel.
God is the Creator.

100

'Waiting upon God' for those who hunger and thirst for His word means they are being still with God.

It is for followers of God who are also lovers of God and choose fellowship with Him.
They wait there in His presence.

"They that wait upon the Lord," is talking about these people.
They wait upon the Lord. They stay there with God in His presence.
They cease all other pursuits and set aside time to wait.

One day you may meet a friend. After asking a question they say, 'I'm waiting on the Lord.'
This is another kind of waiting. With this kind of waiting you can go shopping, drive around town,
carry on with life as usual and still be 'waiting on the Lord'. You may be waiting for His timing,
an answer to prayer or for God to bring an event to pass.
There is much wisdom to wait upon God in this way too.
It is an essential part of following Jesus.
The waiting we refer to here is the other kind of waiting. A person waiting alone with God
for their time of intimate, loving fellowship.
Like an experience in a waiting room it is understood that a follower of Jesus
has chosen to physically invest in this specific time,
in this specific place
set apart for this blessed reason.

Then, they mount up with wings like an eagle, run without being weary and walk without fainting.
These are mighty, supernatural activities. They are performed by all who follow Jesus - even those
who live to their seventies, eighties and nineties! Being with God and waiting upon Him enables
Him to do these things for you. It is also very much intended for the young children.

You are in a love relationship with Jesus Christ your Saviour, Creator and Shepherd.
You need Him to do things for you. You are waiting upon Him because He is the expert.

He has all the answers.

He knows exactly what your needs are in that very moment.

"If you make the Most High your dwelling" (Psalm 91:9).

A personal dwelling is not a place you visit once in a while.

It is your own. It belongs to you. You are able to relax and let down your guard there.
You have say over what happens there.

If you live in a home where there is turmoil, abuse, chaos and fear - then there is good news
for you! Your fellowship with the Lord is still possible!
His habitation or dwelling is spiritual
and not of the natural realm.
Here is what the Lord says He will do:

"If you make the Most High your dwelling - even the Lord, who is my refuge - then no harm will
befall you, no disaster will come near you tent. For he will command his angels concerning you to
guard you in all your ways; they will lift you up in their hands, so that you will not strike your foot
against a stone. You will tread upon the lion and the cobra; you will trample the great lion and the
serpent. 'Because he loves me,' says the Lord, 'I will rescue him; I will protect him, for he
acknowledges my name. He will call upon me, and I will answer him; I will be with him in trouble,
I will deliver him and honour him. With long life will I satisfy him and show him my salvation"
(Psalm 91:9-16).

Where is boasting then? Who is going to do all this for you? Who is going to take care of you
like a good Shepherd takes care of His sheep?
God, that's who. If you must boast then boast in the Lord Jesus.

In order to be a fellowship and a dwelling at the same time,
it must be your only refuge.
The place where you meet with God in reverence and awe.
Drawing near to Him in order to listen.

In a home of turmoil and ungodliness, you will be limited in how you express your faith.
You may not be able to do the things other Christians are normally doing.
You will be able to make God your refuge.
In this supernatural dwelling place He will, 'show you His salvation.'

How wonderful! The Lord will fill your life with the wisdom and understanding you need.
You will do His will in the midst of opposition.
He will show you that He is 'with you' and 'in you' even if you are limited outwardly.
God is a great God.

He is with you in your hard times.

He is with you especially in those hard times!
The Son of God has the power to turn everything for good all the time!

He really is that powerful.

The Son of God is All-Powerful.

102

All night long Jesus has been there for you.

This morning He eagerly looks forward to taking care of you.

A loving parent is like this.
There are many parents in the world
who do not have a fine suit of clothes for the one so precious to their heart.
But they dress that little person with all the love in their heart.

It may not be possible to prepare a tiny, tasty meal though they would gladly give anything to do so.
Their offering may cause them pain for they know it is not the best. But it is the best they can do.

God is there to take care of that parent
and also to take care of that child.

"The Lord is good to all; he has compassion on all he has made" (Psalm 145:9).
"Because of the Lord's great love we are not consumed, for his compassions never fail"
(Lamentations 3:22).

May you know today that God's love is there for you.

He wants to take care of every parent and every child at the start of a new day.
If you receive the Lord then you are His child and He will take care of you.
Who will receive Him? Who will permit Him to pour love and care and light into their
home and heart as the day begins?

You probably don't have the best situation and you probably feel things aren't exactly
as they should be. As you spend time with Jesus today - whatever time of day it is - may you know
that His blessing is prepared just for you.

In the midst of your circumstances and relationships how much does Jesus love you?
In difficulty, suffering and sorrow -
how much does your heavenly Father love you?

Your Father loves you so much that He asked His Son Jesus to be obedient and go to the cross.

God gave
His best.

Hallelujah, God gave His best for you.

103

It took a terrible sacrifice for True Love to flow into this world.

It is the blood of Jesus that brings salvation and power over the demons of hell and Satan.

Satan is the deceiver, liar and defeated ruler of darkness.
It is neither your learning nor zeal that overcomes the power of darkness.
It is the Shepherd who steps in and battles for the sheep. The power needed to overcome
does not originate in a human source.

It is the blood of Jesus.

"They overcame him (the devil) by the blood of the Lamb and by the word of their testimony; they
did not love their lives so much as to shrink from death" (Revelation 12:11).

Your heavenly Father loves you.
His Son Jesus loves you.
The Holy Spirit loves you.

The defeat of Satan by Jesus Christ offers to each believer a precious freedom.
Each of God's precious children is able to approach Him at any time.
That is the freedom - nothing can stop you from running to Jesus.
You find perfect love and perfectly bless His heart
every time you exercise this freedom.
You can never be denied the benefits and blessings of love that you seek from your precious Jesus.
This is realized in the intimate fellowship.

Nothing will ever be able to interfere with His love relationship.
No matter what is going on
a born again follower of Jesus will have intimate fellowship.
Nothing can stop it.
It is a birthright freely bestowed upon those who belong to God.

This is the apex of what Jesus did for you.

"Who shall separate us from the love of Christ? Shall trouble or hardship or persecution or famine
or nakedness or danger or sword? As it is written: "For your sake we face death all day long; we are
considered as sheep to be slaughtered." No, in all these things we are more than conquerors

through him who loved us. For I am convinced that neither death nor life, neither angels nor demons, neither the present nor the future, nor any powers, neither height nor depth, nor anything else in all creation, will be able to separate us from the love of God that is in Christ Jesus our Lord" (Romans 8:35-40).

104

His power and His blood will not prevent you from going through fiery trials.
His power and His blood ensure that you will never lack His fellowship, safe-keeping and love.

"Dear friends, do not be surprised at the painful trial you are suffering, as though something strange were happening to you. But rejoice that you participate in the sufferings of Christ, so that you may be overjoyed when his glory is revealed. If you are insulted because of the name of Christ, you are blessed, for the Spirit of glory and of God rests on you" (1 Peter 4:12-14).

He has the power to save and the power to keep.

"Unless the Lord builds the house, its builders labour in vain. Unless the Lord watches over the city, the watchmen stand guard in vain" (Psalm 127:1).

Dear Reader here is a precious mystery just for you.

If the Lord
builds the house
then He remains to guard the house.
It is a coin with two sides. One side always compliments the other.

You let God guide you, remain obedient to Him
and you will be a house that He has built.
You will then be well guarded because God was the author and finisher of all you have become.
He loves to hang around and delight in what He has done.
Remember the story of the elderly widow with only two mites for the collection
that morning in church?
Where was Jesus?

Jesus was faithful even though she had so little to offer in her own strength.
I pity the individual who would mess with that senior citizen!

Guarding something is not a passive thing.

Like I said - pity those who mess with the sheep.

105

Though mankind endures all manner of suffering and trial you will never be in a position where the enemy can prevent you from running to your refuge in Jesus Christ!

Never!

This is the victory freely given to you by Jesus Christ!
Right now you are more than a conqueror.
His finished work does not prevent you from sharing with Him in the fellowship of His sufferings.
What Jesus has done is make sure you will have access to Him no matter what you will go through.
You will never be separated from His love.
This is the victory He has freely given to you.

As you continue to abide in His love He will lead you through to the victory
prepared in advance for you! You have victory over all the power of the enemy!

"For we are God's workmanship, created in Christ Jesus to do good works, which God prepared in advance for us to do" (Ephesians 2:10).
"I did not see a temple in the city, because the Lord God Almighty and the Lamb are its temple. The city does not need the sun or the moon to shine on it, for the glory of God gives it light, and the Lamb is its lamp. The nations will walk by its light, and the kings of the earth will bring their splendour into it. On no day will its gates ever be shut, for there will be no night there. The glory and honour of the nations will be brought into it. Nothing impure will ever enter it, nor will anyone who does what is shameful or deceitful, but only those whose names are written in the Lamb's book of life" (Revelation 21:22-27).
"He who listens to you listens to me; he who rejects you rejects me; but he who rejects me rejects him who sent me." The seventy-two returned with joy and said, "Lord, even the demons submit to us in your name." He replied, "I saw Satan fall like lightning from heaven. I have given you authority to trample on snakes and scorpions and to overcome all the power of the enemy; nothing will harm you. However, do not rejoice that the spirits submit to you, but rejoice that your names are written in heaven" (Luke 10:16-20).

106

For now man has a free will to do good or evil.

"When tempted, no one should say, "God is tempting me." For God cannot be tempted by evil, nor does he tempt anyone; but each one is tempted when, by his own evil desire, he is dragged away and enticed. Then, after desire has conceived, it gives birth to sin; and sin, when it is full-grown, gives birth to death" (James 1:13).

Because God is allowing mankind to exercise free will and do whatever they please it will be difficult for you at times.

"As you know, we consider blessed those who have persevered. You have heard of Job's perseverance and have seen what the Lord finally brought about. The Lord is full of compassion and mercy" (James 5:11).

Always your Lord will be there. Pouring out all the love in His heart. Pouring out His very best. Let His love embrace you. One day you will be with Him forever and you will never know sorrow, tears and pain again. Heaven, Dear Reader, has become your blessed hope.

"For the grace of God that brings salvation has appeared to all men. It teaches us to say "No" to ungodliness and worldly passions, and to live self-controlled, upright and godly lives in this present age, while we wait for the blessed hope - the glorious appearing of our great god and Saviour, Jesus Christ, who gave himself for us to redeem us from all wickedness and to purify for himself a people that are his very own, eager to do what is good" (Titus 2:11-14).

107

"Praise be to the God and Father of our Lord Jesus Christ! In his great mercy he has given us new birth into a living hope through the resurrection of Jesus Christ from the dead, and into an inheritance that can never perish, spoil or fade - kept in heaven for you, who through faith are shielded by God's power until the coming of the salvation that is ready to be revealed in the last time. In this you greatly rejoice, though now for a little while you may have had to suffer grief in all kinds of trials. These have come so that your faith - of greater worth than gold, which perishes even though refined by fire - may be proved genuine and may result in praise, glory and honour when Jesus Christ is revealed. Though you have not seen him, you love him; and even though you do not see him now, you believe in him and are filled with an inexpressible and glorious joy, for you are receiving the goal of your faith, the salvation of your souls" (1 Peter 1:3-9).

The goal of your faith is the salvation of your soul.
 It isn't something you are able to measure with your deeds.
The goal is the salvation of your soul.

The greatest faith of all is a consistent fellowship with Jesus for a lifetime.

Mark the life that satisfies the timings, the obedience, and the consistency of being in God's perfect will. That life lived in agreement with the scripture - to press on in intimate relationship with Jesus to the salvation of the soul.

"Therefore, since we are surrounded by such a great cloud of witnesses, let us throw off everything that hinders and the sin that so easily entangles, and let us run with perseverance the race marked out for us" (Hebrews 12:1).

Starting the race of grace with Jesus, running the race step by step,
abiding in and waiting upon Jesus.
Afterward you will be presented holy and blameless before the Father by Jesus.

"Consider it pure joy, my brothers, whenever you face trials of many kinds, because you know that the testing of your faith develops perseverance. Perseverance must finish its work so that you may be mature and complete, not lacking anything." "Blessed is the man who perseveres under trial, because when he has stood the test, he will receive the crown of life that God has promised to those who love him" (James 1:2, 12).
There is no way to persevere under trial unless you are running to your shelter at every turn.
That means time alone with God as oft as you are able.
Certainly every day.

"Let us fix our eyes on Jesus, the author and perfecter of our faith, who for the joy set before him endured the cross, scorning its shame, and sat down at the right hand of the throne of God" (Hebrews 12:2).

108

Your faith in Jesus Christ will bring blessing and trial into your life.

You can't have one without the other.

That is why your 'blessed hope' is so important to you.
Your reward and God's justice await a time when all of His work on earth is finished.

When Jesus walked on earth and had come to the end of His Father's will He said, 'it is finished.'
He was raised from the dead three days later and was seen by many people.
However, the overall plan to redeem mankind was not yet finished.
The rest of the plan included you.
You were yet to be born and then redeemed by that same Jesus.

God wanted to create you
because your fellowship with Him
would so please Him.

He is not like a farmer who looks at a tractor and says,
'could I ever plough with that.'
Or a fine team of work horses or water buffalo,
'could I ever pull with those.'
Or a piece of fine wood and say,
'I want that because I have a fence to fix.'

God created you and then sent His Son to redeem you like the Shepherd who sees a dear sheep and gives up everything to save and care for that little sheep.

Oh Dear Reader,
you are so precious.

"What do you think? If a man owns a hundred sheep, and one of them wanders away, will he not leave the ninety-nine on the hills and go to look for the one that wandered off? And if he finds it, truly I tell you, he is happier about that one sheep than about the ninety-nine that did not wander off. In the same way your Father in heaven is not willing that any of these little ones should perish" (Matthew 18:12-14).

"As a father has compassion on his children, so the Lord has compassion on those who fear him; for he knows how we are formed, he remembers that we are dust. The life of mortals is like grass, they flourish like a flower of the field; the wind blows over it and it is gone, and its place remembers it no more" (Psalm 103:13).

Do you want to be remembered no more?
When your life is done do you want every trace to vanish?
You bring nothing with you as soon as you die. What you leave behind including the memories of you cherished by your friends and loved ones will eventually disappear.
It will be as if you never lived nor accomplished anything at all.
However you will bring all your intimate times of fellowship with Jesus
directly into eternity forever!

This is the only thing that belongs to you when you stand before God.
The only offering you are entitled to present to Jesus.

Psalm 51:17 "The sacrifices of God are a broken spirit; a broken and contrite heart, O God, you will not despise."

It will all come down to your free will.
You chose to spend time with Jesus!

Of God it says,

"but there is a friend who sticks closer than a brother" (Proverbs 18:24b).
"But few things are needed - or indeed only one. Mary has chosen what is better, and it will not be taken away from her" (Luke 10:42).

How sweet the fellowship.
How deep the sacrifice and how far Jesus went to redeem you.
All of it,
all of it points to
how very
very valuable
you are to God.
Therefore, it will never be about what you have done
or what you ever will do.
You are valuable
like a chunk of gold just has to sit there
and is valuable.

Let Jesus become your first love.
His relationship is central to the shining value and beauty
you were created to be.

I really mean it.

To God you are super valuable.

109

If you want to be part of His family and His plan, ask Him to enable you to be in a love
relationship with Him.

You also can ask Him to enable you to spend time with Him each day.

Since 1981 I have sought the Lord as best I can. In those initial years it was plain enjoyable to get
alone with God. It certainly wasn't due to any talent or ability of my own. Though I was extremely
thankful, it is because He had mercy upon me.
I ended up seeking Him quite a lot. It occurred to me with this new journey that I should have an
overarching quest.
This one thing I asked of the Lord was to hear His voice.

So, in those early years I read the bible a lot. I had not yet the understanding or His sweet refining
to seek the Person of Jesus Christ at the same time. Perhaps the notion that God was intent on a
personal relationship with me was entirely implausible to my human understanding.
I had been a sinner. I had offered myself as a servant to the enemy of Jesus.
Now I was saved. Who am I that He would give me the opportunity now to become an intimate
friend? I was most happy to completely surrender to Him. He had cleansed my dark and
disrespectful heart. I could not even consider I was worthy of any more attention than that of
forgiveness of sin. I was amazed that He had enough love to accept me back.

I didn't know how powerful His forgiveness would be. I didn't know He had the power to love me
the same as He already loves His only sinless Son the Mighty Lord Jesus Christ of Nazareth.

I didn't know He felt that way the moment He had taken me back!

Then in 1986 in second year at bible college, at just the right time,
He asked me to look up Psalm 123. With this leading came an understanding that there was more
personal blessing in the Christian life. This blessing would be mine if I were to become singularly
devoted to the person of the Holy Spirit. I was encouraged to look to the Lord God as portrayed in
Psalm 123. The blessed Holy Ghost would take care of the process of becoming better acquainted.
The direction given in Psalm 123 was that of submission to God,
the privilege of being in the presence of a great Master
and confidence in Him to care about me with my utmost good in mind.

"However, as it is written: "What no eye has seen, what no ear has heard, and what no human mind has conceived" - the things God has prepared for those who love him - these are the things God has revealed to us by his Spirit" (1 Corinthians 2:9-10).

I still depend upon the Lord to enable me to seek a relationship with Him above all else.

I have never become 'self-sufficient' as if any person could acquire a secret, hidden ability to want God above all other things.
Every day, it is grace and mercy of God that brings me around to the quiet place with Him.

At times, I have actually confessed helplessly that I did not have the resolve to seek Him.
On one occasion I was unusually weary. I should take the opportunity to be alone with Him just as naturally as I was expecting to eat my next meal that day. Crestfallen, after sitting awhile unable to focus, with sadness I said, "I really do want to spend time with You and I know how important it is to be with you . . . " and as I was in the process of saying, "but I guess this isn't going to happen right now . . . ,' the Holy Spirit poured out upon me with great power and love! I didn't ask for Him to do this. We were communicating - wow, God is always listening when we go aside to be with Him!
His precious Holy Spirit became the strength of God within me. Well, I stayed put with Him on that occasion! By the mercy of God it was time to fellowship. By the grace of God.

One day when life is through I will be able to bring with me the intimate times we have spent together. I will know Him. He will know me. We will have known each other.

That is intimacy.

It is like that in marriage. In latter years the times spent getting to know one another define the relationship. If there has been little intimacy and time spent together then a couple may feel lost with one another. They may say things like, 'you never got to know me.' 'I don't seem to know you.' 'I don't feel close to you.' 'Can we get to know one another after living together all these years?'

And yet, getting to know Jesus even over a lifetime is nothing to boast about.

I do not understand why He has brought me this blessing.
I do not deserve it in any way. I never have.

It is His mercy and His grace.

110

"So, if you think you are standing firm, be careful that you don't fall!" (1 Corinthians 10:12).

Belonging to Jesus is about a precious sharing of hearts.
It is all about Jesus and His grace.

I pray each day, 'Lord, please help me to spend time with you as I should,' until the hour of my final rest. The blessed end of my race.
The day when I can finally be with Jesus forever. Oh happy day!

Many things that are only temporary appear to matter so much.
Later in life when looking back we wonder why we worried so much about things.
In hindsight they appear so inconsequential and unimportant.

Jesus said to Mary, only one thing mattered to Him.
It is truly the one thing that is needed.
He told Mary she had chosen the better thing.
Those who carry on without acknowledging the mandate from Jesus shall do so at their own peril and the peril of their friends and loved ones. Fear God. Do what He asks.

Here is the whole matter neatly set before you from God's Holy Word.

"This day I call the heavens and the earth as witnesses against you that I have set before you life and death, blessings and curses. Now choose life, so that you and your children may live and that you may love the Lord your God,
listen to his voice,
and hold fast to him for the Lord is your life," (Deuteronomy 30:19-20a).

111

If you spent an hour or two each day with a champion golfer you would become very knowledgeable about golf.

If you spent an hour or two with a successful investor every single day you would become very knowledgeable about investing.

If you wanted to be great at golf or investing you would seek out the best teacher you could find and you would endeavour to spend time with them.

Dear reader, you already know that the more time you spend with someone the more they will influence your life. As the time passes they could not help but offer tips and nuggets of understanding. Whatever they say would represent a lifetime of diligence, canny insight, personal successes and failures.

Jesus is like that, only better.

He will say exactly the right thing for you.

He will offer the love that you need exactly when you have that need.
He will supply your every good need and give you the desires of your heart.

"And my God will meet all your needs according to the riches of his glory in Christ Jesus" (Philippians 4:19).
"Take delight in the Lord, and he will give you the desires of your heart" (Psalm 37:4).

112

When you are sick there is Someone who cares about you.

Feeling alone and lonely is a difficult part of being sick.

But Somebody Precious loves and accepts you.
This love and acceptance flows to your heart from the throne of God.
God really cares about you.
He cares at the times when you figure He wouldn't care.
Why would someone who loves you be all enthused about you when you are sick in bed?
Wouldn't they be better served to wait until you feel better?
When you are feeling better it would seem a more worthwhile time to be involved with you.
You know, wouldn't it be better to go about happily doing other things
until a sick friend gets up out of bed?

But not God the Father,
Jesus Christ His Son,
and the wonderful Holy Spirit.

They stay with you.
Oh glory, their love compels them to be with you always.

"Never will I leave you; never will I forsake you" (Hebrews 13:5b).
"And surely I am with you always, to the very end of the age" (Matthew 28:20b).

113

The Person of the Holy Spirit is your friend.

Jesus felt the Holy Spirit was essential to your salvation experience.

Before leaving earth Jesus said it was better for us that He departs so that His Father could send the Holy Spirit.

He is generally invisible to the human eye.
Sometimes when He is at work you will see like a shimmering, or form of supernatural light or maybe another indication He wants you to see. When I used to speak for Full Gospel Businessmen's Fellowship International the Holy Spirit would enable me to see these qualities above or upon an individual. Upon observing God already at work in that precious life it only

remained to call upon them to step forward and receive what the Lord had prepared for them. Always, the Holy Spirit would lead very specifically. That is because this is His work.

He showed me just a glimpse.

He took care of the rest and usually did this through prophecy and the gifts of the Spirit.

God's angels are also invisible to the human eye if this is God's plan at the time.

Angels are able to be seen if needed.

It is possible to have interactions with an angel and not know it at the time.

"Do not forget to show hospitality to strangers, for by so doing some people have shown hospitality to angels without knowing it" (Hebrews 13:2).

But the Holy Spirit most definitely wants you to know He is involved with you.

He enables you to sense His presence.

"For the kingdom of God is not meat and drink; but righteousness, and peace, and joy in the Holy Ghost" (Rom 14:17).

The precious Holy Ghost is central to our New Testament experience of God!

The righteousness and peace and joy are all in the Holy Ghost!

If you truly know the Lord then you are led by His Spirit.

"For as many as are led by the Spirit of God, they are the sons of God" (Romans 8:14).

Here is a prayer for today:

'Dear Holy Spirit. You are a person and Jesus sent you to the earth after returning to His Father. Please come Holy Spirit and be my friend. To lead me and guide me, reveal Jesus unto me, baptise me and fill me with You. You have come to live inside me when I believed in Jesus and received Him as my Saviour. May I be sensitive to your leading in Jesus name I pray, Amen."

"In my former book, Theophilus, I wrote about all that Jesus began to do and to teach until the day he was taken up to heaven, after giving instructions through the Holy Spirit to the apostles he had chosen. After his suffering, he presented himself to them and gave many convincing proofs that he was alive. He appeared to them over a period of forty days and spoke about the kingdom of God. On one occasion while he was eating with them, he gave them this command: "Do not leave Jerusalem, but wait for the gift my Father promised, which you have heard me speak about. For John baptized with water, but in a few days you will be baptized with the Holy Spirit." Then they gathered around him and asked him, "Lord, are you at this time going to restore the kingdom to Israel?" He said to them: "It is not for you to know the times or dates the Father has set by his own authority. But you will receive power when the Holy Spirit comes on you; and you will be my witnesses in Jerusalem, and in all Judea and Samaria, and to the ends of the earth." After he said this, he was taken up before their very eyes, and a cloud hid him from their sight. They were looking intently up into the sky as he was going, when suddenly two men dressed in white stood beside them. "Men of Galilee," they said, "why do you stand here looking in to the sky? This same Jesus, who has been taken from you into heaven, will come back in the same way you have seen him go into heaven" (Acts 1:1-11).

114

When the Holy Spirit comes into your life and baptizes you, your life becomes different.

It is one thing to accept Christ as your Saviour and become born again.

It is true the Holy Spirit immediately lives inside of you. But after being saved, God wants to baptize you in the Holy Spirit. He is ready and willing and able to fill you with power from on high. All you have to do is ask God to do this.

The bible calls it 'receiving power from on high.'

Let us have but one goal when we ask for the baptism of the Holy Spirit.
That God would empower us with His love for others.
"I am going to send you what my Father has promised; but stay in the city until you have been clothed with power from on high" (Luke 24:49).
"But you will receive power when the Holy Spirit comes on you; and you will be my witnesses in Jerusalem, and in all Judea and Samaria, and to the ends of the earth" (Acts 1:8).

115

Each day you need to ask for His wisdom, understanding and obedience.

Something like this, "Oh God, let me be obedient to only You."

May you fulfill your obedience only to Jesus as you walk in the power of His love.

Always say, 'yes' to Jesus.

"I pray that out of his glorious riches he may strengthen you with power through his Spirit in your inner being, so that Christ may dwell in your hearts through faith. And I pray that you, being rooted and established in love, may have power, together with all the Lord's holy people, to grasp how wide and long and high and deep is the love of Christ, and to know this love that surpasses knowledge - that you may be filled to the measure of all the fullness of God" (Ephesians 3:16-19).

"Above all, love each other deeply, because love covers over a multitude of sins" (1 Peter 4:8).

Always say, 'yes' to Jesus.

116

The Ephesians prayer is about love.
The power of Jesus is in His love.
His love is the ultimate manifestation of His power.

The most powerful manifestation of God is His love.
It tells us there in Ephesians 3:16 - 19 that the power of God works within us
to bring us ever deeper into the knowledge and reality of God. You will grow ever deeper
in the knowledge of His love.
That love is for you.
God loves you.

When my dear wife and I pastored for a short while we used to picture the church as a circle of
people holding hands. We felt to compel them not to stand with their backs to the center of the
circle ever reaching out. Focusing on inviting more people, doing more for the church,
gazing ever outward for some breakthrough or crashing new experience. Instead, our vision was a
circle of people looking toward the center of the circle and therefore able to behold one another.
Seeing their brother and sister, aware of the needs of others by the power of the Holy Spirit.
Agreeing with what the Lord is doing in our midst.
Rejoicing in who God already is and what He has done to bring us together.

"A new command I give you: Love one another. As I have loved you, so you must love one another"
(John 13:34).
"Now about brotherly love we do not need to write to you for you yourselves have been taught by
God to love each other" (1 Thessalonians 4:9).
"Keep on loving each other as brothers" (Hebrews 13:1).
"This is the message you heard from the beginning: We should love one another" (1 John 3:11).
"And this is his command: to believe in the name of his Son Jesus Christ, and to love one another
as he commanded us" (1 John 3:23).
"Dear friends, let us love one another, for love comes from God. Everyone who loves has been born
of God and knows God" (1 John 4:7).
"And now, dear lady, I am not writing you a new command but one we have had from the
beginning. I ask that we love one another" (2 John 1:5).

In all your experiences in life the reality of God's love will ground you.
He will sustain you.
The power of God is already with you that you might learn of His love. That is what is says in this
passage in Ephesians. 'The power of God is with you that you may know this love.'
For years when I read this passage I was unable to stay true to what was written. When I came to
the part about power, my mind would wander off to miracles, raising the dead, casting out demons,
prophecy and stuff like that. As the Lord showed mercy to me, as time went on I came to realise
that the passage speaks for itself. The power reveals the love of God. God is Love.
God's power is manifest in love. God moves because of His love.
The love Jesus has for you will keep you. Jesus will bring meaning to your challenges in life as you
grow in His love. It is all for love.

Your walk with God exists because of His love for you.

"For God so loved the world that he gave his one and only Son, that whoever believes in him shall
not perish but have eternal life" (John 3:16).

"And God raised us up with Christ and seated us with him in the heavenly realms in Christ Jesus, in order that in the coming ages he might show the incomparable riches of his grace, expressed in his kindness to you in Christ Jesus" (Ephesians 2:6).

'The incomparable riches of His grace is expressed in His kindness to you in Christ Jesus.'

His grace is expressed in His kindness to you.

I love that part.
May the Lord bring this back to your remembrance as often as you need it.

You are transformed when you receive the wonderful Saviour of the world Jesus Christ.
There is a destiny for you.
There is a destiny within you.
You have a future. This is because the most powerful influence in existence has adopted you.
You are now in the care and keeping of the Sovereign Lord.
You are being watched over continually by your creator.
There is a spiritual reality that has become a constant in your life.

"And God raised us up with Christ and seated us with him in the heavenly realms in Christ Jesus," (Ephesians 2:6).

'You are seated with Him in heavenly places in Christ Jesus.'
It means you may have intimate fellowship with Him at any time - guaranteed.

It is your birthright.

Because you have received Christ if you were to die at any time you are ready!

Do not fear death at any time Dear Reader, Dear Soldier of the cross!

This is an appointment set by God!
You are in good hands and you are not going anywhere unless God says so.

"And as it is appointed unto men once to die," (Hebrews 9:27a King James Version).

He will receive you into glory because you have His righteousness.

"You guide me with your counsel, and afterward you will take me into glory"
(Psalm 73:24 New International Version).

It means the judge of all mankind has pardoned you.

Through the blood of Jesus you are now a member of the family of God.
It means you belong to God. You are forever in a position of authority
because the devil and his power was defeated.
When our Father raised Jesus from the dead He conquered sin, death and hell.

"Where, O death, is your victory? Where, O death, is your sting?" The sting of death is sin, and the power of sin is the law. But thanks be to God! He gives us the victory through our Lord Jesus Christ" (1 Corinthians 15:55-57).

Though you will face the trials and testing's of life along with all the other people God has created, all the resources of heaven will be available on your behalf.

"He causes his sun to rise on the evil and the good, and sends rain on the righteous and the unrighteous" (Matthew 5:45b).

Latest news headline!

JESUS WILL BE THERE FOR YOU IN THIS LIFE!
and take care of everything for the next life!

119

"I give them eternal life, and they shall never perish; no one can snatch them out of my hand. My Father, who has given them to me, is greater than all; no one can snatch them out of my Father's hand" (John 10:28-29).
"See, I have engraved you on the palms of my hands;" (Isaiah 49:16a).

When you are loved by someone you naturally desire to be with them.

For those fortunate to have a beloved partner, it brings the privilege of being close in ways that go beyond friendship.

Sitting extra close, having an arm around one or the other - holding the hand of your loved one.

Here in John 10 God saying your place with Him is to be held right there in the hollow of His hand. He makes no secret of how close the two of you are. In His eyes you are both very close. In fact, He makes such a fuss over being with you that it comes across as a 'triumphal procession.'

"But thanks be to God, who always leads us in triumphal procession in Christ and through us spreads everywhere the fragrance of the knowledge of him. For we are to God the aroma of Christ among those who are being saved and those who are perishing. To the one we are the smell of death; to the other, the fragrance of life. And who is equal to such a task?" (2 Cor. 2:14-17).

You will have to resist the inclination to prove your love by keeping the law and pouring your strength into 'dos and don'ts' for God.
You can count on His Holy Spirit to relieve the pressure.

You will be tempted to perform. It will seem necessary in some way
to earn the precious love of your heavenly Father. To earn His closeness.
To be good enough somehow.
It may seem He surely has a favourite son or daughter ahead of you.
Someone with a big name or lots of ministry success.
Someone with far less troubles than you have.
How can He love all of His sheep the same?
"I have loved you with an everlasting love;" (Jeremiah 31:3b).

When you wonder how much God loves you, or in those times when you wonder if He loves you, may you be reminded

He has an everlasting love for you.

It isn't a news headline.
That is because it is an intimate expression shared in secret between two people.
Don't miss your opportunity to be with Him today.

These words and expressions of love between the two of you
mean everything to Him.
What pleasure as He gently whispers
to your heart.

You are betrothed after all.

Where else would He be today but with you.

120

"Not everyone who says to Me 'Lord, Lord,' shall enter the kingdom of heaven, but he who does the will of My Father in heaven" (Matthew 7:21).

Who will go to heaven?

When it comes to other people's lives we will have to wait and see.

"But the Lord said to Samuel, "Do not consider his appearance or his height, for I have rejected him. The Lord does not look at the things man looks at. Man looks at the outward appearance, but the Lord looks at the heart" (1 Samuel 16:7).

Who would look into the eyes of Jesus, call Him by name, only to be denied a place in heaven?
People who live apart from Jesus.
Those who did not obey the Lord.
People who never believed in Him.
People who knowingly denied the Lord and did not receive Him would already know there is no place for them. It will be too late and they will be consumed with regret and dread.
Desperate to escape the words they know are coming.

"But whoever disowns me before men, I will disown him before my Father in heaven"
(Matthew 10:33).
"Then I will tell them plainly, 'I never knew you. Away from me, you evildoers!" (Matthew 7:23).

"Just as man is destined to die once, and after that to face judgment, so Christ was sacrificed once to take away the sins of many people; and he will appear a second time, not to bear sin, but to bring salvation to those who are waiting for him" (Hebrews 9:27-30).

121

It will be a terrible thing to live all the way through this life pleasing oneself only to stand naked, alone, silently, in front of all humanity - looking into the eyes of Jesus Christ with Him looking right back.

How much worse to live without God, to be mistreated and suffer through life only to face hell in the end.

One day when you will stand before Jesus you will look into His eyes and be astonished to see that He is looking right back into your eyes too. For that span of time you will have the complete attention of the creator of the universe.

He loved everyone.

While you were alive on earth His heart was filled with love for you too.
From the highest of society to the least important, He was even involved with the outright filthy and rejected. Every person was created in His image.

He will be able to comfortably look at you and look right into your eyes.
He never made a mistake. He is perfectly just. He gives everyone an opportunity to serve Him.
Imagine having Jesus Christ silently looking right at you, looking into your eyes, Jesus Christ focusing totally upon you.

You've heard His name used innumerable times as a swear word. You have heard about His birth every Christmas for as long as you can remember. You have known historically that He really did exist and walk on this earth and was hung upon a cross with nails. Now, here He is.
This is the real Jesus. Every person is going to face Jesus Christ.

It will be like time is standing still. There will be no appointment to go to. No TV show to see. No emails to read or send. You won't be wondering which latest movie you will be going to see, your collection of favourite music, the bills to pay. Sending and receiving text messages will end for all eternity.

You will not
have the choice to return to the home you lived in.
It is no longer your home.

You have died but you are somehow still very much alive.
How did this happen?
You had made up your mind that after death there was nothing.
Or chose to believe eternity did not include Jesus.

What happens now
is forever out of your control
because you are facing judgement.

You will see and stand right in the midst of people you have seen in the news: movie stars, celebrities, athletes and politicians. Rock stars and criminals and doctors, lawyers and judges. You may be amazed to be alongside a great actor or musician. People you would never have the opportunity to see or speak to in this life. There will be no class distinction. Policemen and rapists, murderers and outwardly fervent church goers.
All will stand together before a great and holy God because life has ended and it is now time to give an account. All personal items will be left behind, even special collections and treasures.
No cleaning to do and no health problems either.
Every person will see Jesus Christ in this way.

They will see the scars in His hands and in His feet.
They will see the radiant face more bright than the sun itself.
They will see His total love.
They will see the overwhelming love that He has for them.

Friends, this is going to happen for every person who has ever lived.

123

Jesus Christ truly did arrive on this earth at one time.

He has lived and died and been raised from the dead and He will be waiting to meet you.

Of all mankind, who will be glad to see the Lord?
Those who received Him, believed, were forgiven of their sins
and chose to make the Lord their refuge.

Among them will be the millions and millions of murdered children. The ones who went into the abortion clinic but didn't come back out - except out the back door in the garbage.
Momma went home
and they got a free ride in a big truck to the landfill, or dump or maybe just down the drain into the sewer.

Here is the truth.
Those little ones went directly into the arms of Almighty God.
Each abortionist along with their assistants, administration, staff and the blind Politian's who fastened themselves to votes with the flesh and blood of unborn human beings will be looked upon by their once helpless victims.

Now, Jesus is in the house. It is reckoning time with God Almighty.
It's judgement time in the Holy Place and you don't want to be there.
The Bad Shepherd has shown up in His own timing
and there is hell to pay.

I don't know who is going to heaven. No one is in a position to know on this side of eternity.
Going to church is far from a guarantee. But we know Jesus Christ is longing for followers
who will love Him,
and be loved by Him.

"Guard your steps when you go to the house of God. <u>Go near to listen</u> rather than to offer the sacrifice of fools, who do not know that they do wrong. Do not be quick with your mouth, do not be hasty in your heart to utter anything before God. God is in heaven and you are on earth, so let your words be few. As a dream comes when there are many cares, so the speech of a fool when there are many words" (Ecclesiastes 5:1-3).
"Come near, you nations, and listen; pay attention, you peoples! Let the earth hear, and all that is in it, the world, and all that comes out of it!" (Isaiah 34:1).
"Go near and listen to all that the Lord our God says. Then tell us whatever the Lord our God tells you. We will listen and obey" (Deuteronomy 5:27a).

The heart of God longs for people who draw near to listen
rather than saying too much.
People who actually care about what Jesus is thinking, how He is feeling
and how they can minister to Him.
People who will say, 'yes' in all He asks of them.

They will enter into "the joy of the Lord" on that Day and never, never look back.

"His master replied, "Well done, good and faithful servant! You have been faithful with a few things; I will put you in charge on many things. Come and share you master's happiness!" "
(Matthew 25:23a).

Jesus loves you with an everlasting love.

He will always draw the line at the right time if you are going to be inappropriately treated.

I have grown to count on Him to say, 'that's it, enough is enough.'
This has endeared my heart to Him. He cares about me.
He is the one to decide if and when someone will mistreat me.

Jesus Christ is into mental health.
It will never be His will to want you to be abused.
He will always make an escape so that you can escape abuse.

I have a rule of thumb.

If you would not tolerate your child being abused that way,
then don't allow yourself to be abused that way.

"No temptation has seized you except what is common to man. And God is faithful; he will not let you be tempted beyond what you can bear. But when you are tempted, he will also provide a way out so that you can stand up under it" (1 Corinthians 10:13).

Being mistreated is a part of following Jesus.

"Here is a trustworthy saying: If we died with him, we will also live with him; if we endure, we will also reign with him. If we disown him, he will also disown us; if we are faithless, he will remain faithful, for he cannot disown himself." (2 Timothy 2:11-13).
"You, however, know all about my teaching, my way of life, my purpose, faith, patience, love, endurance, persecutions, sufferings - what kinds of things happened to me in Antioch, Iconium and Lystra, the persecutions I endured. Yet the Lord rescued me from all of them. In fact, everyone who wants to live a godly life in Christ Jesus will be persecuted, while evil men and impostors will go from bad to worse, deceiving and being deceived. But as for you, continue in what you have learned and have become convinced of, because you know those from whom you learned, and how from infancy you have known the holy Scriptures, which are able to make you wise for salvation through faith in Christ Jesus" (2 Timothy 3:10-15).

If some believers can reasonably expect to die for their faith
once the authorities in their country find out they love Jesus and follow Him,
what does it mean, 'God will make a way of escape' for His beloved followers?

We would think God values our life.
He would surely decide to protect us from evil doers.
This is exactly what God does.

Even as a follower of Jesus loses his or her life because of their faith
they will not depart from the hollow of His hand
from His Holy presence
from the promise of spending all eternity in heaven.

Whether we live or die we belong to the Lord.
God promises He will keep us from 'eternal harm'.

Believers who die of smoke inhalation in a house fire
or struck down and killed in a traffic accident,
or the victim of a heinous crime are all in God's hand in life and in death.

"Just as man is destined (appointed) to die once," (Hebrews 9:27a).

The Lord has an appointment set for each person. To God it is precious.

"Precious in the sight of the Lord is the death of His saints" (Psalm 116:15).
"Therefore, since we are surrounded by such a great cloud of witnesses, let us throw off everything
that hinders and the sin that so easily entangles, and let us run with perseverance the race marked
out for us. Let us fix our eyes on Jesus, the author and perfecter of our faith, who for the joy set
before him endured the cross, scorning its shame, and sat down at the right hand of the throne of
God" (Hebrews 12:1-2).
"To him who is able to keep you from falling and to present you before his glorious presence
without fault and with great joy - " (Jude 1:24).

125

If you are being led by the Holy Spirit - when you pray you are in the work of the Holy Spirit.

Why is this so?

It is because the Lord says only He will build His church.

"Unless the Lord builds the house, its builders labour in vain" (Psalm 127:1).
"When the Counsellor comes, whom I will send to you from the Father, the Spirit of truth who
goes out from the Father, he will testify about me" (John 15:26).

God did not say He needed to send another religious leader to add to the message of the bible,
reinterpret the message of the bible,
or set up a unique church that claims to be the only one with the truth.

He simply said He would send the Holy Spirit.
The Holy Spirit is the Spirit of truth.
If you want the truth let the Holy Spirit lead you.

His agency of love in the earth is the precious Holy Spirit.
We are not the agency of love on the earth today, the Holy Spirit is.
When the Holy Spirit is free to work
He ultimately wants to lead people to Jesus
for Jesus is the Way.

There is a lot of waiting when God is leading by His Spirit.
He needs us to constantly defer to Him.
A servant of God is always ready to step aside
and allow the Holy Spirit to do as He pleases.

Most of the time the Holy Spirit is asking me to pray for someone after meeting them
instead of asking me to say something to them about God.

If you are led by the Holy Spirit you become His agency of love in the earth today.
His hands and His feet. God will put you into all manner of situations.
Afterward He shows you how He wants you to pray about that situation.
He sometimes shows you how to pray when you are right in the situation too.

When we are led by the Holy Spirit we have the money He needs and the possessions He needs
even if it doesn't seem like it to us at the time. He can't fail you when you really need Him because
His children are led by His Spirit. His sons and daughters.
How important is it that we are led by the Holy Spirit?

"because those who are led by the Spirit of God are sons of God" (Romans 8:14).

God includes both women and men in the leading of His Holy Spirit when He says, 'sons'.

"Now that faith has come, we are no longer under the supervision of the law. You are all sons of
God through faith in Christ Jesus, for all of you who were baptized into Christ have clothed
yourselves with Christ. There is neither Jew nor Greek, slave nor free, male nor female, for you are
all one in Christ Jesus. If you belong to Christ, then you are Abraham's seed, and heirs according
to the promise" (Galatians 3:25-29).

In this particular bible reference the bible does not identify the manner of work.
Neither does God say how much work needs to be done.
It simply says the members of God's family are led by His Spirit.

You need no other pedigree, permission or premise.

If you are led by the Spirit of God
you are a member of His family here on earth.

Oh, and He enables you to be available to do His true work as well.

God doesn't 'farm out' the work of the church.

He doesn't go throughout the face of the earth for smart people or super religious people
to sit down and figure out how to set things up for Him.

It is true that some people have been deceived into thinking that is exactly what they are supposed
to do. Some are in the Christian church, and others are in churches they made up for themselves.
Interestingly enough, some of those 'churches' won't acknowledge that God is with the other ones.
Only 'their' rules, writings, secrets, plans and adherents have the answer.
They even think their interpretation of the bible is the only accurate one.
No one else has the inside track with Almighty God!
Really?
Remember what Jesus said.
Isn't Jesus the center of the whole Christianity thing?
It all comes down to whether or not Jesus is able to say He 'knew you' or not.

If joining the right group is so important why did Jesus say He will need to know you?
Why didn't He say you will have to belong to one particular church instead? He said those who go
to hell are told, 'I never knew you.' Not, 'you failed to belong to the right church?'

Jesus is God and therefore He is perfect. It seems strange that He failed to mention the specific
name of a certain church if it were the only church. Doesn't that strike you as odd?
He is raised from the dead and about to ascend physically up into heaven but fails to mention that
belonging to the right church on the planet and pledging your allegiance to a mere man who would
show up centuries later will get you to heaven? Wouldn't he at least know the name, possibly the
address or phone number of the person in all history who is supposed to bring this new revelation
to mankind on His behalf?
Oh, wait a minute, didn't Jesus say 'He' is the truth?
Yeah, He did.
The truth is found in Jesus Christ alone.
Get a New Testament.
Ask God for His help as you read it.
Get to know Jesus for yourself.
Lay aside the copious, bamboozling stacks of religious writing you are told you can't do without
in order to understand God.

Jesus came for you.
Your leaders are not God.
Only Jesus is God. Only He is the Shepherd appointed by God the Father
once and for all mankind.
Go to Him yourself. Find out why He died and rose again on your behalf!
Is there any religious leader on earth who did anything anywhere near that significant for you?

"For there is one God and one mediator between God and men, the man Christ Jesus, who gave himself as a ransom for all men - the testimony given in its proper time" (1 Timothy 2:5-6).

127

"Jesus answered, "I am the way and the truth and the life. No one comes to the Father except through me" (John 14:6).
"The thief comes only to steal and kill and destroy; I have come that they may have life, and have it to the full" (John 10:10).

The thief has come to steal you away from your intimacy with Jesus.

To keep you busy doing anything but developing your friendship.

"I no longer call you servants, because a servant does not know his master's business. Instead, I have called you friends, for everything that I learned from my Father I have made known to you. You did not choose me, but I chose you and appointed you to go and bear fruit - fruit that will last. Then the Father will give you whatever you ask in my name. This is my command: Love each other" (John 15:15-17).

Jesus is a Person and there is nothing more important in the entire world
than for you to be caught up in the passion and the love of your own relationship with Him.
He already has a member of the trinity here on earth to bring it to pass!
His precious Holy Spirit.
Imagine that, all the followers of Jesus need to do is allow the Holy Spirit to move
and the works of God will come into being.
In fact our God insists upon it.

"Unless the Lord builds the house, its builders labour in vain. Unless the Lord watches over the city, the watchmen stand guard in vain" (Psalm 127:1).

128

Lots of people doing lots of labour all the time is not what God is all about.

The kingdom of God is about a few people like Mary (Martha's sister) who give reverence and awe to God.

A few people who are willing to sit quietly and listen to what the voice of God would bring to their heart.

I know it sounds extreme.
But Jesus told Mary and Martha only one thing mattered.
Jesus sounds extreme eh?

126

Those who seek Him follow on a narrow path.

"Then Jesus asked, "What is the kingdom of God like? What shall I compare it to? It is like a mustard seed, which a man took and planted in his garden. It grew and became a tree, and the birds of the air perched in its branches." Again he asked, "What shall I compare the kingdom of God to? It is like yeast that a woman took and mixed into a large amount of flour until it worked all through the dough" (Luke 13:18-20).

This is good news for those paying the price to wait upon the Lord and listen for the leading of the Holy Spirit. Sometimes if feels like there are only a few people out there whom God is using in this manner.
Fortunately Jesus kept saying the small contributions will create His biggest impact.
The mustard seed, the little bit of yeast - God has planned to do a lot with a little for those who are led by the Spirit.
The work of God is really all about prayer. That's what Jesus told us.

'It is written,' he said to them, 'My house will be called a house of prayer,' but you are making it a 'den of robbers' (Matthew 21:13).
"these I will bring to my holy mountain and give them joy in my house of prayer. Their burnt offerings and sacrifices will be accepted on my altar; for my house will be called a house of prayer for all nations" (Isaiah 56:7).
Jesus quotes this next verse in Isaiah 56:7. "And as he taught them, he said, "Is it not written: " 'My house will be called a house of prayer for all nations'? But you have made it 'a den of robbers' " (Mark 11:17).

129

There is so much joy in letting the Holy Spirit minister to your heart!

The Holy Spirit's ministry is your life.

If He is not personally guiding you then you have 'nothing' to show
for all of your efforts
to be a Christian.

Unless you call your best ideas on how to serve God - 'something'.
Unless you are content to simply do what you are told
and presume that because you are in church that everything is therefore totally God's will.
Or, because it was your pastor or church higher-up giving you opportunity or instruction
then it is just like God telling you.

The Lord's will is the result of unity in the Holy Spirit.

"Make every effort to keep the unity of the Spirit through the bond of peace" (Ephesians 4:3).

I share this with you from personal experience only this morning. I was awakened in the middle of the night. So I had a seat in a comfortable chair in the quiet of our bedroom. After waiting upon the Lord the Holy Spirit began to minister. His presence was unmistakeable. The room was filled with the peace that passes understanding. Such a sense of love and well-being.
I had to wait quite a while this time before He arrived with anointing power. He was no doubt busy taking care of hindrances and other obstacles put in place to keep me from the love of God.
After warring on behalf of my family and me He turned His attention to my desire for face-time with Jesus and my heavenly Father. The Holy Spirit is a fighter as well as a lover.
He is a wonderful friend to have on your side!
Give Him time when you go aside to meet with your Jesus.
He will work on your behalf.

"I will bless those who bless you, and whoever curses you I will curse; and all peoples on earth will be blessed through you" (Genesis 12:3).

You will be led in kindness and compassion by a God who never slumbers nor sleeps.

130

We all want so much to please the Lord.

This is the story of Mary and Martha.

Martha wanted to please the Lord so she got busy for Jesus. Mary wanted to please the Lord, so she humbled herself to sit with Jesus and listen to what He would teach her - to devote herself to His love.
It sounds so different and it is very different in God's eyes.

"But Samuel replied: "Does the Lord delight in burnt offerings and sacrifices as much as in obeying the voice of the Lord? To obey is better than sacrifice, and to heed is better than the fat of rams" (1 Samuel 15:22).

"I desire obedience and not sacrifice," He said. What does this mean?
People who permit God to tell them what He wants offer God obedience.

People desiring sacrifice become busy then ask God to bless what they have done.

When they sense the moving of the Holy Spirit they jump into action instead of waiting to hear what is on the mind of the Holy Spirit. They move ahead before they actually enquire of the Lord.

Often it is to duplicate what He has done on prior occasions.
Sometimes they have already decided in advance He is going to do, what they have heard about Him doing in other places, what they believe for Him to do - but none of it is in obedience to the still small voice.

128

They develop an astoundingly impressive appearance of Godliness without paying the price
to find out just exactly what God was up to. That means the critically needed ministry of the Holy
Spirit has been brushed aside in favour of human ability, capability, opportunity and sinful flesh.

Some folks are willing to forsake the approval of God for the approval of man.
But in the end, when standing directly in front of Jesus Christ Himself,
what will all the approval of man amount to?
Will Jesus have to ask, 'why didn't you come to Me instead of running around and being so busy?'

I love when He sends His word to my heart.

The important thing is to let Jesus talk to you now, in this life.
I know for sure that He has a great plan for your life.

"For I know the plans I have for you," declares the Lord, "plans to prosper you and not to harm
you, plans to give you hope and a future" (Jer. 29:11).

131

Will you ask the Holy Spirit to help make the concept in this story real within your heart?

Perhaps He will use this example in story-form to help bring understanding.

At precisely 2:00 p.m., without prompting, three people in eighth grade class stood up, quickly and
quietly walked out the door. The rest of the class sat bewildered. The teacher remained motionless.
Silent. Finally when she did speak, she said, "the three students who just walked out 'were listening'
and they were 'obedient'. The rest of you did not hear what I said. Earlier today I said, "at two
o'clock I want you to get up and walk out of this room without any talk or fuss." The three students
now outside the classroom were obedient. From now on I hope you choose to 'listen more closely'."

Does that story help? We automatically link obedience with listening.
The teacher in the story said her students must choose to listen more closely.
The obedient students had listened.

God is the same way. He said Mary pleased Him utterly because she was listening to what He
taught her (Luke 10:38 - 42). Jesus knew she wanted to do what pleases Him.
He knew Mary loved Him and she understood how He felt about obedience.

"If you love me, you will obey what I command" (John 14:15).

Before she could obey she would have to find out what was on His heart.
She would have to give God an opportunity to speak to her.
It was a vital way to share His love with her.
It would happen each day in a personal encounter with Him.

She entered into joyful, loving service because she first listened to Him.

Her obedience was the Spirit's overflow touching every deed.

"I have been crucified with Christ and I no longer live, but Christ lives in me. The life I live in the body, I live by faith in the Son of God, who loved me and gave himself for me" (Galatians 2:20).

132

There comes a time for most every Christian when a certain conflict will arise in their heart.

It is the time when the Holy Spirit is telling them one thing, and their church, pastor, leader, teacher, mentor or another religious 'voice' is saying something completely different.

It might be about a little step of obedience asked by the Holy Spirit.

What should a person do?

It seems a simple answer but in real life it is not.
When the 'church' is in conflict with the still, small voice of the Holy Spirit in your heart here is what you should do. Go back to the Lord as soon as you can with the whole dilemma. Give this situation over to God. Tell Him you need His wisdom in the matter.
Give God time, wait upon Him, be still before Him then obey God in whatever He puts upon your heart. Do what He tells you to do. Tell Him you will trust Him and you desire only to please Him. Always say, 'yes' to Jesus.
God comes to build His kingdom. The only avenue He has is through obedience in His beloved children.

"Once, having been asked by the Pharisees when the kingdom of God would come, Jesus replied, "The kingdom of God does not come with your careful observation, nor will people say, 'Here it is,' or 'There it is,' because the kingdom of God is within you" (Luke 17:20-21).

Jesus holds you safely in the palm of His hand.
He will protect you from those who disagree with you.

Some will even be fellow church people.

"I give them eternal life, and they shall never perish; no one can snatch them out of my hand" (John 10:28).

133

He has prepared the earth
and then created mankind.

In compassion and mercy He has not left your activities up to chance.
God has a very specific idea of what He would like to accomplish.
He is reaching out with this loving guidance to every person.

"This is my Father's glory, that you bear much fruit, showing yourselves to be my disciples"
(John 15:8).
"But the fruit of the Spirit is love, joy, peace, patience, kindness, goodness, faithfulness, gentleness
and self-control. Against such things there is no law" (Galatians 5:22-23).

As surely as He had a specific place in the heavens for each star
there is a magnificent plan and order prepared for each individual.

"So God created man in his own image, in the image of God he created him; male and female he
created them" (Genesis 1:27).

He had all kinds of ideas long before a person walked upon the earth.

"For we are God's workmanship, created in Christ Jesus to do good works, which God prepared in
advance for us to do" (Eph. 2:10).

He did not wait for us to show up to figure out how to run the universe.
His plan will bring out the very best in you.
His plan for you will stand up for the aeons to come.

134

When mankind was created our heavenly Father had already been in existence for countless ages of
eternity past.

He is without end.

Before time and the earth itself. Everlasting into all eternity.
God calls Himself, 'I am'. That means He is beyond human imagination of greatness, of time,
of love, of death and the meaning of life. That is who your God is.

"Moses said to God, "Suppose I go to the Israelites and say to them, 'The God of your fathers has
sent me to you,' and they ask me, 'What is his name?' Then what shall I tell them?" God said to
Moses, "I AM WHO I AM. This is what you are to say to the Israelites: 'I AM has sent you' "
(Exodus 3:13-14).
"And I say also unto thee, That thou art Peter, and upon this rock I will build my church; and the
gates of hell shall not prevail against it" (Matthew 16:18 King James Version).

Be joyful always as you consider the work of God.
He will always have a plan.

To seek to build the work of God without Him is not wise.
To enter into an activity without having 'been with Jesus' is like sitting in the captain's seat
of a jet aircraft because you believe it will fly. Having faith you can fly a plane without training
or experience is not the enablement God intends for His representatives.
Notice though,
what great things are accomplished by even a novice
in the care of a Mighty God.

David and Goliath. 1 Samuel 17
Moses and the parting of the Red Sea. Exodus 14:21 - 31

"Jesus looked at them and said, "With man this is impossible, but with God all things are possible"
(Matthew 19:26 New International Version).

135

"But God chose the foolish things of the world to shame the wise; God chose the weak things of
the world to shame the strong" (1 Corinthians 1:27).
"That is why, for Christ's sake, I delight in weaknesses, in insults, in hardships, in persecutions, in
difficulties. For when I am weak, then I am strong" (2 Corinthians 12:10).

If we are the ones spending time with Him,
seeking Him,
why does He say <u>He</u> is building His church?

This is where the Precious Holy Spirit and His ministry are explained.
We come to the Lord
for His sweet fellowship.
We come to the Lord for the love we crave.
In His presence there is healing.
There is hope and deliverance.
He reaffirms your righteous identity in Christ Jesus.
Intimacy with Almighty God is all about what He has in mind.

Your heavenly Father has already prepared in advance the way for the church to be built.
Your destiny is fulfilled right there in the quiet place with Him.
It is because of your weakness that you are so dearly esteemed by your creator.
He has chosen the weak things of this world.
Faithful is he who calls you who also will do it.

"God chose the weak things of the world to shame the strong" (1 Corinthians 1:27b).
"The one who calls you is faithful and he will do it" (1 Thessalonians 5:24).
"being confident of this, that he who began a good work in you will carry it on to completion until
the day of Christ Jesus" (Philippians 1:6).

When we gather with other 'like minded people' to seek the Lord, there is agreement to enable Him to bring His will to pass.

"Do two walk together unless they have agreed to do so?" (Amos 3:3).

This is because each one is hearing from God.
Each person has purposed in their heart to seek the Lord Jesus Christ.
He is free to bring them together with each person having the mind of Christ.

It is the Holy Spirit who communicates the mind of Christ to us.

"How good and pleasant it is when brothers live together in unity" (Psalm 133:1).

Unity is a wonderful phenomenon made possible by the Holy Spirit.

It is more than people getting together who agree about what to do.
Or people who agree in a kind of belief system.
It is more than people agreeing who is in charge and unquestioningly doing what they are told.

Unity is a state of being.

Unity is a blessing bestowed from heaven by God.

Unity cannot be manufactured by man.

Unity is a spiritual condition shared by a group of people who have agreed to seek Jesus Christ and allow Him to be the Lord of all that takes place.
It is in the seeking of Jesus that He is found.

"You will seek me and find me when you seek me with all your heart" (Jeremiah 29:13).

They are ordinary people committed to doing His perfect will and they settle for nothing less.
In their complete surrender He meets with them and leads them as a group.
To surrender your heart means you will allow him to lead you in His will for your life.
Also, it means you are willing to surrender your own will and desires
when He shows you what He wants.

Like the selection of colours on an artist's palette each person becomes a unique reflection, observation, perception and unique experience of God.

Drawing near to the Lord when you gather with other Christians is a most favourable goal.

137

Unity can only be established by God Himself.

"Unless the Lord builds the house, the builders labour in vain" (Psalm 127:1a).
The work of the church is entered into from many points of view.

Many beliefs and protocols find their way into Christian church activity.
There are many workmen eager to build the church for God.
They are always working.
They are always ready to influence individuals and groups of people and tell them what to do.

When God is honoured above all other things in your heart,
Jesus Christ takes His place as 'the' builder.

"Let us fix our eyes on Jesus, the author and perfecter of our faith," (Hebrews 12:2).
"for it is God who works in you to will and to act according to his good purpose"
(Philippians 2:13).
"he saved us, not because of righteous things we had done, but because of his mercy" (Titus 3:5a).

Jesus exercises His dominion with a sweet, winsome, over-arching gentleness and glory.

138

Jesus exercises His All-powerful, sovereign influence in your life.

You are of all people kept safe in your complete surrender to your loving God.

You are shaped by the Master-potter like clay upon His potter's wheel.
There will be only One builder when your life is completely surrendered to God.
This surrender is realized in the intimate fellowship you enter into with God.
It is not something you do when you get to church.
God needs intimacy.

That is because you are not called to surrender to man, his protocols and special teachings.
It is service to God from your heart.
"Above all else, guard your heart, for it is the wellspring of life" (Proverbs 4:23).

When the Lord builds the house the other workmen are out of a job.
They are unable to do their work to influence the outcome of your soul.
They will try, but the Master has you securely placed upon His potter's wheel.
He is in charge
and they will never do any work that touches your precious soul.

Anything they do will
1) recoil back to where it came from
2) God will work it all together for your good no matter how much devastation their influence brings upon you.

"Surely God is my help; the Lord is the one who sustains me. Let evil recoil on those who slander me; in your faithfulness destroy them" (Psalm 54:4-5).

Jesus you see,
is your Shepherd and you will only follow Him.

"My sheep listen to my voice; I know them and they follow me" (John 10:27).

Can you pick up the nuance?
God knows all things.

Yet He says all His sheep follow Him and, 'He knows them'.
For those who love and care for the body of Christ this word brings peace.

Ultimately the Sheep are unable to follow another shepherd. They are kept by the Good Shepherd.

Your brothers and sisters of the faith are kept by God. Sometimes those sheep can be in a situation that appears to compromise their good keeping.
But God's word is surer than anything the sheep will endure. Jesus loves His sheep.
He gave His life for them. He will save them to the uttermost.

None can be taken out of His hand.

Dear Reader. This is another expression of intimate love.
When Jesus says He 'knows them' it speaks of singular intimate sharing.
Becoming known to Him in a sacred place where hearts and secrets are shared one of another.
A vulnerable quality unlike any other relationship.
No one can replace the refuge that is God.

It is true God knows all things.
There are those who draw near to Him and seek Him
and Jesus proclaims that He knows them.

May Jesus say of you one day, "I know you" expressing the love and tenderness
of your dearest friend.
The One to whom you were betrothed before the world was made.

Do not fear, for God loves you and He is with you.
Oh yes dear one,
God loves you.

139

When the Lord is building a person's life
He delights to have them meet someone else who is likewise surrendered to His care.
There is unity.

There is like-mindedness.
There is instantaneous pleasure for both God and man not possible by a thousand builders
working all night and all day for many years.

"How good and pleasant it is when brothers live together in unity" (Psalm 133:1).

It is good and pleasant to man.
It is good and pleasant to God.
Both events occur together.

From our perspective it brings an overwhelming awareness of being right with God.
Unity floods the meeting of a brother or sister of the faith with God's love. The people in His care
are flooded with the sensation of divine, supernatural love.
God's love for them,
love for one another
and the freedom to follow the Holy Spirit's guidance in unison.

At the same time, this awareness is but a reflection of the pleasure in the heart of God
with the work He is accomplishing.

It is a reflection of the joy He has with His beloved children.

It is His will being done in earth as it is in heaven.
The perfect will He would like to see take place on earth is being done.

His Holy Spirit come to do the heavenly Father's will right there in your midst.

"your kingdom come, your will be done on earth as it is in heaven" (Matthew 6:10).

140

'Not by might, nor by power, but by my Spirit,' says the Lord Almighty (Zechariah 4:6b).

Here is the verse written in the bible for all believers in every moment of history.
It is the Holy Spirit who takes the place of supreme honour in individual lives and church activity.

"for it is God who works in you to will and to act according to his good purpose" (Philippians 2:13).

The Holy Spirit's role is to direct everything in the life of the sheep in God's care.
He is a Person living within a born again person.
Once a believer has received Jesus as Saviour the Holy Spirit lives within that person.
Afterward, it is essential to ask God for the Baptism with the Holy Spirit.
This will endue a believer with power from on high.
As we have seen, it is not possible to be in the service of God without being led by the Holy Spirit.

When the Holy Spirit is denied His preeminent role
there are traditions,
fads,
rules,
protocols,
good ideas and religion.
Becoming an identifiable member of church activity is limited to those who can stand up to the rigors imposed by workmen usurping the True Builder of the church.
The weak and vulnerable are 'culled' out.
Their desire to hear from God is not accommodated.
They are easily pushed out of the picture by those aligned with a wrong motive in their heart
and people in church that are dead to the Spirit.

How the Lord weeps as good people work their hearts out
trying to do what they think God wants
when they are just doing what their leadership tells them to do.
Pushed on in dead works
by those who have chosen to live apart from God's heart.
A Laodicean leadership who never take time to stop and ask God,
'exactly what is it that You want me to do'.
Not taking time to enjoy His presence.
No desire to humble themselves under God's mighty hand.

How sad for dedicated church attendee to hear, 'I never knew you,' when they face Jesus in eternity.
'Who sought Me to establish their work?', Jesus will be asking.
'Did you permit the Person of the Holy Spirit, the One sent to earth by Me, to tell you what I wanted accomplished in the earth?'
There will be no traction for the argument, 'speaking in tongues is of the devil,' or 'that was only happening with the original disciples,' or 'I was told I couldn't belong if I believed in that stuff.'

"However, as it is written: "No eye has seen, no ear has heard, no mind has conceived what God has prepared for those who love him" - but God has revealed it to us by his Spirit. The Spirit searches all things, even the deep things of God. It is the Spirit that takes the deep things of God and reveals it unto *you*" (1 Corinthians 2:9-10).

You are so blessed that Jesus sent the Holy Spirit to take up residence in you.
Ask the Holy Spirit to be real in your life today!
Ask Him to take the deep things of God and reveal them unto you.

You will be praying His perfect will for this is written in the bible for those who choose to follow Jesus Christ.

141

If you are afraid because I am talking about the Holy Spirit it is alright.

Please follow along as we get to know Him a bit better.
Here is today's news headline.

A PERSON CALLED THE HOLY SPIRIT LIVES INSIDE ALL PEOPLE WHO RECEIVE JESUS CHRIST OF NAZARETH!
He will go unknown by most converts!
Many won't ask what His purpose is inside of them!
The Holy Spirit is very lonely!

You may have come to think you can live without involving the Holy Spirit after seeing or hearing about strange and ungodly things done and attributed to the work of the Holy Spirit.
But the Holy Spirit is hardly Someone to be afraid of since He is a member of the Trinity.

God the Father, Son and Holy Spirit. There, you said it.
God the Holy Spirit (there, you said it again).

'Dear Holy Spirit, please lead me into all Truth. Do the work for which my heavenly Father sent you to this earth. Guide me in my walk with God. Reveal Jesus and His love unto me.
You live within me. I welcome your total influence in my life. Amen.'

You have done well.
Wait upon the Lord.

Be with Him in His presence.
Let the peace of God rule in your heart.

"Let the peace of Christ rule in your hearts, since as members of one body you were called to peace. And be thankful" (Colossians 3:15).

142

As the Holy Spirit becomes more real to you His presence will also become more important to you.

He lives to bring people to God.

You need Him for He is your inspiration.
He alone enables you to be intimately involved with Jesus.

"This is the word that came to Jeremiah from the Lord: "Go down to the potter's house, and there I will give you my message." So I went down to the Potter's house, and I saw him working at the wheel. But the pot he was shaping from the clay was marred in his hands; so the potter formed it into another pot, shaping it as seemed best to him. Then the word of the Lord came to me: "O house of Israel, can I not do with you as this potter does?" declares the Lord. "Like clay in the hand of the potter, so are you in my hand, O house of Israel" " (Jeremiah 18:1-6).

Because we are likened to clay upon the potter's wheel we readily accept the need for God to be the One to accomplish His work within us. We are called to an intimate relationship with God in which His Holy Spirit - the Person living within - brings God's influence to bear upon us. Just as clay is unable to be shaped of its own volition, power or creative energies.

Clay must be pliable for the Potter to bring shape and change.

"No one can come to me unless the Father who sent me draws him, and I will raise him up at the last day" (John 6:44).
"Now when they had gone throughout Phrygia and the region of Galatia, and were forbidden of the Holy Ghost to preach the word in Asia, After they were come to Mysia, they assayed to go into Bithynia: but the Spirit suffered them not" (Acts 16:6-10 King James Version).

From the very start of your walk with God
you need the Holy Spirit to do what He has purposed in His heart.
He is the only agency on earth that brings you to God.

God's broken hearted servants desire the fellowship of their Creator.
Unless the Father draws them there is no coming to Jesus in fellowship.
Necessary and life giving fellowship is made possible by the Holy Spirit. Clay contributes not.

"I said to the Lord, "You are my Lord; apart from you I have no good thing" (Psalm 16:2).

143

There isn't anything in you that God can use to redeem you.

The whole process is born of His Spirit through the blood of Jesus. Here is that verse again.

"Unless the Lord builds the house, the builders labour in vain. Unless the Lord watches over the city, the guards stand watch in vain" (Psalm 127:1).

Don't just read about Jesus. Don't just talk about Jesus.
Don't neglect seeking God because you go to church and you are told about Jesus.

Be bold and daring and abandon yourself to His Holy embrace.
Get alone with Jesus Christ today and be changed.
It will not be for the reason of becoming better at serving Him.
The whole idea is for you to share yourself with Him
and get to know Him.

As years advance and little by little your skill set is diminished,
having someone who cares about you enough to spend a little time with you
becomes so much more important.

Start now.
Develop this life-long friendship.

"The Lord your God is with you, he is mighty to save. He will take great delight in you, he will quiet you with his love, he will rejoice over you with singing" (Zephaniah 3:17).
"I do not set aside the grace of God, for if righteousness could be gained through the law, Christ died for nothing!" (Galatians 2:21).
"So too, at the present time there is a remnant chosen by grace. And if by grace, then it is no longer by works; if it were, grace would no longer be grace" (Romans 11:5-6).

144

This time alone together can never be taken from you.

Your time alone together is the one thing Jesus said you need.

Jesus knows what is good for you.
Spending time alone with Him is the fullness of His purpose
after He has saved and completely washed you from sin.

The tears He shed,
the painful prayers in the Garden of Gethsemane,
His willingness to be brutally treated
through the ripping and tearing of His flesh -
His desire is made complete when you believe and embark on a journey of friendship with Him.
Getting to know one another
face to face,
Person to person
completes His mission.

Imagine the joy He has
when even one person is willing to say,
'yes Lord,
I will take time to get to know you.'

His agony and sorrow endures daily for every soul indifferent to the loving settlement meted out in His physical body so long ago on the cross.

He is at the ready, poised to restore from sin and eternal damnation.

The degree of His concern can be seen in the depths of sorrow, pain and self denial He willingly suffered.

Those who hate Jesus,
misrepresent Jesus
and pass Him by
are unwittingly
but a heartbeat this side
of the burning flames of the devil's hell.

Any person without God is literally suspended by a single, frail strand of life.
That person is ready to be inconveniently devoured by utter,
unimaginable torment the very moment their spirit
leaves their body.
For the righteous it is not so.

"We are confident, I say, and would prefer to be away from the body and at home with the Lord"
(2 Corinthians 5:8).

No, we do not live our 'hell here on earth'.
That is because the 'experience' of hell is forever.
Unending.
Without pause or remission.
Jesus knew all about this.
So He did whatever He needed to do - just for you.
"I consider that our present sufferings are not worth comparing with the glory that will be revealed in us" (Romans 8:18).
"For our light and momentary troubles are achieving for us an eternal glory that far outweighs them all. So we fix our eyes not on what is seen, but on what is unseen. For what is seen is temporary, but what is unseen is eternal" (2 Corinthians 4:17-18).

How remarkable that His joy is made complete when only one person expresses interest in spending time together! Glory, glory, glory to His name for ever and ever!
So merciful. So kind. So wonderful is our Jesus!

"I tell you that in the same way there will be more rejoicing in heaven over one sinner who repents than over ninety-nine righteous persons who do not need to repent" (Luke 15:7).

"for it is God who works in you to will and to act according to his good purpose" (Philippians 2:13).

The precious Holy Spirit has been sent to live within you as a follower of Jesus.
He is working there to do His good pleasure.

It will be so important in your walk to allow the Holy Spirit to guide you, empower you,
baptise you, and also to make His desire known to you.
This is included in your experience of spending time with the Lord.

The Holy Spirit will communicate with you.
You will need Him to do this because your love for the Lord
is expressed in obedience
to what He wants.

"If you love me, you will obey what I command" (John 14:15).

Notice it doesn't say, 'if you love me you will -
study really hard,
give lots of money,
do overseas mission work,
evangelise door to door or on the main street,
attend church a lot,
make sure you witness to people,
get your healing,
believe everyone else is going to hell except the people who belong in your group.'

Remember the example of the students who obeyed their teacher?
To those who did not obey she said, 'you did not listen.'
The Holy Spirit has a role in your life to communicate on behalf of the Father and the Son,
Jesus Christ. He is working in you to do His good pleasure.

He will carefully enable you to fulfil your obedience to the Lord Jesus Christ.
He will tell you what He wants,
He will open the door of His leading for you
and He will enable you to be obedient.

"What he opens no one can shut, and what he shuts no one can open. I know your deeds. See, I
have placed before you an open door that no one can shut. I know that you have little strength, yet
you have kept my word and have not denied my name" (Revelation 3:7b-8).

"For I know the plans I have for you,' declares the Lord, 'plans to prosper you and not to harm you, plans to give you hope and a future" (Jer. 29:11).

It is a wonderful day!

That is because God has a plan for your life.

All of your confidence, all of your trust is in 'who' is taking care of you. When you desire to know Him above any other desire, you will see your heavenly Father cares for you exactly as He does His own Son Jesus Christ. He cares for you 'right now' with the same perfect love, resolve and power.

"I have made you known to them, and will continue to make you known in order that the love you have for me may be in them and that I myself may be in them" (John 17:26).

When our heart is set on how we think things should turn out
there is trouble grasping events from God's perspective.
For instance, if things don't turn out the way we had hoped,
it is a time to be thankful for God's care.
Trusting that He has made a decision with only our best interest at heart we can
- through tears sometimes - tell Him of our love for Him.

Continue to get alone with Him and experience the joy as the Holy Spirit lifts up your soul!
He will comfort and reassure you with His presence.

Get your bible open and read where He leads you. The Psalms are good.

If this is a difficult time for you, there is such comfort to know God is with you
and able to handle whatever your problem is.
He can handle it. Your God is powerful enough to turn everything for your good.
He has chosen to love you and take care of you.
It has been His decision to do so with love and joy until the end of time and all eternity.

"You did not choose me, but I chose you and appointed you to go and bear fruit - fruit that will last. Then the Father will give you whatever you ask in my name" (John 15:16).

That means nothing can happen to exclude you from the relationship He has in mind.
Talk about power!
All of His plans revolve around His everlasting love for you. He will use all that happens in your hard times to deepen your relationship. He knows how important this relationship is for you.

Jesus answered, "It is written: 'Man does not live on bread alone, but on every word that comes from the mouth of God' " (Matthew 4:4).

Who IS the real God?

Your God is the real God, that's who!

Your God reigns on high.

"Let the name of the Lord be praised, both now and forevermore" (Psalm 113:2).

"And we know that in all things God works for the good of those who love him, who have been called according to his purpose" (Romans 8:28).

He has amazing resiliency.
Flawless, really. But it is not His perfection that births passion in His dear ones.
Though He is thoroughly resolved to make you a success, it is how much He cares
that brings your hearts together.

"But I, with a song of thanksgiving, will sacrifice to you. What I have vowed I will make good.
Salvation comes from the Lord" (Jonah 2:9).

Belonging to God is a treasure that can never be taken from you.
He
wants
you.
He wants to love you and take care of you now and for evermore.
He has prepared His plans for you before He made the world so He is ready
to handily guide you through the challenges that will arise in your life!

"For we are God's handiwork, created in Christ Jesus to do good works, which God prepared in advance for us to do" (Eph. 2:10).

The challenges He allows will try you beyond your own natural ability to cope.

In truth, the trials will be 'common to mankind.'

Death of a loved one.
Rejection,
betrayal,
loneliness,
stresses of life,
misunderstanding - in this world you will encounter many things beyond your control.

"No temptation has overtaken you except what is common to mankind. And God is faithful; he will not let you be tempted beyond what you can bear. But when you are tempted, he will also provide a way out so that you can endure it" (1 Corinthians 10:13).

The faithful, kind and loving Holy Spirit will always be there for you.
Through the years of daily fellowship with Him you will be shaped.
He is so lovely, so endearing and such a servant.

It will be like the strands of a cord slowly entwining around each other
as your hearts grow in intimacy.
In His loving guidance the entwining of your heart will translate
into something worth more than gold.

Trust.
Confidence.

You will grow in your trust of the One who loves you so very, very much.
You will be blessed with reliance upon Him. It won't be through your strength.

In Him you will find your place of refuge.

"The name of the Lord is a strong tower; the righteous run to it and are safe" (Proverbs 18:10).
"For you have been my refuge, a strong tower against the foe" (Psalm 61:3).

150

When God the Father is pleased with you it doesn't matter what anyone else thinks.

Sometimes He may be the only supportive voice in your life.
When you come to God and He expresses His pleasure
it is wonderful to be given the feeling that all is well.
Often when the Lord has chosen
and set His eternal love, forgiveness and favour upon a tender hearted soul
there is sudden opposition from people around them.
They do not understand the change.

No longer interested in selfishness, excessive drinking, taking drugs, telling lies, committing adultery. And the change in appearance! The born again believer will have a noticeable change in their facial appearance. This radiance in the eyes and features is called someone's 'countenance'. Their countenance ceases to be dark, gloomy, glum, and common. There is a beauty shining forth.

"The path of the righteous is like the first gleam of dawn, shining ever brighter till the full light of day" (Proverbs 4:18).

God's redeeming power radiates from deep within.
At times a person appears to 'glow'.
Being forgiven for every sin you have ever committed can do that for you!
Being picked up and claimed by the eternal Son of God
can do that to you too!
Knowing instantly what will happen if you were to die
can certainly do that to you!
You know within your heart
that you no longer fear death
because of what Jesus did.
Receiving Christ is truly the singular important decision you will ever make
in this life.

Jesus answered him, "I tell you the truth, today you will be with me in paradise" (Luke 23:43).

Who can promise you something like this?
Only God Almighty - and He is your friend!

Any man who would give their word that they are responsible for your eternal life is taking you for a fool. What mortal man can offer you eternal life?
No man can do this. Only the Son of God is able to do this.

While you were still a sinner, it is Christ who died for you!

"We love because he first loved us" (1 John 4:19).
"You see, at just the right time, when we were still powerless, Christ died for the ungodly. Very rarely will anyone die for a righteous man, though for a good man someone might possibly dare to die. But God demonstrates his own love for us in this: While we were still sinners, Christ died for us" (Romans 5:6-8).

151

You are obedient, contrite and seeking to know Him above all other things.

Right in the middle of blissful fellowship with God calamity happens in your life!

Have you done something wrong?
Have the dark spiritual forces suddenly discovered how to uproot you from your faith?
Here is the good news. Nothing can change God.

"Jesus Christ is the same yesterday and today and forever" (Hebrews 13:8).

He is the only true God.

He *was* the King of Kings
is the Kings of Kings
and always will be the King of Kings!

He is perfectly powerful and sold out in His love for you.
He loves you with an everlasting love.

Then what is happening? Why have you been led right into suffering
when things could have been so much easier for you?
These are called 'fiery trials'.
God knows about them.
He was looking after you when He opened the door for you to experience such things.

"Beloved, think it not strange concerning the fiery trial which is to try you, as though some strange thing happened unto you: But rejoice, inasmuch as ye are partakers of Christ's sufferings; that, when his glory shall be revealed, ye may be glad also with exceeding joy. If ye be reproached for the name of Christ, happy are ye; for the spirit of glory and of God resteth upon you: on their part he is evil spoken of, but on your part he is glorified" (1 Peter 4:12-14 King James Version).

It is your destiny to go through life right in the midst of the toil, trauma and heartache
faced by every other human being all over the world. These trails are not new nor are they unique.
They are carefully planned as part of God's perfect will for your life.

'I have told you these things, so that in me you may have peace. In this world you will have trouble.
But take heart! I have overcome the world' (John 16:33 New International Version).

Jesus is your best friend.

"but there is a friend who sticks closer than a brother" (Proverbs 18:24).

He was careful to finish the work His Father planned for Him.
It meant enduring a death He did not deserve.
Jesus Christ allowed His precious blood to be spilled
right there in His Father's perfect will.
Love sustained Him. Oh, Jesus Christ is one cool individual! He doesn't back down.
What a hero!

Jesus Christ - the original Super Hero!

John 19:30 "When he had received the drink, Jesus said, "It is finished." With that, he bowed his head and gave up his spirit."

Now it could be said,
"Therefore he is able to save completely those who come to God through him, because he always lives to intercede for them" (Hebrews 7:25).

Because He is your friend and the Saviour of mankind at the same time,
He says, 'be of good cheer.'

In the face of any trial you endure you will be upheld by Him.

"for everyone born of God overcomes the world. This is the victory that has overcome the world, even our faith. Who is it that overcomes the world? Only he who believes that Jesus is the Son of God" (1 John 5:4-5).

There is no mention there of special learning for this victory.
Only that he or she who believes that Jesus is the Son of God has the victory
that overcomes the world.

"for everyone born of God overcomes the world. This is the victory that has overcome the world, even our faith" (1 John 5:4).

Some people are blessed with freedom to travel.
They have the time, money and the understanding of their loved ones to devote themselves
to special gatherings and lectures. They live in a country that doesn't shoot Christians or douse
them with gasoline and set them on fire.
But many, many dear brothers and sisters have only the Lord to depend upon.
That is the only freedom they have got. They can't even take a shower because there are no
facilities. They go without basic personal hygiene and medical care for themselves and their loved
ones and it breaks their hearts. These dear ones, who are such champions of the faith, are given
the victory that overcomes the world immediately with their faith in Jesus Christ the Son of God.

Can you picture 'lion classes' back in the time of the Coliseum in Rome?
You know, 'this is how you get chased and have the victory before the lion eats you'.
Dear brother and sister, Dear Reader, in our freedoms we have gotten a little bit carried away!
Carried away from intimacy with Jesus Christ. I imagine while in the rotten, stinking holding cells
beneath the ground those followers of Jesus were worshiping and ministering one to another.
They would be drawing near to Jesus and confessing their love for Him. I am not sure they were
praying to get out of there. Would it be more likely they were commending their lives into God's
care saying, 'thy will be done.'?
Please ask yourself today, 'am I devoted to the institution of Christianity or to Jesus Christ?'

Here is another little example. I hope it helps.
A husband is lying in bed about to die from an illness.
His devoted wife is lovingly attending to him.
<u>Husband</u>: I believe in marriage.
I uphold the whole premise of monogamy.
It is entirely a good thing to commit to one other person for the rest of your life.

148

I am committed to everything marriage means.
Good-bye dear. You are going to be ok. I believe it. Don't worry.

Wife: (Listening without being given the opportunity to say anything)

Is this love? Is this intimacy?
Is this communication? It is if you are lecturing.
It is communication if you don't need to know the person you are talking to.
It fills time, sounds great, makes a person appear committed
and definitely substantiates a belief system.
But there is no intimacy here in this relationship.

Here is the same scene with a demonstration of intimacy,
love and selflessness
between two loving hearts.

(and yes, I was thinking of my dear wife while writing this
as she is the ultimate example of God's love and faithfulness to me).

(Husband listening)
Wife: Are you doing OK dear?
Husband: Your love has meant so much to me throughout this ordeal.
(Husband listening)
Wife: There is no where else I would rather be dear. I wouldn't change a thing. I regret nothing.
You are the one I have always loved.
(Husband still listening)
Wife: (Quiet, now sobbing)
Husband: (Quietly watches the person he has adored for so very long. She is more beautiful now
than any time he could possibly remember. Everything he thinks about her brings him joy.
She has always been so selfless)
Wife: (Looking into her husbands eyes)
Husband: (Looking back into his wife's eyes)
-Time Passes -
Husband: I've taken care of our legal needs as best I can. Is there anything you need me to do?
Wife: (Unable to speak. She leans over from where she is sitting at the bedside and leans upon
him. Tenderly they enjoy each others warmth and embrace. They have done so more times than
any person can count)
Husband: (He has learned to accept that when she is silent that her actions speak louder than her
words. He counts himself the more fortunate than any man alive to have been the recipient
of such love. There was so much love)
[He will never know why he had been so favoured, so fortunate all these years.
With everything in him, he could sense that their love for one another had finally erased her fears.
He knew so well this dear girl he had married so long ago. He knew how it felt to read her
emotions and he knew she was not afraid anymore. She was just sad and there was nothing he
could do about that. There was nothing he could do, for she loved him so much.

She could not help but be sad]
(They held each other and they both felt so blessed for their embrace lasted as long as they wanted it to)
[It had always been this way. The tender give and take with the only love you have
in the entire world. It would be ok. They withheld nothing from each other.
They gave all they could give - gladly]
Husband: (Thinking to himself, 'I hold in my arms the only treasure God gave me in this life.')
"I love you dear."
Wife: "I will miss you but I will be ok." (She spoke the truth, knowing how important it was for her husband to know she remained confidant in spite of the pain they shared with each other)

In the Christian Religion
people become good at being 'Christian'.

Intimacy with Jesus is a thrilling and rewarding way of life. Please think about it.

Are you really involved with Jesus as your intimate, loving friend? Or are you fulfilled just knowing you have the right belief system. Your lack of persecution means you are somehow successfully doing the Christian thing the way it was meant to be done?

Get real with the Son of God.
Don't shut Him out with your beliefs.

Be still before Him.
Adore Him.
Glorify Him.
Stand in reverence and awe of Him.

Go near to listen.

153

As you are lifted up by God the Holy Spirit He will do wondrous, supernatural things with your grief.

He will give a 'crown of beauty' in exchange for the ashes in life.

He has the 'oil of gladness' to displace mourning.
He has a 'garment of praise' to decimate a spirit of despair.

"and provide for those who grieve in Zion - to bestow on them a crown of beauty instead of ashes, the oil of gladness instead of mourning, and a garment of praise instead of a spirit of despair. They will be called oaks of righteousness, a planting of the Lord for the display of his splendour" (Isaiah 61:3).

In the first part of this verse we see that God is well able to deal with your problems and handle whatever befalls you.
The second part describes what the people around you will perceive about your life.
They will see God eventually lifting you up, turning all things for good.
They won't be able to keep from enquiring how you have been able to survive.

Shining through your sincerity and mountain moving faith will be the Person
you have grown to love. Jesus is with you. All will be well. You survive and prosper
because you have believed that Jesus Christ is the Son of God.

You overflow with the comfort of the Lord as you continue to realise the goal of your faith which is the salvation of your soul.

"They will be called oaks of righteousness, a planting of the LORD, for the display of his splendour" (Isaiah 61:3b).

154

An oak tree does not move.

It has roots.

A tree is planted in one place.
It neither runs away nor does it have a master plan of escape from the stress.
If it starts to snow or the wind picks up or lightning strikes,
that tree remains where it has been planted.

Planted in one place, it stands.

The tree is able to weather the storms that befall it.
It is able to draw strength from the elements. The soil the sun and water.

"He is like a tree planted by streams of water, which yields its fruit in season and whose leaf does not wither. Whatever he does prospers" (Psalm 1:3).
"He will be like a tree planted by the water that sends out its roots by the stream. It does not fear when heat comes; its leaves are always green. It has no worries in a year of drought and never fails to bear fruit" (Jeremiah 17:8).

We are very much like a tree.
That is why we are referred to as the 'planting of the Lord'.

He becomes our survival, strength and provider in times of draught, misadventure and setback.
As we stand fast and simply gaze upon His beauty He sustains us supernaturally.

Because a tree is unable to provide its own defence or resources against an adversary
it must depend upon the elements.
Choosing to depend upon God guarantees the survival and prosperity of the tree.

"One thing I ask of the Lord, this is what I seek: that I may dwell in the house of the Lord all the days of my life, to gaze upon the beauty of the Lord and to seek him in his temple. For in the day of trouble he will keep me safe in his dwelling; he will hide me in the shelter of his tabernacle and set me high upon a rock Then my head will be exalted above the enemies who surround me; at his tabernacle will I sacrifice with shouts of joy; I will sing and make music to the Lord"
(Psalm 27:4 - 6).

"I don't know how you have been able to do it," caring loved ones will say.

"God is our refuge and strength, an ever-present help in trouble" (Psalm 46:1).

Jesus. Jesus.

Beautiful,
lovely
Jesus.

155

"What will 'following Jesus' look like?"
Many people wonder about this when they get saved.

How about the thief on the cross
who believed in Jesus?

"Jesus answered, "I am the way and the truth and the life. No one comes to the Father except through me" (John 14:6).

Don't worry about the 'doing' part of a relationship with God when you get saved!
If you do you will just get frustrated.
Just love Jesus. The wondrous exaltation when you first believe is called your first love.
It is a special love God wants you to have for Him for the rest of your life.

Think of the thief on the cross next to Jesus.
He got saved while he was nailed to a cross.
What a frustrating thing if he thought he had to do stuff for Jesus!
I would think he was half-dead at the time.

He loved Jesus!
He worshiped Jesus!

This would have pleased the Lord.
Jesus did not tell Him to do anything.
Jesus did not correct him or give him special instructions.

At the same time the thief couldn't help mention his faith to the other man hung up to die
on the other side of Jesus. Does this picture tell you something about salvation? Did Jesus say
anything about 'doing good works' to the man who had just believed while hanging on a cross?

"One of the criminals who hung there hurled insults at him: "Aren't you the Christ? Save yourself
and us!" But the other criminal rebuked him. "Don't you fear God," he said, "since you are under
the same sentence? we are punished justly, for we are getting what our deeds deserve. But this man
has done nothing wrong." Then he said, "Jesus, remember me when you come into your kingdom."
Jesus answered him, "I tell you the truth, today you will be with me in paradise" (Luke 23:39-43).

156

The criminal on the cross beside Jesus was about to achieve the goal of his faith, the salvation of his
soul.

'Today you will be with me in paradise,' Jesus said.

"for you are receiving the goal of your faith, the salvation of your souls" (1 Peter 1:9).

Did he have faith to move mountains? Jesus doesn't mention it . . .
but He does say,

'you
will be
with me.'

That is a big deal.

Here we see the magnificent heart of God.
This is a criminal almost dead. Justly condemned to die for his crime.
Jesus is nailed to the cross beside him physically tortured beyond recognition.
Both men are in bad shape and both of these men were written off by the rulers,
law makers and religious people
of their day.
But no!

Defiant. Compassionate. Jesus.

'This day YOU will be with me in paradise."
The devil will not get this man. Not with Jesus on the scene!

In spite of His wounding there is power in the word of the Lord.
Jesus said it out loud and people could hear him.

Isn't this why they hung him up? Accused of claiming to be the Messiah?
They even put a sign upon his cross in three different languages
to mock that He was the King of the Jews.
Only, He actually is the Messiah.
'This day you will be with ME in paradise.'
Take a moment and say this out loud! Put the emphasis on the word, 'Me.'
Can you perceive the heart of a Shepherd?
Can you feel how it must have impacted the criminal to be spoken to with such 'protective love'?

How comforting for that dying thief for Jesus Christ to be so focused and fully in command
in spite of being so physically broken. He was not leaving this man behind.
His love is too great to miss even one of His sheep.

A Shepherd's heart. 'You will be with ME in paradise.'
The end of all fear.
Jesus has taken charge in a life headlong toward hell itself. It is not just 'power' it is 'love'.
Jesus loved this man so despised and outwardly worthless.
But that is only the man we see with our human eyes.
God looks upon the heart.

In the end the criminal got what he deserved.
Grace.
Tender loving regard.
Redemption.

"For God did not send his Son into the world to condemn the world, but to save the world
through him" (John 3:17).

This word is absolutely true. Nothing could stop Jesus from saving anyone who trusts in Him
and He did it right there on the cross before He died physically.
Jesus looked at this criminal and saw someone made in His own image.
Jesus heart went out to him.
What is Jesus heart?
No one has to go to hell! All may be redeemed! He has come that the whole world might be saved
and He is going to do it if a person will trust in Him instead of in their 'dead works'.
He is going to do it one soul at a time.
Hebrews 6:1 - 3 says that the things we do without a relationship in God are called 'acts that lead
to death.' It says our foundation begins to be built when there is repentance from these works.

"Therefore let us leave the elementary teachings about Christ and to on to maturity, not laying
again the foundation of repentance from the acts that lead to death, and of faith in God,"
(Hebrews 6:2).

'Not everyone who says to me, 'Lord, Lord,' will enter the kingdom of heaven, but only he who does the will of my Father who is in heaven' (Matthew 7:21-23).

Not to mention the parents of that thief if they had been present to see their son slowly die. Parents have a way of knowing there is good in their children.
They have been with them since birth. Known them in their innocent beginnings.
They know what they have been through and have a grasp as to why they have done the things they have done. The bible doesn't say why this thief behaved the way he did,
but we will find out in heaven.
Hopefully we will meet the parents of the thief who died on the cross beside Jesus.

We will definitely meet the thief himself!

157

So how does someone look who is a born again Christian?

In reality one would observe the follower of Jesus daily spending time with God.

Just like one would observe a couple engaged to be married
and how they are just always doing things together.
Bound together by their love,
appreciation for each other and their fervent hope for the future they will share.

Because we are talking about a spiritual love it would look like a person sitting, kneeling, standing, pacing or prostrate on their face
in the presence of Almighty God.

Jesus said He is the 'door' or the 'gate'.

"I am the door. If anyone enters by Me, he will be saved, and will go in and out and find pasture" (John 10:9).

158

"What do I 'do' as a Christian?"

We naturally want to find a way to give Jesus what He wants without waiting to find out what He is looking for.

Being active in the perfect will of God is the Divine process undertaken by God the Holy Spirit.
We are become clay being shaped by the hand of God. Does the clay contribute?
Yes it does! It contributes by yielding to the artful hand of the Potter.
It is part of our human nature to want to earn His love.

God's grace means from the very start His love is a free gift.

"For it is by grace you have been saved, through faith - and this not from yourselves, it is the gift of God - not by works, so that no one can boast" (Eph 2:8-9).

Receiving His love is a matter of believing in Him, loving Him and following Him.
Not one of His precious children is destined to depend on their 'works'
in order to be loved.

Because it is all about Jesus and what He has already done for each person, at the end of life is the comfort of knowing their faith in God was enough.

159

Due to circumstances beyond their control some folks will have little or nothing to outwardly show for a lifetime of loving God.

This is an enormously difficult burden to bear.

Only the shield and refuge of God's fellowship
sustains the soul deprived of opportunities to offer God something substantial
in the realm of Christian service.

"The eternal God is your refuge, and underneath are the everlasting arms" (Deuteronomy 33:27a).

Such comfort enfolds them as they discover anew that Christ really has become their salvation.

Reflected in the light of His love is the reality
that good works in no way constitute who Jesus has become in you.
Jesus is your hope.
There may not always be the health, freedom, energy
and constitutional freedom to do all the things
you like to do for Christ.

"To them God has chosen to make known among the Gentiles the glorious riches of this mystery, which is Christ in you, the hope of glory" (Colossians 1:27).

Since His love never was based upon our own works, your rest will always be complete.
Christ in you, the hope of glory. Not by works lest any man should boast.

"To him who is able to keep you from falling and to present you before his glorious presence without fault and with great joy - to the only God and Saviour be glory, majesty, power and authority, through Jesus Christ our Lord, before all ages, now and forevermore! Amen"
(Jude 24-25).

It is in your daily times alone with God where you discover the importance of the fellowship of His love.

The 'plan' of God for your life does not begin with an inventory of what you will be able to do for Him.

"I have seen something else under the sun: The race is not to the swift or the battle to the strong, nor does food come to the wise or wealth to the brilliant or favour to the learned; but time and chance happen to them all" (Ecclesiastes 9:11).

What are we supposed to look like as Christians anyway?
Where are we supposed to go to church? What church is right for us?
What role does the Holy Spirit have in our life?
Which churches misrepresent the singular role of Jesus in your salvation?
So many questions.

Here is a mystery: God's purpose for you is hidden.
As long as you are looking for it you will never find it!
That is because we assume we are strong in some areas
and also assume we know what God would ask of us.
God levelled the playing field for one and all.
His kingdom is revealed in His love.

Any person who 'lives' outside of a relationship with Jesus will not find His plan for their life.

"For you died, and your life is now hidden with Christ in God" (Col.3:3).

There you have it. Your life is hidden with Christ. The person you once were has been reborn and the 'old you' has effectively died. You are a new creation.

"Therefore, if anyone is in Christ, he is a new creation; the old has gone, the new has come!" (2 Corinthians 5:17).

Has your leader expounded and exposited and with all subtlety entreated you to seek God's will in your life without consistently pointing to God's Christ?
You may even have the impression slowly arising in your understanding
that he or she has achieved a fantastical spirituality far beyond the norm.
Certainly beyond where you are presently are.

But God's will for your life is 'hidden with Christ in God'.

How will you find anything at all that is hidden?

Ah, dear believer,
all that you need is able to be found where it is hidden!
Look to Jesus Christ.
He is the Way, the Truth and the Life.

Are things looking more clearly for you now?
First and foremost, every day, continue your journey where it is easily found.

Get alone with the author and finisher of your faith.

"Let us fix our eyes on Jesus, the author and perfecter of our faith, who for the joy set before him endured the cross scorning its shame, and sat down at the right hand of the throne of God" (Hebrews 12:2).

161

The believer is held in the everlasting arms of God.

That is our singular place of refuge.

All that perplexes us is mercifully addressed day in and day out in the light of His glorious grace.
In that personal, quiet place of meeting with God.

Typically, we stumble and trip in our devotion in our early years of faith. This may be the result of things told to us. If the person who stands at the front to preach is not spending at least a few hours a day alone in the presence of God (like Mary did from the 'Mary and Martha story')
then they can only share with us the 'trial and error' of their faith. This is not faith in God at all.
"Try this approach like I did", "pray like I did " and "seek like I did".
It can even go to the extreme.
'When you pray you will sound like I do, pray what I pray, pace around like I do.'

Oh, how church people have their precious time wasted
gathering in God's name to listen to this religious purge.
Most of the time we hear this and conclude, 'what a great man or woman of God!',
because of what they do,
or say they have done.
This is true - they are 'great in themselves'. Their teaching can only point their followers one way -
to themselves.

Sadly, building oneself up as 'a man or woman of God' becomes an addiction.
Positive things spoken about what they do for God becomes the cornerstone of their faith.
They are no shepherd of God.
They are nothing like Jesus
for Jesus often went off on His own to spend time with His Father.

God can only be a dwelling and not a visiting place.

Seeking God once a week or once in a while
makes His fellowship a visiting place
not a refuge.
If He doesn't have your whole heart He is forced to spew you out of His mouth
like a lukewarm beverage.

So, we are to conclude
that it is not the quantity of the works being done or spoken of.
It is rather,
the heart of the individual
which only God can know through intimate love.

This is not to include the acts of sinfulness.
Deeds of sin also reflect a heart taking rest elsewhere from God.

It is also important to note that there are wonderful, Christ-centered ministries doing the work of God that are large and prolific, doing a great service both to God and mankind.

"To the angel of the church in Laodicea write: These are the words of the Amen, the faithful and true witness, the ruler of God's creation. I know your deeds, that you are neither cold nor hot. I wish you were either one or the other! So, because you are lukewarm - neither hot nor cold - I am about to spit you out of my mouth. You say, 'I am rich; I have acquired wealth and do not need a thing.' But you do not realize that you are wretched, pitiful, poor, blind and naked. I counsel you to buy from me gold refined in the fire, so you can become rich; and white clothes to wear, so you can cover your shameful nakedness; and salve to put on your eyes, so you can see. Those whom I love I rebuke and discipline. So be earnest, and repent" (Revelations 3:14-19).

Here is a reference to the laying a foundation of faith we looked at earlier.

The antidote is not to work harder, but to repent from dead works.

162

Spending time alone with Jesus fulfills His mission here on earth.

He came to live among men in order to take away the sin that keeps us apart from His love
and fellowship.

It would literally be impossible for someone who does not relate to God as a 'dwelling' to introduce people to the Person of Jesus Christ. Impossible.

That is because they do not abide with Him as a refuge.

"When they saw the courage of Peter and John and realized that they were unschooled, ordinary men, they were astonished and they took note that these men had been with Jesus" (Acts 4:13).

Intimate knowledge of someone you seldom spend time with amounts to a carnal version of someone you 'know about'. Tragically for the leader and for the flock they misrepresent, this is how most Christian leaders live. May God, may God raise up true spiritual leaders. Followers of Jesus.

" 'Not everyone who says to me, 'Lord, Lord,' will enter the kingdom of heaven, but only he who does the will of my Father who is in heaven. Many will say to me on that day, 'Lord, Lord, did we not prophesy in your name, and in your name drive out demons and perform many miracles?' Then I will tell them plainly, 'I never knew you. Away from me, you evil doers!' "(Matthew 7:21-23).

"Lord, may we be true to you in our own heart. Grant that we follow you hand in hand, spending time with you each day. Oh Lord, please bring your guidance into the lives of the many people having no one to share Jesus with them. Guide us, your people, to others who know you intimately. Have mercy upon those who speak of you without knowing who you are. Amen."

163

If they have not spent time with Him, then He doesn't know them either.

"Then I will tell them plainly, 'I never knew you" (Matthew 7:23a).

"Then he said to them all: "If anyone would come after me, he must deny himself and take up his cross daily and follow me" (Luke 9:23).

Here is the glorious truth.
This cross is not a physical cross!
Taking up your cross daily can be done by a dear 90 year old woman or man!
Those in hospital. By the poor and marginalized!

Your path is 'lived' by you right where you are at.
God has made it possible for you to blossom as an individual!

A follower of Jesus Christ grows and matures into a unique person!
There are no two followers of Jesus alike! Like the many snowflakes that fall from the heavens, God's design is expressed in profound diversity.

The purpose of God is realized in the fellowship He cultivates with each one of His children!

This is the heart of God's plan.
To love you personally and explore His wondrous plan together for the rest of your days and then for all eternity!

"Why, you do not even know what will happen tomorrow. What is your life? You are a mist that appears for a little while and then vanishes" (James 4:14).

With our lifespan said to be here then gone like a wisp of smoke,
getting saved and following Jesus is important in the extreme.

"I tell you, now is the time of God's favour, now is the day of salvation" (2 Corinthians 6:2b).

It is so important to accept Jesus into your heart as Saviour without delay.
'Today' is the day of salvation. It is the day for your salvation.

"Jesus, You have come to this earth to forgive me of my sins. You have a plan for my life which includes heaven on the day that I die. Please forgive me of all my sins. Come into my heart and lead me in the path you have prepared for my life. Let me live as a devoted friend of yours."

164

Though a life lived in Jesus is about faith and obedience to Him alone, you will discover with great joy your heart's desire is fulfilled right there in His plan for your life.

There is no greater fulfillment than to know His pleasure and favour.

Living to please only God brings blessing and peace.

"And the peace of God, which transcends all understanding, will guard your hearts and your minds in Christ Jesus" (Philippians 4:7).

It is very difficult, no, it is impossible to believe that Jesus is all you need in life.
That is why spending time with Him is imperative. He is your only source and supply.
He is your refuge.

Jesus spent a lot of time alone in prayer.
In this way He was refreshed in His beautiful love relationship with His Father.

165

"And being in anguish, he prayed more earnestly, and his sweat was like drops of blood falling to the ground" (Luke 22:44).

Endless devotion to His heavenly Father from eternity past enabled Jesus Christ to walk through the agony of Gethsemane's garden.

Part of His agony was conceptualizing the cost of obedience.
In obedience to His Father

Jesus would allow the makers of the law to take hold of Him under false accusation.

How deep the meaning as He turned to the thief on the cross beside Him.
In spite of all the punishment for being called a blasphemer,
being called the Saviour of the Jews, the Son of God and the Messiah - now near death Jesus said,
'This day you will be with Me in paradise.'

He went ahead and saved that thief right there and then.

How great, how wonderful is this Jesus!
They did everything they could to stop Him.
The devil did everything necessary to kill Jesus Christ.

There is your precious Jesus reaching out.
Yes, He did exactly what His Father sent Him to do.
This is the same wondrous Person who has reached out to you.
He truly was and forever is the Messiah, the Saviour of the world.

"I want to know Christ and the power of his resurrection and fellowship of sharing in his sufferings, becoming like him in his death, and so, somehow, to attain to the resurrection from the dead. Not that I have already obtained all this, or have already been made perfect, but I press on to take hold of that for which Christ Jesus took hold of me. Brother, I do not consider myself yet to have taken hold of it. But one thing I do: Forgetting what is behind and straining toward what is ahead, I press on toward the goal to win the prize for which God has called me heavenward in Christ Jesus" (Philippians 3:10-14).

He allowed the people who hated Him to finally apprehend Him.
At the same time knowing this would forever curtail His outreach here on earth.

He knew He had to go, but how He must have loved
connecting with the people created in His own image.
Surely there were experiences He would have longed to revisit.

The walks. Teaching His humble and eager followers.
Worship being poured out at His feet by those He forgave.
His joy in those who had counted the cost and were willing to completely
surrender their lives to Him. The absolute thrill to physically touch those He loved so much.

He would miss those times terribly for He knew death waited.

He must have ached within for He knew He would not have the freedom to see many of His beloved followers until the Holy Spirit raised Him from the dead.

Finally after his 33 years on earth Jesus would be restored through death to His Father
who loved Him so much.

They would rejoice together in their victory over the world, the flesh and the devil!

Another part of His agony was the innocent indifference of His dearest followers and friends
who could only grasp a small portion of His grand mission
here on earth.

Limited by their humanity, His inner circle whom He cherished and depended upon,
were unaware of His deep need.

Jesus Christ must have felt so alone.

He knew and loved them and understood how different He was from His devoted followers.
He knew He was about to die

but they did not know.

"Now Judas, who betrayed him, knew the place, because Jesus had often met there with his
disciples. So Judas came to the grove, guiding a detachment of soldiers and some officials from the
chief priests and Pharisees. They were carrying torches, lanterns and weapons. Jesus, knowing all
that was going to happen to him, went out and asked them, 'Who is it you want?' " (John 18:2-4).

His men would miss the opportunity to minister to Him at the time of His greatest need.
He had plainly told them so.

'The Son of Man must be delivered into the hands of sinful men, be crucified and on the third day
be raised again.' (Luke 24:7).

Do you care about Jesus? The great and wondrous things He is aware of?
What is His burden for the billions of souls
following each other into hell and separation from God for all eternity?
'Enter through the narrow gate. For wide is the gate and broad is the road that leads to destruction,
and many enter through it' (Matthew 7:13).

Just a note, remember Jesus said He is the gate? It is narrow because there is only one gate, one way
to salvation. It is a narrow because there is no other.

A narrow way meaning there are no other choices.

Do you care about how the Son of God feels at this very moment?

He is presently overwrought with surrender to passionate prayer.

We are told He is in deep intercession at this very moment.

"Therefore he is able to save completely those who come to God through him, because he always lives to intercede for them" (Hebrews 7:25).

He is in the deepest kind of prayer that is possible.
His mission continues for now until every last person is brought into His kingdom,
into His care.
Jesus is praying for the people His Father has given to Him.
He is totally surrendered to the place of intercessory prayer
because it is said He will not lose one person given to Him by His Father.

Oh, dear and precious Jesus, the lover of your soul and of all mankind.

"And this is the will of him who sent me, that I shall lose none of all that he has given me, but raise them up at the last day" (John 6:39).
"This happened so that the words he had spoken would be fulfilled: "I have not lost one of those you gave me" (John 18:9).

Would you like to share the burden Jesus is carrying?

Right now, as you are reading this text, Jesus is interceding.
Jesus really cares about His Father and He really cares about you.
When you minister to the Lord, you are taking the opportunity to do something even the disciples were unable to do in the Garden of Gethsemane. You will be able to stand with Him in the time of His intense need. Jesus is praying right now. Will you watch with Him one hour?

Will you attend to the need of Someone who is already in prayer on your behalf?
What an honour to volunteer to lift up Jesus,
lift up His Holy Name as He carries the responsibility for every soul who has ever lived.
He is extending mercy to the profane, loving the most reviled,
pouring out His longsuffering and mercy upon the self-righteous and hypocritical,
those who hate themselves and those who don't care anymore about anything.

Minister to the Lord.
Love the Lord.
Care about the Lord.
Take time to be with Him during the final moments of His ministry on behalf of all mankind.

As you stand with Jesus and minister your love, worship, adoration and praise to Him,
He will be endearing your hearts together.

One day when your life has ended there will be such joy when you meet the Lord in person!
The feeling of completeness, the feeling of accomplishment.
It will be overwhelming!
Beyond anything you could imagine here on earth.

'You took your stand with Jesus the Son of God.'
'You helped during His time of harvest as He was reaching out to every last soul on earth.'
'You shared together the tears, the joys, the heartaches.'

He lifted you up and guided you like a Shepherd. He never failed, not once, to meet with you
whenever and wherever you turned your gaze upon Him. You met people who hated Jesus, but you
remained steadfast because He loved you so much. Always there to comfort. Always caring. Making
you feel like there was no one but you to share His time and deep friendship.
You will be amazed to see the truth alive within you as Jesus presents you Holy and blameless
before the Father! Your Friend will be beaming! Thinking so highly of you!

"To him who is able to keep you from falling and to present you before his glorious presence
without fault and with great joy - " (Jude 1:24).

You will see that His outstanding power made every last thing work together for good in your life!

"And we know that in all things God works for the good of those who love him, who have been
called according to his purpose" (Romans 8:28).

To meet with Jesus after this life will bring the light of His truth
into every part of your conscious mind.
The way things turned out in the end,
all the things that happened in your life - it will all make perfect sense.

"Beloved, now are we the sons of God, and it doth not yet appear what we shall be: but we know
that, when he shall appear, we shall be like him; for we shall see him as he is. And every man that
hath this hope in him purifieth himself, even as he is pure" (1 John 3:2-3 King James Version).

For now it is all about seeking Jesus Christ.
Daily, ministering to Him.
For He is worthy.

"Thou art worthy, O Lord, to receive glory and honour and power: for thou hast created all things,
and for thy pleasure they are and were created" (Rev. 4:11).

You were created for His pleasure!
Give Him all the love you have in your heart.

He is worthy.

169

The Lord Jesus Christ has made the ultimate sacrifice for you.

You are walking in the perfect result.

Going to the cross gave mankind a perfect view
of perfect surrender to our heavenly Father.
In the form of man living in the flesh we could see His relationship with His Father.
Jesus always did His Father's will.

"The one who sent me is with me; he has not left me alone, for I always do what pleases him"
(John 8:29 New International Version).
"And he said unto them, How is it that ye sought me? wist ye not that I must be about my Father's
business?" (Luke 2:49 King James Version).
'Why were you searching for me?' he asked. 'Didn't you know I had to be in my Father's house?'
(Luke 2:49 New International Version).

When Jesus prayed that His Father has loved Him before they created the world,
we are shown in what manner Jesus Christ and His Father lived throughout eternity past.

Jesus loved His Father and lived His days on earth to please Him.
Jesus loved His Father and His heavenly Father loved Him.

This everlasting love relationship has enfolded you.

You belong to the God who finishes what He starts.

"being confident of this, that he who began a good work in you will carry it on to completion until
the day of Christ Jesus" (Philippians 1:6).
"Now unto him that is able to keep you from falling, and to present you faultless before the
presence of his glory with exceeding joy," (Jude 1:24).

He is going to keep you from falling.
He never failed to do His Father's will.

Because of His perfect, sinless obedience - He will keep you from falling and He will present you
faultless before the presence of His glory with exceeding joy.
This is how it will be for you one day. You know now how this journey will end.

Do not look at your own feeble flesh! Don't weigh your deeds in the balance and make
a judgement about yourself already made by Jesus Christ the holy, perfect, sinless only Son of God!

He will finish what He started in your life.
He chose you Dear Reader!

"You did not choose me, but I chose you" (John 15:16a).

It cannot be changed, it has been written.

Jesus your Champion,
the King of Kings,
the Lion of the tribe of Judah has won the victory.

It has all been for you.

170

"We had previously suffered and been insulted in Philippi, as you know, but with the help of our
God we dared to tell you his gospel in spite of strong opposition" (1 Thessalonians 2:2).

'With the help of our God.'

There is One who will always be there for you dear reader.
He stands alone

above all other loves.

His only request of His children is to permit Him to become their dwelling.
He also calls Himself a hiding place.

"Therefore let everyone who is godly pray to you while you may be found; surely when the mighty
waters rise, they will not reach him. You are my hiding place; you will protect me from trouble and
surround me with songs of deliverance" (Psalm 32:6-7).

His greatest gift to your heart is His love so costly and unequalled.
Jesus paid such a high price before dying.
And then in dying
He gave everything for you.

Before His life slipped away on the cross
He said, "it is finished." His Father's will was finished.

Oh, how He looked forward to your arrival one day and the opportunity to love you.

At no time did Jesus disobey His heavenly Father.

"When Jesus therefore had received the vinegar, he said, It is finished: and he bowed his head, and gave up the ghost" (John 19:30).

Jesus died.
His Father had asked for Jesus to be obedient
and Jesus
was obedient.
Jesus had always known this time of horror would come.

Have you ever had a test to write, an interview to go to?
Something coming that made you nervous or distressed?
Maybe you were to tell someone that plans had changed.
That is not a pleasant thing to do.

But our Jesus, alive from eternity past
stretching back, back, back for all infinity -
He knew.
He always knew the cross was set before Him.

Jesus Christ is God and therefore He knows all things.
He also knew a time of suffering was set before Him.
When His hour had come He still prayed to get out of it.
He did so because He was fully man and fully God.
The degree of the impending carnage was at times too much for Him.
It had become time for Jesus to face the cross.
Instead of relief -
with the cross soon out of His life forever -
He was in agony. Not relief but agony. Why?
Because it was going to be difficult.

At the same time, taking all the sins of the world upon Himself
would separate Him from His Father.
For the first time,
for the only time,

Jesus would be alone.

Alone on one little blue planet in the vacuum of space and time

where He would die.

172

Remember Jesus praying, 'Father you have loved me before the earth was made.'?

Jesus knew the cross would come and His Father's perfect love was all He had ever known.

But He was willing to endure the deepest,
most costly penalty
because Jesus and His Father had enough love to save the whole world.

Jesus had known this precious love for all eternity past.
He also knew how dreadful the cost of hell
would be for each soul
thrown
down
there.

The outrageous cost meted out one by one

to the damned for eternity.

Jesus loved each soul
and would pay any price

because He considered each one to be priceless.

He knew how much it would mean to the lost people of this world.
This became the joy that was set before Him - each person He would save.

"Looking unto Jesus the author and finisher of our faith; who for the joy that was set before him
endured the cross, despising the shame, and is set down at the right hand of the throne of God"
(Heb 12:2).

173

So, His Father's love meant more to Jesus than anything.

He lived to obey His Father no matter what He was asked to do.

Jesus faced two terrible things.
Torture
and the moment His Father would turn away from Him
while He drooped helplessly on the cross.

"And he was withdrawn from them about a stone's cast, and kneeled down, and prayed, Saying, Father, if thou be willing, remove this cup from me: nevertheless not my will, but thine, be done" (Luke 22:41-42).

"And about the ninth hour Jesus cried with a loud voice, saying, Eli, Eli, lama sabachthani? that is to say, My God, my God, why hast thou forsaken me?" (Matthew 27:46).

Their forever love was ended.

Jesus had the sins of the whole world upon Him.
His Father looked away,

Jesus died.

"My God, My God, why hast thou forsaken me?"

With that reality,
with that sorrow beyond all sorrows
Jesus said, 'it is finished.'

Friend, today, will you spend time with this same Jesus?

Jesus said, "stay here and keep watch with Me" (Matthew 26:38).

When He returns to earth let Him find you fervently keeping watch - with Him.

174

"For I, saith the LORD, will be unto her a wall of fire round about, and will be the glory in the midst of her" (Zechariah 2:5 King James Version).

When you feel all alone, there is someone who has already paid the price
for your freedom and the privilege of loving you.

We remember His loss on the cross - willing to die in obedience to His Father.

Jesus loved His Father and our Heavenly Father loved His only Son Jesus.

You matter to your Lord.
At this very moment He is a wall of fire around you!
He knew of your struggle at the time of His death.
That difficult moment in your life was in His heart and mind while being scourged - growing faint from the loss of Holy, precious blood.
But there was joy set before Jesus.
He could see your victory in the cost of His life.

Though He was being wrongfully punished
He was on His way to conquering sin, death and hell.
Do not assume
that His present invisible nature prevents Him
from laying waste to the powers of hell!
Though He is meek and lowly

do not mistake His awesome defeat of all that opposes Him.

He is your wall of fire!
He lives as the glory within that terrifying, Holy wall.
You are cherished.

You are precious.

"And they overcame him by the blood of the Lamb and by the word of their testimony; and they loved not their lives unto the death" (Rev. 12:11 New International Version).

The powers of hell are no match for the precious blood of your Saviour Jesus.

Ask for His blood to be upon you and upon all.
You are an overcomer because of His blood shed freely for you.

"Neither is there salvation in any other: for there is none other name under heaven given among men, whereby we must be saved" (Acts 4:12).

He is Lord! He is King of Kings! He is your champion with His fire round about you!
Worship Him today. Worship Him right now!

He is the glory in your midst.

175

Time does not matter when one is waiting upon the Lord.

He is busy interceding. He is transforming hearts, lives and nations.
Everything is going to work for good.

"And we know that in all things God works for the good of those who love him, who have been called according to his purpose" (Romans 8:28).

It is Jesus who keeps bringing things into line with this word.
Things may appear to be heading in wrong directions,
it may seem all is about to be lost.

Sometimes it will appear that the enemy has accomplished his will.
But do not mistake your praying, Sovereign Ruler.
Mighty King of Kings!

Where is Jesus?

"Therefore he is able to save completely those who come to God through him, because he always lives to intercede for them" (Hebrews 7:25).

That's where Jesus is!
He is totally in charge.

Nothing happens on this earth,
nothing happens in your life
except what is permitted through His prayers
and through His promise to work everything for your good.
Death? Insults? Sickness? Persecution? Rejection, abandonment, loss and misunderstandings?

"For our struggle is not against flesh and blood, but against the rulers, against the authorities, against the powers of this dark world and against the spiritual forces of evil in the heavenly realms" (Ephesians 6:12).

All manner of consequence to befall you are known in advance and have been settled by your loving Saviour through His death, resurrection and intercession on your behalf.

176

"I declare to you, brothers, that flesh and blood cannot inherit the kingdom of God, nor does the perishable inherit the imperishable. Listen, I tell you a mystery: We will not all sleep, but we will all be changed - in a flash, in the twinkling of an eye, at the last trumpet. For the trumpet will sound, the dead will be raised imperishable, and we will be changed. For the perishable must clothe itself with the imperishable, and the mortal with immortality. When the perishable has been clothed with the imperishable, and the mortal with immortality, then the saying that is written will come true: 'Death has been swallowed up in victory.' 'Where, O death, is your victory? Where, O death, is your sting?' The sting of death is sin, and the power of sin is the law. But thanks be to God! He gives us the victory through our Lord Jesus Christ" (1 Corinthians 15:50-57).

It is true! The goal of your faith is the salvation of our soul!
Since Jesus is the cornerstone of that faith
you are certain to be delivered from the sting of death
and the power of sin.
Through all of life's hardships and setbacks you have an anchor to your soul.
You have assurance that your Saviour is faithful and an ever present help in time of trouble.
He will not let you go through anything alone.

In the end He will work all things together for good -
and you are assured of a place with Him in heaven for eternity.
The goal of your faith is the salvation of your soul through your intimate relationship
with Jesus Christ Almighty.

"for you are receiving the goal of your faith, the salvation of your souls" (1 Peter 1:9).

Oh dear one, rejoice today!
Rejoice by faith that the Lord of glory Jesus Christ Himself
has you lifted up in prayer and abides with you now and forevermore.

"But because of his great love for us, God, who is rich in mercy, made us alive with Christ even
when we were dead in transgressions - it is by grace you have been saved. And God raised us up
with Christ and seated us with him in the heavenly realms in Christ Jesus," (Ephesians 2:4-6).

Amen

176

Jesus said He is the Light of the world.

"I have come into the world as a light, so that no one who believes in me should stay in darkness"
(John 12:46).

The Light of Jesus illuminates,
brings revelation for all who would simply gaze upon Him.

The Son of Man must be lifted up.

"Just as Moses lifted up the snake in the desert, so the Son of Man must be lifted up, that everyone
who believes in him may have eternal life. 'For God so loved the world that he gave his one and
only Son, that whoever believes in him shall not perish but have eternal life. For God did not send
his Son into the world to condemn the world, but to save the world through him. Whoever
believes in him is not condemned, but whoever does not believe stands condemned already
because he has not believed in the name of God's one and only Son. This is the verdict: Light has
come into the world, but men loved darkness instead of light because their deeds were evil.
Everyone who does evil hates the light, and will not come into the light for fear that their deeds
will be exposed" (John 3:14-20).

He brings an invitation to 'see' the Light of His Truth.
That truth reveals the immediacy and fellowship of His Father's love!
The Light brings forgiveness of sin,
healing of mind and body and God's invitation for Divine relationship
starting now with all the rights and privileges His covenant bestows.

Without a love connection He is limited as to how much He is able to be involved in your life.
Sell-out to Him. Keep the goal of your faith in mind.

Don't let the troubles of this life and the misdeeds of others influence your faith.
Do not reject God when you see others misrepresent Him
and live a life of hypocrisy in His precious name.

There was no hypocrisy there on the cross.
There was sincerity and commitment.
There was courage, boldness and obedience.
There was supernatural power and resurrection life in the Holy Spirit.

Simply take your eyes off of man and let them rest upon the Holy One of God - Jesus Christ.
Waste no more of your time wrestling with the impurities and imperfections of man.
It is your own soul that is at stake.
Look to Jesus. Believe in Jesus with your goal in mind - the salvation of your soul.

His love and the power of the Holy Spirit will see you through.

177

Your understanding of time is rooted in the present.

It is viscerally tied to the date of our birth.

Since you were not alive and able to experience historical events prior to your birth
your grasp of reality is dependant upon historical sources.
This provides a rich but temporal understanding at best.

Personally, I am fascinated by dinosaurs.
There is a lot of information and evidence to bear witness to their existence.
I once found a fossilized shell inside a rock after breaking it open with a hammer at the public
lakefront where I grew up. How incredible it would be however, to observe the thriving dinosaurs
first hand. Witness and experience first hand how the dinosaurs behaved.

Much closer to the birth of our generation is the Second World War and the tragedy of the Jewish
Holocaust. There are precious folks who can provide first hand accounts of loved ones lost at the
extermination camps. There are also written records, photographs and news reels of this historical
tragedy. The terrible treatment of the Jewish people by the individuals and world nations who
rejected their exiles is painfully fresh. Precious Jewish families alive today are able to recount the
gaps in their lineage and point to these events. They communicate the pain. The quandary.
Their loss on a personal level.

Jesus lived on earth a long time ago. It was 2000 years ago.

Getting to know about Jesus may be quite easy depending upon the country where you live. If Christianity is outlawed in the country you live then learning historical facts about Jesus would prove very difficult. The written account of His life and even the mention of His name would be forbidden.

Jesus did not come to earth to become a history lesson. Unlike other historical events Jesus is alive! He can speak for Himself.

You can find God in the Holy Bible and pursue a living relationship with Him through the Holy Spirit when you are alone and caught up in the wonder of His love.

178

Getting to know Him is what you need.

You can know Him, and getting to know Jesus first hand will mean eternal life to you.

Please consider. Here is truth.
Many people in a society that grants freedom to practice a religion
merely settle for the temporal experience
of knowing 'about' God.

By freedom, I mean it doesn't cost them anything to be a church-going person.
There is no persecution if you are seen with a bible, no imprisonment, and no confiscation of goods. No ramifications with regard to their career of choice and relatively no chance of being ostracized by the community at large. They will not be sought out by those who plan to physically harm them because of their faith. Their homes will not be ransacked nor invaded by people who want to convince them to recant their faith.
The local police will not take them out back, douse them with gasoline, set them on fire and return to their desks to take care of the rest of the day's business and finish their cup of tea.
After they wash the smell of petrol from their hands, of course.

"In fact, everyone who wants to live a godly life in Christ Jesus will be persecuted,"
(2 Timothy 3:12).

Most people who teach and preach about God do so based upon their temporal experience. They restrict their experience within their comfort zone. They decide how much they are going to let Jesus guide them and freely offer Him a fragment of their life. They may not want to upset a family member be it a mother or father. They may want to hang onto a certain financial status and freely offer Jesus anything He wants with the rest of their life.
Inevitably they hold onto an area as sacred - but give Jesus the rest.
This is why Jesus said the first thing a person needs to do is deny themselves.

I believe your relationship with God does not start until you have completely denied yourself.

With God, He said if you do not deny yourself on every level you are not worthy of Him.

"Then Jesus said to his disciples, "If anyone would come after me, he must deny himself and take up his cross and follow me" (Matthew 16:24).
"and anyone who does not take his cross and follow me is not worthy of me" (Matthew 10:38).

1) Deny Himself
2) Take up own cross
3) Follow Jesus.

179

You will need to break free in your own experience and not settle for being 'good enough' for God.

Know God yourself.

Get away from all your ideas about what is keeping God happy and step away from all the outer observances demanded by your group.

Go all the way
with total surrender to Him.
Give Him your all.
Deny yourself.

That doesn't mean doing some extreme act of devotion.
Jesus said He is only looking for someone who will get to know Him
with a lifetime of intimate fellowship!
Then, because He said only one thing is needed,
give that one thing to Him
(remember the story of Mary and Martha and what Jesus said).

Here it is.
Your time and attention alone in prayer where you come directly to Him
with your desire to listen.
Have your own bible with you to read. The New Testament is awesome.

IMPORTANT: Let it be the bible embraced by the Christian church all over the world, not just the one interpreted and espoused by one particular group.

When you read ask the Holy Spirit to reveal Jesus to you. Ask the Holy Spirit to take the deep things of God and reveal them unto you. The bible says that is what He does.
You will be praying according to the bible.
How could your leadership be offended with you for praying according to the bible
and then obeying Jesus? Jesus said we show our love for Him by obeying what He asks of us.

You will find great joy, peace and love within when you follow the Master.

He is a good Shepherd.

The Good Shepherd asks that you follow Him.
He did not add that there is only one church able to fulfil His mandate on earth.
He was most specific that eternal life is found in Him alone. The Christian church is peopled by many different denominations and 'flavours' of worship.

I think Jesus would have been careful to mention if all of the churches were wrong except for one.

"Then he (Jesus) said to them all: 'If anyone would come after me, he must deny himself and take up his cross daily and follow me" (Luke 9:23).

He needs people to <u>follow Him</u>.

An intimate relationship is only entered into with your complete surrender.
Remember repentance from 'dead works' - works done because we think it is what He wants?
There is a cross for you to carry. Jesus says it is your own. Walking in unity with Jesus is to be lavished with the very kindness of God!

"the incomparable riches of his grace, expressed in his kindness to us in Christ Jesus" (Ephesians 2:7b).

When alone with God include a journal if you are able. This is the name for a note book to write down the loving communication, thoughts and verses you share with your beloved.
The One to whom you have been betrothed.

Get to know Him. Listen to Him. Follow Him.
Jesus
Jesus

Jesus.

Be accepted, forgiven, cherished, and valued by Him.

180

Notice Acts 4:12 says there is no other 'name' given among men.

It does not say, 'no other church' given among men.

Dear Reader, Jesus Christ said clearly that your obedience and allegiance is only unto Him.

Please don't get mixed up by religiosity and the dead works of the cults. Church people who insist you pledge allegiance only to their brand of church or to their own founder or leader. There is no other name given among men. If there is no other name given among men, then why would they insist you acknowledge their founder in your declaration of faith? Only a fool would step between Jesus and the sheep and insist upon their loyalty to a group or person - dead or alive.

Oh yes, the very demons of hell are pulling the strings behind the scene.

These teachings effectively rob the precious, well meaning people of an intimate relationship with Jesus. Dear Reader, Jesus is the only One who can save you to the uttermost.

"Salvation is found in no one else, for there is no other name under heaven given to men by which we must be saved" (Acts 4:12).

When you become aware of God's offer to forgive you must decide if you will believe in Him.
Your only opportunity is offered to you within the short span of your life on this earth.
Even though Jesus lived so long ago and loved people way back then,
He has loved you for a long time.
Jesus didn't start to love you within the span of your life.
He has loved you from eternity past
and knew you even before the world was made!

There is no one who can love you like this!
If Jesus loved you then He also had complete knowledge of you.

"For he chose us in him before the creation of the world to be holy and blameless in his sight" (Ephesians 1:4).

Think about this Dear Reader. Pause, stop, and consider this truth.
The bible says that Jesus loved you before the world was made. He was your Redeemer
before mankind even came into existence!
Before anyone was created!

Why would He appoint someone else, a mere human being, to take His place when He already loved you completely and knew you? Every person to be born on this earth would be the beneficiary of this sacred love. Each would have the opportunity to receive the kindness and grace of the Lord Jesus Christ. He has not appointed any man to step in and take His place.
Jesus Christ alone retains forever His position as leader of the church.

"That power is like the working of his mighty strength, which he exerted in Christ when he raised him from the dead and seated him at his right hand in the heavenly realms, far above all rule and authority, power and dominion, and every title that can be given, not only in the present age but also in the one to come. And God placed all things under his feet and appointed him to be head over everything for the church, which is his body, the fullness of him who fills everything in every way" (Ephesians 1:19b-23).

Dear Reader, please take a moment and consider.

Are you following your church's teachings, its leadership, its tradition and its rituals?

Or do you know Jesus who has been appointed the head over everything for the church?

This is good news for you! It means you are able to go directly to Jesus. I expect that is why He said anyone who comes to Him He will not drive away.

Since Jesus Christ is the head of the church where else would He expect people to go?!

Here is a simple check list. Would you please consider these three helpful pointers?

1) Does my group teach that they are the only church that will go to heaven?

2) Do they provide a sacred text and insist that it is a higher authority or equally sacred as the Holy Bible itself? Is it a text only accepted and adhered to by one church?

3) Do they teach that Jesus Christ is the One and only God and able to save all people without the need to work for salvation?

If they add conditions and works to your salvation they have stripped Christ of His Divinity.

Only Jesus Christ was God in the flesh. There is only one Son of God that dwelt among men.

If these three elements are in your church then you are in a cult.

You are in a church that will deceive and damn your soul to hell.

Show kindness. Show love. But get out. Leave and don't ever return.

Get saved. Go to Jesus and see what great salvation He has made available to anyone

who will come to Him and believe. The Holy Spirit can be trusted to direct you to a fellowship

of people who are in unity with the same Spirit that lives within you!

Rest. Rest in that love eternal.

Through Jesus, men, women and children are made holy and blameless in the sight of God.

Hallelujah!

You have a refuge and a spiritual home through your faith in Jesus Christ.

Be still, and make Him your dwelling.

In finding Jesus you have received your sight.

Let His word be entreated to your heart in the dwelling you share together for the rest of your days.

181

Yet at the same time many even among the leaders believed in him. But because of the Pharisees they would not confess their faith for fear they would be put out of the synagogue; for they loved praise from men more than praise from God. Then Jesus cried out, 'When a man believes in me, he does not believe in me only, but in the one who sent me. When he looks at me, he sees the one who sent me. I have come into the world as a light, so that no one who believes in me should stay in darkness' (John 12:42-46).

How precious, Jesus deferring to His Heavenly Father.

'When a person looks at Me they see the one who sent Me.'

In perfect humility He beseeches His hearers to acknowledge the existence and purpose
of God the Father Almighty.
'Look at Me,' He proclaims. 'You will see! In this marvellous gift of sight,
take in the wonder of your Father in heaven.'

He spoke this to all people!
ANYONE who looks at Me!
Not the favoured, the connected, the talented or the outwardly zealous.
No! Jesus came that all may see.
Anyone who comes to Him will have life
and He will in no means turn anyone away.

"People were bringing little children to Jesus to have him touch them, but the disciples rebuked
them. When Jesus saw this, he was indignant. He said to them, 'Let the little children come to me,
and do not hinder them, for the kingdom of God belongs to such as these. I tell you the truth,
anyone who will not receive the kingdom of God like a little child will never enter it.' And he took
the children in his arms, put his hands on them and blessed them" (Mark 10:13-16).

Even children are entirely suitable to grasp all the whole message of the creator.
The little children are ready
to enter into the kingdom of God.

There is an abundance of mercy, revelation, truth, light and wisdom
to all who look unto Jesus.
"Let us fix our eyes on Jesus, the author and perfecter of our faith," (Hebrews 12:2a).

In God's eyes children are wise beyond their years and station in life.
They posses little or nothing.
Have little opportunity to exercise the right to self determination.
Yet through Christ they are candidates to become a royal heir of salvation.
Through Christ they are entirely a Royal Priesthood
set apart by God and wealthy
beyond all comprehension.
'Do not store up for yourselves treasures on earth, where moth and rust destroy, and where thieves
break in and steal. But store up for yourselves treasures in heaven, where moth and rust do not
destroy, and where thieves do not break in and steal. For where your treasure in, there your heart
will be also' (Matthew 6:19-21).

Let the little children enjoy their Saviour's embrace.

Who but Jesus helps us to perceive the value of the very young and the very old.

The common and the nondescript.
The poor and the pitiful,
broken and discarded.

All are entitled to easily become members of the flock in the Chief Shepherds good care.
Where is the Saviour's love?

Look there. Look to His flock.

"But not a hair of your head will perish" (Luke 21:18).
Do not be afraid of those who kill the body but cannot kill the soul. Rather, be afraid of the One who can destroy both soul and body in hell. Are not two sparrows sold for a penny? Yet not one of them will fall to the ground apart from the will of your Father. And even the very hairs of your head are all numbered. So don't be afraid; you are worth more than many sparrows. 'Whoever acknowledges me before men, I will also acknowledge him before my Father in heaven' (Matthew 10:28-32).

182

Jesus the Son of God 'will GIVE you life' will GIVE you sight.

Your blinded eyes will see! Oh Hallelujah!

If you do not fancy yourself a spiritually gifted person, no matter!
Jesus, will bring you sight.

Without Jesus you are blind!
You will assuredly see a certain future in heaven for all eternity with Jesus!

"Just as man is destined to die once, and after that to face judgment," (Hebrews 9:27).

You see dear one,
with no saving grace you will be assigned
along with the most vial and despicable forces
to a Godless eternity.

You will be in the company of the devil and all the demons for an endless eternity.
There will be no love, no kindness, no one will ever show any interest in you ever again.
The only interest will be to torment you unceasingly.
Without a Saviour now in this life you will walk
and suffer and hurt yourself and others
and then with great inconvenience you will end up in the devil's hell.

It was for you that Jesus wept, and lived and died.

Afterward He was raised from the dead.
Because He lives you too may also live.
Ask for forgiveness from the only One able to free you from sin.
He has taken your place and paid the penalty for all you have done
and all you will ever do.

Will you humble yourself today and receive Jesus Christ as your own personal Saviour?

"Jesus, will you forgive me of all my sin. I ask you into my heart and that Your Holy Spirit will come into my life and baptise me with fire from above. I want you to teach me how to live for you. Take me into your care now and forever. Amen."

183

There is a place where you are highly thought of.

Do you have regrets? All people have them.

They come to mind every so often.
They sometimes stay away from our conscious mind because we push them away.
It is our attempt to bury them deep down inside where they won't bother us.
But there is a place where you are very well thought of.
You are loved and valued by the God who created you.

"So God created man in his own image, in the image of God he created him; male and female he created them" (Hebrews 1:27).
There is a great purpose for you.

But first you are in need of redemption. You need to be redeemed.
There is something keeping you from your eternal destiny.
Did you know you have an eternal destiny?

"He has made everything beautiful in its time. He has also set eternity in the hearts of men;" (Ecclesiastes 3:11).

'And you, my son Solomon, acknowledge the God of your father, and serve him with wholehearted devotion and with a willing mind, for the Lord searches every heart and understands every motive behind the thoughts. If you seek him, he will be found by you; but if you forsake him, he will reject you forever.' (1 Chronicles 28:9).

Where are you going to spend eternity?

Let's talk about how important it is that you get into a right relationship with God.

If you have not prayed to receive Jesus as your Saviour,
the one who will forgive you all your sins,
now is the time.

"I tell you, now is the time of God's favour, now is the day of salvation" (2 Corinthians 6:2b).

Will you pray today?
Will you pray and ask for Jesus to save your soul?

"Just as man is destined to die once, and after that to face judgment," (Hebrews 9:27).

Go for it.
Eternity is a long time.
Eternity is forever.

Let the Lord of glory share all of His love with you.
Through faith in Jesus Christ you instantaneously become His friend and a full heir
of His glorious kingdom to be fully revealed
on the final Day.

It is for this reason that He came.

"For God did not send his Son into the world to condemn the world, but to save the world
through him" (John 3:17).

184

Won't you take Jesus' hand today?

There is nothing to stop you from an intimate sharing of hearts.

He said nothing will be able separate you from His love.

"For I am convinced that neither death nor life, neither angels nor demons, neither the present nor
the future, nor any powers, neither height nor depth, nor anything else in all creation, will be able
to separate us from the love of God that is in Christ Jesus our Lord" (Romans 8:38-42).

Nothing can separate you from His love.
Why are there so few people who know the Lord?
Why are so many caught up in their sin bringing harm to themselves and others?

"But small is the gate and narrow the road that leads to life, and only a few find it" (Matthew 7:14).

There are so many people doing what they want to do.

They treat others as though there is no eternity,
as if being unkind or deceitful is a lifestyle choice.
But it is not.
It is not.
It is the evidence of a failure to seek God.
It is a choice to live without acknowledging
the existence of God.
It is not more convenient to live without God.

There is only one life.
There are however two deaths.
"But the cowardly, the unbelieving, the vile, the murderers, the sexually immoral, those who practice magic arts, the idolaters and all liars - their place will be in the fiery lake of burning sulphur. This is the second death" (Revelation 21:9).
"Blessed and holy are those who have part in the first resurrection. The second death has no power over them," (Revelation 20:6a).
"Then death and Hades were thrown into the lake of fire. The lake of fire is the second death" (Revelation 20:14).
"He who has an ear, let him hear what the Spirit says to the churches. He who overcomes will not be hurt at all by the second death" (Revelation 2:11).

Yet, there are fine people who live without God.
Kind, generous and thoughtful people. Intelligent, learned and accomplished people.
Talented, famous and respected people. Great people who can be a wonderful friend.
But who is Jesus if not a remarkable person who said that He and God the Father are One.
"Jesus answered: 'Don't you know me, Philip, even after I have been among you such a long time? Anyone who has seen me has seen the Father. How can you say, 'Show us the Father'?" (John 14:8).
"I and the Father are one" (John 10:30).

Finally, Jesus pronounced clearly,
"I am the way and the truth and the Life. No one comes to the Father except through Me" (John 14:6).

No earthly accomplishment compares to the decision to accept Jesus Christ as Sovereign and Lord.
He alone is the answer to the question of where you will spend eternity.
Now is the time to get to know Him.
One day,
if life be taken away from you without an opportunity for a reckoning
and saving experience with Jesus
                                    it will be too late for His saving grace.

"For he says, 'In the time of my favour I heard you, and in the day of salvation I helped you.' I tell you, now is the time of God's favour, now is the day of salvation" (2 Corinthians 6:2).

Take His hand.

Do you want to know about Jesus or do you want to 'know' Jesus.

Settle this important question in your heart
at your journey's beginning.
This alone will determine what will become of your encounter
with this living, All-powerful Creator.

That is because He has not come to condemn
nor cajole
nor force you
to become a deep, dear friend of His.
No,

He will only become intimately involved with those who take the time to invite Him in.
Invite Him 'in what'? Invite Him 'where'? Where does Jesus share all the depths of His wisdom,
love and intimacy? Why, it is within you! That's where!
This verse is written to members of the church. Jesus has come to a church member. He is seeking
access. Even though they belong to Him it appears there is no fellowship. No intimacy.

"Here I am! I stand at the door and knock. If anyone hears my voice and opens the door, I will
come in and eat with him, and he with me" (Revelation 3:20).

In this life you will not fully see how much Jesus esteems you,
values you.
Even your most compelling experience of His love is but a glimpse.
There is only so much you can take because you are yet in your earthen body.
When you humble yourself
and surrender your heart
the King of Kings will immediately serve and embrace you.
Making you His number one priority - whenever you call.

He is already knocking at the door.

"I no longer call you servants, because a servant does not know his master's business. Instead, I have
called you friends, for everything that I learned from my Father I have made known to you"
(John 15:15).

Jesus makes this known to those who open the door and let Him in.

He is not going to go knocking on the door of an unsaved person. They will say, 'who are you?'

The context in Revelation shows that Jesus is seeking an invitation to intimacy
with someone who is already a member of the church.

Don't physically 'go somewhere' in order to encounter God!
Those in prison can't up and go somewhere to encounter God.
Those precious elderly saints confined to a room in an assisted care ward aren't going anywhere.
The little bitty children in good or bad circumstances at home are unable to decide that they are
going to go to a location of their choice to encounter God.

Get alone with Jesus Christ
where you and your creator are able to share together
the intimate love that awaits you.
We already know He is prepared to share 'everything He has learned from His Father'.

Who is wise but those who welcome Jesus and open that door that 'He may come in and share with
them.'

186

Take time to get to know Jesus.

It takes time to maintain an automobile.

It needs to be lifted up off the ground sometimes. We need to make an appointment for it to
receive special attention. As the years pass the plastic, metal and wire will deteriorate beyond repair.
Some parts will ultimately cease to exist and return to the dust. This is an ordinary car or van.
A pick-up truck, limousine a dump truck or bus.

Dear Reader, you are not an inanimate object. You are a person.

Incredibly precious - yet your body is subject to decay.

"Therefore we do not lose heart. Though outwardly we are wasting away, yet inwardly we are being
renewed day by day" (2 Corinthians 4:16).

Your body will return to the dust like some of the parts of a car.
But you require much more special care than your automobile.

'You',
the human spirit within your 'shelf life' physical body,
will emerge intact from decay and dismantling.

There you will be!
Have you taken steps to maintain the real you?

The unseen you?

"I praise you because I am fearfully and wonderfully made; your works are wonderful, I know that full well" (Psalm 139:14).

Please. Don't delay. Permit Jesus to redeem your inner spiritual being before the 'outer' you keeps the appointment with death.

It is critical for Jesus to be able to say that He knows you on that appointed day.
Does He know you?

You alone have the incredible power to change all of that right now!
Give your life to Jesus Christ and He will be careful to maintain you now and forever more.

"For the Lord God is a sun and shield; the Lord bestows favour and honour; no good thing does he withhold from those whose walk is blameless" (Psalm 84:11).

187

The most precious gift you can give God your heavenly Father . . . is your time!

The most powerful manifestation of His Holy Spirit . . . is love!

What wife treasures her husband's status or provision above his commitment
that makes her the center of his world?
Making a special appointment for coffee or tea to give her his undivided attention.
Would she rather choose to drive around for awhile in a fine car?
Is that what sustains her soul, her true sense of self-worth as a wife or mother?

Would she rather make an appointment at the bank or ATM machine to gaze upon the numbers
on the paper or screen? Would it be more enriching to run or walk through their home tantalized
and inspired by the decoration or design in order to restore the romance with her spouse?
A woman married to a man she truly loves,
has her peace restored and sustained
in the comfort of his love.

While paying attention to her needs he finds a unique fulfillment. He is grounded and finds
direction in life in their times together. He confides in her unlike any other.
When she speaks he listens intently.
More than physical intimacy
she is endeared to him for this reason more than any other.

'He listens to me.'
'He knows me.'

She wants to share everything with this man.
All that is in her heart.

Is it any wonder that Jesus, who owns all things, finds His greatest fulfillment
when we make an appointment to be alone with Him.

Who listens to Jesus?
Who cares about Jesus in a manner that fulfills His heart?
All creation is His footstool.
But the only thing He treasures is you.

The greatest gift you have for Jesus is your next appointment to be alone together.

188

"Six days before the Passover, Jesus came to Bethany, where Lazarus lived, whom Jesus had raised
from the dead" (Luke 9:1).

Notice, it says 'six days' neither five nor seven.

Jesus knows where His heavenly Father wants Him to be from one moment to the next.
Jesus was always about His Father's business.
But here we read that He was meant to be in Bethany on this sixth day before the Passover.
Why is this? You will never fully search out the wisdom and mind of God.

'As the heavens are higher than the earth, so are my ways higher than your ways and my thoughts
than your thoughts' (Isaiah 55:9).

Jesus was found in Bethany six days before the Passover.
It was perfect. It was purposeful. His Father had planned this before the foundation of the earth.

To know God dear one, is to encounter matters unsearchable.
Jesus was found in this place because it was the perfect fulfillment
of a perfect plan
by a perfect God.

Do you want to follow Jesus? Don't try to be perfect like Jesus.

Don't look upon the unfolding events of your life through the religious filter of being perfect.
It was Christ's perfection that brought the new birth to humankind.
In fact, the measure of your perfection can't be found in what you will or will not accomplish.

"For you died, and your life is now hidden with Christ in God" (Colossians 3:3).

Dearest reader, you cannot find something that is already hidden. It was Jesus who invited you to 'follow'
not to 'find'.

"Then he said to them all: "Whoever wants to be my disciple must deny themselves and take up their cross daily and follow me" (Luke 9:23).

The person you follow is the one you are near to.
The one you listen to.
The one you obey.

Can you see the difference between religion and an intimate relationship with Jesus Christ?

A religious commitment says,
'I know therefore I conclude that I am His.'
An intimate relationship with Jesus Christ says,
'let me be found in His intimate love that I may fulfill the desire of His heart.'

Now it is time for you to draw near to Him
that He may share His life with you.

The life that is hidden in the warmth of His fellowship and total love for you.

189

"And he said, "The Son of Man must suffer many things and be rejected by the elders, the chief priests and the teachers of the law, and he must be killed and on the third day be raised to life" (Luke 9:22).

On the third day Jesus Christ was raised to life.
Not the second day. Not the fourth day. Amen.
Jesus Christ was raised to life with certainty and Sovereignty and perfection on the third day.
This is where the Lord was to be found the third day after His death.

It came to pass by design in a plan established before the world was made. As His follower you will become part of the sensational purpose of God prepared before the world was made.
God has plans for your life too!
Thankfully it is not based upon your ability.

"I have seen something else under the sun: The race is not to the swift or the battle to the strong," (Ecclesiastes 9:11a).
"His pleasure is not in the strength of the horse, nor his delight in the legs of a man; the Lord delights in those who fear him, who put their hope in his unfailing love" (Psalm 147:10-11).

"Even youths grow tired and weary, and young men stumble and fall; but those who hope in the Lord will renew their strength. They will soar on wings like eagles; they will run and not grow weary, they will walk and not be faint" (Isaiah 40:30-31).

Can you see it?
God's invitation is for you.

Do you have nothing to offer this great lover of your soul? Don't measure your value.
Christianity is not an experience based upon great things you can do for God.
It is a love relationship made rich with entitlement because God cares about you
and wants to give you the kingdom.

There is favour.
There is also a family of faith.
Who is the most spiritual person in this family?
I would say without reservation, 'Jesus is the most spiritual'.
The name of a man or woman doesn't even enter into my mind.

"The Spirit and the bride say, 'Come!' And let him who hears say, 'Come!' Whoever is thirsty, let him come; and whoever wishes, let him take the free gift of the water of life" (Revelation 22:17).
As the Scripture says, 'Anyone who trusts in him will never be put to shame' (Romans 10:11).
"In times of disaster they will not wither; in days of famine they will enjoy plenty" (Psalm 37:19).

His perfect salvation is offered to all who are willing.
Don't count yourself out just because you feel inadequate or undeserving.
On the third day He was raised to life. No longer was it necessary to qualify or quantify
the righteousness of mankind through sacrifice.
His perfect salvation is for the old,
the infirm,
the prisoner behind bars,
the most undeserving
and the unclean.
On that third day human history began anew.
There was now a new and living Way.

Be loved today Dear Reader.
You have a hidden purpose set before you. Let your search begin and end with your Lord Jesus.
Though your life is hidden with Christ in God
you will be well able to find it there.
All are entitled to participate in His marvellous plan.
All can partake through the Lord Jesus Christ.
He is Lord and you are the object of the desire of His heart.
Jesus has invited you to be a person who is 'entitled'.
His followers walk around with a 'Divine entitlement'.
Each is forever precious in His eyes.

"Anyone who loves his father or mother more than me is not worthy of me; anyone who loves his son or daughter more than me is not worthy of me; and anyone who does not take his cross and follow me is not worthy of me. Whoever finds his life will lose it, and whoever loses his life for my sake will find it" (Matthew 10:37-39).
"For whoever wants to save their life will lose it, but whoever loses their life for me will save it" (Luke 9:24).

'but whoever loses their life for me . . .'

Dear reader, don't try to save your life. Get ready to lose your life for Jesus.
Meaning,
your marvellous value and purpose
could never be perceived through mere human accomplishment.

There comes a time when you realise,
in the marvellous care of your loving Jesus,
that all the effort
you can
or will
or have ever made
has not before nor ever will
equate to a knowledge of the meek and lowly Saviour.
Whoa. That is a mouthful.

Though your purpose is hidden with Christ in God,
at the same time your purpose is hidden with the Light of the World.

"For you died, and your life is now hidden with Christ in God" (Colossians 3:3)

Jesus is the Light that can't be hidden.
If you chose to lose your life for Jesus,
you will find your life through Jesus!

"Whoever finds his life will lose it, and whoever loses his life for my sake will find it"
(Matthew 10:39).
"Whoever tries to keep his life will lose it, and whoever loses his life will preserve it" (Luke 17:33).

He is not saying you have to die physically to find your life.

"I have come that they may have life and have it to the full" (John 10:10b).

The laying down of your life begins and ends in your personal fellowship time with Jesus!

It is there that He can communicate the pure desire of His heart and endear your life to His. You have to love Him.
It is there that you discover His will for yourself and for the other people in your life.
He does this imperceptibly at times.
Like a potter with clay the work faithfully continues as it should.

"This is the word that came to Jeremiah from the Lord: 'Go down to the potter's house, and there I will give you my message.' So I went down to the potter's house, and I saw him working at the wheel. But the pot he was shaping from the clay was marred in his hands; so the potter formed it into another pot, shaping it as seemed best to him. Then the word of the Lord came to me: 'O house of Israel, can I not do with you as this potter does?' declares the Lord. 'Like clay in the hand of the potter, so are you in my hand, O house of Israel' " (Jeremiah 18:1-6).
"Yet, O Lord, you are our Father. We are the clay, you are the potter; we are all the work of your hand" (Isaiah 64:8).

191

When you truly lose your life for God you become a lover of God.

It is too easy to love the things we do as Christians.

The ritual,
the ceremony,
the personalities the fads the fashions and the teachings!

There are wonderful people who attend Christian events.
There are wonderful people in your church too!
In the end you will be fulfilling your true destiny
when you stand before Jesus Christ because you loved one another.
As you and Jesus gaze into each others eyes when your eternity begins
let the exchange you share be one of exhilaration, hope and relief.

Exhilaration

because He will be so much more beautiful,
so lovely,
so kind,
loving and merciful than anything you came to know of Him.
Far surpassing your human understanding though you met with each other almost every day.
Overcome with hope and anticipation as you realise how meaningful eternal life will be.
This too will far surpass any ideas of heaven because there is no way
to clearly see what is to unfold there.
Your tremendous value is hidden behind a veil for the time being.

"Now we see but a poor reflection as in a mirror; then we shall see face to face. Now I know in part; then I shall know fully, even as I am fully known" (1 Corinthians 13:12).
"Dear friends, now we are the children of God, and what we will be has not yet been made known. But we know that when he appears, we shall be like him, for we shall see him as he is" (1 John 3:2).

Relief
for though you always knew He had taken your place in order to save you,
the true riches and consequence will become crystal clear. The strength of His love will be
forcefully impressed upon you as you see the holes in His hands and feet.
This is the penalty He bore for you on the cross because of your need for redemption.
Those marks that have changed His appearance for all eternity.
Only because of His sacrifice, because of this One humble servant,
you will stand with an ultimate sense of well being.

At the same time you will see the unsaved summarily ushered forthwith into a Godless eternity.

An eternity without Jesus
is a Godless eternity.

The true meaning of hell will be sharply exposed for what it is -
banishment from God and His goodness forever.

How sad that it really all came down to one personal decision to live without Jesus.

"Whoever believes in the Son has eternal life, but whoever rejects the Son will not see life, for God's wrath remains on them" (John 3:36).

Pray today that Jesus would safely lead you. Pray also for those who do not know Him before it is too late for them to exercise their free will in the matter.

Their eternal destiny depends upon it.

192

"Then he said to them all: "Whoever wants to be my disciple must deny themselves and take up their cross daily and follow me" (Luke 9:23).

Daily.

Who among us can go to church daily? No, that is not what Jesus was saying. Who among us can perform a religious act daily without fail?
We are human and by nature inconsistent and prone to failure.

"Yet man is born to trouble as surely as sparks fly upward" (Job 5:7).

Daily we are being offered the invitation to dine with Jesus.
To join with Him at His table of fellowship.
To find our purpose is to seek Him daily in the private, intimate place of fellowship with Him.

"Here I am! I stand at the door and knock. If anyone hears my voice and opens the door, I will come in and eat with him, and he with me" (Revelation 3:20).

Because of His love He came to the earth on your behalf.
It wasn't a decision to love you. Jesus can only offer love when He thinks of you.

God is love.
He loves because it is all He can do.
He wanted to come and get you.

"For God so loved the world that He gave His one and only Son" (John 3:16).
"And so we know and rely on the love God has for us. God is love. Whoever lives in love lives in God, and God in him" (1 John 4:16).

193

Love without consent is force.

It is the denial of an individual's free will.

Jesus could not come into this world out of love if mankind had no choice.

"So God created man in his own image, in the image of God he created him; male and female he created them" (Genesis 1:27).

You are created to have fellowship with Almighty God!
When you are redeemed by the blood of Jesus (who is able to forgive all your sin) you freely receive His righteousness. God becomes your best friend!
Your rightful place will be with God in heaven one day for all eternity.

"And you also were included in Christ when you heard the word of truth, the gospel of your salvation. Having believed, you were marked in him with a seal, the promised Holy Spirit, who is a deposit guaranteeing our inheritance until the redemption of those who are God's possession - to the praise of his glory" (Ephesians 1:13-14).

It is a profound blessing to have a friend.

A dear pet is also a great treasure it is true.
We value and are blessed by the pets given to us by God to look after.

We need our friends and our brothers and sisters in the faith.
But there is an exchange that takes place when we are with God that is unlike any other.

You are so much like God that you can use your free-will to tell God to 'get lost'.
You can outright deny the Holy Spirit from working on your behalf.

You can walk away from His invitation to believe and enter into fellowship.
There is no other being on earth with this power.

People like you and me, we are the only ones.

Remember earlier when we considered the tears of a loving God for those who do not know Him?
How much more poignant to consider it only takes a decision to keep the Lord at arms length.
To guarantee an eternity without Him.
An eternity in hell.

Once again today, may we lift up the unsaved.
Praying they will consent to being loved, forgiven, washed with the precious blood of Jesus Christ and aware of His marvellous plan for their life.

"Someone in the crowd said to him, 'Teacher, tell my brother to divide the inheritance with me.' Jesus replied, 'Man, who appointed me a judge or an arbiter between you?' Then he said to them, 'Watch out! Be on your guard against all kinds of greed; a man's life does not consist in the abundance of his possessions.' And he told them this parable: 'The ground of a certain rich man produced a good crop. He thought to himself, 'What shall I do? I have no place to store my crops.' "Then he said, 'This is what I'll do. I will tear down my barns and build bigger ones and there I will store all my grain and my goods. And I'll say to myself, "You have plenty of good things laid up for many years. Take life easy; eat, drink and be merry." ' "But God said to him, 'You fool! This very night your life will be demanded from you. Then who will get what you have prepared for yourself?' "This is how it will be with anyone who stores up things for himself but is not rich toward God" (Luke 12:13-21).

194

"What good is it for someone to gain the whole world, and yet lose or forfeit their very self?" (Luke 9:25).

You see, it comes down to your priorities and your time doesn't it?

Who among us is able to gain the whole world?

Usually it is someone who has invested their life and their time in an all consuming pursuit.

The athlete who ceaselessly, daily exercises and repetitively practices his sport.

Until the day comes when his body is unable to meet the standards of competition.
The musician who neglects friends and family to be shut in the studio. Devoted to a life of touring on the road or endless hours of practice each and every day. Until a new, younger performer shows up and redefines the rules of performance.

It would be a serious temptation
to be offered 'the whole world'.

"Again, the devil took him to a very high mountain and showed him all the kingdoms of the world and their splendour. "All this I will give you," he said, "if you will bow down and worship me." Jesus said to him, "Away from me, Satan! For it is written: 'Worship the Lord your God, and serve him only.' " Then the devil left him, and angels came and attended him" (Matthew 4:8-11).

Being offered 'the whole world' is a scam. That is because the devil is a liar and the Father of lies. The devil would offer anything to keep you from serving God with your whole heart.

He can offer you the whole world but you will loose your own soul.

"He was a murderer from the beginning, not holding to the truth, for there is no truth in him. When he lies, he speaks his native language, for he is a liar and the father of lies" (John 8:44b).

Satan and the demons' only reward for you in the next life
is an existence of torment, torture and infernal loneliness in hell.

Specifically in a place called, 'the lake of fire.'

'Then he will say to those on his left, 'Depart from me, you who are cursed, into the eternal fire prepared for the devil and his angels' (Matthew 25:41).

195

Satan is behind this whole misconception about the riches of this world.
Who on their death bed will cry out,
"if only I had just an hour more to spend at the office!"
"If only I had more money in my pockets! Hurry, hurry stuff it in! I feel I'm fading."
"If only I had more real estate! I could have had that investment! It was right there for the taking!"

Most people, would prefer their end of their life to take place in their old age. They want to be in a serene, quiet bedside setting. They want their loved ones to be all around them - be they family or friend. They want to have their mental faculties, to be lucid right to the end. Some will say they want the right to decide when they will die.
Satan will gladly promise (remember, he is the liar!) all of this to any person who will bow down to worship him.
Anyone who denies the Lord Jesus Christ bows to Satan by default.

"No one can serve two masters. Either he will hate the one and love the other, or he will be devoted to the one and despise the other. You cannot serve both God and Money" (Matthew 6:24).
"The god of this age has blinded the minds of unbelievers, so that they cannot see the light of the gospel of the glory of Christ, who is the image of God" (2 Corinthians 4:4).

Jesus is wise.
He said,
'no, there is only one God and I will honour Him. Though you can offer Me all the treasure of the earth, I will make my choice. With My choice I will deny you Satan and I will worship only my Father in heaven.'

The importance of riches becomes much clearer if your time of death is a protracted event.
God forbid, through the tragic news that you have a terminal illness. You will experience an approaching precipice. It will demand that you leave behind or give up all you have come to know in the full measure of your lifetime.

Jesus had to make a decision about the world and all its riches on the day He renounced Satan's offer. Jesus would not bow down to worship Satan even when offered the entire world and all its riches.

There comes a time and place when you will make a decision to reject or accept either God or Satan. You can't serve both.
You have the power of choice!
Use it wisely!
Choose Jesus and live. Choose Jesus and be blessed.
Choose Jesus and not the god of this world as your master and keeper.

For it is sure you will belong to and come face to face with one or the other - on the other side.
"Don't you know that when you offer yourselves to someone to obey him as slaves, you are slaves to the one whom you obey - whether you are slaves to sin, which leads to death, or to obedience, which leads to righteousness?" (Romans 6:16).

196

Do you fear death?
"But he said to them, "it is I; don't be afraid" (John 6:20).
"Hearing this, Jesus said to Jairus, "Don't be afraid; just believe, and she will be healed" (Luke 8:50).
"Then Jesus said to them, "Do not be afraid. Go and tell my brothers to go to Galilee; there they will see me" (Matthew 28:10).
"The Lord is with me; I will not be afraid. What can man do to me?" (Psalm 118:6).
"In this way, love is made complete among us so that we will have confidence on the day of judgment, because in this world we are like him. There is no fear in love. But perfect love drives out fear, because fear has to do with punishment. The one who fears is not made perfect in love. We love because he first loved us" (1 John 4:17-19).

Isn't that last verse beautiful? There is so much meaning in this passage.

Tomorrow we will look at some more verses like these.

197

Today, let's consider more verses like the ones from yesterday's devotional.

"Peace I leave with you; my peace I give you. I do not give to you as the world gives. Do not let your hearts be troubled and do not be afraid" (John 14:27).
"Do not be anxious about anything, but in everything, by prayer and petition, with thanksgiving, present your requests to God" (Philippians 4:6).

Who could possibly have this much power.

"That day when evening came, he said to his disciples, "Let us go over to the other side." Leaving the crowd behind, they took him along, just as he was, in the boat. There were also other boats with him. A furious squall came up, and the waves broke over the boat, so that it was nearly swamped. Jesus was in the stern, sleeping on a cushion. The disciples woke him and said to him, "Teacher, don't you care if we drown?" He got up, rebuked the wind and said to the waves, "Quiet! Be still!" Then the wind died down and it was completely calm. He said to his disciples, "Why are you so afraid? Do you still have no faith?" They were terrified and asked each other, "Who is this? Even the wind and the waves obey him! "Even the wind and the waves are subject to Him" (Mark 4:35-45).

Won't you take His hand today?
You are valuable enough and precious enough to save!

"Jesus answered, "I am the way and the truth and the life. No one comes to the Father except through Me" (John 14:6).

Receive the Lord today. He is right there with you right now.

He is waiting for your invitation.

"For it is by grace you have been saved, through faith - and this not from yourselves, it is the gift of God - not by works, so that no one can boast." (Eph 2:8-9).

198

God's purpose for your life is . . . something you will discover with each step in the short amount of time you will live here on earth.

It is a short time.

Ask any person who has lived many years and they will tell you
it passes by quickly.
As you spend time with the Lord each day
life brings unexpected surprises.
Things may not go according to plan.
What if a health issue arises?
What if a trusted companion suddenly changes and you are no longer able to walk together
in the Lord. You find you are no longer able to be in agreement.

"Can two walk together, except they be agreed?" (Amos 3:3).

There is a place for change in Godly relationships.
Relationships can change with two people who serve the Lord.

You may have steady, consistent contacts with other people.
Life for some will be a series of relationships.
Each will be meaningful in its own way.

Some will end pleasantly.
                    Some will end with difficulty.
Some will have to be terminated with haste
                    bringing disappointment and remorse.
Some will end naturally through death,
or painfully with rejection.

Dear reader, let us look at a very meaningful scripture that will shed much necessary light upon the
challenge we will all face with other people.

"To the angel of the church in Philadelphia write: These are the words of him who is holy and true,
who holds the key of David. What he opens no one can shut, and what he shuts no one can open.
I know your deeds. See, I have placed before you an open door that no one can shut I know that
you have little strength, yet you have kept my word and have not denied my name"
(Revelation 3:7-8).

The Lord carefully opens up doors that bring people together.
He will close doors at the right time and in the way necessary to create opportunity
and to open new doors.

When you feel overwhelmed because these things are out of your control,
take comfort that you are God's sheep. He is opening and closing doors.
We see joy, pain, sadness, opportunity discovery or wonderment.
God in His love, sees a door open or close for your good.

He does all of this for you with the permission you gave Him to lead you, care for you and bring
His best for your life.

Others may be allowed to see what God has you doing.

That is the outward part of your relationship with God.

You may find that God in His wisdom chooses to hide
your faithful obedience.
He may choose to delight in you all by Himself.
He may take pleasure
yet be the only one to see your costly obedience.

Who is available to help an elderly person cross the street?
God can see this.
Who is available to speak to one or two people at a home bible study?
God is there
and thrilled to see unity, companionship and compassion.

Who would be willing to take time to invest in the life of a confused and broken person?
An unimpressive person with no evidence of going anywhere in life or faith.
It may be a person God wants to reach.
This may not impress others but it will deeply touch God
if you follow His leading and love the confused and downcast.

He patiently pursues the lost soul who sits alone in darkness.
He patiently pursues each person who accepts Him as Lord and Master.
Because our loving Jesus
is such a great friend.

He plans to make His time with you the absolute jewel of His day.
The purpose of God in your life, the part between you and God is to be loved by Him
and to love Him in return.
It is a love relationship with Him that will compel and enable you to do things for His good
and for His glory.
Often on the surface it will not appear to be to your own advantage.
You will find your solace in the challenges of life however, for the time you spend in His presence
is always filled with meaning and purpose. You will be aware of His guidance
because you have taken refuge in Him.
At the same time,
you may not always know exactly what He is up to. That is what trust is all about.

God's love is so deeply textured with meaning that it will overflow and cover every aspect of life.
Having a refuge will become the inspiration you need when things become difficult.
He will be all that you need when you seek Him.

He belongs to you as much as you belong to Him and He is your dwelling place.

Jesus Christ is God.

"God is our refuge and strength, an ever-present help in trouble" (Psalm 46:1).

200

There is nothing that can stop you from moving forward in the perfect will of your Father in heaven!
That is because it is not based upon whom you are.
If you make Jesus your refuge, a dwelling place you run to each day,
then you can be sure that amazing supernatural principles apply directly in your life.
Here is remarkable little piece of advice given to you by your God.

"give thanks in all circumstances, for this is God's will for you in Christ Jesus"
(1 Thessalonians 5:18).

We have recently referred to trials that befall you in life.

Unexpected things. Difficulties for which you never spent a second
figuring out what you would do should it happen to you. But here you are.

Now you are armed with this great advice from the Lord in Thessalonians.
You already know one thing to do no matter what befalls you.
Dwell upon reasons to be thankful.

You can be thankful on behalf of loved ones. It can apply to your town, possessions, your country, the nations - this little piece of supernatural advice applies in all things. It is very, very powerful.

Tomorrow we will expand upon this profoundly efficient solution given graciously to you by God.

201

Perhaps you have tried to be thankful since our last devotional.

If not, don't be anxious dear reader.

Do you know that God loves you the same today as He did yesterday?
Let's make that our headline in the news today!

GOD LOVES YOU THE SAME TODAY AS YESTERDAY!

"Jesus Christ is the same yesterday and today and forever" (Hebrews 13:8).

Being thankful is a good first step in any situation.
That is what God asks you to do.
He knows how hard life can be.
He knows we can be caught up with events at times and feel shook up.

He is looking to you when the 'dust settles' and you have gotten over the shock.
When you are thinking clearly and things have gotten back to a manageable footing.
When you are thinking clearly God is thrilled when you give Him thanks!
Telling Him you will serve Him no matter what happens.
When you say, 'my God is good. He has always been good to me.
He will always be there for me and has never made a mistake on my behalf.'
Look out for the next news headline!

PLANS OF SATAN CRUSHED BY LOCAL SENIOR!
Assisted by 6 year old girl they both gave thanks to God again today!
Witnesses at the scene overheard them saying,
'He does all things well' and 'perfect love casts out fear'.

Even before you know what is to befall you,
God has offered a powerful spiritual strategy with the instruction,
'be thankful in all things'.

Yes, we also call it a 'command' to be thankful.

It is like a parent who says, 'look both ways before you cross the street.'
This is a command given out of love. A loving parent brings blessing and life to a cherished son
or daughter through certain commands.
How sad for children with no one to teach them right from wrong.
Let's pray for neglected children during our time with Jesus today ok?
Here is a prayer the weakest follower of Jesus is able to say.
"Thank you Lord Jesus. Thank you heavenly Father. Thank you Holy Spirit.
I don't know why _____ has happened but you do!
I express my love for you by offering thanks to You.
I express my faith in you by thanking you.
I express my desire to be led in your perfect will by thanking You."

By all means, feel free to open up right now to God.
If you feel led by the Holy Spirit,
lift up your heart and voice with thanksgiving and song.
Faith! Love! Truth! Surrender to His plan and purpose for your life.
'In everything give thanks.'
At first we are often overwhelmed in circumstances.
Once the mercy and grace of God enables us to gather our thoughts and to focus on the Lord, He
will enable us to open up with thanksgiving.

You often won't understand fully the reason why God has permitted events to transpire around you that bring testing, trial, sadness, loss.

It is crushing at times.

Without the Lord and His faithful care in our life it may have the potential to bring about your personal undoing.

"For God, who commanded the light to shine out of darkness, hath shined in our hearts, to give the light of the knowledge of the glory of God in the face of Jesus Christ. But we have this treasure in earthen vessels, that the Excellency of the power may be of God, and not of us. We are troubled on every side, yet not distressed; we are perplexed, but not in despair; Persecuted, but not forsaken; cast down, but not destroyed; Always bearing about in the body the dying of the Lord Jesus, that the life also of Jesus might be made manifest in our body" (2 Cor. 4:6-10).

That darkness around you is defeated by the blood Jesus shed upon the cross. Defeated by His resurrection from the dead. There is a power within you. You have been bought with a price.

"Do you not know that your body is a temple of the Holy Spirit, who is in you, whom you have received from God? You are not your own; you were bought at a price, Therefore honour God with your body" (1 Corinthians 6:19-20).
"And if the Spirit of him who raised Jesus from the dead is living in you, he who raised Christ from the dead will also give life to your mortal bodies through his Spirit, who lives in you"
(Romans 8:11).

There are phenomenal benefits because you belong to Jesus Christ the King of Kings. This battle is fought and won not through your own ingenuity but by the resurrection life within you!

"Can a mother forget the baby at her breast and have no compassion for the child she has borne? Though she may forget, I will not forget you!" (Isaiah 49:15).

Whose Spirit dwells inside of you? I have to ask this question because it is central to this phenomenon. Have you been dwelling with your God? If you have made the Lord your dwelling place then His resurrection life within you will bring all things together in the exact plans God has for you! His resurrection life will quicken your mortal body. You will fear no evil.

Sometimes things won't go your way. You will be held safely in His arms and still feel overwhelmed at times. The resurrection life of the Holy Spirit within you shall rise up. You will be led in the victory prepared for you by your God.

You will be led as a Shepherd leads the sheep in His care.

There is beauty in the world.

There is beauty in you.

There is beauty *in you*.

In all the world there is nothing more beautiful to the Lord Jesus than you are right now.

Do you say, 'but look at me. Look at what I've done.'
Or do you say, 'look at how badly I have failed you Lord.'
'I have failed.'
'There is no reason for God to love me.'
'I have cursed God.'
'I have served the devil.'
'I have wounded and hurt many others.'
'I hate myself.' 'I am dirty and unclean.'
'My pastor does not approve of me.'

Or do you merely repeat to yourself a damning or negative word spoken to you in early years?
'You are stupid.' 'You are ugly.'
'You are a disappointment.'
'You will never amount to anything.'
'My life would have been better if I never had you children.'
Let the tears flow precious reader.
Allow your Saviour to bring His love and His presence right into the very center
of that wicked and hurtful area.

Jesus needs to be there with you right now.
Let Him have access to all that pain. Invite Jesus right into the very center of that pain.
You are His purchased possession. He wants to look after you.
He is able to look after you. He cares about you and will make you whole.

"And you also were included in Christ when you heard the word of truth, the gospel of your salvation. Having believed, you were marked in him with a seal, the promised Holy Spirit, who is a deposit guaranteeing our inheritance until the redemption of those who are God's possession - to the praise of his glory" (Ephesians 1:13-14).
"Which is the earnest of our inheritance until the redemption of the purchased possession, unto the praise of his glory" (Ephesians 1:14 King James Version).
"Do you not know that your body is a temple of the Holy Spirit, who is in you, whom you have received from God? You are not your own; you were bought at a price. Therefore honour God with your body" (1 Corinthians 6:19-20 New International Version).

Dear, dear reader.
Look to your Redeemer.

Look to Jesus right now.

204

You are beautiful to Jesus.

Jesus loved you long before you were born.

He knew everything about you. In order to love you he had to really know you.
Love means He thought about you unceasingly.
You have always been in His heart.
We may conclude that you were in the heart of God
from eternity past and you are in His heart now.
As His betrothed you will remain there in His heart for all eternity.

"For he chose us in him before the creation of the world to be holy and blameless in his sight. In love he predestined us to be adopted as his sons through Jesus Christ in accordance with his pleasure and will - to the praise of his glorious grace, which he has feely given us in the One he loves. In him we have redemption through his blood, the forgiveness of sins, in accordance with the riches of God's grace that he lavished on us with all wisdom and understanding" (Eph. 1:4-8).

Can you see what God's perfect love is all about? A love for you in the deep, deep heart of God existing from eternity past before you were born.
Dear Reader, for God to love you it means He has to know everything about you.
He would have to know you fully. That is because He is perfectly just.
In His justice He would have to know about you completely
before He made the decision to die for you.
He did so with great joy because He understood it would enable Him to wash away your sin.
That means when He was thinking about you it included everything you would do.

He knew it all
and because He is perfect love
He saw your redemption as the only way forward.
Jesus Christ loved you just the way you are before He made the world.

"And hope does not disappoint us, because God has poured out his love into our hearts by the Holy Spirit, whom he has given us. You see, at just the right time, when we were still powerless, Christ died for the ungodly. Very rarely will anyone die for a righteous man, though for a good man someone might possibly dare to die, But God demonstrates his own love for us in this: While we were still sinners, Christ died for us. Since we have now been justified by his blood, how much more shall we be saved from God's wrath through Him! For if, when we were God's enemies, we were reconciled to him through the death on his Son, how much more, having been reconciled, shall we be saved through his life!" (Romans 5:5-10).

"For you know that it was not with perishable things such as silver or gold that you were redeemed from the empty way of life handed down to you from your forefathers, but with the precious blood of Christ, a lamb without blemish or defect. He was chosen before the creation of the world, but was revealed in these last times for your sake. Through him you believe in God who raised him from the dead and glorified him, and so your faith and hope are in God" (1 Peter 1:18-21).

Because God is love
there is never a doubt that He loves you.
There is nothing you could ever do to stop Him absolutely loving you.
That is because He already knows what you will do in the tomorrows of your life
and committed Himself to die for you in advance.

"The Spirit and the bride say, "Come!" And let him who hears say, "Come!" Whoever is thirsty, let him come: and whoever wishes, let him take the free gift of the water of life" (Revelation 22:17).

Are you ready to let God reach your heart? It is time to give Him all your hurt, your pain, your past. He knows all about it.
It is time dear reader.
It is time - for He is love.
God bless you.
You are loved.

205

"We give thanks to God always for you all, making mention of you in our prayers" (1 Thessalonians 1:2).

God loves all of His dear people.

The men who personally walked with Jesus and were taught by him.

Those men prayed for the church in Thessalonica.
They had previously met the brothers and sisters in the faith.
A deep bond
was established in their hearts.

When they remembered the Thessalonica church they gave thanks
for all of the members.
They gave thanks all the time,
for all the members.
Not one person was excluded from the love
and thanksgiving lavished upon them.

206

Everyone was included.

There must have been times when one or the other was having problems. Maybe they felt they didn't measure up. After all, they were being guided by men as imperfect as themselves.

But the Holy Spirit, praise God, led the disciples to be thankful in their hearts for every person.

Imagine being so deep in God
where you are able to perceive the absolute value
of every person in the church.
They were not necessarily deeper than you or I.
They were just busy gazing upon the beauty of the Lord.
Through Him they could see His love at work.
It was not their effort building the church but the work of His Holy Spirit.

"Selling their possessions and goods, they gave to anyone as he had need. Every day they continued to meet together in the temple courts. They broke bread in their homes and ate together with glad and sincere hearts, praising God and enjoying the favour of all the people. <u>And the Lord added to their number daily those who were being saved</u>" (Acts 2:45-48).

"Do nothing out of selfish ambition or vain conceit, but in humility consider others better than yourselves" (Philippians 2:3).

You see, from God's perspective
each person in the gathering now fully belonged to Him.
They were His responsibility.

Every person was subject to the fullness of His care.
Each person had been instantly initiated into God's glorious plan and purpose in the earth.
From the oldest to the youngest, both male and female,

they were living out God's will on earth.

For I know the plans I have for you,' declares the Lord, 'plans to prosper you and not to harm you, plans to give you hope and a future' (Jeremiah 29:11 NIV).

Dear reader,
you are no different
from these early believers when you have been born-again
and are led by the Holy Ghost!

"because those who are led by the Spirit of God are sons (and daughters) of God" (Romans 8:14).

Being led by the Holy Ghost is a matter of friendship with the Divine.
He chose you and loves you. He is looking for someone who cares enough to be His friend
when things aren't going well. Isn't that what a friend is for?
The mighty Holy Spirit will enable you to uphold your end of the friendship. He will work in you.
He will give you such a heart for friendship with God.

You will thank Him, praise Him, and stick with Him to the end!

The Holy Spirit will empower you to be a great friend of God!

"How if we are children, then we are heirs - heirs of God and co-heirs with Christ, if indeed we share in his sufferings in order that we may also share in his glory" (Romans 8:17).

All that power from on high will enable you to share with Him in His sufferings.

'Let the weakling say, 'I am strong!' (Joel 3:10b).

206

You are completely acceptable to God through the Living Truth.

The Living Word.

The Living wonder of the Righteous Son of God, Jesus Christ.

"For we know brothers loved by God, that he has chosen you," (1 Thessalonians 1:4).

To be chosen Dear Reader is a great honour.
We know to be chosen in sports says everything about your talent and your skill.
To be chosen first is a great honour. Everyone knows only the best
are chosen ahead of everyone else.
God has chosen you.

You belong to Him.
He has purchased you through the death and resurrection of His Son.
You must be the very best He could find.
You are a member of His Royal Priesthood.
You are unique and wonderful,
fearfully and wonderfully made.

"But you are a chosen people, a royal priesthood, a holy nation, a people belonging to God, that you may declare the praises of him who called you out of darkness into his wonderful light" (1 Peter 2:9).
"I praise you because I am fearfully and wonderfully made; your works are wonderful, I know that full well" (Psalm 139:14).

His plan is taking place in you because the same Spirit that raised Jesus from the dead also lives in you!
With His Holy Ghost living in you
you are the handiwork of God.

"And if the same Spirit of him who raised Jesus from the dead is living in you, he who raised Christ from the dead will also give life to your mortal bodies through his Spirit, who lives in you" (Romans 8:11).

Amen.

You are safely in His hands through faith in Jesus Christ.
May you be encouraged today in how much potential you have in God.

"How great is the love the Father has lavished on us, that we should be called children of God! And that is what we are! The reason the world does not know us is that it did not know him. Dear friends, now we are the children of God, and what we will be has not yet been made known. But we know that when he appears, we shall be like him, for we shall see him as he is" (1 John 3:1-2).

207

"Knowing, brethren beloved, your election of God" (1 Thessalonians 1:4 King James Version).

This is a compelling part of your new spiritual foundation.

Instantly you were changed
because Someone loved you so much.

It is really about power and will.
God has the power.
The power of His absolutely perfect love.
God's love and His meekness to serve and to save are linked together in perfect agreement.

"For even the Son of Man did not come to be served, but to serve, and to give his life as a ransom for many" (Mark 10:45 New International Version).
"just as the Son of Man did not come to be served, but to serve, and to give his life as a ransom for many" (Matthew 20:28).

God has the will.

God has the heart of a servant.
It defines His behaviour toward those purchased by His precious blood.
He gave His life
and shed His blood - it took that great a ransom.

Once the ransom was paid on your behalf nothing would ever
be able to hold your soul captive
ever again!

The devil and the demons are unable to hold your soul captive.

Time for a news headline!

RANSOM PAID! BELIEVERS NO LONGER CAPTIVE!
JESUS GAVE LIFE - ALL SIN CAN BE FORGIVEN!
SATAN'S POWER CRUSHED. BE FREE IN JESUS NAME!

208

"Knowing, brethren beloved, your election of God" (1 Thessalonians 1:4 King James Version).

The verse says, 'your election of God.'

How wonderfully confident the church leaders were because they knew.

They knew the followers of Jesus in the church of Thessalonians
were elected by God
and added to the church by God.

They were chosen.

These people,
the whole lot of them in Thessalonica,
shared together in the election process of God!
In the next verse it mentions 'preaching the gospel' in their midst.

"because our gospel came to you not simply with words, but also with power, with the Holy Spirit
and with deep conviction. You know how we lived among you for your sake"
(1 Thessalonians 4:5 New International Version).

The church people not only heard the gospel from these followers of Jesus
but they glimpsed first hand the lives of consecrated leadership.
This all came together as the 'message'.
There was
power,
the Holy Spirit
and deep conviction.

Conviction.
This term is not referring to impending punishment.
Punishment is given on the path that leads to death.

210

Because you are chosen and elected grace is freely given when you humble yourself
and respond to conviction from the Lord.

Conviction shines a light upon that which displeases God in your heart and life.
It is the God's mercy. It is His love at work all over again!
Conviction from God is a loving work of the Holy Spirit.
It brings about a godly sorrow.

"Godly sorrow brings repentance that leads to salvation and leaves no regret, but worldly sorrow
brings death" (2 Corinthians 7:10).

Instead of feeling down and beaten up -
NO! The Holy Spirit sweetly comes alongside
to indicate problem area(s) that will hinder and harm you now and in the future.

Repent.
Be forgiven.
It is your birthright
to avail yourself of His forgiveness.
Who but those who love Jesus will respond to the cry to receive forgiveness through His blood.

You are chosen. You of all people in the world are most uniquely blessed.
God will forgive you.
God will restore you.
He is responding to your desire to walk in the Light.
His forgiveness is a blessing beyond all riches - and you deserve to be forgiven because of His love.

There is a wholesale rejoicing and joy for what the Lord has in store for those who have received
the message! Believing in Jesus Christ is your beginning of eternal life.

Have you believed in Jesus Christ?
Have you received the gospel message?
Does the Holy Ghost now live in your heart?
When you have,
there is much cause for rejoicing.
You are elected of God.
You belong with those precious individuals who are considered a friend of Jesus.
Along with the believers in Thessalonica
you are now one of the children of the Most High God.
You are an heir of salvation.

Think of the most incredible Christian you can think of.

You dear reader, are prayed for and loved right along with them!

Where would you be without the Holy Spirit?

He is chosen of God to lead people in fellowship with God the Father in heaven.

"No one can come to me unless the Father who sent me draws him," (John 6:44).

This is written in the bible. It is what God decided to tell us about Himself.
Who are we to contradict God when He is mercifully reaching out to us?
He carefully points to His Holy Spirit as the only Person able to bring God's truth to our heart.

"But God has revealed it to us by his Spirit. The Spirit searches all things, even the deep things of God" (1 Corinthians 2:10).

The Holy Spirit brings the reality of God's embrace to your life.

He surrounds you in a most tangible way at times.
A deep, intimate relationship with God
is only possible when the Holy Spirit is honoured.
Respected.
Reverenced.
Listened to.
Obeyed.
Followed.
Adored.
Submitted to.
It is a comfort for the follower of Jesus when one realises the Holy Spirit is already present
to lead and to guide.

He does not need to be enticed or impressed.

He is not outside the room waiting to come in the window when the singing is just right.
Or when there is the correct atmosphere, or there are enough consecrated people in the room.
Before you even begin your time with Jesus dear reader, the Holy Spirit is there waiting for you.

Those who forgo the manifestation of the Holy Spirit do so at their own peril.
The precious Holy Spirit was commended to us by Jesus Christ Himself
just before He was seen going up into the clouds following His resurrection.

"And I will ask the Father, and he will give you another Counsellor to be with you forever - the Spirit of truth. The world cannot accept him, because it neither sees him nor knows him. But you know him, for he lives with you and will be in you" (John 14:16-17).

Today I am bringing an invitation to you dear reader,
to invite the Holy Spirit to reveal your heavenly Father's love.
This is the reason Jesus came to earth. It was because of His love for the whole world.
That means He loved the absolute worst sinner possible in all of human history.
The whole world includes all people.

Of course this will take a measure of time once you go aside to be in His presence.

In that quiet, alone place - go there
to meet with God.
Let God share Himself with you as He pleases. Do you know a lot about God? No matter.
God loves everyone. It is time to renew your commitment to 'know God'.

Many people know about God.
Even non Christians freely tell Christians what they should be like.
Take courage today to renew your commitment to 'know God' rather than to know about God.

You need the Holy Spirit. Not a belief in the Holy Spirit - you need to experience Him as a person.

You need Him to work day to day. You need Him.

210

"You became imitators of us and of the Lord; in spite of severe suffering, you welcomed the
message with the joy given by the Holy Spirit" (1 Thessalonians 1:6).

The Holy Spirit is your friend.

He gives you joy.

How close He is to you if He is the reason for your joy!
The Holy Spirit lives inside you and He gives you the ability to follow Jesus.

"So he said to me, 'This is the word of the Lord to Zerubbabel: 'Not by might nor by power, but by
my Spirit,' says the Lord Almighty" (Zechariah 4:6).

The Holy Spirit enables you to perceive God's will for your life.
Those who take time alone with God to listen are able to perceive the instruction
God has for them. Remember the story of the children who obeyed their teacher?
She said they had 'listened'.
They had listened to her. They were obedient.
God will give you the ability and opportunity to fulfill His perfect will.

Even if you have severe suffering you are still able to walk with Jesus.

That is because you have become the place where the Holy Spirit dwells.

The bible says your body has become a temple.

"Do you not know that you are the temple of God and that the Spirit of God dwells in you?"
(1 Cor. 3:16).

211

"for it is God which worketh in you both to will and to do of his good pleasure" (Philippians 2:13).

He is not an unknown phantom.

If you have decided in advance not to be open to His guidance and His council then you might
imagine the Holy Ghost to be strange and unknowable.
The Holy Spirit is already with you as an intimate friend.

Jesus prayed for the Spirit to come to earth.
Once Jesus ministry on earth had been completed and He ascended to His Father
He said the Holy Spirit will be with each believer and will be in each believer.
These are the very words of Jesus Christ.
"The Holy Spirit will be with you and He will be in you."

The Holy Spirit lives inside of you when you are saved.
He is ready to share everything with you that you need.
He enables ordinary people to walk in a deep,
intimate relationship with an unseen God!

The Holy Spirit is so accessible and sincere. He readily shows His willingness to become your most
intimate friend. Very quickly you will see His desire for you to get to know one another.
This is the cornerstone of intimacy - to communicate openly and transparently.

He is ready to share with you. He is your joy.
He takes the deep things of God and reveals them unto you.

"because our gospel came to you not simply with words, but also with power, with the Holy Spirit
and with deep conviction" (1 Thessalonians 1:5a,b).

To make it a relationship you need to take the step
and open up two-way communication.
He is ready to listen and share. The Holy Spirit was critical to your salvation.
He worked in your heart as you responded to the gospel message.
He is waiting for you to make a place in your life
to listen and share with Him.

214

It is like this, you can know about your next door neighbour.
But if you were to invite them for tea or coffee every day for a week in your own home,
then you would 'really' know your neighbour. It would not be the same as before.
Things would be different between the two of you.
Now, you 'really' know one another.

The Holy Spirit is very similar to this.
It takes your commitment to know Him and to be known by Him.

When you seek God, lean heavily upon the work of the Holy Spirit.
Do not take any credit to yourself. Time spent with God is all a work of grace.
There is no boasting in it. Not by might, nor by power but by the Holy Spirit
a relationship has taken place.

If we look at a successful marriage, spending consistent time together
with openness and communication lends itself to a successful marriage.
A couple that rarely has time together often falls apart.
'We were too busy.'
'We never saw each other.'

Then they split up.

This is often the case with successful people who are in the public spotlight. Their careers are in
conflict with the love that brought them together. Success comes between them. They don't spend
time together. Time passes and the tender love they celebrated becomes elusive. Then it is gone.
The reason for intimate sharing vanishes. Like the rest of us, as ordinary people, it all comes down
to getting to know one another. Just like with God.

They didn't put together a relationship. How wonderful if they had gotten to know each other.
There would have been such treasure to nurture - and enjoy!

Maybe even for a lifetime.

212

"However, as it is written: 'No eye has seen, no ear has heard, no mind has conceived what God has
prepared for those who love him - but God Has revealed it to us by his Spirit. The Spirit searches
all things, even the deep things of God" (1 Corinthians 2:9-11).

Let us take this day to consider the deepest mysteries.
Though this sounds like a scary proposition,
we are not talking about the might and power of man.
That kind of power always fades and is forgotten forever.
We are going to consider the 'source' of the deepest mysteries!

We need to separate human talent, capability, skill and enthusiasm
away from the kind and loving heart of the Lord Jesus Christ.

He said His truths are revealed by His Spirit!

They are not revealed by the Spirit - selectively to the ones on the upper level!
The ones whose family have founded the church or gave the most money.
Who preach with the loudest voice.
No! The Lord knows and He has already said He looks at qualifications within the heart.

"Humble yourselves, therefore, under God's mighty hand, that he may lift you up in due time"
(1 Peter 5:6).
"The sacrifices of God are a broken spirit; a broken and contrite heart, O God, you will not
despise" (Psalm 51:17).
"Who may ascend the hill of the Lord? Who may stand in his holy place? He who has clean hands
and a pure heart, who does not lift up his soul to an idol or swear by what is false. He will receive
blessing from the Lord and vindication from God his Saviour. Such is the generation of those who
seek him, who seek your face, O God of Jacob" (Psalm 24:3-6).

213

Deep truth is not strewn about in the unseen realm.

Actually there is Someone
who calls Himself the Truth.

He said He is the Way,
the Truth
and the Life.

You get into Jesus and you will get into all the Truth you can handle.

Looking singularly unto Jesus Christ
enables *Him*
to bring the fullness of spiritual revelation.

He safely guides and generously bestows wisdom and understanding to those who sincerely ask.

"If any of you lacks wisdom, he should ask God, who gives generously to all without finding fault,
and it will be given to him" (James 1:5).

God has been revealed to us in the 'flesh'.
That means when Jesus no longer wanted to be unseen and invisible
His form became just as our own. We are created in His image after all.

216

Can you possibly discover any more truth and revelation than in the face of God?
There is no One more in tune with you than this precious, dear, loving servant named Jesus.

"Jesus answered, 'I am the way and the truth and the life. No one comes to the Father except through me" (John 14:6).
"Therefore he is able to save completely those who come to God through him, because he always lives to intercede for them" (Hebrews 7:25).

214

You have Someone to help you.

He will choose what to reveal to you.

He will carefully give you only what you can handle.
He has prepared your entire future and knows what you need.
He is kind and loving.
His forgiveness and His mercy knows no end.
He is faithful.
He will be faithful to you until your very last breath on this earth.

"I will praise you, O Lord, among the nations; I will sing of you among the peoples. For great is your love, higher than the heavens; your faithfulness reaches to the skies. Be exalted, O God, above the heavens, and let your glory be over all the earth. Save us and help us with your right hand, that those you love may be delivered" (Psalm 108:3-6).
"Your love, O Lord, reaches to the heavens, your faithfulness to the skies. Your righteousness is like the mighty mountains, your justice like the great deep. O Lord, you preserve both man and best. How priceless is your unfailing love! Both high and low among men find refuge in the shadow of your wings. They feast on the abundance of your house; you give them drink from your river of delights. For with you is the fountain of life; in your light we see light" (Psalm 36:5-9).
"For we are God's workmanship, created in Christ Jesus to do good works, which God prepared in advance for us to do" (Ephesians 2:10).

There is just nowhere else to go in the vast heavenly realm to gain access to great spiritual truth.
Remember, truth is found in a Person. His name is Jesus.

"Oh, the depth of the riches of the wisdom and knowledge of God! How unsearchable his judgements, and his paths beyond tracing out!" (Romans 11:33).
"Your life is hidden with Christ in God." (Colossians 3:3).

You won't need someone to search the far reaches of earth to reveal the magnitude
of God's love for you. God will do that Himself.
Nor will you need another person to search to the far side of the sea
to bring back these mysteries to share with you.

Jesus Christ is the altogether lovely one.

"Now what I am commanding you today is not too difficult for you or beyond your reach. It is not up in heaven, so that you have to ask, 'Who will ascend into heaven to get it and proclaim it to us so we may obey it?' Nor is it beyond the sea, so that you have to ask, 'Who will cross the sea to get it and proclaim it to us so we may obey it?" (Deuteronomy 30:11-13).

While you are looking for your life without putting Christ in the center of your own personal universe you will come up with nothing worthwhile.
You can't find something that is hidden no matter how hard you look.

Truth is hidden unless you receive Jesus Christ and follow Him.

"Then he said to them all: 'If anyone would come after me, he must deny himself and take up his cross daily and follow me" (Luke 9:23).

215

"For this commandment which I command thee this day, it is not hidden from thee, neither is it far off. It is not in heaven, that thou shouldest say, Who shall go up for us to heaven, and bring it unto us, that we may hear it, and do it? Neither is it beyond the sea, that thou shouldest say, Who shall go over the sea for us, and bring it unto us, that we may hear it, and do it? But the word is very nigh unto thee, in thy mouth, and in thy heart, that thou mayest do it" (Deut. 30:11-14 KJV).

Do you see?

God has your spiritual journey all planned out.

You don't have to become 'spiritual'! A lover of Jesus no longer follows a path based upon the common influences in society. Without even trying your life becomes entirely spiritual.

Positionally you exist under the cover of His love.
Through Him you are transformed.
From His perspective you are continually being kept by Him.
Cared for by Him.
Nurtured by Him.
Overshadowed by Him.
You are one with Him.

"And God raised us up with Christ and seated us with him in the heavenly realms in Christ Jesus," (Ephesians 2:6 New International Version).
Dear reader, this devotional is not aimed at reaching people who want to be spiritual.
It is especially not going to be helpful to those who want others to think of them as 'really spiritual'.
It is written simply for 'followers'.

Those who desire with their whole heart to follow Jesus Christ.

Being oriented to the spiritual realm is a living, breathing reality
the moment you receive Jesus Christ as Saviour.

From that moment of faith in Jesus Christ you are in the safekeeping of the King of Kings.

"And God raised us up with Christ and seated us with him in the heavenly realms in Christ Jesus,"
(Ephesians 2:6).

216

Jesus Christ is your good shepherd.

He is the epitome of Spirituality
and has taken responsibility with your own personal revelation of His love.
The love of God -
this is the locus of Jesus'
revelation to you
for the rest of your days.

"One thing I ask of the Lord, this is what I seek: that I may dwell in the house of the Lord all the
days of my life, to gaze upon the beauty of the Lord and to seek him in his temple" (Psalm 27:4).

People are spiritual based upon what they do not in telling people what they do.

If what they do is spend time with Jesus they are as spiritual as they can get.

He places His Holy Spirit in the heart of all of His followers. They have been changed from the
inside out. They are His temple forever
if that is what they want.

Each and every believer can have their own deep personal relationship with God.

You will be a spiritual person through the life of the Holy Spirit within you.

There is a rich relationship waiting to unfold.
Deep, intimate, personal fellowship with God awaits you!

Relationship can only proceed if you meet God's desire with your own.
Willing to put yourself in the place of intimate fellowship with Him.
Time spent with your beloved.
The place of meeting with God.
Your life is found in the risen Son of God.

His Holy Spirit, now living in you,
will take the wonderful reality of the spiritual realm
and bring to you all that you are to know.
But more importantly, He will impart the understanding of how greatly He values you.

You will be consumed with the knowledge that Jesus loves you enough to lay His life down for you.

After suffering death just to get to know you,
think of how fulfilling it is for the risen Son of God to actually get to spend time with you.
After giving His life for you each moment you allow Him to minister to you
is beyond precious for this meek, omnipotent Servant.

"just as the Son of Man did not come to be served, but to serve, and to give his life as a ransom for many" (Matthew 20:28).
"Here I am! I stand at the door and knock. If anyone hears my voice and opens the door, I will come in and eat with him, and he with me" (Revelations 3:20).

How meek.
He gave His life
but doesn't make you love Him.
Many know about Jesus.
Not very many
really love Jesus.

He has asked for nothing in return
only a request to be your friend.

And it's entirely at your convenience.

217

So great is the cost of a soul lost for all eternity.

A car rusts.
A taxi, scooter or bicycle eventually falls apart and is not worthy of repair.
A house inevitably disintegrates even if cared for with love and attention to detail.
A home one hundred years old is considered rare. It may have a plaque of special recognition.
Currency from an ancient civilization - Rome, India, Malaysia, Africa, North America
and all the rest - is no longer in circulation. If it exists at all it is locked up, tucked away
and kept secure because it is so scarce.

But a soul.
Your human soul.
The wealth of the whole world cannot compare.

"Yet when I surveyed all that my hands had done and what I had toiled to achieve, everything was meaningless, a chasing after the wind; nothing was gained under the sun" (Ecclesiastes 2:11).
"What good is it for a man to gain the whole world, yet forfeit his soul?" (Mark 8:36).

Do you know?
Do you know you are this valuable?

Jesus knew.
He knew about your value.

"I praise you because I am fearfully and wonderfully made; your works are wonderful, I know that full well" (Psalm 139:14).
"So God created man in his own image, in the image of God he created him; male and female he created them" (Genesis 1:27).
"Therefore, if anyone is in Christ, he is a new creation; the old has gone, the new has come!" (2 Corinthians 5:17).

218

Jesus knew full well of your value along with your heavenly Father and the Holy Ghost before the world was made. That means you were known to God from eternity past.

How can we possibly grasp our worth?

From eternity past, with love beyond measure,
God looked forward
to your arrival.
He did not spot something really nasty about you
and change His mind about your birth.

Before you did anything good or bad you have always been on God's mind.

Often the things we love
are at the forefront of our thoughts.
We bring them to mind because it is pleasurable.

You dear reader, have always been on God's mind.

If you chose not to receive His Son and be forgiven, imagine the sense of loss
in your Heavenly Father's heart. He created you in His own image.
He considers you a member of His family if only you would believe.
You are intrinsically the most valuable thing in all of God's creation.
'What, me?" you might ask.
More important than the beautiful water falls in Africa, the rain forest, the Taj Mahal?

More significant than the mighty Blue Whale, a hummingbird, a bumble bee or the soaring eagle?
Jesus says,
'yes'.

He proved this by obeying His Father and dying for you.
His love is that personal.

He knew about you, your trials and sorrows.
Your highs and lows.
Your passion and your disappointments.

He knew all about you when He hung up there on that roughly hewn cross.
His profound passion for intimate fellowship was shining forth for all to see.
It shines through His willingness to die.

You are worth it.

219

"The Spirit and the bride say, 'Come!' And let him who hears say, 'Come!' Whoever is thirsty, let him come; and whoever wishes, let him take the free gift of the water of life" (Revelation 22:7).

When it was time to step up and pay the price Jesus did not hold back.

Just the thought of what His Father was asking Him to do compelled Him
to return to His Father's presence
again and again.
That is what the garden of Gethsemane was about.

Again and again it seemed alright.
He understood what His Father wanted.
He would leave the place of prayer but become overwhelmed
by the burden of it. The enormity of the price.

He was about to take upon Himself the sins of the whole world.
He had to seek His Father again
because this loving Servant couldn't take it in His mind.
He had to go back to that place of prayer.

Jesus did not have a low pain threshold.
He was not reticent to suffer.
The physical aspect of crucifixion
was not His greatest burden to bear.

Notice later on how willingly He submitted to the process in His Father's will.
For now in the garden though, that blessed, Son of God pressed in until He was 'sweating blood'.
That is where that saying originated.

It was lived out by the Son of God in His passionate love for His Father and for you dear reader.

"And being in anguish, he prayed more earnestly, and his sweat was like drops of blood falling to the ground" (Luke 22:44).

220

Pleasing His Father meant your freedom from death and hell.
Jesus Christ purchased your freedom with a love that is an everlasting love.

The greatest of all loves.

"Greater love has no one than this, that he lay down his life for his friends" (John 15:13).

There is enough power in His precious blood to forgive anyone who asks for forgiveness.
Jesus can wash away all sin no matter how grievous.
Even if every person in the world at the same time asked for forgiveness - the blood Jesus shed 2000 years ago would be sufficient. There is room for everyone.

There will always be room for you dear reader.

"This is how God showed his love among us: He sent his one and only Son into the world that we might live through him" (1 John 4:9).
"For God did not send his Son into the world to condemn the world, but to save the world through him" (John 3:17).

When Jesus was crucified He shed His blood.
That sacrificial blood is able to forgive any and all sin.

"They overcame him by the blood of the Lamb and by the word of their testimony; they did not love their lives so much as to shrink from death" (Revelation 12:11).
"If we confess our sins, he is faithful and just and will forgive us our sins and purify us from all unrighteousness" (1 John 1:9).
"Come to me, all you who are weary and burdened, and I will give you rest" (Matthew 11:28).

221

Do you have a tough sin deep down inside of you?

Is your life a sinful mess?

One that is extra dark, extra sordid?
GLORY TO GOD!
He will cleanse you from ALL sin!
That is Truth.
That is Light.
That work is already prepared for you by Jesus!

There is no place so dark or peculiar that God can't stand alongside
and love you,
love you,
love you.

"For we do not have a high priest who is unable to sympathize with our weaknesses, but we have one who has been tempted in every way, just as we are - yet was without sin. Let us then approach the throne of grace with confidence, so that we may receive mercy and find grace to help us in our time of need" (Hebrews 4:15-16).

"Suppose one of you has a hundred sheep and loses one of them. Does he not leave the ninety-nine in the open country and go after the lost sheep until he finds it?" (Luke 15:4).

Are you that, 'one' today?
Lost.
Without a sense of your cosmic worth.

You are loved.

You have value.

222

You can't be compared to a large diamond because you are worth so much more.

Gold?

Property?
Vehicles?
Money?
Nothing on earth can be compared to your worth dear reader.

"In him we have redemption through his blood, the forgiveness of sins, in accordance with the riches of God's grace that he lavished on us with all wisdom and understanding" (Ephesians 1:7-8).

Before anything in the material world existed
you were known by an all-knowing God of love.

He has had you in mind before you were even born.
You exist in His eternal mind
and that is why your heavenly Father
asked Jesus to die for you.

Your heavenly Father needed above all things
to bring you into fellowship with Himself.
This would not be easily done

for God is perfect in every way
and you and I have a sinful nature.
He would have to make a way to cleanse us from sin.
Deliver us from death and give us eternal life in heaven with Him once life here is over.

It has to be a free gift
because it is not possible to earn our way to righteousness.
You see, Jesus Christ came to earth for you.
God loves you and God is unable to do wrong.
He can't sin.
He cannot lie.

"Paul, a servant of God and an apostle of Jesus Christ for the faith of God's elect and the
knowledge of the truth that leads to godliness - a faith and knowledge resting on the hope of
eternal life, which God who does not lie, promised before the beginning of time," (Titus 1:1-2).

He is able to be in every place all the time.
God is beyond what we understand as 'time'.

"I am the Alpha and Omega, the First and the Last, the Beginning and the End"
(Revelation 22:13).

In your heart of hearts you might have to ask,
"How could you love 'this'?
How could God love me with all I am and all I've done?
How could God love someone made filthy from being abused?"

You rightfully belong to God
and your God has come down to get you.

You are created in His image and nothing can change that.
You were uniquely created because God framed everything about you in His mind
and brought you into existence.
Your worth has been determined by the unsearchable intellect of the Creator.
This value God sees in you is so very,
very high.

Only through the giving of a life could He redeem your life.

Jesus paid the price for your sin.

"Salvation is found in no one else, for there is no other name under heaven given to men by which we must be saved" (Acts 4:12).

223

Your free will.

This separates you from God.

The power to accept or reject the forgiveness of God.
At the same time - 'free will' is the very thing that makes you just like God.
He created you in His image.
He has invited you to become His follower
but Jesus will not force you to make the decision.

There is no other creature in existence on this planet that has a free will.
Mankind alone has the image of God.

"Know that the Lord is God. It is he who made us, and we are his; we are his people, the sheep of his pasture" (Psalm 100:3).
"But small is the gate and narrow the road that leads to life, and only a few find it" (Matthew 7:14).

If you have not chosen to be a sheep in His care
He will wait.
He will wait for you.
You will not be forced to love, because that is not love.

Jesus would like to reveal the 'full extent of His love to you.'

"It was just before the Passover Feast. Jesus knew that the time had come for him to leave this world and go to the Father. Having loved his own who were in the world, he now showed them the full extent of his love." The evening meal was being served, and the devil had already prompted Judas Iscariot, son of Simon, to betray Jesus. Jesus knew that the Father had put all things under his power, and that he had come from God and was returning to God; so he got up from the meal, took off his outer clothing, and wrapped a towel around his waist. After that, he poured water into a basin and began to wash his disciples' feet, drying them with the towel that was wrapped around him" (John 13:1-5).

224

Consider how much sheep need their kind and devoted Shepherd.

"I am the good shepherd. The good shepherd lays down his life for the sheep" (John 10:11).
"I am the gate; whoever enters through me will be saved. He will come in and go out, and find pasture" (John 10:9).

Only in the care and love of Jesus can you know your great value.
Do you want God or not? That is the question.

"I tell you, now is the time of God's favour, now is the day of salvation" (2 Corinthians 6:2b).

Don't wait. Don't hesitate.
Now,
today - this is the moment of decision.

Let Him save

forgive

love
and bless you.
You will know you are bound for heaven!
You will have discovered one of life's great mysteries Dear Reader -

'what happens to you when you die'?

In Jesus Christ you will have eternal life!
Be there!
Make your decision.

I want to see you there - in heaven one day.

225

A soul lost for eternity...there is no greater loss.

If you do not know where you are going after death then you are lost.

To tell someone they are spiritually lost is a serious thing.
It is peculiar to live your life as you see fit and still be lost.
Doesn't it matter that you are doing your best, had a bad background,
got in with the wrong crowd or that you go to church?

It comes down to your decision for Christ to keep you from being lost.

Being lost while on a trip through a forest
would be a terrible occurrence.
Though you have the strength and determination
to walk around you are so
not in control.

Time actually becomes your enemy.
You move forward but the sense of loss just keeps growing. It is taking longer and longer
just to get where you want to go. You become acquainted with the feeling of hopelessness.
It takes advantage. It tackles you,
sucking you into a craven, heedless partnership.
It is a formidable contender - a thief in your heart and mind,
growing stronger as you venture further along.
This is not 'your' hike because it feels more like survival. This isn't a hike at all.
You feel smaller and smaller in your mind. Without putting it into words you are being consumed
by despair. You are owned by the spirit of fear and loss.
You become concerned about food and water. It might rain and you with no shelter.
Becoming prey to a wild animal chokes your thoughts and night approaches.
Dear reader I hope you will never be lost in a forest.

This example helps you grasp what being lost - truly lost - is like while you are yet in this short life.

"Why, you do not even know what will happen tomorrow. What is your life? You are a mist that
appears for a little while and then vanishes" (James 4:14).

Being lost is an unsavoury predicament.

Dear reader,
you are spiritually lost if you live without heeding the words
of the Good Shepherd.

Please read on.

To be aware of lost people around you
is to share with Jesus Christ His heart for mankind.
God your Father has only one goal. To bring you into fellowship.

"Your word is a lamp to my feet and a light for my path" (Psalm 119:105).

He loves each person the same as He loves His Son Jesus. Life is hard though.
There is selfishness, deceitfulness, abuse, lying, murder, rape, lust, loss, rejection and hopelessness.
People choose to do these things of their own free will.
Is free will a bad thing?

228

No.

Free will gives you the opportunity to choose God.

It is now and forever your personal decision.

It is the most important decision you will ever make bar none.

At the end of life will you be lost or will you be saved by the grace of God?

"by grace are you saved by faith not of yourself. It is the gift of God not of works lest anyone should boast" (Ephesians 2:8-9).

226

Your God is timeless.

He has always existed and will exist without end.

Your precious life is measured in days.
Within each day there are many seconds,
minutes and hours.
In the backdrop of eternity
how might we describe the full span of a human life?

"Why, you do not even know what will happen tomorrow. What is your life? You are a mist that appears for a little while and then vanishes" (James 4:14).

It seems your years are measured as fleeting in their breadth.
Fragile in their fullness.
Uncertain,
because you are as permanent as a puff of smoke
that is here and then gone.

"Rise in the presence of the aged, show respect for the elderly and revere your God. I am the Lord" (Leviticus 19:32).
"Gray hair is a crown of splendour; it is attained by a righteous life" (Proverbs 16:31).

There is a great deal of wisdom in the testimony of the aged.
The older folks have the benefit of hindsight.
They are more in tune with the truly important ingredients of life.

To reach out and touch the divine
at any point of your 'wisp of smoke'
is important above all things.

"Suppose one of you has a hundred sheep and loses one of them. Does he not leave the ninety-nine in the open country and go after the lost sheep until he finds it? And when he finds it, he joyfully puts it on his shoulders and goes home. Then he calls his friends and neighbours together and says, 'Rejoice with me; I have found my lost sheep.' I tell you that in the same way there will be more rejoicing in heaven over one sinner who repents than over ninety-nine righteous persons who do not need to repent" (Luke 15:4-7).

Life on earth is infused with meaning when the author of Life
has reached out and taken hold of you!

227

With such a short time to take in all that life has to offer
can there be one thing important above all else?

The person falling overboard has only so much time.

When a lifeline is cast out why not grab it.
Toward the end of a long life fully lived,
it grows increasingly important to prepare for the experience of death.

Life after death is more important than the wisp of smoke that precedes it.
There is an endless eternity out there.

Dear Reader, Jesus is your lifeline.
Let's put a news headline in here.

HEAVEN IS REAL! YOU WILL GO THERE
IF YOU BELIEVE IN JESUS CHRIST!
COST OF ADMISSION COVERED BY THE RISEN SAVIOUR!

No time spent communing with Jesus is wasted.
All through your life eternity is waiting just over another horizon.

Most people can't know how many days are ahead.

There may be many
there may be few.

"Salvation is found in no one else, for there is no other name under heaven given to men by which we must be saved" (Acts 4:12).

Take hold once again today with your Life-line.

Open up your heart to Jesus
and be forgiven,
washed with His precious blood.

Know right now that you have become safely and successfully prepared
for the endless ages to come.

228

"Thou whom I have 'taken' from the ends of the earth, and called thee from the chief men thereof, and said unto thee, Thou art my servant; I have chosen thee, and not cast thee away. Fear thou not; for I am with thee: be not dismayed; for I am thy God: I will strengthen thee; yea, I will help thee; yea, I will uphold thee with the right hand of my righteousness. Behold, all they that were incensed against thee shall be ashamed and confounded: they shall be as nothing; and they that strive with thee shall perish. Thou shalt seek them, and shalt not find them, even them that contended with thee: they that war against thee shall be as nothing, and as a thing of nought. For I the Lord thy God will hold thy right hand, saying unto thee, Fear not; I will help thee"
(Isaiah 41:9-13 King James Version).

"I 'took' you from the ends of the earth, from its farthest corners I called you. I said, 'Your are my servant'; I have chosen you and have not rejected you. So do not fear, for I am with you; do not be dismayed, for I am your God. I will strengthen you and help you; I will uphold you with my righteous right hand. "All who rage against you will surely be ashamed and disgraced; those who opposed you will be as nothing and perish. Though you search for your enemies, you will not find them. Those who wage war against you will be as nothing at all. For I am the Lord, your God, who takes hold of your right hand and says to you, Do not fear; I will help you"
(Isaiah 41:9-13 New International Version).

We all share a craving for personal intimacy.

A person kind and pure of heart touches your shoulder, your hand - reaches out for a moment
to touch your arm.
There is a deep response within.
Instantaneously it rises up in your soul.
You are overwhelmed and feel blessed.
It surpasses all accomplishments if we discover someone wants us.
To be chosen.
To be wanted.

Don't you long inside for that kind and loving person to reach out to you.
On the phone.
In person.
By email.
A letter.

All of these communicate to your soul that you have value.

Dear Reader, if I am going to talk about the Christian faith.
About becoming a follower of Jesus Christ.
It is about an invitation to begin a very personal journey.
It starts with Jesus, the Lord our God.

"For I am the Lord, your God, who takes hold of your right hand and says to you, Do not fear;
I will help you" (Isaiah 41:13 New International Version).

It isn't about how much good you are able to do,
it is because you have been chosen to share
with the Love of all loves.

Jesus Christ has not called you to be His yard implement.
A lawn mower, a shovel or sprinkler.
The ability you will demonstrate as His follower does not come from your own might,
power or strength. Therefore, you do not go on alone without His fellowship.

Our salvation is in a God we get to know along the way because He first reached out to us.

229

"I <u>took</u> you from the ends of the earth, from its farthest corners I called you. I said, 'You are my servant'; I have chosen you and have not rejected you" (Isaiah 41:9).

Consider the words in the verses from yesterday's devotional [Isa. 41:9-13] with God saying He has 'taken' you from the ends of the earth.

When you catch your first glimpse of the wondrous majesty of our God,
it seems He has had to reach a great distance to find you.

The sinfulness that isolated you from a God of mercy
now washed away with the precious blood of Christ.
There is an unmistakeable cleansing within.
It is a sudden transition from feeling alone or just one among billions
to the brilliant radiance of God's love through Jesus Christ.
To be filled with the knowledge that you are forgiven,
created for a purpose
and one day definitely going to heaven.

You were rightfully destined to be saved and loved with an everlasting love.

It is a discovery to find out you have been far from the love of God.

Your best efforts can't take hold of this revelation of His love and mercy.
But from a great distance He reaches down to touch,
heal,
save,
deliver
and claim you as His own.

When you are 'taken' by God
it is His gift.
It is an experience man is unable to contrive nor duplicate.

"Jesus answered him, 'I tell you the truth, today you will be with me in paradise" (Luke 23:43).

It is entirely supernatural.

"For it is by grace you have been saved, through faith - and this not from yourselves, it is the gift of God - not by works, so that no one can boast" (Eph 2:8-9).
"For the wages of sin is death, but the gift of God is eternal life in Christ Jesus our Lord"
(Romans 6:23).

230

"Now this is eternal life: that they may know you, the only true God, and Jesus Christ, whom you have sent" (John 17:3).
"And this is the testimony: God has given us eternal life, and this life is in his Son. He who has the Son has life; he who does not have the Son of God does not have life. I write these things to you who believe in the name of the Son of God so that you may know that you have eternal life"
(1 John 5:11-13).

The original disciples told people about God in this manner.

The Holy Spirit moves within the human soul.

The Holy Ghost our friend and counsellor, becomes a power within us.
He shares with others the knowledge of our heavenly Father
and the touch of His love from within our heart.

'Taken' by God,
even though it is from a great distance,
is 'to be bound fast',
'to be attached',
'to make firm',
'to support',
'to hold fast'.

When Almighty God saves you it does not matter
that He has had to come a great distance to deliver you from your sin.
It is the beginning of the most intimate fellowship you will have in this life.
God 'takes' you and immediately you are His friend. You are lifted from the greatest depth
of being alone, religious, forsaken, filthy, self-righteous, foolish, dull, rejected, strange, peculiar,
popular, talented, lonely, abandoned, addicted, abusive, abused and lost.
Suddenly you are received by your God who loves you the same as He loves His own Son.

231

It is here in the position of being 'taken' by God that a remarkable change suddenly takes place.

When you believe in Jesus Christ and receive Him as your Saviour
it says you are 'taken' by God.

It is hard to understand because this change
is both supernatural and permanent at the same time.
You are still the same person outwardly
but totally transformed.
For many there is a brightness that shows forth. It continues after death! GLORY TO GOD!

"Do not fret because of evil men or be envious of those who do wrong; for like the grass they will
soon wither, like green plants they will soon die away. Trust in the Lord and do good; dwell in the
land and enjoy safe pasture. Delight yourself in the Lord and he will give you the desires of your
heart. Commit your way to the Lord; trust in him and he will do this: He will make your
righteousness shine like the dawn, the justice of your cause like the noonday sun" (Psalm 37:1-6).

It will exist from now on into the endless ages of eternity future.
It also means you are no longer separated from God.

From God's perspective you are now fully righteous as surely as His only Son Jesus is righteous.

232

"For by one offering he hath perfected <u>for ever</u> them that are sanctified" (Heb 10:14).

There's that word,
'for - ever'.

Your spiritual transformation is complete
and profoundly consequential.
For the rest of your life you will be treasured by your heavenly Father
the same as He loves His dear Son Jesus.
It will mean the end of your crippling low self esteem.

234

Why?

Difficulties and trials no longer determine your success.

The Holy Ghost faithfully points out that Jesus Christ will forever
be the measure of WHO YOU ARE.

"God made him who had no sin to be sin for us, so that in him we might become the righteousness
of God" (2 Corinthians 5:21).

Your gaze will be faithfully guided to the Person of Jesus as your likeness,
explanation of your being and absolute justification!
If you feel condemnation on some level you will have none of it!

Ever!

"Therefore, there is now no condemnation for those who are in Christ Jesus" (Romans 8:1).
"Being justified freely by his grace through the redemption that is in Christ Jesus" (Rom 3:24).
"Herein is our love made perfect, that we may have boldness in the day of judgment: because
as he is, so are we in this world" (1 John 4:17).

Dear reader, if there is a key understanding for you,
it is that you should not be put down in your own mind.
When thoughts come that condemn you it is time to believe once again what Jesus said.
You are righteous as Christ is righteous.
There is no basis within you to be judged with regard to your right standing in God.

The following verse explains that God has given you the wisdom, righteousness,
holiness and redemption of His Son.

"It is because of him (God the Father) that you are in Christ Jesus, who has become for us wisdom
from God - that is, our righteousness, holiness and redemption" (1 Corinthians 1:30).

While you spend time with Jesus everyday and live in obedience to Him
you are living in His blessed shadow.

"He who dwells in the shelter of the Most High will rest in the shadow of the Almighty"
(Psalm 91:1).
"But now the righteousness of God <u>without the law</u> is manifested, being witnessed by the law and
the prophets; Even <u>the righteousness of God which is by faith of Jesus Christ</u> unto all and upon all
them that believe; for there is no difference: For all have sinned, and come short of the glory of
God; <u>Being justified freely by his grace through the redemption that is in Christ Jesus:</u>"
(Romans 3:21).

When God takes you to be His own the Holy Spirit is sent to live inside you.

You are the residence of the Person of the Holy Spirit.

"Don't you know that you yourselves are God's temple and that God's Spirit lives in you? <u>If anyone destroys God's temple, God will destroy him; for God's temple is sacred, and you are that temple"</u> (1 Corinthians 3:16-17).

God's protective love . . . endears my heart to Him.
Yes, He cares about the unsaved and wants the whole world to be saved
but He also cherishes me.
He will not let me be unnecessarily mistreated.
He has the power and He will deal with anybody
who messes with me in a manner that displeases Him.
Protection is part of the package when you surrender
your obedience to the Most High God.

"Do you not know that your body is a temple of the Holy Spirit, who is in you, whom you have received from God? You are not your own; you were bought with a price. Therefore honour God with your body" (1 Corinthians 6:19-22).
"Not by works of righteousness which we have done, but according to his mercy he saved us, by the washing of regeneration, and by renewing of the Holy Ghost" (Titus 3:5).

The Spirit that lives in you is the same Spirit that raised Jesus from the dead!
You have access to Someone who was a witness when they crucified the Lord of Glory.
The Holy Spirit was there with Jesus and raised Him from the dead within three days.
He now lives in you.

Imagine the power to bring the dead back to life!

The Holy Spirit conquered death!

"And if the Spirit of him who raised Jesus from the dead is living in you, he who raised Christ from the dead will also give life to your mortal bodies through his Spirit, who lives in you" (Romans 8:11).

Why not talk to Him?
Take some time to listen and see what He wants to talk about with you.

It is amazing, but the Holy Spirit is your friend.

This is quite an important Person to be in love with you.

The glow that can be seen upon your face at times shines from deep within you.

This is your 'countenance'.

As the temple of the Holy Spirit you radiate His presence.
Would it amaze you to know that the same Spirit that raised Jesus from the dead
also lives right there inside of you?

"And if the Spirit of him who raised Jesus from the dead is living in you, he who raised Christ from the dead will also give life to your mortal bodies through his Spirit, who lives in you"
(Romans 8:11).
"And you also were included in Christ when you heard the word of truth, the gospel of your salvation. Having believed, you were marked in him with a seal, the promised Holy Spirit, who is a deposit guaranteeing our inheritance until the redemption of those who are God's possession - to the praise of his glory" (Ephesians 1:13-14).

God completely loves you and He immediately takes up residence in you.
His Holy Spirit enters you.
He begins the process of shaping you because you are like clay in the hands of a Master potter.
All throughout eternity-past God the Father was in love with you.
When you accept Jesus Christ by faith
your heavenly Father finally gets to dwell within you
by His Holy Spirit.

You are invincible with the Holy Spirit of God living right inside of you.

"O house of Israel, can I not do with you as this potter does?' declares the Lord. 'Like clay in the hand of the potter, so are you in my hand, O house of Israel" (Jeremiah 18:6).

Do you feel confident that God will bring His will to pass in your life?
If you are confident in the Lord you will be fine.
If you derive your confidence by might or by power
in time these sources will definitely fail you.
Your walk with God is by the Holy Spirit after all.
Along the way He will shape your life to prevent you from establishing your confidence
outside of His everlasting love for you.

He will open and close doors
of experience and opportunity
and shape you as clay.

This is a great thing for you because He does all things well.

Jesus commanded them not to tell anyone. But the more he did so, the more they kept talking about it. People were overwhelmed with amazement. 'He has done everything well,' they said. 'He even makes the deaf hear and the mute speak' (Mark 7:36).

235

The Holy Spirit is God.

He is a member of the Trinity.

God is three persons at the same time.
He is God the Father, God the Son and God the Holy Spirit.

When the Holy Spirit begins to live within you it is a wondrous occasion.
You have an opportunity to begin your friendship with God.

"Then he said to them all: 'If anyone would come after me, he must deny himself and take up his cross daily and follow me. For whoever wants to save his life will lose it, but whoever loses his life for me will save it" (Luke 9:23-24).

Jesus said you must deny yourself.
This is the first step.
It is a surrender only God can see.

You sincerely give over every part of your life to Him.
You freely put Him in the place of ownership of all you are,
all you own and all you will become.
This is a conscious decision and a process at the same time.
Jesus said after denying yourself completely
you are in a position to take up your own cross.
After this
you are able to respond to His instruction and wisdom for your life.

The Holy Spirit is able to perfectly guide an unselfish soul.
The dear soul at rest has surrendered their life completely to God.
They have denied themselves saying, 'here am I Lord, use me.'

Wherever, however and with whomever You have planned.

"For we are God's workmanship, created in Christ Jesus to do good works, which God prepared in advance for us to do" (Ephesians 2:10).

236

Jesus Christ must have all of you or He has none of you.

His surrender becomes your example of spirituality and Godliness.

Jesus obedience to His Father was love.
It was His loving surrender that pleased His Father
not how much Jesus did or where He did it.

Jesus had to set aside His own interests and concerns.
Each day was all about being in His Father's perfect will.

Jesus is your example of obedience.
Your life is the Spirit of God within.
Let Him have His way.

He lives within you because you are fully acceptable to God
no matter what you have done up to that point in time.
This is your forgiveness.
Forgiveness is a gift given to you by Jesus Christ the Lord.

He is a loving and forgiving and merciful God.

"We love because he first loved us" (1 John 4:19).
"You see, at just the right time, when we were still powerless, Christ died for the ungodly. For if, when we were God's enemies we were reconciled to him through the death of his Son, how much more, having been reconciled, shall we be saved through his life! Not only is this so, but we also rejoice in God through our Lord Jesus Christ, through whom we have now received reconciliation" (Romans 5:6,10,11).

Immediately you are invited to be in a family relationship.
You are fully redeemed by God through His Son.
When you act upon this truth your relationship with God will blossom.

Do you want this relationship to blossom?

Take a step toward God today by spending some time with Him.

"Come near to God and he will come near to you" (James 4:8a).

237

Now that you belong to Him He will always be there to share His deep love with you.

A good picture of this kind Shepherd Jesus is given in Rev 3:20.

"Here I am! I stand at the door and knock. If anyone hears my voice and opens the door, I will come in and eat with him, and he with me."

Do you see how love works?
He is ready to share everything with you
but insists upon your free will in the matter.

Do you want His love?

Then open the door of your heart.
Settle down and be still before the Lord.
Invite Him to spend time together with you.

That is love for God.
Doing things together.
Being agreed.
Always having Someone who wants to spend time with you.

The amazing thing is that He is always there whenever you chose to spend time with Him.

That is how important you are to your faithful God.

"I have come that they may have life, and have it to the full" (John 10:10b).

238

It is a natural thing to want to do something for God.

As long as we have vast freedoms
to express our desire for God
we tend to exploit it.

Wanting to do something for God is not the same
as walking in a love relationship with God.
It is natural to think if we can do something for God
it must be what He wants us to do.
This is our natural thinking though.
The plan of God begins and ends with relationship.

It only starts
with our complete surrender.
Having first denied ourselves.

Else, how could the paralyzed in body be members of His kingdom?
How could the elderly and infirm,
the deaf mute and the imprisoned be considered fruitful?
Each is physically restricted.
There is something that limits the expression of their physical ability.

Man thinks, 'act'. God lavishes love.

Man thinks, 'ability'. God bestows acceptability.

239

"Come to me, all you who are weary and burdened, and I will give you rest" (Matthew 11:28).
"Whosoever will may come" Jesus said in Revelations 22:17.

That is all I require of you He says to those who will listen.

It is My whole will.

All of My desire is fulfilled
if you will just come unto Me
that I may love you.

Just come to Me that we may share together.

Just come to Me. Oh yes 'whosoever' includes the quadriplegic, the blind, the deaf, the mute,
the hospitalized, the elderly and decrepit and the little children, babies and those within the womb,
those in prison and psychiatric institutions. The tortured, misunderstood, raped, abused
and all that are inwardly maimed.
Jesus asks for all people to just come to Him.
He looks upon the heart.
Man looks upon the outward appearance.
God is looking at the heart, inviting those who are deeply, deeply in sin

to come to Him.

"Come now, let us reason together," says the Lord. "Though your sins are like scarlet, they shall be
as white as snow; though they are red as crimson, they shall be like wool (Isaiah 1:18).

Trust in Him.

Jesus really does care about you. His gift is equally for you
as much as it is for the outwardly whole and privileged. Is He not the potter?
The Shepherd who does all things well?

This helps us understand the mystery of God's love.

"It was just before the Passover Feast. Jesus knew that the time had come for him to leave this world
and go to the Father. Having loved his own who were in the world, he now showed them the full
extent of his love. Verse 4. so he got up from the meal, took off his outer clothing, and wrapped a
towel around his waist. After that, he poured water into a basin and began to wash his disciples'
feet, drying them with the towel that was wrapped around him" (John 13:1,4,5).

God had so much love to give.
Each of the disciples had ministered in extraordinary ways.
Miracles and casting out of demons. People believed their message
and sins were completely forgiven. People instantly set free and saved. But being face to face
with Jesus Christ was a different thing
altogether.

Allowing God to touch them personally in mundane aspects of life
meant Jesus could be involved where He was needed.
They would have to let Jesus see their weakness
and trust Him with it.

In this example, with the mundane job of washing their dirty feet.

This was not a way to prove their love for Him through their own strength and ability.
It required them to humble themselves,
to face their weakness,
acknowledge it and submit to Jesus for His help.
Much easier to offer God something big and special.
But it was in their human need that they permitted Jesus to share the full extent of His love.

'The full extent of His love,' reveals itself as the greater part.
The important part.
The whole picture of relationship is manifest when Jesus is allowed
to take care of the unseemly, uncomfortable and base aspects of our life.
These parts are shared by all people
but only the humble are willing to face this
and accept it about themselves.

It isn't about being sent
for not all are able to perform physical service for God.
It is about being vulnerable
when you are alone with the Lord.

Allowing Him the time and place
to become involved in the difficulties, hardships
and necessities of life.

"But he said to me, 'My grace is sufficient for you, for my power is made perfect in weakness.'
Therefore I will boast all the more gladly about my weaknesses, so that Christ's power may rest on
me. That is why, for Christ's sake, I delight in weaknesses, in insults, in hardships in persecutions,
in difficulties. For when I am weak, then I am strong" (2 Corinthians 12:9-10).

Finding out that Jesus became your Saviour to share the trials of being human is a liberating truth.

Dear Reader,
invite Him into that place of sorrow hiding within.
Let him become involved in the tangles and misunderstandings.
It is there He reveals the full extent of His love.

He becomes the way through each mess
for He is the Way.
When you seek Him first
He will withhold no good thing from you.
What a great deliverer He is.

Redeemer.

Faithful friend.

"The one who calls you is faithful and he will do it" (1 Thessalonians 5:24).

240

"Even if I should choose to boast, I would not be a fool, because I would be speaking the truth. But
I refrain, so no one will think more of me than is warranted by what I do or say"
(2 Corinthians 12:6).
'He who listens to you listens to me; he who rejects you rejects me; but he who rejects me rejects
him who sent me.' The seventy-two returned with joy and said, 'Lord, even the demons submit to
us in your name.' He replied, 'I saw Satan fall like lightning from heaven. I have given you authority
to trample on snakes and scorpions and to overcome all the power of the enemy; nothing will harm
you. However, do not rejoice that the spirits submit to you, but rejoice that your names are written
in heaven (Luke 10:16-20).

Jesus was saying,
'get excited about being My friend. Consider the opportunity to get to know Me
throughout your lifetime to be your cause of rejoicing. In everything, in good times and difficult,
rejoice. Your knowledge of Me and our friendship will continually grow.'

"I no longer call you servants, because a servant does not know his master's business. Instead, I have called you friends, for everything that I learned from my Father I have made known to you" (John 15:15).

Knowing what God wants from you is the entitlement of every person who has become a believer.

Knowing your Father's business. It is your birth-right once you are saved.
It is not an entitlement
to those with exceptional spiritual capacities.

Dear Reader, can you see that the whole purpose
of the Holy Spirit within you
is to steadily acquaint you with God?

This bodes well, very well,
for those with limits on their freedom
or ability to do outwardly great things for God.
They may be too old, feeble, poor, the wrong gender in their part of the world
or even too young.

Making known the love God has for you.
That is the ministry of the Holy Spirit within you.

It is more important even than understanding
and moving in the love God has for others!

"Praise be to the God and Father of our Lord Jesus Christ, the Father of compassion and the God of all comfort, who comforts us in all our troubles, so that we can comfort those in any trouble with the comfort we ourselves have received from God" (2 Corinthians 1:3-4).

If you are doing things for God without a relationship with Him
you are sadly missing out on your purpose in this life.
Jesus will not say you are welcome into heaven
based upon how much you did
or how big you did it.
He is only able to conclude that you had a relationship with Him or not.

In a gathering of Christians if the question were asked
'who is the most spiritual person here?'
the answer would be easy.
'Jesus.'
The answer would always be the same
'Jesus.'
Jesus the foot washer.

The people - one and all - that gather together in God's name are the sheep in His care.

Be careful Dear Reader.

Do not boast in how God uses you.
It will bring great hindrance to God's kingdom when those listening
'think more of you than is warranted by what you do or say.'
They will belittle themselves in their own thinking.
They will conclude there is a difference in how God leads you
and you live on some higher spiritual level.
That is why the disciple wrote
that he delighted in weaknesses, in insults, in hardships
in persecutions, in difficulties.
Yes Dear Reader, that is why.

It is wrong to continually regale people
with information about what God is saying to you
or has been saying to you, how God is or has used you
and point out the souls you have led to Jesus.
You see, the man who wrote the previous bible verse had an intimate relationship with Jesus.

He knew the Lord. He didn't just know 'about' the Lord.
In the Light of this relationship the disciple understood
that a reputation on earth is worthless.
He was in love with Jesus and took great pains
to prevent his listeners from thinking too highly of him
because of his Christian service.
After He preached he desired for His listeners to be more in love with Jesus too.
He was offended if they overflowing with praise and said 'what a great man of God.'

He actually took steps to help them conclude 'what a great God we serve.'

"In Lystra there sat a man crippled in his feet, who was lame from birth and had never walked. He listened to Paul as he was speaking. Paul looked directly at him, saw that he had faith to be healed and called out, "Stand up on your feet!" At that, the man jumped up and began to walk. When the crowd saw what Paul had done, they shouted in the Lycaonian language, "The gods have come down to us in human form!" Barnabas they called Zeus, and Paul they called Hermes because he was the chief speaker. But when the apostles Barnabas and Paul heard of this, they tore their clothes and rushed out into the crowd, shouting: "Men, why are you doing this? We too are only men, human like you. We are bringing you good news, telling you to turn from these worthless things to the living God, who made heaven and earth and sea and everything in them. Even with these words, they had difficulty keeping the crowd from sacrificing to them"
(Acts 14:8-12,14,15,18).

When you think of it, we are going to be serving God in our earthen body for, oh, a vapour.

Our entire lifespan is measured as a wisp of smoke.

Like the time it takes to appear,
curl upward

and vanish.

Jesus Christ in His wisdom
counselled His disciples
to focus
on getting to know Him.
He wanted them to rejoice in seeking Him above all things.

That is why He said getting to know Him was 'the one thing that is needed'
while teaching Mary and Martha.

The time to harvest is now.

This is because your lifespan is so short a time to be involved in the harvest.

242

Each of God's followers is special to Him above all things.

When you get to know your Father above all things then you will understand
the love behind events unfolding in your life.

You will perceive by faith His purpose unfolding all around you.
You will know of His love in the many episodes of distress and despair
that crop up along the way.

There are times when we do not understand why things happen to us.
He knew we would feel this way.
He knows us so well.

Matthew 6:33 "But seek first his kingdom and his righteousness, and all these things will be given
to you as well."

Those who understand His intense desire for intimacy seek Him
ahead of anything else.

He will gladly add all other things.

"Delight yourself in the Lord and he will give you the desires of your heart" (Psalm 37:4).

243

Our access to God is not measured by how much we do.

"The Spirit and the bride say, 'Come!' And let him who hears say, 'Come!' Whoever is thirsty, let him come; and whoever wishes, let him take the free gift of the water of life" (Revelation 22:17).

'Whoever is thirsty, whoever wishes let him take the free gift' Jesus said

God had mercy upon mankind.
He knew we would feel compelled to somehow prove how much we love Him.
When He abolished the law
as the measure of our righteousness
people could freely approach Him because of His mercy.

"Blessed are those who hunger and thirst for righteousness, for they will be filled" (Matthew 5:6).
"All that the Father gives to me will come to me, and whoever comes to me I will never drive away" (John 6:37b).

Jesus is looking for people to come to him.

Not to impress Him.

Those who hunger and thirst for righteousness will be filled.
Many people can't do great things for God,
but everyone can be hungry and thirsty!
Even little babies are hungry and thirsty!
God fills you.
All you need to do is hunger and thirst.
You get the picture. Anyone as able to be filled to overflowing with the Spirit!

"for God gives the Spirit without limit" (John 3:34b).

We cannot help but feel the more we do
the more we love Him
and the more He loves us
in return.
More and more.
Bigger and better.
Large, vast and more superior.

But Jesus
is the Way the Truth and the Life.
There is no longer a need to show love for God
through strength,
ability,
connections,
family name or denominational attachment.

Some take pride in how long they have ministered as if this measures something.
God is not interested.

His heart is with Mary the sister of Martha.
He shares His heart with her because she has come near to listen.
Jesus said, "no one comes to the Father except through Me."
Through Jesus we are supposed to be coming to the Father.
Our Salvation is thoroughly a relationship-centered phenomenon.

You are devoted to Jesus Christ?
Have you spent time with Him today?
There is no ladder or ascension upward to godliness.

There is only a meek and gentle Saviour.
With the invitation to become a follower once you are saved.
This is because He has become your righteousness.

If you allow Jesus to serve you
as He did for the disciples when they let Him wash their feet
you will receive the full extent of His love.

A love that can't be earned.
Praise God!

His love is for everyone.

244

"Then Jesus said to his disciples, 'If anyone would come after me, he must deny himself and take up his cross and follow me" (Matthew 16:24).

In great mercy God accepts us unconditionally.
We respond with the offering of our life, our service our strength and our abilities.

'Take all that I am and use me', from our heart we sincerely cry.
Then in mercy we are invited to explore the vast riches we now possess.

It is a process
and the Holy Spirit is our faithful guide.
He helps us grasp the value of the many facets of God's work here on earth.

We thrill with Him in the supreme importance of evangelism.
Marvel and agree with the wonder of deliverance from demons.
He brings to us His joy in giving finances to the work of God
as a means of storing up our riches in heaven.
He is leading all the while to the greatest wonder of all things spiritual.

The person of Jesus Christ.

"Let everything that has breath praise the Lord. Praise the Lord" (Psalm 150:6).

In all that pertains to the kingdom of God
you will be led to an understanding
that Jesus Christ is the One who is above all things.

To love His harvest field
is to fail to love Him.
To love prophetic ministry
is to take one's eyes off of the Altogether Lovely One.

You will need Him when life is over.
You will not need your ministry.
Your ministry will be gone for all eternity.
You will not be saving souls in heaven.
You will however, be able to fix your eyes upon Jesus.

He would love for you to do that now and each day.

That is the heart of His perfect will for your life.
He doesn't want you to wait until you get to heaven to become acquainted with Him.
If Jesus doesn't know you when you stand before Him
it won't matter how much you have done in His name.

You will know about Him but you won't know Him
and He will tell you so

in front of everyone.

Open up the door today.
Jesus is knocking on the door of your heart. Invite the Lord of Glory in.

Be surprised at how precious your time with Him shall grow.

"I can do everything through him who gives me strength" (Philippians 4:13).

You have a standing of righteousness.

You are freely given a gift of forgiveness and salvation the moment you believe in Jesus Christ.
Afterward your loving Master awaits the invitation from you
to share His heart and become friends.

The privilege of fellowship is wonderfully seen through an example in the Old Testament.
High Priests were bestowed with the great honour of having a personal encounter with God.
They would enter into a room called the Holy of Holies where God would meet with them.
If they did not go in there would be no meeting.

"But you are a chosen people, a royal priesthood, a holy nation, a people belonging to God, that
you may declare the praises of him who called you out of darkness into his wonderful light"
(1 Peter 2:9).

Choosing to spend time with Jesus is a most precious opportunity.
All who are saved by grace through faith in the Lord Jesus Christ
are now His High Priests.
They are able to enter into fellowship directly with God Himself.
God leaves the choice with you
to meet together with Him.

God speaks to His children everywhere.
Anywhere and at any time the good Lord of glory can speak to the heart of His servant.
What of those who seek for more of God?
How can the hunger and thirst be satisfied?

"Blessed are those who hunger and thirst after righteousness, for they will be filled" (Matthew 5:6).

Dear reader, this hunger is for more of God.
He has invited you to get to know Him.

You can do this face to face.

"I can do everything through him who gives me strength" (Philippians 4:13).

It is the one who comes afresh from the presence of the Lord
who is more than a conqueror.

"No, in all things we are more than conquerors through him who loved us" (Romans 8:37).

You are one of those 'taken' by a mighty God.
Called by Him to do His exploits in this earth.

The lover of God is found daily in the quiet place of fellowship.
The helpless finding purpose,
the neglected lifted high
on wings like an eagle.

The rejected alone no more and suddenly,
seated in heavenly places in Christ Jesus.

"And God raised us up with Christ and seated us with him in heavenly realms in Christ Jesus,"
(Ephesians 2:6).
"He gives strength to the weary and increases the power of the weak. Even youths grow tired and
weary, and young men stumble and fall; but those who hope in the Lord will renew their strength.
They will soar on wings like eagles; they will run and not grow weary, they will walk and not be
faint" (Isaiah 40:29-31).

If you are waiting upon the bus, do you run helter-skelter?
Or if you are waiting upon a Dr. for your appointment
do you wander about the building
or go do some shopping?

Dear reader, if you are waiting upon the Lord
there is but one thing to do.
Be still.
Go near to listen.

Quietly present yourself
and wait where unconditional love
enfolds you every time.
If there is something from God you seek
freely let Him know.

"Do not be anxious about anything, but in everything, by prayer and petition with thanksgiving,
present your requests to God" (Philippians 4:6).

It will be the Holy Spirit's joy to respond to your petitions and bring immediate response.

"Then he continued, 'Do not be afraid, Daniel. Since the first day that you set your mind to gain
understanding and to humble yourself before your God, your words were heard, and I have come
in response to them" (Daniel 10:12).

247

This fellowship, this joining of hearts, becomes the life of the surrendered servant of God.

There is nothing quite so important in a day as the time spent listening
and hearing
while in the superlative care of the wondrous Holy Spirit.

The sense God gives of being in His timing
brings no greater sweetness.

So significant,
so sublime
is the fulfillment acquired in His presence
that it takes its rightful place as the very riches upon which life is based.

"Because your love is better than life, my lips will glorify you" (Psalm 63:3).

Being with God and knowing what is upon His mind
even through storms and affliction
is a personal treat
in all circumstances.

It is in the trial that His love is so captivating.
It is in the midst of loss
that the value of His grace easily overshadows any obstacle.
It is while suffering under unbearable heartache
that His ability to identify with You
endears you to Him a little deeper.

He cannot fail His own.
You see,
'to live is Christ.'
When your hopes are dashed through friend or foe
and your loving Jesus easily shelters you yet another day in spite of it all,
it can be said 'thy loving-kindness is better than life."

"For to me, to live is Christ and to die is gain" (Philippians 1:21)

248

Is this really true, 'to live is Christ'? What of an adulterous affair?

Can it possibly satisfy for an entire lifetime?

There is nothing one could trade for an everlasting love!
A bar of gold?
Enough money to retire on?
No treasure can be exchanged for serving Jesus and the salvation of your soul.

"Then he said to them, 'Watch out! Be on your guard against all kinds of greed; a man's life does not consist in the abundance of his possessions.' And he told them this parable: 'The ground of a certain rich man produced a good crop. He thought to himself, 'What shall I do? I have to store my crops.' 'Then he said, 'This is what I'll do. I will tear down my barns and build bigger ones, and there I will store all my grain and my goods. And I'll say to myself, 'You have plenty of good things laid up for many years. Take life easy; eat, drink and be merry.' **'But God said to him, 'You fool!** This very night your life will be demanded from you. Then who will get what you have prepared for yourself?"' (Luke 12:15-20).

You will draw your next breath on God's terms.
God is not messing around with this topic nor shall I.
We just read that this God of love called someone a fool.

Dear Reader,
though you may not know your incredible worth in God's eyes
do not give up your life in exchange for sin.

There is no safer place to dwell than in the shadow of the Almighty.

"He who dwells in the shelter of the Most High will rest in the shadow of the Almighty"
(Psalm 91:1).

Give God your heart
your soul
and all of your tomorrows.

"O Lord, you have searched me and you know me. You know when I sit and when I rise; you perceive my thoughts from afar. You discern my going out and my lying down; you are familiar with all my ways. Before a word is on my tongue you know it completely, O Lord" (Psalm 139:1-4).

You do not know the day your soul shall be required of you.
Death is inescapable and you cannot control
when you shall leave our flesh behind.

However, you *can* know your destiny before you die.
You can know that there is love
and the fullness of joy awaiting you!
You need come to Jesus now
in the present
while you are still able to exercise your own free will.

There is no finer life to live than allowing all desire
to be poured out in singular longing.
To fulfil the deep passion - I must know the Lord,

I must please the Lord
above any other thing.

I must above all things obey one Master, the Lord of glory.

249

"because those who are led by the Spirit of God are the sons of God" (Romans 8:14).
"Be still, and know that I am God; I will be exalted among the nations, I will be exalted in the earth" (Psalm 46:10).

First be still.

Then, He will lift you up.
God's Holy Spirit
and God's word - the bible -
will never fail you.

"Humble yourselves before the Lord, and he will lift you up" (James 4:10).

250

"Therefore, if anyone is in Christ, he is a new creation; the old has gone, the new has come!" (2 Corinthians 5:17).

Your life begins anew when you believe in Jesus Christ.

Wouldn't you like a clean start?
With the washing of Christ's blood your sins are forever forgiven.
At the same time you are inwardly transformed.
The bible calls it, 'born again.'
'The old has gone, the new has come.'

You feel like a new person because you actually are!
A new start. A new future.

"For I know the plans I have for you," declares the Lord, "plans to prosper you and not to harm you, plans to give you hope and a future" (Jeremiah 29:11).

You have a wondrous journey ahead. You are now in the care of the good Shepherd.

"I am the good shepherd; I know my sheep and my sheep know me - just as the Father knows me and I know the Father - and I lay down my life for the sheep" (John 10:14-15).
"I give them eternal life, and they shall never perish; no one can snatch them out of my hand" (John 10:28).

Okay,
we know that the journey will end in eternal life.
In the mean time Jesus says He is the good Shepherd.
'I know my sheep and my sheep know me.'

The sheep belonging to Jesus actually know Him.

Jesus didn't say, 'I know my sheep . . . and my sheep are always busy.'
'Do great things for Me.'
'Do the best they can.'
'Do what they are told by their leadership.'
'Believe lots of doctrine with all their hearts.'
'Belong to the right church.'
'Are the only ones going to heaven because only one church figured it out.'

In this journey - this new journey bringing you to heaven -
your goal, your mission
is to know the Shepherd.

"I am the good shepherd; I know my sheep and my sheep know me -" (John 10:14).

251

Christianity is as like a garden of beautiful flowers.

A faith expressed in diverse denominations and practices.

God's work is coordinated by the Holy Spirit who teaches us how to love one another.
His work also brings encouragement one to another.
As each individual is getting to know their Shepherd
He directs them in a plan He has prepared just for them.
You will grow in the grace of God.
It is for this reason that no matter which church you attend
your primary place of being rooted and grounded
is with Jesus Christ and the Holy Bible.

Wherever you attend church there should be only one glorious result.
You are growing
in your love

and knowledge
of Jesus Christ your Shepherd.

If, after all of your years of devotion, obedience
and financial contribution to your church
you take a moment and have to admit

'I don't know God,'

then there is good news for you!
This is an important time for you!
Start your journey right now!
Jesus only asked for one thing of His sheep.

That they know Him.

252

To know Jesus means you are in love with Jesus.
When you know someone you have been with them enough to become familiar with them.
If you have not spent time with someone, you have to admit you don't know them.
If you don't know them you can't be in love with them.

If you say you love someone it means you spend time with them.
You know what I mean.

Intimate time with Jesus means you are listening for His word,
you have your bible on hand,
and a journal to record the loving things He makes real to your heart.

When you are listening you are obeying.
People who are listening to God are being used to do His will.

Nothing can take the place of time spent alone with your Saviour.

253

"Because your love is better than life, my lips will glorify you" (Psalm 63:3).

Your heavenly Father is always making provision for you.
He is doing what needs to be done to take good care of you.
If He could not completely take care of you then you could be snatched out of His hand.
"I give them eternal life, and they shall never perish; no one can snatch them out of my hand"
(John 10:28).

Even in hardship He is actively weaving together the decorative strands of your life.

"I lift up my eyes to the hills - where does my help come from? My help comes from the Lord, the Maker of heaven and earth. He will not let your foot slip - he who watches over you will not slumber; indeed, he who watches over Israel will neither slumber nor sleep. The Lord watches over you - the Lord is your shade at your right hand; the sun will not harm you by day, nor the moon by night. The Lord will keep you from all harm - he will watch over your life; the Lord will watch over your coming and going both now and forevermore" (Ps. 121).

God never sleeps.
Why is that?

Isn't it interesting that the bible shows the link between sleep and God's careful oversight for each person belonging to Him?

God will not allow you to be overcome by the evil one because He never sleeps!
He is committed to your spiritual success!
He will ever be the reason for your spiritual success!

He has planned to bring you through your journey to the praise of His glory and grace.

Here is our news headline for today.

YOU WILL SUCCEED! JESUS IS THE REASON!
TRUST HIM TO GUIDE YOU - KEEP YOU - SAVE YOU!
Everything He has belongs to those who know Him!

"Praise be to the God and Father of our Lord Jesus Christ, who has blessed us in the heavenly realms with every spiritual blessing in Christ. For he chose us in him before the creation of the world to be holy and blameless in his sight. In love he predestined us to be adopted as his sons through Jesus Christ, in accordance with his pleasure and will - to the praise of his glorious grace, which he has feely given us in the One he loves. In him we have redemption through his blood, the forgiveness of sins, in accordance with the riches of God's grace that he lavished on us with all wisdom and understanding. And he made known to us the mystery of his will according to his good pleasure, which he purposed in Christ, to be put into effect when the times will have reached their fulfillment - to bring all things in heaven and on earth together under one head, even Christ" (Eph. 1:3-10).

Belonging to God the Father through Jesus Christ
with the Person of the Holy Spirit living within you
makes you an overcomer.

"To him who is able to keep you from falling and to present you before his glorious presence without fault and with great joy -" (Jude 1:24).

At the same time as you are on the road to success in God's eyes
things may not go your way.

You may be in a difficult situation.

Are you trusting God to answer a prayer
and waiting on Him to do so
in His own timing and in His own way?
Intense feelings and thoughts are part of waiting upon the Lord.
It is not easy.

It may seem you have been excluded from God's amazing blessings!
You may see your brothers and sisters in Christ
being blessed while you go without
the very thing you need.

It seems this way
when hoping to meet God's choice for a spouse.
Keeping yourself for the right person
can become impossible to bear.
There is a deep pathos in this process.

It is so much a part of us to love and to be loved in return.

At the same time through Jesus Christ you are able and more than a conqueror
when you continue to stay close to Him day by day.

It is the ministry of the Holy Ghost inside of you that continually enables you
to keep your intimate fellowship with God.

God brings these hardships into the lives of people who deeply love Him.

"But he said to me, 'My grace is sufficient for you, for my power is made perfect in weakness.' Therefore I will boast all the more gladly about my weaknesses, so that Christ's power may rest on me. That is why, for Christ's sake, I delight in weaknesses, in insults, in hardships, in persecutions, in difficulties. For when I am weak, then I am strong" (2 Cor. 12:9-10).

Learning of His ways is to discover He is in love with you when things go well and when they don't.

None of us really understands how to serve God before being saved. That did not stop our heavenly Father from sending His Son to die.

God loved us
when we were deeply flawed
and sinful
and out of relationship with Him.

"For God so loved the world that he gave his one and only Son, that whoever believes in him shall not perish but have eternal life" (John 3:16).
"But God demonstrates his own love for us in this: While we were still sinners, Christ died for us" (Rom. 5:8).

Dear Reader it was His love reaching out to you while you 'were still a sinner'.
You weren't doing anything to earn His love.
That is the point.
You don't have to earn His love.

2 Cor. 4:4 "The god of this age has blinded the minds of unbelievers, so that they cannot see the light of the gospel that displays the glory of Christ, who is the image of God."

The devil is the god of this age.
Yet his power to blind you was NOTHING compared to the power of God's love to save you.
What happens to darkness when you introduce light? There you go!
Jesus Christ has become the God of your salvation.
Now that He has saved you He also has all power to keep you safe!

"For I am convinced that neither death nor life, neither angels nor demons, neither the present nor the future, nor any powers, neither height nor depth, nor anything else in all creation, will be able to separate us from the love of God that is in Christ Jesus our Lord" (Romans 8:38-39).

When your life is ended you will be in heaven for all eternity.
Jesus Christ is Almighty God.

Jesus Christ has become the God of your salvation.

"Surely God is my salvation; I will trust and not be afraid. The Lord, the Lord himself, is my strength and my defence; he has become my salvation" (Isa. 12:2).

256

In times of great distress His love continues to flow unto you.

His invitation to be alone with Him is just as fervent as ever.

He doesn't show His displeasure by sending bad things your way.
Some people say, 'if things are not going right in your life what's wrong with you?'

But God is truly amazing.
His love is wonderful.

It is not a sign of His displeasure if things do not go the way we want them to.
When things don't go the way we think they should.
If things don't go the same as they do for everyone else.

You are always special to God no matter what is happening around you.

Remember when Jesus prayed and said, 'your heavenly Father has always loved you!'

257

In His presence the troubles of mind and body are ministered to by the precious Holy Ghost
until once again we are aware that we remain in His care and all is well.

"He causes his sun to rise on the evil and the good, and sends rain on the righteous and the
unrighteous" (Matthew. 5:45b).

Opportunity and outward blessings of health and wealth are abundant to all people.

"But as for me, my feet had almost slipped; I had nearly lost my foothold. For I envied the arrogant
when I saw the prosperity of the wicked. They have no struggles; their bodies are healthy and
strong. They are free from common human burdens; they are not plagued by human ills"
(Psalm 73:2).

Through the help of the Holy Spirit even the weakest follower of Jesus
is victoriously brought through struggle.
In God's presence the distress and heartache gives way
to praise and the sweetness of the love of God.

This transition is not humanly possible. Oh, but you are now in the care of Jesus . . .
There are times when you are not able to cope because for you simply lack the strength.
In Christ there is no skill you need to apply. His grace will be sufficient.
He will bring you through.

"But he said to me, 'My grace is sufficient for you, for my power is made perfect in weakness.' Therefore I will boast all the more gladly about my weaknesses, so that Christ's power may rest on me" (2 Corinthians 12:9).

"For it is by grace you have been saved, through faith - and this is not from yourselves, it is the gift of God - not by works, so that no one can boast. For we are God's handiwork, created in Christ Jesus to do good works, which God prepared in advance for us to do" (Eph. 2:8,9).

No matter how long you walk with God
you will not be able to pursue a journey with Him
unless you receive His personal touch.
He will touch you every day if you will give Him the opportunity.
You will need to experience His nearness and covering
just as you did from the moment
you first believed.

All of His followers need to be touched on a personal level
that they may know He is still in control.

This is described as mounting up with wings like an eagle.

"He giveth power to the faint; and to them that have no might he increaseth strength. Even the youths shall faint and be weary, and the young men shall utterly fall: But they that wait upon the Lord shall renew their strength; they shall mount up with wings as eagles; they shall run, and not be weary; and they shall walk, and not faint" (Isaiah 40:29-31 King James Version).

258

His love will grow in meaning and truth deep inside of you.

You will grow in your confidence that the Lord is for you.

You will experience the ability to love others.
With the Holy Spirit you will surpass your own understanding
of what it means to be a 'good person'.

Christ has purchased your ability to be free from feeling you have 'been good enough'.
It took the costly price of His blood.
You will find fulfillment through your obedience unto Christ.

'My food,' said Jesus, 'is to do the will of him who sent me and to finish his work'
(John 4:34 New International Version).
"being confident of this, that he who began a good work in you will carry it on to completion until the day of Christ Jesus" (Philippians 1:6).

It is His work within you.

He will carry it on.

He will complete it.

"People were overwhelmed with amazement." <u>He has done everything well</u>, "He even makes the deaf hear and the mute speak" (Mark 7:37).

Dear reader, your Saviour 'does all things well.'

The wonderful relationship He has begun in your life will unfold in just this manner.

259

You are His temple and the Person of the Holy Spirit lives within you.

Your knowledge of God is personal.

God planned it that way for His followers. He said, 'I know my sheep and they know Me.'

He didn't say, 'My sheep work for Me.'

You are transformed through the work of the Holy Spirit inside you.
He heals from memories.
He heals your broken heart.
He enables you to 'forgive others' and teaches why this is important.

But this is not all, He has wondrous things to make known to you!

"'Call to me and I will answer you and tell you great and unsearchable things you do not know" (Jeremiah 33:3).

Dear reader, He will prepare your heart and make things known to you.

Some things you will know about before they happen!

"But when he, the Spirit of truth, comes, he will guide you into all truth. He will not speak on his own; he will speak only what he hears, and <u>he will tell you what is yet to come</u>" (John 16:13).

260

Jesus said to Mary, 'this love can never be taken away from you.'

He endears Himself to your heart.

You will grow through His intimate sharing with your heart.
Without even having to put it into words
you will know Him as an unfailing love.

Like a branch grafted into a vine,
He restores you into hope and intimate fellowship.
God will be there when you need Him.

He will always be there when you seek Him.

"You will seek me and find me when you seek me with all your heart" (Jeremiah 29:13).

He is always looking out for your best.
He is always on our side.

"Though the fig tree does not bud and there are no grapes on the vines, though the olive crop fails and the fields produce no food, though there are no sheep in the pen and no cattle in the stalls, yet I will rejoice in the Lord, I will be joyful in God my Saviour. The Sovereign Lord is my strength; he makes my feet like the feet of a deer, he enables me to go on the heights" (Habakkuk 3:17-20).

He walks with us through the difficult times.
He is trustworthy
and the intimate love He shares when alone with Him
far surpasses any blessing or hard times
you will encounter.

The blessing of your fellowship with Christ really is your life.
He is in love with you in this life and beyond.

So great is His love.

261

The strongest desire of a wise and loving father toward each one of his children
is for them to be as successful as possible.

In the end a loving father just wants them to be happy.

But if a son or daughter were an alcoholic they would not say
'I just want you to be happy. You are happy to drink as often as possible.
I just want you to be happy.'
Or would they say 'you are happy to cheat people in your profession.
As long as you are happy I am happy.'?

Or 'you work day and night and never see your family.
But if you are happy, then I am happy.'

A father both wise and loving would want the best for his children.
The boys and the girls.
He wants them to grow up and avoid mistakes
that would cost them for the rest of their lives.
A wise father or mother would want to see their child on a path of success.

A certain kind of success.

"For I know the plans I have for you," declares the Lord, "plans to prosper you and not to harm
you, plans to give you hope and a future" (Jeremiah 29:11).

Do you see why it is exactly the right thing to do
for you to 'run' to your heavenly Father in both good times and bad?

He wants the right success for you and has the power and the will to give it to you.

262

"The name of the Lord is a fortified tower; the righteous run to it and are safe" (Proverbs 18:10).

Your Father is your refuge.
He is a Person
but He is also a 'place' of refuge.

In His arms you can rest.
There are times you will feel like you are in His arms.
That is why you need to make a movement toward Him if He is to be your fortified tower.
Jesus said this movement is just like opening a door
that allows Him to enter.

When you seek safety from a hail storm or tornado you run or flee for cover.
If it starts to rain you 'run' for shelter.

This is how we respond when we are seeking God
for an intimate relationship.

We flee.
Run.

Or go to Him - making the alone place of fellowship with Him our choice of refuge.

263

He is refuge - for those who seek Him.

Here is a question.

What kind of friend of God do you want to be?

Did you know that He is seeking your friendship
more than anything else?
It comes under the category,
'only one thing is needed.'

A friend of God says,
'Lord, there is only one thing I desire. To be with you.'
In Psalm 27 David used this kind of extreme language.
Dear reader, in truth all of mankind needs a refuge
and there is only one given.

His name is Jesus Christ.

"One thing I ask of the Lord, this only do I seek: that I may dwell in the house of the Lord all the
days of my life, to gaze on the beauty of the Lord and to seek him in his temple" (Psalm 27:4-6).

Just felt to mention.
'To seek Him' is different than 'to seek His provision.'
It is different than
'I just want to praise you Lord.'

"Be still and know that I am God," the bible says.

There comes a time after all of our effort
when we have to actually
'listen'
in order to get to know God.

Dear reader, do this at home on your own.
Do this when you will not be disrupted.
Do this for God's sake.

Do this that you may know Him.

Do this because Jesus said, 'there is only one thing that is needed.'

264

Here is the rest of Psalm 27:4 - 6 once again.

"<u>One thing I ask of the Lord</u>, this only do I seek: that I may dwell in the house of the Lord all the days of my life, to gaze on the beauty of the Lord and to seek him in his temple. For in the day of trouble he will keep me safe in his dwelling; he will hide me in the shelter of his sacred tent and set me high upon a rock. Then my head will be exalted above the enemies who surround me; at his sacred tent I will sacrifice with shouts of joy; I will sing and make music to the Lord."

Have you read the expression, 'only one thing,' somewhere else in the bible?

Here it is in Luke 10:42.
"Jesus said, "<u>But one thing is needful</u>: and Mary hath chosen that good part, which shall not be taken away from her." "

Mary 'chose' that one thing.
She went aside to sit and listen to Jesus.

She had to make that choice.

It will always be the supreme expression of love for God.

265

A friend is someone who seeks God for 29 days.

If disaster strikes on the 30th day
they just do what they have done
for the previous 29 days.

They run into the presence of the Lord
ready to listen to Him
as they do on any other day.

The same thing they do on all the other days
when things were going fine.

Through no strength of their own.
With no special secret formula.

God has become a friend.
They become acquainted with One so kind.
A friend so faithful.
The One who knows all about all things.
This acquaintance becomes a reality because, 'they have been with Jesus.'

It says in the bible even a fool is made wise through fellowship with God.

"Wisdom reposes in the heart of the discerning and even among fools she lets herself be known" (Proverbs 14:33).

Oh, precious reader, no one is counted out of God's great plan.

Jesus came that the whole world might be saved.

266

On the day of distress a follower of Jesus runs for shelter and is troubled, maybe shaken
or maybe even terribly upset.
As the Almighty God,
the Alpha and Omega, the Beginning and the End intervenes by His Holy Spirit -
they that wait upon their Lord discover they are unshakeably confident.

Confident,
knowing God is there!
They have a hidden reservoir to draw upon.

A well, a spring of water that flows within.

"Whoever believes in me, as the Scripture has said, streams of living water will flow from within him" (John 7:38).

It is about the mystery of His love.
When you seek Him He is there! He will always be there for you.

"And surely I am with you always, to the very end of the age" (Matthew 28:20b).

The weakest servant of God will know from experience
that God always shows up when they go aside
to gaze upon Him . . .

"But as for me, it is good to be near God. I have made the Sovereign Lord my refuge; I will tell of all your deeds" (Psalm 73:28).

. . . when they listen to Him and enquire of Him.

"Christ in you, the hope of glory" (Colossians 1:27c).
"I will say, 'Salvation comes from the Lord." (Jonah 2:9c).

This day in God's presence the Lord will have His way in your distressful state.
And we know how God feels about demons or devils, or anything that messes with His children.

"The Lord will grant that the enemies who rise up against you will be defeated before you. They will come at you from one direction but flee from you in seven" (Deuteronomy 28:7).
"The Lord is far from the wicked: but he hears the prayer of the righteous" (Proverbs 15:29).

267

"Yet I am always with you; you hold me by my right hand. You guide me by my right hand. You guide me with your counsel, and afterward you will take me into glory. Whom have I in heaven but you? And earth has nothing I desire besides you. My flesh and my heart may fail, but God is the strength of my heart and my portion forever. Those who are far from you will perish; you destroy all who are unfaithful to you. But as for me, it is good to be near God. I have made the Sovereign Lord my refuge; I will tell of all your deeds" (Psalm 73:23-28).

Who has sinned against you?

Were you harmed as a child?
Did a family member, family friend or someone else defile you at an early age?
Some people go through life wounded.

They have nagging memories of being inappropriately touched.
In some cases the person who abused
has covered it up and lives a prosperous life.
This leaves the broken hearted with no closure.
It is a situation God cares very much about dear reader.

Let God into the very center of that mess inside you
that hurts so badly.
He won't hurt you further.
You need His loving touch.
The Holy Spirit will never fail you nor lead you into deeper suffering in this area.

Jesus has come 'that you may have life.'

Precious reader, be open to forgive.

Everything Jesus does, He does well.
He will walk with you
on a journey of your healing.
It does not have to involve the one who wronged you.
Often someone who preys upon the young and innocent has no desire to get right with God.
You can still move on with life.
Give God time.
Spend time with Him.
You are on a collision course with success dear reader.

Here is Psalm 16 to meditate on. This is a wondrous Psalm that is a truthful declaration of faith.
In there is says, 'the lines have fallen for you in pleasant places.' This describes the certainty that
God wants to bless and satisfy you with the path in life that He has prepared just for you.

"Keep me safe, my God, for in you I take refuge. I say to the Lord, "You are my Lord; apart from
you I have no good thing." I say of the holy people who are in the land, "They are the noble ones in
whom is all my delight." Those who run after other gods will suffer more and more. I will not pour
out libations of blood to such gods or take up their names on my lips. Lord, you alone are my
portion and my cup; you make my lot secure. The boundary lines have fallen for me in pleasant
places; surely I have a delightful inheritance. I will praise the Lord, who counsels me; even at night
my heart instructs me. I keep my eyes always on the Lord. With him at my right hand, I will not be
shaken. Therefore my heart is glad and my tongue rejoices; my body also will rest secure, because
you will not abandon me to the realm of the dead, nor will you let your faithful one see decay. You
make known to me the path of life; you will fill me with joy in your presence, with eternal pleasures
at your right hand" (Psalm 16).

Dear one, you won't be able to 'keep your eyes always on the Lord' through an exercise
of your own will or your own strength.

But when you get alone with the Lord
He will lift you up.

It is ok to be helpless or feel helpless in His presence.
He will lift you up.

Wait upon Him and He will transform your place of need
into a place of loveliness.
Because of Christ you are more than a conqueror.

In that place of intimate friendship
you will be enabled to obey Him
and perceive His thoughts both now and throughout your day.
The time spent with Him will make your obedience
an act of love.

The Master will be walking with you.

Your heavenly Father has always loved you.
You belong to Him
and He will deliver you safely
because He has given His life for you.

How sad it will be for those who did not know how much they needed Him.

"But as for the cowardly, the faithless, the detestable, as for murderers, the sexually immoral, sorcerers, idolaters, and all liars, their portion will be in the lake that burns with fire and sulphur, which is the second death" (Revelations 21:8).
"And when the thousand years are ended, Satan will be released from his prison and will come out to deceive the nations that are at the four corners of the earth, Gog and Magog, to gather them for battle; their number is like the sand of the sea. And they marched up over the broad plain of the earth and surrounded the camp of the saints and the beloved city, but fire came down from heaven and consumed them, and the devil who had deceived them was thrown into the lake of fire and sulphur where the beast and the false prophet were, and they will be tormented day and night forever and ever" (Revelations 20:7-10).
"Then he will say to those on his left, 'Depart from me, you cursed, into the eternal fire prepared for the devil and his angels" (Matt 25:41).
"For the wages of sin is death, but the free gift of God is eternal life in Christ Jesus our Lord" (Romans 6:23).

270

"I love you, O Lord, my strength. The Lord is my rock, my fortress and my deliverer; my God is my rock, in whom I take refuge. He is my shield and the horn of my salvation, my stronghold. I call to the Lord, who is worthy of praise, and I am saved from my enemies" (Psalm 18:1-3).

The Lord is your strength.

He is your rock, your fortress and your deliverer.
He is your refuge, your shield, horn of salvation and stronghold.
When you call to the Lord He saves you from your enemies.

He means from 'all' enemies! Praise God!

Your greatest lifelong treasure is summed up in the occasions you have been alone with God.
He is the creator of the universe
and He always takes time for intimate fellowship with you!
These times can never be taken from you.

Dearest, you have been developing a friendship with Someone in very high places.
Like, there is no more important person to know in this life!
Jesus is the only spiritual leader who put it all on the line making statements such as these:

"Jesus said to her, "I am the resurrection and the life. He who believes in me will live, even though he dies; and whoever lives and believes in me will never die. Do you believe this?" " (John 11:25-26).

Dear reader, do you believe in Jesus?
There is no one else who can keep you safe
from evil's eternal harm.

"And I give unto them eternal life; and they shall never perish, neither shall any man pluck them out of my hand" (John 10:28).

No one else is the 'resurrection and the life.'
If you are not taken from this life suddenly or unexpectedly,
life after death will become very important to you in your old age.
Get to know Jesus now.
Don't have a false hope that you can put off the Son of God.

Be sure you have a place with 'the resurrection and the life' for all eternity - starting today!

271

"I said to the Lord, "You are my Lord; apart from you I have no good thing." I have set the Lord always before me. Because he is at my right hand, I will not be shaken" (Psalm 16:2,8).

We see from the story of Mary and Martha, Jesus explained that Mary had chosen the better part.

She had set the Lord before her.

Those who set the Lord before them will not be shaken.
They cannot be shaken
because they have come to know the Lord God as a shelter
before disaster occurs.
His grace will enable them to continue to meet Him
each day until the disaster has passed.

He can't fail the faithful.

"To the faithful you show yourself faithful," (Psalm 18:25a).
"And everyone who calls on the name of the Lord will be saved" (Acts 2:21).

Dear reader, when God saves you
His love reaches every aspect of your life.
Your everyday needs are not all that He is interested in.
Because you belong to Him
He will uphold both you and your righteous cause.
Lean upon Him in all things.
He will not let you be put to shame!

"If you declare with your mouth, "Jesus is Lord," and believe in your heart that God raised him from the dead, you will be saved. For it is with your heart that you believe and are justified, and it is with you mouth that you profess your faith and are saved. As Scripture says, "Anyone who believes in him will never be put to shame. For there is no difference between Jew and Gentile - the same Lord is Lord of all and richly blesses all who call on him" (Romans 10:9-12).
"in you I trust, O my God. Do not let me be put to shame, nor let my enemies triumph over me" (Psalm 25:2).
"I hold fast to your statutes, O Lord; do not let me be put to shame" (Psalm 119:31).

272

Why wait until there is a disaster?

Why wait until things go horribly wrong to set the Lord before you on a daily basis?

"Then he said to them all: "Whoever wants to be my disciple must deny themselves and take up their cross daily and follow me" (Luke 9:23).

Jesus knew how much we would need Him
to keep us from falling.
He said we need to 'take up our cross daily.'

"For hardship does not spring from the soil, nor does trouble sprout from the ground. Yet man is born to trouble as surely as sparks fly upward. But if I were you, I would appeal to God; I would lay my cause before him. He performs wonders that cannot be fathomed, miracles that cannot be counted" (Job 5:6-9).

Have you got time for Jesus?

That is the all important question.

If you go by what Jesus said it is a daily thing.

Daily we must choose the 'one thing that is needed' like Mary did
when she sat with Jesus to listen.
Do you want to allow Jesus
to become your refuge and strength?
Is it worth the time to become an intimate friend of Jesus?

All it will cost you is a little of your time.

273

"And the Spirit and the bride say, Come. And let him that heareth say, Come. And let him that is
athirst come. <u>And whosoever will, let him take the water of life freely</u>" (Revelations 22:17).
"Come to me, all you who are weary and burdened, and I will give you rest. Take my yoke upon
you and learn from me, for I am gentle and humble in heart, and you will find rest for your souls"
(Matthew 11:28-30).

The follower of Jesus finds . . . rest.

Who is that follower of Jesus?

Whoever receives Jesus as Saviour
and then spends time with Him.
That is all.
Intimacy with God is for everyone who will.

How wonderful that anyone
can have an intimate relationship with Jesus!
There are no barriers.
There is no special denomination, no membership needed to an earthly organisation.

The relationship is given freely from the moment you receive the ever living Son of God.

274

Do not let any man steal this mighty privilege from you!

You get alone with God and you believe ONLY HIM!
The devil will send people from within the church to try and rob you
of your Holy privilege.

"Let God be true, and every human being a liar" (Romans 3:4a).

When it comes down to it dear believer
you trust the voice of the Holy Spirit - such as you have come to know Him and His ways.

Do not think, 'that person must surely know God better than me.
Look how long they have gone to church or been a Christian!'

"You're not ready yet."
"God doesn't work that way."
"You have been listening to demons."
"You are having a nervous break down."

These are but a few things said by church people to the true followers of Jesus.

You might be tempted to conclude of your detractors,
'There must be something to what they are saying.'
'Look at how important they are, look at how the Lord uses them.'
'They seem so concerned for me.'

That is why it says 'every man.'
'Let every man be a liar'
because some of your dissenters will appear so very worthy.
They will come to you and try to rob you
of your obedience to the most High God!

"It is better to take refuge in the Lord than to trust in humans. It is better to take refuge in the Lord than to trust in princes" (Psalm 118:8).
"Cursed is the one who trusts in man, who draws strength from mere flesh and whose heart turns away from the Lord. That person will be like a bush in the wastelands; they will not see prosperity when it comes. They will dwell in the parched places of the desert, in a salt land where no one lives. "But blessed is the one who trusts in the Lord, whose confidence is in him. They will be like a tree planted by the water that sends out its roots by the stream. It does not fear when heat comes; its leaves are always green. It has no worries in a year of drought and never fails to bear fruit" (Jeremiah 17:5-8).

275

People who live through a tornado - they now have a safe room specially built into their new home.

Before the disaster their home was sufficient.
It protected them from all manner of storm.
They felt safe with their home the way it was.
It may even have been in the family for successive generations.
Why have a safe room when you have never needed one before?

"Therefore everyone who hears these words of mine and puts them into practice is like a wise man who built his house on the rock. The rain came down, the streams rose, and the winds blew and beat against that house; yet it did not fall, because it had its foundation on the rock. But everyone who hears these words of mine and does not put them into practice is like a foolish man who built his house on sand. The rain came down, the streams rose, and the winds blew and beat against that house, and it fell with a great crash" (Matthew 7:24-27).

Jesus compared us to a house.
He says we are His temple when we belong to Him.
He is the foundation made of rock.
Those who build their own house without Him have only sand for a foundation.
The whole house will fail one day.

Jesus is the rock of our salvation.

Jesus considers each precious follower a temple wherein His Holy Spirit dwells.
He understands our need for spiritual foundation.

In Psalms 18:1 - 3 it says, "I love you, O Lord, my strength. The Lord is my rock, my fortress and my deliverer; my God is my rock, in whom I take refuge. He is my shield and the horn of my salvation, my stronghold. I call to the Lord, who is worthy of praise, and I am saved from my enemies."

Jesus Christ is the only true spiritual foundation.

276

There comes a time for everyone when a forceful, unexpected storm comes up in life.

A storm might be an unfaithful partner,
a spiritual leader discovered in sin,
being born into an abusive home
or being deceived or manipulated at work.

At some point in time the death of a friend, loved one or family member
may leave you with unanswered questions and the grief of loss.

Dear reader, in a faithful relationship with Jesus Christ
you have a spiritual foundation being carefully built over time.
To be a good foundation it must be straight and true and level.

In John 10:1 - 6 Jesus relates intimacy to the process of hearing His voice.
How wonderful for each sheep to be called by name by such an important Person.

When you listen to someone:
you stop what you are doing;
set aside some time and minimize distracting sounds.

You focus upon the person communicating with you
and ascertain whether you have correctly heard them.
Jesus shows us this is what His followers do.

"Very truly I tell you Pharisees, anyone who does not enter the sheep pen by the gate, but climbs in by some other way, is a thief and a robber. The one who enters by the gate is the shepherd of the sheep. The gatekeeper opens the gate for him, and <u>the sheep listen to his voice</u>, He calls his own sheep by name and leads them out. When he has brought out all his own, he goes on ahead of them, and <u>his sheep follow him because they know his voice</u>. But they will never follow a stranger; in fact, they will run away from him because <u>they do not recognize a stranger's voice</u>.
Jesus used this figure of speech, but the Pharisees did not understand what he was telling them.
V.7 Therefore Jesus said again, "Very truly I tell you, I am the gate for the sheep. <u>All who have come before me are thieves and robbers, but the sheep have not listened to them</u>. I am the gate; whoever enters through me will be saved. They will come in and go out, and find pasture. The thief comes only to steal and kill and destroy; I have come that they may have life, and have it to the full" (John 10:1-6).

As you take time alone with Jesus He steadily puts together
a magnificent house upon the foundation.

Jesus said,
"Therefore <u>everyone who hears these words of mine</u>
and puts them into practice is like a wise man
who built his house on the rock."

In your intimate fellowship
you and your Jesus take turns
listening to one another.
Then as a true follower and lover of Jesus you rise up from the solitary place
and immediately obey His commands.

Jesus has helped us understand the true way to express love and devotion unto Him.
Don't jump up and join another group.
Give more money
or earn another degree.

You don't need to figure this out on your own without your Saviour's help.

He really needs His followers to spend time with Him so they will hear from Him.
Afterwards they are to be willing to follow-through with His will.

To do what He asks.

"If you love me, keep my commands" (John 14:15).

Clearly, Jesus is not looking for busy people.

Instead, day by day He is intimately building
within those who are listening unto Him.

Those who listen unto Him are getting alone with Him
and they are enjoying 'the richest of fare.'
And guess who prepared the spiritual food just for them?
How amazing is that?!

Right from the hand of God.

"Why spend money on what is not bread, and your labour on what does not satisfy? <u>Listen, listen
to me</u>, and eat what is good, and you will delight in the richest of fare" (Isaiah 55:2).

Dear reader, fellowship with God IS your life
because Christ is your life.
Fellowship with God is the work prepared for you,
starting your labour with intimate fellowship.
Waiting upon the Lord and resting in the Lord
you will arise to your labours with a personal knowledge
of the Person you represent.

Without a relationship rooted and grounded in Love you will not be used to sow to the Spirit.

"Do not work for food that spoils, but for food that endures to eternal life, which the Son of Man
will give you. For on him God the Father has placed his seal of approval" (John 6:27).
"Remain in me, and I in you. As the branch can't bear fruit by itself, unless it remains in the vine,
so neither can you, unless you remain in me. I am the vine, ye are the branches. He that abides in
me and I in him, he bears much fruit; for without me ye can do nothing" (John 15:4-5).

Can you see the simplicity?
Abiding in Christ
brings the fruit of love in all that you do.
Fruit that will never pass away.

Doing things for Jesus, no matter how successful it appears,
does not mean you have an intimate relationship with Him.

Bless the Lord for all eternity for He has prepared the richest of fare
for the blind,
the elderly,

the poor,
the forgotten,
those less intelligent,
the war vet . . .
and each person whose life is taken in the womb
without an opportunity to do one thing for God.

"Humble yourselves, therefore, under God's might hand, that he may lift you up in due time. Cast all your anxiety on him because he cares for you" (1 Peter 5:6-7).

278

We may initially think by doing everything we are told by our church leaders
and by supporting church activities it equates to a strong relationship with God.

I believed that at one time.

"It is written," he said to them, "My house will be called a house of prayer,' but you are making it 'a den of robbers' (Matt 21:13).

Jesus sent the money changers out of the church with a whip.
They were in the church but they were not building God's kingdom.

And Jesus did not like it.

Somehow to the natural mind
it is as if the moment we step inside a building
designated as 'church' that everything
we experience and are being told to do is God's will.

Dear reader,
what a disaster awaits those
who will one day discover that they never knew God
in spite of how many times they went to church
and prayed in Jesus Holy name.
If this discovery occurs after this life there will be no chance to make things right.
The next thing they hear our loving, merciful, meek and lowly Saviour say is,
"Depart from me, I never knew you."
They will then be summarily banished.
Never again to be in His presence.

That is a staggering reality in itself
when you consider that Jesus has been available
to the human race for over two thousand years up until that moment.

Once Jesus rejects you as one of the many unrighteous dead
it will be an eternity without God.
Without hope without love.
Life without end with no forgiveness for what you have done.

It will be the last time you have an opportunity to speak to Jesus
or be spoken to by Him
before the burning punishment of hell.
Can you see what a blessing it is to hear the voice of the Lord?
To have an intimate relationship with Him?

In this present life weren't His words always kind and loving?
Didn't He give up everything to give the hope of heaven to all of mankind?
No words will be able to describe the ache in hearts of those
who will never again be aware of the existence of God
and His love.

"Not everyone who says to me, 'Lord, Lord,' will enter the kingdom of heaven, but only the one
who does the will of my Father who is in heaven. Many will say to me on that day, 'Lord, Lord, did
we not prophesy in your name and in your name drive out demons and in your name perform
many miracles?' Then I will tell them plainly, 'I never knew you. Away from me, you evildoers!'
"therefore everyone who hears these words of mine and puts them into practice is like a wise man
who built his house on the rock" (Matthew 7:21-24).
"Once the owner of the house gets up and closes the door, you will stand outside knocking and
pleading, 'Sir, open the door for us.' "But he will answer, 'I don't know you or where you come
from' " (Luke 13:25).

Jesus must have followers who are committed to listening unto Him,
denying themselves,
taking up their own cross daily
and following
Him.

The bible says Jesus is the head of the church.
There is no mention that He will surrender His Lordship
to a leader who comes after Him,
an organisation,
or a book in addition to the Holy Bible written or discovered by someone.

"And he is the head of the body, the church; he is the beginning and the firstborn from among the
dead, so that in everything he might have the supremacy" (Colossians 1:18).

Your pastor or spiritual leader is not Jesus.
You are able to freely find God's will for your life
as Mary the sister of Martha did.

Sitting with Jesus
in order to listen unto Him.

A godly pastor will be wonderfully used of God to confirm what the Lord has already said to you.

They will be grateful for your prayers and the love you have for the work of God.

279

'Therefore everyone who hears these words of mine and puts them into practice is like a wise man who built his house on the rock. The rain came down, the streams rose, and the winds blew and beat against that house; yet it did not fall, because it had its foundation on the rock. But everyone who hears these words of mine and does not put them into practice is like a foolish man who built his house on sand. The rain came down, the streams rose, and the winds blew and beat against that house, and it fell with a great crash" (Matthew 7:24-27).

When disaster strikes, though you may be caught by surprise you are still sustained.

The Lord is your rock.

You have a sure foundation
that will never leave you nor forsake you.
Your foundation has been around since eternity past
and is full of all wisdom and love.
You will be sustained like a house built upon a foundation of rock.
How great and tender is the love that God
your foundation has for you.

You will make it through.

"You, dear children, are from God and have overcome them, because the one who is in you is greater than the one who is in the world" (1 John 4:4).

280

From an eternal perspective a disaster can become a simple seed of blessing watered by tears.

As the dust settles and you reflect upon your human frailty,
many times there is a blessed cry that arises from the heart.

It is an instinctive cry for God and for His help.
In truth,
God is our maker.
This is within the hearts of the saved and the unsaved alike.

"Oh my God!"
"Oh God!"
"Jesus help me!"
"Jesus Christ!"
"Jesus!"

When sudden shock or disaster strikes do people cry out the name of their favourite automobile?
Their entrusted bank? Do they scream out the name of their country?
Their reigning monarch or greatest sports celebrity?
The unbeliever, even a rank atheist,
rather than crying out the iconic name
of an historical spiritual leader, says the same thing.

"Jesus!" "Jesus Christ!" "Oh my God!" "God help me!"

God has invested a supernatural quality into every human being.
Somehow
when things don't go the way we think they should
we can't help but pray.

He has set eternity in the human heart.

"He has also set eternity in the hearts of men" (Ecclesiastes 3:11b).

281

Disaster has a way of showing us our need for God.

We just don't grasp or realise how important Jesus is
until there is no where to go for safety.

All the while
though we feel self-sufficient
we are truly wretched,
poor, pitiful
blind
and naked.

"You say, 'I am rich; I have acquired wealth and do not need a thing.' But you do not realize that
you are wretched, pitiful, poor, blind and naked. I counsel you to buy from me gold refined in the
fire, so you can become rich; and white clothes to wear, so you can cover your shameful nakedness;
and salve to put on your eyes, so you can see. Those whom I love I rebuke and discipline. So be
earnest and repent. Here I am! I stand at the door and knock. If anyone hears my voice and opens
the door, I will come in and eat with that person, and they with me" (Revelations 3:17-20).

282

Reputation may come and go.

Wealth may come and go.

Health may come and go. Friends may come and go.
A beloved spouse may come and go. Houses may come and go.
Churches may come and go. Church buildings may come and go.
Spiritual leaders may come and go. Jobs may come and go.
Success may come and go.
Human exploit and endeavour remains constant - in its inconsistency.

Everything changes.

Through all of life's trials you will be able to retain
your friendship with your loving Jesus.
It is in a time of loss or disappointment,
rejection or misunderstanding
that this truth becomes a little more real.

The truth that you have all you need in Christ Jesus is tested,
tried and proven
in the real issues of life.
Each time you experience affliction it becomes apparent
all over again how central Jesus Christ is
in your salvation experience.
You see Him anew as your life.

To have Jesus Christ is to have life.

"Because thy loving-kindness is better than life, my lips shall praise thee" (Psalm 63:3).

283

To be accepted and unconditionally loved is a wonderful state of being.

This lifestyle belongs to you.

It is yours. Nothing can take it away from you.
Jesus gave it to you.

You can declare, in the midst of all fury
and the storms of hell itself,

"Jesus is mine."
The thief on the cross had this blessed experience when Jesus spoke to Him.
'This day you will be with Me in paradise'.
He was able to say in His heart,
'Jesus is mine.'

What relief, what comfort in the midst of his crisis.

It wasn't Jesus physical power, religious influence,
neither political will nor reputation that would bring His Father's will to pass.
His Father's will would prevail because Jesus is the truth.
He is the Light of the world
and Light overcomes darkness.

The thief believed in Jesus and became a saved man.
It was faith alone
because the thief was nailed to the cross of a criminal
and could not carry out any pious act.
He had nothing to offer God in return
but his breath and a couple of hours
spent in agony.

Jesus spoke to Him. The Son of God spoke His precious word to him. The following verse in Matthew gives us an idea of what it means for each of us to hear from God.

"Jesus answered, "It is written: 'Man does not live on bread alone, but on every word that comes from the mouth of God' " (Matthew 4:4).

You see Dear Reader, even in your storms of life you have a loving Friend.
Jesus will be there and identify with you
in every way.

When He speaks His word to you in that storm - and He will speak to you -
that word is truth and that word will prevail.
His word is Truth and He will prevail over all storms.
In His Light the darkness flees from Him and He loves you.

He will be right there with you no matter what you are going through
because He loves you.

He was there beside the thief on the cross in his hour of need.
Through sheer love alone Jesus was there to save the thief.

Jesus chose to identify fully with the thief.
He identifies with you today, in every possible way, and will not leave your side.

The truth in the words Jesus spoke had the power to bring eternal life to a man about to die though Jesus Himself was nigh unto death.

It is the Truth that sets you free.

It is not you.

"Then you will know the truth, and the truth will set you free" (John 8:32).

You see Dear Reader,
it is the truth that sets you free
and it is the truth upon which you stand.

God's truth is a foundation in your life. It is unshakeable so that you can be unshakeable.

"I have set the Lord always before me. Because he is at my right hand, I will not be shaken. Therefore my heart is glad and my tongue rejoices; my body also will rest secure, because you will not abandon me to the grave, nor will you let your Holy One see decay. You have made known to me the path of life; you will fill me with joy in your presence, with eternal pleasures at your right hand" (Psalm 16:8-11).

For all your days you will belong to One so kind, One so true.
He literally lives to make intercession for you.

That is how dear you are to Him.

"Therefore he is able to save completely those who come to God through him, because he always lives to intercede for them" (Hebrews 7:25).

Dear Reader, up until now, we have been talking together about the gift you freely receive from your loving Jesus.

We have marvelled and stood in awe at the blessing of being bought with a price.
Chosen by Someone special because they are the only One to know your eternal value.
Someone who considers your irreplaceable soul to be a treasure
more valuable than all the worth of the entire world.

We have talked about Someone wealthy enough,
with love enough - desire enough - to ransom you
though it cost them their own greatest love.

God the Father sent His Son to give His life for you.

Jesus was obedient.
With joy He looked forward to delivering you from hell
and being your friend forever.
He knew all the love in His heart would be yours as a gift
just because you believed on His Holy, precious name.

And now, here you are!

Look at you!
The object of all the desire of God!
This is your standing in Jesus the moment you were saved.
If you want to be saved, don't wait. Ask now,
ask Jesus to forgive you and save you.

He will.

286

God has enough love for the whole world.

If everyone were to turn to Him and cry out for mercy all at once they would all be saved!

Not one of them would go to hell!
Talk about power! Talk about love!
That is so much love.
Be one of those who will stand and say, "I am not ashamed. I believe in Jesus."

"I will be glad and rejoice in your love, for you saw my affliction and knew the anguish of my soul.
You have not given me into the hands of the enemy but have set my feet in a spacious place"
(Psalm 31:7–8).

At this juncture, we are going deeper into why all of this is possible.

But do not be concerned that this meaning and truth is only for a chosen few.
You are among the chosen few if you belong to Jesus Christ!

"Do not be afraid, little flock, for your Father has been pleased to GIVE you the kingdom"
(Luke 12:32).

We have previously shared that God has spared nothing
to bring you into fellowship.
Afterward to bring you into glory forever.

Dear reader, let's consider how this is possible
for plain folks like you and me.
How is it possible
that you will immediately come face to face
with your very best friend as soon as you breathe your last breath?
Jesus Christ conquered death and hell and the grave!

Glory, glory, glory Hallelujah!
"GLORY."

"Glory and Hallelujah to Jesus Christ God's precious Lamb, God's precious Son."

287

A deep and winsome relationship with Jesus is given to any and all who will spend time with Him.

"To them God has chosen to make known among the Gentiles the glorious riches of this mystery, which is Christ in you, the hope of glory" (Colossians 1:27).

Because Jesus is in you
there is hope.
Because Jesus will answer any who cry out to Him
there is hope.
Thank God it is not about your human ability or strength.

God has chosen to make Himself known.
You are in good hands Dear Reader.
You cannot fail for He chose to make Himself known to you.

'Not by might nor by power, but by my Spirit,' says the Lord Almighty (Zechariah 4:6b).

288

Jesus ministers to all who come unto Him.

He is near to the broken hearted.

He lifts up those who humble themselves and reverence Him.
Those who hold Him in awe and respect
are blessed with His fellowship.

"Come to me, all you who are weary and burdened, and I will give you rest" (Matthew 11:28).

Your qualifications for intimacy with God are fully met
just by showing up and spending time alone with Him.
But what part does Jesus play in all of this?

It says in Zechariah 4:6 "not by might nor by power but by My Spirit says the Lord of Hosts."
"Christ in you, the hope of glory" (Colossians 1:27).

To say your hope is in Him for a great and winsome relationship of personal intimacy
is a success oriented affirmation.

Christ in you is your hope of glory.
He will accomplish it.
He will be faithful to watch over it.
Your relationship with God through His Son Jesus Christ is destined to succeed.

"You, dear children, are from God and have overcome them, because the one who is in you is
greater than the one who is in the world" (1 John 4:4).

God will perform this in you.
You will be able to walk with Him because of His greatness.

Nothing exists
that is able to prevent you from having your own personal relationship with God.

289

There is Someone totally, irresistibly, unconditionally in love with you.

That is why you are entitled
to your very own deep, intimate relationship with God.
God loves you.
God unconditionally loves you.
The simple truth about the deep mystery
is the manner in which God is committed
to those who seek Him.
He is committed
on the deepest level possible.

Totally forgiving of the repentant heart.

Totally accepting of all who call on His name.

Always ready to share Himself entirely along with all He has
with anyone who wants to know Him.

Absolutely anyone is able to be involved and intimate,
sharing face time with God.
There is no special gift needed.
You don't even need a person in your earthly family to be praying for you.
You only need Jesus.

It is the nature of His giving, generous love
that makes you a prime candidate
to walk with God.

290

From God's perspective you are worthy.

He already considers you His deepest, closest friend.

In fact He considers you to be as close to Him as you can possibly be.
He is more convinced of your intimacy with Him than you are.
Generally you will need Him to express how special the two of you are together.
He does this when you are alone with Him
and He can really let you know
what you mean to Him.

Isn't that what happens when you are no longer with the crowd but in a private place?
Communication moves into a whole new realm. It becomes an encounter.
It becomes one on one.

In John 14:1 - 4 Jesus says to His disciples 'you already trust in God'.
He says therefore, 'trust also in Me'.
In verse 4, 'you already know the way to the place where I am going.'
He tells them they know the way. He cannot lie.
He tells them point blank that they relate to Him on the deepest possible level,
the level of trust,
and that they know where He is going.
Something happens next that is all too human.
Something we will all struggle with from time to time,
what with life's events frequently putting our relationship with God to the test.
These tests give us pause to question,

"do I still love You as I once did?"
"Is my heart right with You, O Lord of glory?"

It may be after a distressful circumstance, or a time when it looks like God
is not taking care of things the way we are used to.

"Search me, God, and know my heart; test me and know my anxious thoughts. See if there is any offensive way in me, and lead me in the way everlasting" (Psalm 139:23-24).

291

In John 14: 1 - 4 Thomas responds to Jesus immediately and says, "Lord *we* don't know where you are going, so how can *we* know the way."

None of the other disciples object to Thomas speaking on their behalf so they must have all been thinking and feeling the same about what Jesus told them.

So Thomas says right back to Jesus, 'no, we don't know you, or trust you as you say therefore we don't know the way.'

Isn't that how it is sometimes?

Isn't it also wonderful how Jesus sees us very differently than we see ourselves?
How remarkable is the work of salvation freely given to us. The power to redeem us
is always beyond our understanding. It escapes our intellectual grasp.

"may have power, together with all the saints, to grasp how wide and long and high and deep is the love of Christ, and to know this love that surpasses knowledge - " (Ephesians 3:18-19a).

No relationship on earth can compare to the riches we have in our fellowship with our precious Jesus Christ. You need Him to affirm . . . how very precious you are.

Right now, regardless of your situation,
Jesus would tenderly say unto you,
"you know the place to where I am going."
Often we don't feel worthy or qualified to relate to Jesus as deeply as He relates unto us.

But He will say, 'It's ok. You already trust Me.'

292

He begins relationship with you on the deepest level.

In terms of intimacy God is being transparent, authentic and sincere.

From the start He relates to you without holding anything back.
You are His friend!
He is not looking to make you worthy of a close walk.

Jesus has already established that privilege for you.

"And by that will, we have been made holy through the sacrifice of the body of Jesus Christ once for all. For by one sacrifice he has made perfect forever those who are being made holy" (Hebrews 10:10,14).

That is how God relates to you from His perspective.

From His perspective
you begin your walk with Him on the deepest possible footing.
You are 'made perfect forever' when you receive Christ.

He was sent into this world with an everlasting love for you.
He relates to you on terms He set in place.

A long time ago Jesus died for you.

When He rose from the dead that beautiful morning three days later
He looked forward with delight to the day you would turn to Him in faith.
His total commitment was in place.

His commitment to have a relationship with you.

Jesus Christ saved you in order to befriend you
and then take you home
at the time of His choosing.

To be with one another forever.

293

Jesus is completely invested in you.

Even before the world was made.

Now you will be saved if you ask Him
to wash away your sins with His precious blood.
Once you have believed in Him and become born again
you are perfect in His sight.
You are true friends right away. Your belief in Him is all He needs
to freely bestow all the benefits of His salvation upon you.

It is all new to you
but Someone kind and gentle has been waiting,
patiently waiting to love you,
love you, love you.

Someone who is already your friend.
Someone who could never hurt you.
Someone you can trust.

"I no longer call you servants, because a servant does not know his master's business. Instead, I have called you friends, for everything that I learned from my Father I have made known to you" (John 15:15).

This means Jesus has already passed through all phases of relationship.

Your relationship begins in a secure place of trust.
This is the kind of commitment it takes
if you were to choose to give up your life
in exchange for another person.

Whether you live for them or die for them.

Look at the historical event of Jesus death on the cross as the evidence
of His trustworthy intentions for you.

294

"Greater love has no one than this, than to lay down ones life for his friends" (John 15:13).

That is why He said to His followers, 'trust in God trust also in Me.'
It was on the basis of solid friendship Jesus laid down His life.
We have studied that God in fact knew us - both the good and bad - before He made this earth.

Dear Reader, His commitment of friendship is a fully informed decision on His part.

How do you possibly trust someone
until you have had time to get to know them?
You would have to first meet,
need a reason to be involved
and then have the opportunity to prove each other.

It would take time.

Both individuals would explore fellowship in a series of special circumstances that develop and demonstrate honesty, consistency and a common interest to pursue success in the relationship.
There would be an open door to invest in each other.
Jesus says, 'trust in Me.' He also means, 'I trust in you.'

It doesn't matter how you see yourself in regard to His love for you.

The death and resurrection explains it all.

Right now He is sold out in love with you!

295

Friendship is all about trusting one another.

An intimate place rich with generosity,
selflessness
kindness
disclosure
and caring.

For any number of reasons - some beyond your control - the wondrous place of trust
with another person may be a rare experience throughout life.

When God opens a door for you to share a trusting friendship with another person
it will be a wonderful season in your lives!
It will also bring a deep unity with the Holy Spirit
if honouring Christ is the desire that brings you together.

Good friends are not easily acquired. For friendship to take hold over time
both people need to share a unity from the very beginning.
In the bible it is described as 'sharing the same mind' or 'having the same mind.'

"Do two walk together unless they have agreed to do so?" (Amos 3:3).

The root of friendship is a united vision.
Having agreement together deep down in your soul.
Rather than an intellectual phenomenon it goes deep into the spiritual realm.

It is not based upon what you have done for God
or what you are equipped to do for God in the future.

It can't be attained through personal effort like saying, 'I agree with you.'
Thankfully, it is only based upon your walk with Jesus Christ.
Your relationships will begin this way and continue in the same manner
until one day your life on earth is over.

"Do you not know that your bodies are temples of the Holy Spirit, who is in you, whom you have
received from God? **You are not your own**; you were bought at a price. Therefore honour God
with your bodies" (1 Corinthians 19-20).

"I would like to learn just one thing from you: Did you receive the Spirit by the works of the law, or by believing what you heard?" (Galatians 3:2).

Once you believe in Jesus Christ you are never the same again.

It is because of the righteousness of Jesus Christ.
You were bought with a price. The death and resurrection of the Lord Jesus Christ.
He was the price paid for your redemption.

"Do you not know that your bodies are temples of the Holy Spirit, who is in you, whom you have received from God? You are not your own; you were bought at a price. Therefore honour God with your bodies" (1 Corinthians 6:19-20).

Unity is said to bring the blessing of God.

"How good and pleasant it is when God's people live together in unity! It is like precious oil poured on the head, running down on the beard, running down on Aaron's beard, down on the collar of his robe. It is as if the dew of Hermon were falling on Mount Zion. For there the LORD bestows his blessing, even life forevermore" (Psalm 133).

Unity is given as determined by God alone.
Unity takes place with believers when in agreement with the Holy Spirit.

The Holy Spirit blesses people who listen unto Him with 'the mind of Christ'.

296

If you meet and greet folks around town or in the workplace it is a wonderful thing
to exchange pleasantries.

There are nice people out there who care if you have a good day
even if you are a stranger.

There are some folks who respond favourably to the presence of the Holy Spirit within you.
These people blossom to the timely expression of love and kindness you share with them.
A little meeting orchestrated by a God who loves them.
It is possible to turn around someone's whole outlook for the day with one encounter.

"He who listens to you listens to me; he who rejects you rejects me; but he who rejects me rejects him who sent me" (Luke10:16).

Thank God for people who care,
people who love others.
Getting along with Jesus is also uplifting.

His personal fellowship fills your soul and satisfies.
It is an entirely different blessing
than the passing interactions with others
that makes up so much of the day.

To Jesus you are so much more than an acquaintance.
You are a member of His family as soon as you receive Him.

He died for you personally.

It is His opinion of you that makes all the difference.
Your value is great.
In truth your value is eternal.

To Jesus you are worthy of His everlasting love.

297

There is a whole realm of relating with Jesus that lives far beyond exchanging pleasantries.

He is uplifting in every sense of the word.

As you abide in your precious Lord Jesus, for the rest of your life He will guide each step.
Your trust in Him will always be growing.
You are kept by your Creator.

"Yet you, Lord, are our Father. We are the clay, you are the potter; we are all the work of your hand" (Isaiah 64:8).
Then the word of the Lord came to me: 'O house of Israel, can I not do with you as this potter does?' declares the Lord. 'Like clay in the hand of the potter, so are you in my hand, O house of Israel' (Jeremiah 18:6).

It all started when you reached out to Him with faith and trust that He would save you.
You exercised faith in an unseen God!

You trusted Him and opened the door of your heart to Him.

298

You trust in things all the time that are visible to your natural eye.

Like the way you trust in your seat belt to protect you from great harm.
Trust in your shoes to protect you from hot pavement.

There is a degree of trust that your information will be safe online
or you would not go online.
You trust your body to last and serve you well
if you treat it properly.

Just as you would trust a life jacket
to prevent you from drowning
you have reached out and received Jesus Christ.

He removes the concern about what will happen to you when you die.
Jesus is the light of the world and you become truly alive once you believe in Him
and His Holy Spirit lives within you.

"Whoever believes in the Son has eternal life, but whoever rejects the Son will <u>not see life</u>, for
God's wrath remains on them" (John 3:36).

He has become your salvation.
You are now eternally safe.

No harm can compromise your eternal soul
because you are in His care.

In His limitless power He will work all things together for your good.

"The watchman opens the gate for him, and <u>the sheep listen to **his** voice. **He** calls his own sheep by</u>
<u>name and leads them out</u>. When **he** has brought out all his own, **he** goes on ahead of them, and
<u>his sheep follow **him** because they know **his** voice</u>. But they will never follow a stranger; in fact,
they will run away from him because they do not recognize a stranger's voice" (John 10:3).

Do you see from this passage in the book of John the emphasis and simplicity of depending
upon Jesus for your salvation?
Why simply going to church is not your salvation?
Salvation is found in no one else.

If you trust in any work that you are doing
apart from a personal relationship with Jesus Christ
then you are building upon the wrong foundation.
 "Salvation is found in no one else, for there is no other name under heaven given to men by which
we must be saved" (Acts 4:12).

Dear reader, believe in Him - receive Him - and then follow **Him**.
It is Jesus who saved you.
It is Jesus you seek.

It is His voice you recognize.

It is His personal leading that enables obedience,
fellowship
and purpose.

Follow Jesus dear reader.

"And we know that in all things God works for the good of those who love him, who have been
called according to his purpose" (Romans 8:28).
"To him who is able to keep you from falling and to present you before his glorious presence
without fault and with great joy - to the only God our Saviour be glory, majesty, power and
authority, through Jesus Christ our Lord, before all ages, now and forevermore!" Amen
(Jude 1:24-25).

Follow Jesus.

299

When Jesus comes into your life He is the best friend you will ever have.

For the rest of your life no one will ever love you as much
or as completely
as your Jesus.
Jesus loves you more than a member of your own family!

He will also stick with you no matter what happens to you.

"A man of many companions may come to ruin, but there is a friend who sticks closer than a
brother" (Proverbs 18:24).

The most loving mother that ever lived
is not the same
as Jesus.

"Can a mother forget the baby at her breast and have no compassion on the child she has borne?
Though she may forget, I will not forget you!" (Isaiah 49:15).

" - He conquered death and hell proclaiming, "All authority in heaven and on earth has been given
to me. And surely I am with you always, to the very end of the age" (Matthew 28:18,20b).

Jesus has all power in heaven and on earth.
Enough power to be with you always, to the very end of the age.

Still He honoured, cherished
and loved His mother.

"Near the cross of Jesus stood his mother, his mother's sister, Mary the wife of Clopas, and Mary Magdalene. When Jesus saw his mother there, and the disciple whom he loved standing nearby, he said to his mother, 'Dear woman, here is your son.' From that time on, this disciple took her into his home" (John 19:26-27).

300

Jesus Christ is meek.

Humble.

A servant.

Courageously His mother stayed with Him throughout His crucifixion.

He lived as an outgoing, strong, healthy young man.
Full of virtue. A man of His word.
A carpenter, a craftsman of wood.

She was proud of Him every day of His life.
How they loved one another.
Mary could always depend upon her Son Jesus.
She stood as closely to His cross as she was allowed and steadfastly looked up at Him.
His gaze was with her right up until
He breathed His last breath.

She did not fear those in authority - their seething hatred for holiness.
Their obeisance to the filth that is Satan.

The mother of God's Son was resolute.
True. Faithful. Lovely. Kind.
She was faithful to her beloved Son . . .
Satan was no match for her Son.
Satan was no match for the love of Jesus mother.
She wasn't going to forsake her precious Son.
Jesus spoke to Mary from the cross

while He was dying

already slipping toward the next life.
He just wasn't quite there yet

until He said,
"It is finished."

"For God so loved the world that He gave his only Son, that whoever believes in him shall not perish but have eternal life" (John 3:16).
"The kingdom of God is... righteousness, peace and joy in the Holy Ghost" (Romans 14:17).

Praise God. Praise the Lord. Hallelujah.
Jesus Christ is Lord. The Son of God was made manifest in the flesh.

Praise His name for ever and ever.

"Let everything that has breath praise the Lord. Praise the Lord" (Psalm 150:6).

301

We are blessed in John 14 with access to a delightful time of private sharing with Jesus and His close friends.

Jesus is doing one of His favourite things.
Telling friends how much they mean to Him.

He relished every part of this process.
He just had to make an occasion to relate how He loved each one of them.

"Whoever does not love does not know God, because God is love" (1 John 4:8).

He was a loving person.
It means everything to a loving person
when they get an opportunity to express what is in their heart.

He began where He was comfortable - speaking the Truth.
'You trust in Your Father (God) and you know where I am going,' He told them.
Jesus knew they couldn't grasp how deep their relationship was.

"And so we know and rely on the love God has for us. God is love. Whoever lives in love lives in God, and God in him. In this way, love is made complete among us so that we will have confidence on the day of judgment, because in this world we are like him. There is no fear in love. But perfect love drives out fear," (1 John 4:16-18a).
"And I pray that you, being rooted and established in love, may have power, together with all the saints, to grasp how wide and long and high and deep is the love of Christ, and to know this love that surpasses knowledge - that you may be filled to the measure of all the fullness of God" (Ephesians 3:17b-19).

Isn't it great that God's measure of our life is not equated to
'doing things right,'
'doing things really well,' or 'doing ANYTHING!'

Dear reader, it is finding out from Jesus and the bible how much He really, really loves you!

Like it says in Ephesians 3:18, 'how wide and long and high and deep is the love of Christ.'
But still, the love in His heart overflowed and with passion He just had to tell them
that they walked together on a level of trust.
He told them directly and candidly.

Thomas spoke on behalf of the others and said,
'we don't fit this paradigm, trusting God and the Son of God
as if we were friends.'

So Jesus said
because they had spent time together and they believed in Him
then they also knew Him.

Now Phillip speaks. It is too wild for him.

Jesus has power to raise the dead,
heal all who are sick
and cast out any and all devils.
Jesus who says He is the resurrection and the life is saying 'you know Me.'

He is telling them,
'our Father in heaven along with you and Me,
we all know each other and we are all friends together.'

In spite of the humble protests of the disciples, Jesus is not able to lie.
He is expressing the truth as He always did.

After Phillip speaks Jesus lovingly makes it plain to His beloved disciples.
There is tremendous pathos here.

The disciples were not aware that this would be the reason
Jesus would soon go to the cross.
After Jesus death and resurrection I am sure these words would come back to the disciple's minds.
It was spoken to them so closely to the event.

'What did Jesus say before He went to the cross'
they would consider in their heart.

Eventually they would be able to conclude that the two events were related.

The love of God and the cross of shame.

302

In John 14 Jesus was speaking to the very individuals for whom He planned to give His life.

Friends, have you seen Me?

You have seen Me!

To which they would have to say,
'yes, we have seen You.'
Dear reader, you have seen the Lord as the disciples did!
Seen Him in as much as you believe in Him
and now know Him as the Saviour of the world
and your personal Saviour too.

The disciples would agree
as surely as Jesus stood before them and spoke to them
that they have seen Him.

Each day the Holy Spirit will entreat you even as Jesus entreated His disciples.
You do trust God. You do know God. You have seen the Lord.
God calls you His friend.

303

Human intimacy, an intimacy of the soul, is a gradual process.

It begins with transparency. Being open with another person.
Letting them see a part of your heart
that no one else has access to.

Opening up to one other person is a process and delight
unlike any material blessing, personal blessing
or even an accomplishment shared in by a whole group of people.

Intimacy is about sharing in the life journey together.

Wanting to know someone
just as you would desire
for them to get to know you.

Really knowing them in their strengths and weaknesses.
Sharing this relationship brings a reward in life unlike any other.

Those with no one to love are sad.

Those who have no one to love them in return
seem sadder.

Life in a world full of people
is lonely when there is no one
to share it with.
This may be an excellent time for you to stop reading - and wait quietly
in the presence of the Lord.

You might remember people who are alone at this time.
Your God may bring you into agreement on behalf of the needs of lonely people.

He might want to touch your heart right now
if you long for someone to love you.

Go ahead.
There is lots of time.
You are so worth it.

In regard to the experience of intimacy, I now refer to its function with regard to human sexuality.

On the surface this can be hugely fulfilling
even if there is only a fractional intimacy of the human soul.

Being with another person in this way
without sharing your heart and soul
is only able to fulfill for the short term.
It may leave you feeling more alone afterward.

There are many single people who are fulfilled in their faith and emotional life
who are not married and involved in physical intimacy.

There are individuals who are married
and share a bed for years with their spouse and yearn more than anything
to share an intimacy of the soul.
In this example given by Jesus, recorded in the Bible for all time,
Jesus reverses the natural progression of intimacy for the human soul!

3. He starts with the supreme bond of 'trust'.

2. He then mentions 'knowing' each other - because they have journeyed for 3 years.

1. Finally He includes the primary ingredient of 'seeing' one another which typically occurs in the initial stages of relationship.

This information Jesus expressed is in John 14. Please read it, taking all the time you need. The Holy Spirit will most definitely speak to your heart about God's longing for relationship in this lively exchange with Jesus and His closest followers.

306

1. To see someone.

2. To get to know someone.

3. To grow in trust with someone.

Jesus turned around the order.
He said,

'you already trust Me,
you know Me,
you have seen Me.'
They responded,

'we don't really think we trust You',
'yes we do know You but not like you think,'
and, 'Ok. We have seen you.'

Isn't this the opposite progression
of intimacy and all its wonder
as it unfolds from a human perspective?

In the natural, we first 'see' the other person.
If that part checks out, then we begin an event-filled exchange over time
enabling us to get to know that special person.
Finally, in a rare instance, we progress to the stage where we 'trust' that person.
Maybe to trust them with our life if need be.
Jesus loves His followers.

Spiritually,
truthfully,

you are in the deepest relationship possible with your Lord Jesus Christ.

You are on no different footing then the disciples.
You have become completely acceptable to God through Jesus Christ.
You do not need to add anything else to incur more love or trust
in your relationship with God.
It is because your relationship has been established for you
on God's terms.
He has received you.

You belong to Him now.

"For it is by grace you have been saved, through faith - and this not from yourselves, it is the gift of God - not by works, so that no one can boast" (Ephesians 2:8-9).

307

It is the reaction from the disciples that presently draws our attention to John 14:1 - 10.

" "Do not let your hearts be troubled. Trust in God; trust also in me. In my Father's house are many rooms; if it were not so, I would have told you. I am going there to prepare a place for you. And if I go to prepare a place for you, I will come back and take you to be with me that you also may be where I am. You know the way to the place where I am going." Thomas answered, "I am the way and the truth and the life. No one comes to the Father except through me. If you really knew me, you would know my Father as well. From now on, you do know him and have seen him." Philip said, "Lord, show us the Father and that will be enough for us." Jesus answered: "Don't you know me, Philip, even after I have been among you such a long time? Anyone who has seen me has seen the Father. How can you say, 'Show us the Father'? Don't you believe that I am in the Father, and that the Father is in me? The words I say to you are not just my own. Rather, it is the Father, living in me, who is doing his work."

Understandably they are taken aback and nonplussed.

Jesus can't wait any longer!
He decides to tell them
how close they are
and what their intimacy means to Him.

He puts His heart on His sleeve without fear of being rejected.
Forevermore
there is no guess work when it comes to how much God loves you.

"There is no fear in love; but perfect love casteth out fear" (1 John 4:18a).

They react as we would.

Over and over again for the rest of your life
you will need the Holy Spirit to reassure you
just as Jesus kindly did for His dear disciples.
You will feel in your heart,
'Jesus, I don't really think I am as close to You as I could be.'

But you are!

Through no other qualifications than belonging to Jesus Christ 'by grace through faith' -
you are altogether acceptable to God through Him.
You are now on the most intimate terms with God as possible.
You are free to become friends because He has ransomed you
from darkness, sin, death and hell.

'Our relationship is one of trust,' Jesus said.

He must have been just glowing when He said that!

Jesus was laying it all on the table.
He was putting it all out there.
He was being completely vulnerable saying, 'you guys are my best friends.'

"From this time many of his disciples turned back and no longer followed him. "You do not want
to leave too, do you?" Jesus asked the Twelve. Simon Peter answered him, "Lord, to whom shall we
go? You have the words of eternal life. We believe and know that you are the Holy One of God" "
(John 6:66 - 69).

You see?
That was enough. The disciples were positioned to be in intimate relationship with God.
'We believe.'
'We know you are the Holy One of God.'

They had seen Jesus. They had gotten to know Jesus. They trusted in Jesus.

How could they know how pleasing this had become for the Most High God?
How can a mere mortal think it is possible to be in such a sweet place of acceptance
with Someone who is perfect, sinless and all powerful?
Jesus knew He would have to tell them.

He will do so with you for the rest of your life.
He will do so with the same vulnerability,
the same pleasure
as He did so long ago.

Jesus loves you so much.

You are so pleasing to Him.

He will delight in making this known to you as often as He delights to do so.

Your friendship is His greatest treasure.

"What good will it be for a man if he gains the whole world, yet forfeits his soul? Or what can a man give in exchange for his soul?" (Matthew 16:26).

Your soul is worth more than the whole world.

Nothing pleases God more than saving you and being in a friendship with you
for the rest of eternity.

308

No wonder the disciples were unable to grasp the meaning and substance
of the Lord's expression of love and friendship for each of them.

That same everlasting love reaches out to you today.

The same Jesus overflowing with the same love and intent.

Similarly, we are in need of His tender entreaty with regard to the depth of love
He is expressing day by day.

Though you may be submitted to Him with all of your being,
it remains that Jesus Christ is still God.
You are His,
but you carry His Spirit within your frail, flawed earthly body
that will one day outwardly perish.

This body of yours will die some day at the time of God's choosing.
The timing and circumstances of your death may be a complete mystery.
It often is for those left behind.

"Therefore we do not lose heart. Though outwardly we are wasting away, yet inwardly we are being renewed day by day." (2 Corinthians 4:16).
"But we have this treasure in earthen vessels, that the excellency of the power may be of God, and not of us" (2 Corinthians 4:7).

So there you go. His Holy Spirit within you is 'treasure'. This treasure resides in a vessel (container) that came from the dust. Yet the treasure, His Holy Spirit, abides forever. Because of your treasure you will most assuredly abide forever in heaven after you die. You will not 'see' death!

"Even though I walk through the valley of the shadow of death, I will fear no evil, for you are with me; your rod and your staff, they comfort me" (Psalm 23:4).
"For the perishable must clothe itself with the imperishable, and the mortal with immortality. When the perishable has been clothed with the imperishable, and the mortal with immortality, then the saying that is written will come true: "Death has been swallowed up in victory." "Where, O death, is your victory? Where, O death, is your sting?" The sting of death is sin, and the power of sin is the law. But thanks be to God! He gives us the victory through our Lord Jesus Christ. Therefore, my dear brothers, stand firm. Let nothing move you. Always give yourselves fully to the work of the Lord, because you know that your labour in the Lord is not in vain"
(1 Corinthians 15:53-58).

309

What great extremes man will go to in search of treasure during his brief time on earth.

The depths of the sea, the deepest jungles, the heat of the desert.

Digging, smashing, tunnelling the rocks beneath the ground.
Treasure hunters gain a reward.
It will one day pass away and so will they.
But have they gained eternal life with gold, antiquities, precious stones, fame and fortune?

Does being mentioned in a magazine resolve the issue of pain suffered through childhood?

Does fleeting fame smooth over a besetting sin such as adultery, alcoholism,
lying, cheating
or stealing?

Will more and more wealth cover over and absolve guilt or shame?

Has the sacrifice to gain temporary treasures brought peace to the home,
unity and faithfulness in the marriage and a close and healthy bond
with the children?
Is death no longer something to fear? Have riches provided an understanding of what happens
in the afterlife and where they are going on the other side?

Do the treasures surround their soul with an everlasting love and the knowledge
that they themselves are bought with a price and are precious beyond *all* earthly treasure?

"Do you not know that your body is a temple of the Holy Spirit, who is in you, whom you have received from God? You are not your own; you were bought at a price. Therefore honour God with your body" (1 Corinthians 6:19-20).

Please,
let us pray for the lost that they may turn to Jesus
and escape their destiny of an eternity in hell.

310

The wounded in spirit and soul.

Those who once followed our Lord and Saviour but lost their way perhaps due to sin.

The many sincere believers deeply hurt by the church.

In the last days your greatest enemies
will be the members of your own household.
This may be family members,
or church people - members of the house of God.

"Whoever acknowledges me before men, I will also acknowledge him before my Father in heaven. But whoever disowns me before men, I will disown him before my Father in heaven. "Do not suppose that I have come to bring peace to the earth. I did not come to bring peace, but a sword. For I have come to turn " 'a man against his father, a daughter against her mother, a daughter-in-law against her mother-in-law - a man's enemies will be the members of his own household.' "Anyone who loves his father or mother more than me is not worthy of me; anyone who loves his son or daughter more than me is not worthy of me; and anyone who does not take his cross and follow me is not worthy of me. Whoever finds his life will lose it, and whoever loses his life for my sake will find it" (Matthew 10:32-39).

Let us pray for all of the 'members of our household' with a complete surrender
of our heart unto Jesus Christ.

Ask for wisdom.

Ask to be filled with His love for you and His love for others.

311

The disciples were fully aware that Jesus was God.

They saw Jesus do miracles, signs and wonders.

"Believe me when I say that I am in the Father and the Father is in me; or at least believe on the evidence of the miracles themselves" (John 14:11).
"In the beginning was the Word, and the Word was with God, and the Word was God" (John 1:1).

Jesus was God walking around right in their midst.
No bodyguards, press agents or head office.

He meant for people to know He was in the Father
through His teaching and truthful proclamation.
If this was not sufficient He told them to believe
on the basis of His miracles.

With His proclamations and miracles
people would be able to conclude He was God in the flesh.
Jesus left no hindrance to believing in Him.

"Jesus answered, "I am the way and the truth and the life. No one comes to the Father except through me" (John 14:6).

He wanted people to know He was God.

"I and the Father are One." Again the Jews picked up stones to stone him, but Jesus said to them, "I have shown you many great miracles from the Father. For which of these do you stone me?" "We are not stoning you for any of these," replied the Jews, "but for blasphemy, because you, a mere man, claim to be God" (John 10:31-33).

The people who listened got the message loud and clear. 'This guy is saying he is God!'

For some it was good news.

312

Jesus answered: "Don't you know me, Philip, even after I have been among you such a long time? **Anyone** who has seen me has seen the Father. How can you say, 'Show us the Father?' (John 14:9).

Isn't that a beautiful thing to say?

Jesus said, 'anyone'.
Jesus didn't specify, 'if you are a theologian you have seen the Father.'

Jesus also didn't say,
if you are on the high enough spiritual level.
If you come from the correct religious upbringing.
Have the right family name.
If you prove yourself to your spiritual leader.
If you have had enough inner healing.
If you pray the right way 'in Jesus name'.
If you believe key scriptures.

If you get your healing.
If you are first delivered from demons.
If you are not from an abusive background.
Have taken time to be trained.
Have permission from your pastor or spiritual leader.
Belong to the 'right' church.
Belong to the only church that will go to heaven.
Pledge allegiance to an earthly institution.
Follow religious instructions.
Get approval from head office somewhere.

There are so many of these hellish,
demonic,
religious charades.

God came to set people free. People like the thief on the cross.

If anything else were needed for the thief to be saved then he would have missed out.
But you and I both know the thief is now in paradise.
Can I give you some personal guidance
in regard to all of these bondage making instructions?
If you are being told, no, forced to accept any of the warnings listed above,
walk away from the person who is foisting them on you.
Jesus said, 'whosoever will may come.'
No one is exempt from experiencing Jesus first hand.

You will never find Jesus where any of these conditions are being flimflammed on those who would
know the Lord. If you are a leader who has never been intimate with God then it is time
to humble yourself - and come to Jesus.

A leader who knows Jesus puts no obstacle in front of the people.

The Holy Spirit will have them invite people to freely come to Jesus.
Just like Jesus demonstrated in the example of allowing the children
to freely approach and sit on His lap.
Jesus was showing that He has no conditions that need to be met
in order to have a heart to heart,
one on one encounter with Him.

Jesus said 'anyone' who sees Him has seen the Father
and He meant 'anyone.'

'Anyone who has seen Me.'

Anyone.

Anyone.
Anyone.
Anyone.
Anyone.

Anyone who believes in Jesus shall see God.

"There is neither Jew nor Greek, slave nor free, male nor female, for you are all one in Christ Jesus" (Galatians 3:28).

313

Jesus is reaching out to you dear reader.

Seeing Jesus begins with being born again.
Being recreated inwardly through the forgiveness of sins.
The bible uses the term 'washing and rebirth'.
You will be changed from the inside out.

"But when the kindness and love of God our Saviour appeared, he saved us, not because of righteous things we had done, but because of his mercy. He saved us through the washing of rebirth and renewal by the Holy Spirit, so that, having been justified by his grace, we might become heirs having the hope of eternal life" (Titus 3:4-8).

Receive Him! Receive Him and be born again!

Receive Him today and know that your home will be in heaven
for all eternity in the loving presence of God.
He is all glory, majesty, honour, power and praise.

'Anyone' means 'you' dear reader.

You are able to see, you are able to believe and you are able to follow Him.

314

"Suddenly Jesus met them. "Greetings," he said. They came to him, clasped his feet and worshiped him" (Matthew 29:9).

Oh yes, people were getting the message!

They believed in Jesus Christ. They accepted His message!

They could not help but express their love to Him.

He was God walking in their midst
and they got right down in front of everyone and worshipped Him.
They did not need to get permission from any other person to do so.

They came to Him, and in order to clasp His feet with their hands
they would have to bow low to the ground before Him.

Then the verse says,
'they worshiped Him.'
Oh yes.
They took hold of the feet of God
and worshiped Him right there in public.

No one was turned away. Whoever wanted to worship bowed down and did so.

I want you to know that I worship God too. I worship Jesus Christ my Saviour.
He has never turned away my worship
It occurs to me
I am worthy through His love and grace for me.

Jesus was busy letting people know that 'anyone' who has seen Him has seen the Father.
Those who hated Jesus were busy telling people it is not that easy.

Friend, it is that easy.
Don't ever let anyone get between you and the Lord
when you offer your worship
or your obedience to the leading of God's Holy Spirit.

Jesus welcomed those newly saved people.
There is no 'better' more 'advanced' way to love the Lord!
There are no levels. Man has made 'the levels' up.
Man stepping between you and your Jesus.

You get alone.
Spend time with Jesus. Bring your bible. A journal will also come in handy.
What He says is more important
than a thousand
who would tell you otherwise.

You can and you will fulfill the plan of God in your life.

"Let God be true, and every man a liar" (Romans 3:4b).
"Therefore he is able to save completely those who come to God through him, because he always lives to intercede for them" (Hebrews 7:25).

What do you worship dear reader?

Did you know that you can worship God?

You,
can worship the Lord Jesus Christ.

When you worship something or someone you make it the center of your universe.
It becomes the focus of your thoughts, finances, time and ambition.
It is possible to miss this fact if you yourself
are the center of your universe.

You would be surprised at what people worship!

Humbling yourself to Jesus Christ is true spiritual worship.
Sitting quietly in His presence is also a form of worship.
Singing to Him and even raising up your hands in holy surrender unto Him
is also true spiritual worship.
Sometimes it seems there is nothing else to do but to lay face down on the ground
in His Holy, awesome presence.
Generally this activity is expressed in your own, personal prayer time with Jesus.

When we are 'still' before the Lord - this is also a place of true spiritual worship.

"Be still, and know that I am God;" (Psalm 46:10a).
"Yet the time is coming and has now come when the true worshipers will worship the Father in spirit and truth, for they are the kind of worshipers the Father seeks. God is spirit, and his worshipers <u>must worship in spirit and in truth</u>" (John 4:23-24).

He will guide you,
help you in your expression of worship unto Him.
It says, 'His worshipers <u>must</u> worship.' You can start by telling Him thank you Jesus.
Praise you Jesus.

I love you, Jesus.

"give thanks in all circumstances, for this is God's will for you in Christ Jesus"
(1 Thessalonians 5:18).

Nothing can stop you from doing God's perfect will if you want to follow Jesus.

If you are following Jesus it means He will work everything out.

Even when things appear to be going wrong
God is still on your side.
At the immediate time it is just not possible to see His master plan
from His perfect point of view.

He will work things out for your good.
In time you will see.

"And we know that in all things God works for the good of those who love him, who have been called according to his purpose" (Romans 8:28).

One thing that is His will is to give thanks unto Him all the time.
In all circumstances.
Since the bible says it is God's will for you
then you will be able to do it!
At first this practice will feel awkward.
You will wonder if it is a good idea.

It is both faith affirming and warfare in the spiritual realm so you will be accomplishing a number of things at the same time.

"Now what I am commanding you today is not too difficult for you or beyond your reach" (Deuteronomy 30:11).

317

It is consistent with your faith in God when disaster happens to offer thanks to Him
for still being in control of all things.

Of course, because you are still in your earthen body, you initially feel shaken and dishevelled
in a disaster.
God understands this
and He also knows your heart.

I mean to offer thanks unto God
once you get your wits about you again
and are thinking clearly.
Your God quietly watches
and is greatly glorified
when you affirm with your heart
that He remains in complete control.

He is delighted to receive from you your offering of thanksgiving.
You are bringing great damage to the devil and the forces
that would bring disaster.
By rising up and proclaiming the truth and proclaiming your love for God
you are crushing the enemy's ability to carry out his plans
to bring further trouble
through his actions.

One of the things our family does is pray with compassion
if we see a vehicle wreck. Covering that situation with the blood of Jesus.
Praying for everything to work out for good for all involved.
We thank God by faith that He has the power to turn this for good.
The people involved have no idea that this is happening as we drive by.
They are loved by God even though they have been in an accident.
A gift of thanksgiving to God is a lethal form of spiritual warfare.

Instead of taking advantage in a difficult situation, the unseen forces of evil are overcome
and have to flee from you as you thank, worship and praise God.

318

Nothing can stop you from praising God.

No situation will ever be hidden from God's sight, for His eye is always upon you.

"For the eyes of the Lord are on the righteous and his ears are attentive to their prayer, but the face of the Lord is against those who do evil" (1 Peter 3:12).
"He does not take his eyes off the righteous; he enthrones them with kings and exalts them forever" (Job 36:7).
"In the Lord I take refuge. How then can you say to me: "Flee like a bird to your mountain. For look, the wicked bend their bows; they set their arrows against the strings to shoot from the shadows at the upright in heart. When the foundations are being destroyed, what can the righteous do?" The Lord is in his holy temple; the Lord is on his heavenly throne. He observes the sons of men; his eyes examine them. The Lord examines the righteous, but the wicked and those who love violence his soul hates. On the wicked he will rain fiery coals and burning sulphur; a scorching wind will be their lot. For the Lord is righteous, he loves justice; upright men will see his face" (Psalm 11).

No matter what befalls you it cannot keep you from seeing the face of God!

"You will seek me and find me when you seek me with all your heart. I will be found by you,' declares the Lord," (Jeremiah 29:13-14a).

As a follower of Jesus you have 'crossed over' and now live in a higher reality
than those without the Holy Spirit.

'I tell you the truth, whoever hears my word and believes him who sent me has eternal life and will
not be condemned; he has crossed over from death to life' (John 5:24).
"We know that we have passed from death to life, because we love our brothers. Anyone who does
not love remains in death" (1 John 3:14).

You belong to Jesus.

Now and forever.

You are a temple of God because His Holy Spirit lives inside of you.
You are able to be governed by the words of the bible.

'A new command I give you: Love one another. As I have loved you, so you must love one another.
By this all men will know that you are my disciples, if you love one another' (John 13:34-35).

With the living words of the bible the Holy Spirit enables you
to purposefully respond to the occurrences of life.

For instance, even if it doesn't appear to be a situation in which you can give thanks to God,
there is mighty power when you thank Him.
That is why God says to give thanks at all times!

These are living words because in fact,
Jesus said He was the 'word made flesh.'
Jesus is the Word.

"The Word became flesh and made his dwelling among us. We have seen his glory, the glory of the
One and Only, who came from the Father, full of grace and truth" (John 1:14).
"In the beginning was the Word, and the Word was with God, and the Word was God" (John 1:1).
To belong to Jesus for evermore means you never need to give up.
You never need to respond to your circumstances
as if they will be your undoing.
This means we can still offer thanks to God
no matter what is happening.

Why is this?

God is all powerful.

He can take any situation and turn it for good.

"And we know that in all things God works for the good of those who love him, who have been called according to his purpose" (Romans 8:28).

320

Jesus has promised He will never put you in a situation beyond your ability to cope.

"No temptation has seized you except what is common to man. And God is faithful; he will not let you be tempted beyond what you can bear. But when you are tempted, he will also provide a way out so that you can stand up under it" (1 Corinthians 10:13).

Jesus -

not an ordinary person or organization
has given you this comforting reassurance.

You have to ask yourself Dear Reader, are you placing your trust anywhere else?
A 'patriarch' type of person in your denomination?
The writings unique to your group?
The size and strength and history of your group?
Anywhere else?

Only precious Jesus has sold out completely for you.
He has already promised that He will never
put you in a situation too great for you to bear.

Do not allow anyone else to get between you and Jesus.
No organization has the power to regulate all of your life's activities and no person
nor organization can even begin to turn everything for good for you and your loved ones.

Only Jesus.
"Trust in the Lord with all your heart and lean not on your own understanding; in all your ways acknowledge him, and he will make your paths straight" (Proverbs 3:5-6).

321

God's help comes directly to you through Jesus Christ.

"God is our refuge and strength, an ever-present help in trouble" (Psalm 46:1).

Your help does not need to pass through an administrative process here on earth.

It does not need to be approved by someone else.
This is about your relationship with Jesus.
He will work things out with you.

"for it is God who works in you to will and to act according to his good purpose" (Philippians 2:13).
"Commit your way to the Lord; trust in him and he will do this: He will make your righteousness
shine like the dawn, the justice of your cause like the noonday sun. Be still before the Lord and
wait patiently for him; do not fret when men succeed in their ways, when they carry out their
wicked schemes" (Psalm 37:5-7).

322

Jesus can't lie.

He said, "I am the truth." John 14:6.

Thankfully, He freely cares for you
intimately and personally.

You are not beholden
to an organization.

Far be it from anyone to worship,
bow the knee
or glorify
anything that reflects the efforts or artefacts of man.

It is the Person living inside of you (the Holy Spirit)
that accomplishes the will and good pleasure of God.

You need to walk intimately with a 'Person' in order
to do the will of God in your life.

"None of the rulers of this age understood it, for if they had, they would not have crucified the
Lord of glory. However, as it is written: "No eye has seen, no ear has heard, no mind has conceived
what God has prepared for those who love him" - but God has revealed it to us by his Spirit. The
Spirit searches all things, even the deep things of God. For who among men knows the thoughts of
a man except the man's spirit within him? In the same way no one knows the thoughts of God
except the Spirit of God. We have not received the spirit of the world but the Spirit who is from
God, that we may understand what God has freely given us" (1 Corinthians 2:8-12).

Dear reader, in the midst of your calamity,
know that your way through it all
is 'freely given' directly unto you.

Oh yes, Jesus is the Way.

Hallelujah!

323

Critical moments in life will happen from time to time.

Times that try you, test you - make you feel so very small.
You will be alone, or feel alone.
Now it will be up to Jesus and you.
Do not fear,
for it is Jesus and you.

Do you know how big your Jesus is at a time like this?

"Your love, O LORD, reaches to the heavens, your faithfulness to the skies" (Psalm 36:5).

How far, how wide, how high
how vast is the very sky - the very heavens themselves!
His love and faithfulness alone
fills all of this and more. Dear reader, I confess, I am boasting in the Lord Jesus Christ!
"God fulfills His purpose for me."

Again, in Psalm 57:2-3. "I cry out to God Most High, to God, who fulfills his purpose for me. He sends from heaven and saves me, rebuking those who hotly pursue me; God sends his love and his faithfulness."

324

When you conclude that you are all alone in your struggle that is only how it seems.

There are angels all around you!

There are other followers of Jesus all over the world
commissioned by God Himself to pray for you.
And, there is the great God Himself.

"Keep your lives free from the love of money and be content with what you have, because God has said, "Never will I leave you; never will I forsake you" (Hebrews 13:5).
"The angel of the Lord encamps around those who fear him, and he delivers them" (Psalm 34:7).

Critical times can come through setbacks.

"That is why, for Christ's sake, I delight in weaknesses, in insults, in hardships, in persecutions, in difficulties. For when I am weak, then I am strong" (2 Corinthians 12:10).

The follower of Jesus will often see setback.

The follower of Jesus will have occasions where things don't work as expected.

The follower of Jesus is at times very weak.
Broken like a pot of clay
though held in the hand of love eternal.

"This is the word that came to Jeremiah from the Lord: "Go down to the potter's house, and there I will give you my message." So I went down to the potter's house, and I saw him working at the wheel. But the pot he was shaping from the clay was marred in his hands; so the potter formed it into another pot, shaping it as seemed best to him. Then the word of the Lord came to me: "O house of Israel, can I not do with you as this potter does?" declares the Lord. "Like clay in the hand of the potter, so are you in my hand, O house of Israel" (Jeremiah 18:1-6).

Oh the mercy.
Oh the sweet loving-kindness.

To be in the hand of the Master potter!

To have life's hardships fit us for God's deepest love,
His deeper embrace.

There are no levels to His love
however in those deep valleys the wonder of His love is staggering.
He is up to any challenge
and will resolutely be there
sharing with you in your suffering.

"Praise be to the God and Father of our Lord Jesus Christ, the Father of compassion and the God of all comfort, who comforts us in all our troubles, so that we can comfort those in any trouble with the comfort we ourselves have received from God" (2 Corinthians 1:3-5).

He is great and greatly to be praised for His mysteries are altogether wonderful.

So great, so great are His benevolent thoughts toward you all the time!

Sometimes it comes down to Jesus and you at tough times of decision making.

After seeking the counsel of trusted friends you many still be left with a few good options.

"Make plans by seeking advice; if you wage war, obtain guidance" (Proverbs 20:18).
"for waging war you need guidance, and for victory many advisers" (Proverbs 24:6).

For many, the decision to marry is an intense process.

This is in keeping with the impact marriage brings in life.

Marrying the right person is the most significant step you will ever take
once you have accepted Christ - aside from choosing
whether you will spend time with Jesus each day.

'Martha, Martha,' the Lord answered, 'you are worried and upset about many things, but only one
thing is needed. Mary has chosen what is better, and it will not be taken away from her'
(Luke 10:41).

1. Only one thing is needed.
Spending personal time with Jesus in order to listen for His precious, life sustaining word.

"She had a sister called Mary, who sat at the Lord's feet listening to what he said" (Luke 10:39).

2. It is a decision left to each one who believes in Jesus.
Whether to know about Him, or get to know Him.

3. The rewards, intimacy and richness of fellowship can never be taken away.
Oh the joy in this reality!

"Why spend money on what is not bread, and your labour on what does not satisfy? Listen, listen
to me, and eat what is good, and your soul will delight in the richest of fare" (Isaiah 55:2).

327

When you take a stand for what is right it can be a time of great pressure.

"We do not want you to be uninformed, brothers, about the hardships we suffered in the province of Asia. We were under great pressure, far beyond our ability to endure, so that we despaired even of life. Indeed, in our hearts we felt the sentence of death. But this happened that we might not rely on ourselves but on God, who raises the dead. He has delivered us from such a deadly peril, and he will deliver us. On him we have set our hope that he will continue to deliver us, as you help us by your prayers. Then many will give thanks on our behalf for the gracious favour granted us in answer to the prayers of many" (2 Corinthians 1:8-10).

There will be occasions when it isn't enough to know what others would do, but what does God want you to do?

328

Thanksgiving and worship is part of the experience of communing with your Jesus.

You are not forced to be thankful.

You are not forced to be worshipful.

An intimate relationship flourishes
with expressions of the heart
offered one to another.

The appreciation and thankfulness of all they share - there is joy in the expression of love.

Is a belief system akin to true spiritual worship?
A belief system is useful but does not equate to intimacy with God.

"You believe that there is one God. Good! Even the demons believe that - and shudder"
(James 2:19).

Possessing a systematic theology
is not akin to actually taking the step
to share intimate personal time
alone with Jesus Christ.
Neither is advanced theological study
or great prowess of the mind
akin to friendship with God.

"may have power, <u>together with all the saints</u>, to grasp how wide and long and high and deep is the love of Christ, and <u>to know this love that surpasses knowledge</u> - that you may be filled to the measure of all the fullness of God" (Ephesians 3:18-19).

Oh dear reader, it is the moving closer together of two hearts.

The expressions of love,
neediness,
vulnerability
and personal feelings.
There isn't an academic setting necessary
when it comes to intimacy.

God is,
and He lives in you.
God inhabits His temple.

329

He sees all that you do.

He is always attentive to the cry of your heart.

Jesus has set you free!

"So if the Son sets you free, you will be free indeed" (John 8:36).

You will be able to walk with Him
and He will take care of you always.

Should you abandon yourself to a Holy God
in a cry for help?
In thanksgiving or in praise?
Indeed!

Surrender to the Holy Spirit.
Respond humbly with freedom to your inner response
to His presence and loving-kindness.

It is only love that binds your hearts together for all eternity.
He has loved you with an everlasting love.
He loves you now and forever.

"The Lord appeared to us in the past, saying: "I have loved you with an everlasting love; I have drawn you with loving-kindness" (Jeremiah 31:3).

Indeed dear reader. Abandon yourself to the Lord.
Extol Him.
Praise Him.
Know this,
in your affliction He has drawn very near unto you.
He will hear the cry of your heart.

"I will extol the Lord at all times; his praise will always be on my lips. My soul will boast in the Lord; let the afflicted hear and rejoice. Glorify the Lord with me; let us exalt his name together. I sought the Lord, and he answered me; he delivered me from all my fears" (Psalms 34:1-4).
"The righteous cry out, and the Lord hears them; he delivers them from all their troubles. The Lord is close to the broken-hearted and saves those who are crushed in spirit" (Psalm 34:17-18).
"The eyes of the Lord are on the righteous and his ears are attentive to their cry; the face of the Lord is against those who do evil, to cut off the memory of them from the earth. The righteous cry out, and the Lord hears them; he delivers them from all their troubles. The Lord is close to the broken-hearted and saves those who are crushed in spirit. A righteous man may have many troubles, but the Lord delivers him from them all;" (Psalm 34:15-19).

330

So precious unto Him are the crushed.
Those He has led into hardship.

"Fear not, for I have redeemed you; I have summoned you by name; you are mine. When you pass through the waters, I will be with you; and when you pass through the rivers, they well not sweep over you. When you walk through the fire, you will not be burned; the flames will not set you ablaze" (Isaiah 43:1b-2).
"Yet, O Lord, you are our Father. We are the clay, you are the potter; we are all the work of your hand" (Isaiah 64:8).

So precious to Him are those who steadfastly turn to Him
and hide away in His safety.
Taking refuge though so weak within.
Running to sweet fellowship whatever befalls them.

"Therefore let everyone who is godly pray to you while you may be found; surely when the mighty waters rise, they will not reach him. You are my hiding place; you will protect me from trouble and surround me with songs of deliverance" (Psalm 32:6-7).

The Lord is faithful.

He is faithful beyond all that is faithful, never to leave nor forsake you.

Oh Reader! Read these holy scriptures and inwardly rejoice!
Faithful is the One who calls you,

ever faithful.

"May God himself, the God of peace, sanctify you through and through. May your whole spirit, soul and body be kept blameless at the coming of our Lord Jesus Christ. The one who calls you is faithful and he will do it" (1 Thessalonians 5:23-24).

What will God do in your life, ultimately?

"To him who is able to keep you from falling and to present you before his glorious presence without fault and with great joy" (Jude 1:24).

He is able!
It is all about His saving and keeping power.
Take joy in this great Saving God, our Lord Jesus Christ.

Rejoice, for the whole responsibility for presenting
you as 'blameless' is already safely hidden in Christ.

"Since, then, you have been raised with Christ, set your hearts on things above, where Christ is seated at the right hand of God. Set your minds on things above, not on earthly things. For you died, and your life is now hidden with Christ in God" (Colossians 3:1-3).

Go ahead and set your heart on things above, with Christ.
Do not fear if you are in His care.

How faithful He is to keep you unto the end.

Do you need the Lord to take hold of your heart today dear reader?

Is your need of intimacy with Him so great that you simply say, "Jesus please love me."

May you be comforted today in knowing
it is for this reason He has called you.

"But God <u>chose the foolish things of the world</u> to shame the wise; God <u>chose the weak things of the world</u> to shame the strong. <u>He chose the lowly things</u> of this world <u>and the despised things</u> - and the things that are not - to nullify the things that are, so that no one may boast before him" (1 Corinthians 1: 27-28).

You have been chosen
on purpose -
by God!

You did not have to pass a test, measure up to some standard or do better
when compared to others.

"But God demonstrates his own love for us in this: While we were still sinners, Christ died for us" (Romans 5:8).

333

It is not because you can do great things that God is impressed with you.

God does not need to be impressed.

It is not because you have an angle on religion others don't have.
His own precious Son is 'the Way, the Truth and the Life'.

"Then Jesus came to them and said, "All authority in heaven and on earth has been given to Me" (Matthew 28:18).

God doesn't need new ideas about religion.

It is all because God has chosen you dear reader.
And you need Him
more than anything else on earth.
He wants to love you
with all the love you can possibly hold.
He wants to pour His love into you until it overflows.

He has more love than you will ever be able to fathom in this lifetime.
In fact, God loves the whole world.

He wants to share that love with you.

He is the potter and you are the clay.

Yet your life at times is so complex.

So many difficulties, insurmountable obstacles
and so much heartache.
If not in your own life, then in other people's lives and world around you.

From His perspective looking after you
is a task that is powerful, hopeful,
victorious, creative,
intimate, personal and endearing.

God is the potter.
He is your potter.
A precious soul in His hand
is like clay moulded on His potters wheel.

The entire process is His to perform.

He selects the clay.
He places it on the wheel.
He moulds it to specification.
He never makes a mistake with the final outcome!

There will never be any other hand upon you.
Only His hand dear reader.

"Unless the Lord builds the house, its builders labour in vain" (Psalm 127:1a).

When you deny yourself to take up your cross, when your surrender to Christ is absolute
then you have only one Person to build your life. If your surrender is not absolute and you do not
completely deny yourself when taking up your cross then you will automatically have the influence
and input of many builders.
You will only amount to the influence of the strongest prevailing 'winds' at the time.

"Then we will no longer be infants, tossed back and forth by the waves, and blown here and there
by every wind of teaching and by the cunning and craftiness of men in their deceitful scheming"
(Ephesians 4:14).

Glory, glory, glory!

"being confident of this, that he who began a good work in you will carry it on to completion until the day of Christ Jesus" (Philippians 1:6).

Jesus has started a good work in you.

He will complete it.

335

With skill and creativity you are shaped.

How long does a potter work on a cherished vessel?

All day?
Half a day?
The process is deftly and masterfully completed with utmost care and precision.
It is not a long process once it begins.
Your life will unfold from beginning to end like a wisp of smoke.
So does the span of time unfold on the Holy, Omnipotent Potter's wheel.

"What is your life? You are a mist that appears for a little while and then vanishes" (James 4:14b).

How good it is to know that the One who started the work
will take ownership of the work
right up until it is completed.
His intent when you were chosen is to finish what He started.

And He will.

"Greater love has no one than this, that he lay down his life for his friends" (John 15:13).

336

"I tell you the truth, unless a kernel of wheat falls to the ground and dies, it remains only a single seed. But if it dies, it produces many seeds" (John 12:24).

How does this verse involve you dear reader?

God has given another simple example, this time taken from nature.
To help understand the challenges encountered while in His will, He directs your attention
to a seed. It is natural for a seed to follow the path described in John 12:24.

"I tell you the truth, unless a kernel of wheat falls to the ground and dies, it remains only a single seed. But if it dies, it produces many seeds."

So it is for a born again believer.
The seed is healthy and full of life
yet initially it abides alone.
There is purpose for the seed though it is solitary by nature.

There is no indication present that it will move beyond a solitary existence.

Those held in the safety of God's grasp resemble the living seed.
To be in God's hand is to live and yet die.
A seed belonging to God.
In the care of God alone.

"I have been crucified with Christ, and I no longer live, but Christ lives in me. The life I now live in the body, I live by faith in the Son of God, who loved me and gave himself for me" (Galatians 2:20).

In the verse describing the life of the seed it says,
'if a kernel of wheat falls to the ground and dies it produces many seeds.'

Have you ever wondered why it seems you are driven to seek the Lord day by day?

One reason is because, like the seed, you are alive
yet in a process of the Holy Spirit that brings a death to self.
This is a term we have not used until now.
'Death to self.'

To continually surrender to God saying, 'not my will but thy will be done O Lord,'
means you have abandoned all other hope but for God alone.
It means you are His servant being used to build His kingdom.
You are no longer functional or appropriate for use by the world, the flesh or the devil.
Your only purpose is 'hidden'.

"For you died, and your life is now hidden with Christ in God" (Colossians 3:3).

Dear reader, though you be a good person,
your life is not found in good works you offer to God.
It is not found by attending a church as if you are offering a service to God.

Anything that is done in Jesus name must spring forth as a consequence of 'having been with Jesus.'

There is a place of abiding in the Lord.
There is a fellowship made possible
because Jesus surrendered His life to a horrible death.

The place of intimate relationship with God is your hiding place.

You are free to find all that you need in that place
and along with your needs,
your life as well.

"For you died, and your life is now hidden with Christ in God" (Colossians 3:3).

Your life is hidden in your deep, intimate fellowship with Christ Jesus.

You participate in a transforming process in which God's will
is being done on earth as it is in heaven.

This is the truest meaning of life.

To be in one accord with the Almighty.

337

In your fellowship with the Lord Jesus you are whole and complete.

My goodness, He accepts you as you are!

It doesn't matter what your background is
or even if other people think you are 'all screwed up'!
Oh the comfort and confidence He instils in your heart!
You, are His dear love.

I have never once felt condemned while in His presence!
And I am far from a perfect human being!
Neither has He ever left me with the impression that it is a struggle for Him
to spend time with me
instead of my other brothers and sisters in the Lord.
You know what?
He has always made me feel that it is the highlight of His day
just to be with me.

I know that Jesus will make you feel that way too!

He loves you so much!

Like I said,
the wonder of it
is that I really don't have any reason
to deserve His great fellowship!
That's just the way He is.

God is awesome! I'm so glad He loves me.
Jesus will love you too,
just the way you are.
He is the most wonderful
the most precious and kind
friend you will ever have.

Jesus is your best friend in life and in death. To have God in your life is the greatest of all blessings.
Tell this to a follower of Jesus that is in prison or in a country where Christians are openly
persecuted. They will agree that they lack nothing because of Jesus and His love for them.

They have fulfillment because they dine with Jesus at the table of His fellowship
as often as they choose.
It is a feast.
Jesus asks for us to do the same.

"You prepare a table before me in the presence of my enemies" (Psalm 23:5a).

They have companionship. He furnishes them with His everlasting love.
With His love for them they also receive the same assurance Jesus gave
to the thief on the cross, 'this day you shall be with Me in paradise.'

"Jesus answered him, "Truly I tell you, today you will be with me in paradise" (Luke 23:43).

The suffering follower of Jesus
understands a little more of the meaning of His statement.

If your walk with Jesus means you go to church faithfully without spending time with Him
you won't understand the watershed revelation
in what Jesus said before He died on the cross.

We are going to look into this truth now, for the benefit of those who are yet to believe in the Lord
and for those who never spend time with Jesus.

Notice Jesus didn't say to the thief,
'I'm sorry. You will only have a few hours. Too bad you could only be saved for a short time.
But you will end up going to paradise with Me.'
He didn't say,
'It's too bad you won't have a lot of time to serve Me.'
Jesus didn't mention that the thief on the cross would be at a disadvantage in any way.

That is because of who Jesus is.
The thief who believed just before death was going to receive the goal of his faith.
The salvation of his soul.
Jesus said to him, 'you will be with Me.'

There you go! To be with Jesus for eternity is the real goal of our faith!

"for you are receiving the goal of your faith, the salvation of your souls" (1 Peter 1:9).

The love of the Lord Jesus,
the gift of His friendship - is infinitely beyond being compared to anything.
To be with Jesus, to benefit from the fruit of His fellowship, this is life.

It is the only thing worth living for.

338

His love offered freely is called grace.

God freely gives His grace
and thereby bestows the greatest of all riches
to anybody who believes in Him.

"For it is by grace you have been saved, through faith - and this is not from yourselves, it is the gift
of God - not by works, so that no one can boast" (Ephesians 2:8-9).

Would there be any disadvantage
in any possible way
if you are a follower of Jesus?
No.

Once you accept Jesus you are now in the singularly most important relationship
you will ever have in this life. Relationship is what you have been saved to.

That is why accepting Jesus on your death bed is awesome.

That is why accepting Jesus at any time is awesome.

If you believe in Jesus already,
let the Lord just love you.
Accept what He has done for you. Know that if you had only an hour left to live,
you would still benefit fully from the sacrifice He made for you on the cross.

From Jesus' perspective, with great excitement and anticipation He would look at you and say,
'this day you will be with Me in paradise.'

As if there was no one else in the entire world He came to save.

There is nothing to stop you from following Jesus.

"Enter through the narrow gate. For wide is the gate and broad is the road that leads to destruction, and many enter through it. But small is the gate and narrow the road that leads to life, and only a few find it" (Matthew 7:13-14).

Once you believe and are transformed into a temple of the Holy Ghost,
take time to marvel at the wonder of God's love for you.

Take a lot of time to marvel at the wonder of God's love for you.
This is the most important thing in your life.
You are now on a path
that one day brings you to heaven.

Unlike a ticket to board a train or bus or plane to get to a location,
getting to heaven is a 'process'. The bible says it is like running a race.
Thankfully the process is not about an individual getting 'better and better'.
There are no levels in this relationship. It is all about being in the care of the Shepherd.

No one thinks of sheep this way.
God doesn't think of you this way.

It is a process that takes place when we choose to be close to our Shepherd.
Staying closely to the Shepherd does not produce a better sheep.
It just makes a difference
in the life of that one sheep.

The sheep would simply say,
'I would rather be right here beside our Shepherd, than standing over there.'
There really wouldn't be anything else to say about it.

To say, 'I am better than the other sheep' or 'at a deeper level than the other sheep'
would not apply. That would be boasting. It would not reflect the humble heart in a servant
of God and man. It would reflect the lifestyle of someone who has set religious demands upon
themselves and upon others and is meeting these 'religious obstacles' in their own strength.

They are a tremendous hindrance to the work being done on earth as it is in heaven.

"So the last will be first, and the first will be last" (Matthew 20:16).

Being near the Shepherd isn't anything we have done.

It is just the way it is.

How could a sheep think they are better or superior because of where they stand?
They are still the same sheep. Take them away from their Shepherd
and they would be like all the other sheep.
The only difference is where they are standing.

The Shepherd is the One who makes the difference.

It is not really necessary to look up to someone who lives near the Shepherd.
Like everyone else, they do deserve
lots and lots of love.

"Let no debt remain outstanding, except the continuing debt to love one another, for he who loves
his fellowman has fulfilled the law" (Romans 13:8).

Some sheep feel they really need to be looked up to.
They tend to say just enough
in just the right way
to get you a little more excited with them

than in your Shepherd.

Over a length of time a slight change takes place inside of you.
It takes time for them to change you, so you won't notice it.
If you listen to enough of what this sheep says
you will no longer esteem the voice of your Shepherd as you once did.
Even though the Shepherd's voice is the only voice you should be listening to.

Can you see how silly that is?

Look up to the Shepherd. Fix your eyes firmly upon Him
and not upon a mere patriarch or matriarch.
Why get excited about another sheep?
Come close to the Shepherd yourself!
Share in that love.
Let's just all fix our eyes on Jesus.

A word for what happens in this process
is 'relationship'.

"And you also were included in Christ when you heard the word of truth, the gospel of your salvation. Having believed, you were marked in him with a seal, the promised Holy Spirit, who is a deposit guaranteeing our inheritance until the redemption of those who are God's possession - to the praise of his glory" (Ephesians 1:13-14).

"But we all, with open face beholding as in a glass the glory of the Lord, are changed into the same image from glory to glory, even as by the Spirit of the Lord"
(2 Corinthians 3:18 King James Version).

"I lift up my eyes to you, to you whose throne is in heaven. As the eyes of slaves look to the hand of their master, as the eyes of a maid look to the hand of her mistress, so our eyes look to the Lord our God, till he shows us his mercy" (Psalm 123:1-2 New International Version).

341

Assurance of success in your journey is not found in this world.

It is not the result of belonging to the right group.

It is not because you have studied hard enough
or pleased the correct leadership.
It isn't even because you say you believe in God.

"You believe that there is one God. Good! Even the demons believe that - and shudder"
(James 2:19).

You are saved because of your intimate relationship with the person who comes to live within you.
That is the guarantee.
The Holy Spirit is a deposit. He is sent to live within you as your assurance that you belong to God.

"And you also were included in Christ when you heard the word of truth, the gospel of your salvation. Having believed, you were marked in him with a seal, the promised Holy Spirit, who is a deposit guaranteeing our inheritance until the redemption of those who are God's possession - to the praise of his glory" (Ephesians 1:13-14).

Those who belong to God have the Holy Spirit take up residence within them.
The Holy Spirit is the Person who is keenly interested
in introducing you to this God
who has saved you.

Do you allow the Holy Spirit to guide you?

Are you baptised in the Holy Spirit? Most likely you will speak in tongues once you have been baptised in the Holy Spirit.
Have you allowed the Holy Spirit to bring you the understanding
and wisdom you need each day?

"And if the Spirit of him who raised Jesus from the dead is living in you, he who raised Christ from the dead will also give life to your mortal bodies through his Spirit, who lives in you" (Romans 8:11).

When you obey God, you are being led by the Holy Spirit.

"because those who are led by the Spirit of God are sons of God" (Romans 8:14).

342

With the Holy Spirit living inside there is power to resist sin and the works of the devil.

Interestingly enough,
He is not working within you to adhere to a mission statement or set of doctrinal rules.

That is why we must not revere the words written by man that talk about what God is.
Revere the bible because it is the Word. And Jesus is the Word.

"In the beginning was the Word, and the Word was God, and the Word was with God" (John 1:1).

Jesus is the head of the church.
That is a relief.
It also means there are many good churches out there.

Jesus is the head of the church.
He said our love for Him, not our appearance of love for him,
is based upon our obedience to Him.
To be a son or daughter of God we must be led by the Spirit of God.

That is why it is possible to appear to be doing everything right
yet still not be in love with God or others.
Outward observance is impressive and also very misleading at the same time.
That makes it a little difficult
to really know the heart of an individual.
They may appear to be totally consecrated to God
yet not walk in obedience to God.
The motive of their heart may not line up with what pleases God.

They may not be in the timing of God because they do not wait upon Him for His opportunity.
Rushing ahead they are forcing open doors of opportunity in their own strength.
Pushing ahead through their own ability or with the help of key members
in their religious organisation, some folks miss out on their inheritance in heaven.

Choosing to receive their reward now in this life.

Though God clearly lets you know what He wants you to do -
it is left up to you to accept and obey.
That is what makes your love for God
a free will offering.

You are free to choose to serve Him or reject His leading.

"Your word is a lamp to my feet and a light for my path" (Psalm 119:105).

343

"Your word is a lamp to my feet and a light for my path" (Psalm 119:105).

Seek the Lord. Seek Him to know what He has on His mind.

When you seek the Lord, who is the head of the church,
the lamp of His word will clearly illuminate your direction.
This is meant to give assurance to your heart!
You will find the way if you seek direction from God alone!

He will gladly show you what you are to do.

Do you see why it is important to have a leader who is also a follower of Jesus?
When you are listening to the things they say God will use their words to magnify the Lord.
The communication will confirm and be in unity with the same Spirit that lives in you.
You will share in your Teacher or Pastor's love for Jesus.
You too will hunger and thirst for God and His righteousness.
You will be seeking to know the Lord together.
You will continually be affirmed in knowing that your life is found sitting with Jesus,
listening for His word for you.
You will share his or her passion to know the Lord.

You will be able to say you are getting to *know* the Lord - not just getting to know more and more *about* the Lord.

344

"Preserve my life according to your love, and I will obey the statutes of your mouth" (Psalm 119:88).
"Now what I am commanding you today is not too difficult for you or beyond your reach. It is not up in heaven, so that you have to ask, "Who will ascend into heaven to get it and proclaim it to us so we may obey it?" Nor is it beyond the sea, so that you have to ask, "Who will cross the sea to get it and proclaim it to us so we may obey it?" No, the word is very near you; it is in your own mouth and in your heart so you may obey it" (Deuteronomy 30:11-14).

A leader who doesn't know or follow the Lord will tell their audience
that they have gone many places, learned many things
and done many things.

They will say with all their travels to distant places
and personal experiences
that they are now in a position to be the one to bring all this back
in order to teach you.

They plainly make it known how fortunate you will be to sit under their leadership
because of the unique information they can share with you.
Here in Deuteronomy it plainly says God's sheep don't need someone to go
to the other side of the sea, or even go up to heaven for fantastical spiritual experiences
in order for them to know the very wonder of God.
Sadly, you could be faithful to listen to a leader like this for years
but in the end you will admit - "I don't know God."
You will think you are devoted to learning about God and yet you will never really get down to it.
Never get down to just finding out who God is for yourself.
The revelation is swirling and swirling around the 'man', and not revealing the 'Maker'.

A leader who knows God just directs you to God.
They stand at the door of God's house like a doorkeeper.
With joy they beckon you to come through the door but they do not follow you in
and establish themselves as the object of your attention.
The doorman just remains where they are posted.
They have done their job to usher you in to the place where you meet with the Lord for yourself.
They see this as the only reason you have come to God's house.

To meet with the Lord.

"Better is one day in your courts than a thousand elsewhere; I would rather be a doorkeeper in the
house of my God" (Psalm 84: 10a - b).

They know that God has prepared something special for each sheep
and only He can provide it for them.
They understand the desire God has for His sheep to be properly fed.
They have experience with the ability God has to feed His sheep - even the weakest -
as long as that sheep comes to God.
A leader who really knows God would never think of getting in the way.
Of getting in-between God's sheep and their Shepherd by acting out a ministry
they have contrived in their own mind.

Mark these words. You will know what Jesus wants you to do. At the same time He will enable you
to trust Him to guide you in the path that is right for you. That is because He is always with you.
That is what the passage from Deuteronomy says.

That is what the thief saved by Jesus found out just before his death on the cross.
That is what little children already know. And no one ever needed to preach to a baby in the womb before it was aborted

with great stories gleaned from world travels or great ministry experiences
up in heaven or across the sea

just before that little baby was received straight into the arms of Jesus.

345

You will be very much aware of your own will or desire.

This is the plan you want to hold onto because you think it will make you happy.

The conflict between God's point of view and yours
will be clear within your soul.

You are married. You feel a mutual attraction with another man's wife.
God's general revelation about His plan
is that you remain faithful to your own wife.
Your will - to satisfy a desire to be happy for the moment - is to be unfaithful.

Who's will do you follow?
God's will or your will?

Fidelity in marriage is an example of God's will that is a universal plan for all people.
The faithfulness of God to make His will known in personal aspects of daily life is just as necessary.
For example, whether He wants you to move to a new home or when He wants you to move to another home. If you should pursue further education, wait until later
or do something different altogether. He wants to guide you in everything.

God will be faithful and you will know if your decision is His best for you.

346

Dear reader, if you are in a time of trial take the way of escape He provides
in order to do what pleases your God.

"No temptation has seized you except what is common to man. And God is faithful; he will not let you be tempted beyond what you can bear. But when you are tempted, he will also provide a way out so that you can stand up under it" (1 Corinthians 10:13).

Take a step back from the situation.

Cast your cares upon the Lord.

Don't default to your leader's stories of their own experiences
as if God has changed His way of guiding His sheep.
Let God show you the way that pleases Him.

Even in the eleventh hour He will be pleased with your obedience.
The Lord sometimes brings a door of opportunity past the hour that you feel you needed it.
It will always prove to be perfect timing
when you wait upon the Lord.

Your obedience to Him is the expression of love He requires of you.
Give to Him this day
your obedience.
Keep your fellowship with Him intact.
Your fellowship with Him is after all,
His utmost desire.

"I am the vine; you are the branches. If a man remains in me and I in him, he will bear much fruit;
apart from me you can do nothing" (John 15:5).

In addition to this encouragement to trust in the Lord,
be thankful if the Lord has given you a godly, kind and loving church leader.

There are an unlimited number of ways God will use a faithful pastor, teacher or leader
to assist the followers of Jesus.
God will use that leader to often confirm to you
the things God gives you in your own heart.

Rejoice, for it is a blessing to benefit from the ministry of someone who is also a follower of Jesus.

Another person who takes time to be alone with Jesus and listen to Him everyday.

347

Our examination of intimacy with your Lord Jesus Christ brings us into a rather involved area
at this time.

It is an area not well understood by many church folks.

In a previous devotional we referred to a scripture where Jesus speaks of His followers
as those who 'believe' and then 'eat'.

Believing in Jesus and eating the Bread of Life.

I am hoping it will be a relief for some of my brothers and sisters in the faith to be given a grasp of what Jesus is referring to here. It is in the bible, and may have eluded your understanding up until now. Jesus has in no way loved you less for this! He has never failed to provide every good thing that you have needed and that includes bible understanding. It may be that this is just His timing to bring these truths to your heart. In Christ you have never lacked any good thing.

May the Holy Spirit illuminate these verses for your edification.
Here they are once again to bring them to your remembrance.

"I am the bread of life. Your forefathers ate the manna in the desert, yet they died. But here is the bread that comes down from heaven, which a man may eat and not die. I am the living bread that came down from heaven. If anyone eats of this bread, he will live forever. This bread is my flesh, which I will give for the life of the world" (John 6:48-51).

I promise you dear reader that I am not going
to get weird on you right now.
This examination will be bible based.
These daily writings will be a little longer than usual.
Read and re-read them as often as you see fit.

We are going into a little detail with parts of this understanding.
The detail is meant to greatly enhance your perspective so please read through this section.

You will be glad you did.

Jesus began to talk about the true followers.
He said they need to eat manna that has been sent from heaven.
Manna is bread.

Jesus said, "I am the bread of life."

"Then Jesus declared, "I am the bread of life. He who comes to me will never go hungry, and he who believes in me will never be thirsty" (John 6:35).

What is Jesus explaining here when He connected loving and following Him
with not being hungry?

When you buy bread, do you set it on your counter or table to look at?
Is it presented in your home simply to admire and adorn your décor?
Do only the best homes in town have a loaf of bread in their possession?
Is it on your table to be a thought provoking object of discussion?
Do you buy it only once then take it home and set it in a safe place?

Is it a comfort to know the loaf of bread you've owned for years
(or was passed down to you as an inheritance)
is secure and untouched in the last place you left it?

For what reason would you have this bread in your possession?

348

We know that bread is only meant for one thing.

It is skilfully baked,
delivered as quickly as possible

and 'eaten'

at the peek of freshness.

Bread is not able to be used in woodworking, gardening, vehicle repair,
school or educational purposes nor the construction of a rocket to put a person in space.
It can't fuel an engine nor construct a building or be worn as clothing.
Bread is bread.

Bread is only good for eating.

Come to think of it, it is not even thought of
as having any insulation value of any kind.

Jesus said if you 'come to Him', you 'will never go hungry'.

This can only mean one thing.

Jesus is the bread of life and His followers partake of this bread.
That is why they will never go hungry.

What do the followers of Jesus do
if they will never go hungry?
What do they do with the 'bread of life'?
There has to be a process in which they consume the bread that has been offered on their behalf.
We know that this is the only reason bread is offered.

Dear reader may it be a comfort to you to know that you have already been reading
about this process all this past year! We have just not spoken about your time alone with Jesus
in this paradigm of believing and eating.
To help understand deep intimacy it was Jesus who referred to Himself as 'the bread of life.'

Now, may I ask you.
Is this weird?
People eating bread - is that a weird thing?

Jesus likened Himself to a common,
readily attainable commodity
available to almost all people in all walks of life.

What else do you do with bread?

How else will bread fulfill its purpose?

349

Followers of Jesus do what He asks of them.

They show their love for Him through their obedience to Him.

This is a much freer outlook on faith than rules and religious customs
created by man trying to do something for God.

Jesus simply asked us to obey Him.

"After six days Jesus took with him Peter, James and John the brother of James, and led them up a high mountain by themselves. There he was transfigured before them. His face shone like the sun, and his clothes became as white as the light. Just then there appeared before them Moses and Elijah, talking with Jesus. Peter said to Jesus, "Lord, it is good for us to be here. If you wish, I will put up three shelters - one for you, one for Moses and one for Elijah." While he was still speaking, a bright cloud enveloped them, and a voice from the cloud said, "This is my Son, whom I love; with him I am well pleased. Listen to him!" When the disciples heard this, they fell facedown to the ground, terrified. But Jesus came and touched them. "Get up," he said. "don't be afraid." When they looked up, they saw no one except Jesus. As they were coming down the mountain, Jesus instructed them, "Don't tell anyone what you have seen, until the Son of Man has been raised from the dead" (Matthew 17:1-9).

Here is an example from the bible that shows how easy it is to get busy and think up something to do for God.

In Matthew 17:4 Peter said to Jesus, "Lord, it is good for us to be here. If you wish, I will put up three shelters - one for you, one for Moses and one for Elijah."

Peter was saying that they should build three religious memorials because they had seen Moses and Elijah talking to Jesus on the mountain. He did not realise how easy it would be for people to mistake the shelters as a symbol that ordinary men like Moses and Elijah could be compared to the

Son of God. Jesus, the Son of God is the only individual appointed by God to bring mankind into fellowship with Himself. There was no other man nor will there ever be another man appointed by God except for Jesus Christ and Him alone.

The disciples had seen a wondrous thing.

They responded in the natural without waiting to be directed by Jesus.

They enthusiastically applied themselves to create a religious practice. In this case it was to build three shelters. One dedicated to Moses, the other Elijah and the other to Jesus.

It was after they firmly decided what they were going to do that they heard from God.

Low and behold, it was a voice from heaven - no less.

The voice came without invitation and with no prompting.

It was God the Father

Himself.

They were making a mistake.

Their heavenly Father stepped in right away because they were way off track.

Here is what the disciples had done.

They decided among themselves that they could set up a place of remembrance by making and setting up three shelters.

They thought this would please God in some way.

Jesus had not asked them to set up three shelters.

They had not listened and received His instruction.

Did they get ahead of God, was that the problem?

Actually they were right out of the will of God in their thinking.

The bible calls this 'sowing to the flesh', or 'sowing to the sinful nature'.

"Do not be deceived: God cannot be mocked. A man reaps what he sows. The one who sows to please his sinful nature, from that nature will reap destruction;" (Galatians 6:7-8a).

They had failed to hear from God before launching ahead in their own efforts. Possibly the disciples were about to pray: "Dear Lord please bless these shelters. We commit them to your service and to your glory. Please bless our efforts. In Your name we pray."

'Master, it is good for us to be here. Let us put up three shelters - one for you, one for Moses and one for Elijah.' (He did not know what he was saying.) While he was speaking, a cloud appeared and enveloped them, and they were afraid as they entered the cloud. A voice came from the cloud, saying, 'This is my Son, whom I have chosen; listen to him' (Luke 9:33b-35).

There's that word again, 'listen'.

Listen to Jesus above all else.

How exciting this is! The word of God is shaped and moulded
to convey the simple cry in God the Father's heart to be your friend!

If you are 'committing your own work to the Lord',
please receive this wisdom.
Find out if this is what the Lord wants you to do
by receiving His word in your heart
either before you begin or afterward like the disciples did here.
It is never too late to respond to anything the Lord says to you!

When the disciples were off track in their thinking God intervened by sending His word to them.
They had all they needed to remain in the will of God in the word He spoke to them.

He can keep you from getting off track each day as you listen to the word He sends to you.

350

"After six days Jesus took with him Peter, James and John the brother of James, and led them up a
high mountain by themselves. There he was transfigured before them. His face shone like the sun,
and his clothes became as white as the light. Just then there appeared before them Moses and
Elijah, talking with Jesus. Peter said to Jesus, "Lord, it is good for us to be here. If you wish, I will
put up three shelters - one for you, one for Moses and one for Elijah." While he was still speaking, a
bright cloud enveloped them, and a voice from the cloud said, "This is my Son, whom I love; with
him I am well pleased. Listen to him!" When the disciples heard this, they fell facedown to the
ground, terrified. But Jesus came and touched them. "Get up," he said. "don't be afraid." When
they looked up, they saw no one except Jesus. As they were coming down the mountain, Jesus
instructed them, "Don't tell anyone what you have seen, until the Son of Man has been raised from
the dead" (Matthew 17:1-9).

So, the voice from heaven - the voice of God the Father - was reminding the disciples to just listen
and walk with the Lord. Nothing else was asked of them.
Neither did their Father condemn them. That is the kindness of God.

"yet now I am happy, not because you were made sorry, but because your sorrow led you to
repentance. For you became sorrowful as God intended and so were not harmed in any way by us.
Godly sorrow brings repentance that leads to salvation and leaves no regret, but worldly sorrow
brings death" (2 Corinthians 7:9-10).

No other 'works' or labour was needed to make God happy.

Only to listen
hear
and obey
His express instruction.

Remember the words Jesus spoke in His visit with Mary and Martha?

"only one thing is needed" (Luke 10:42a).

An intimate love for Jesus is found in listening to Him.
How merciful.
How gracious.
How kind.

This means not one of His followers are excluded from a passionate,
intimate relationship
with the Son of God.

Think of it, even someone who is physically deaf is able to have an intimate relationship with God.
No one is excluded.

In Psalm 27 David says looking to God and enquiring of Him
was his only desire
for the rest of his life.

But doesn't it sound extreme?
'There is only one thing I will seek for the rest of my life.'

Here is that beautiful verse in Psalm 27.

"One thing I ask of the Lord, this is what I seek: that I may dwell in the house of the Lord all the days of my life, to gaze upon the beauty of the Lord and to seek him in his temple" (Psalm 27:4).

David lets us know what the payoff is in this kind of relationship when God is your Father.

"For in the day of trouble he will keep me safe in his dwelling; he will hide me in the shelter of his tabernacle and set me high upon a rock. Then my head will be exalted above the enemies who surround me; at his tabernacle will I sacrifice with shouts of joy; I will sing and make music to the Lord" (Psalm 27:5,6).

In the final verse, he alludes to our need
to really let the Lord be the author and finisher of all we do.

"Wait for the Lord; be strong and take heart and wait for the Lord" (Psalm 27:14).

Having a 'perspective' like this is another way of saying, 'not my will but thy will be done.'
'Perspective' is a helpful word here as opposed to the word 'focus' because the experience
is the result of God's gracious care and not what we are able to manufacture in our own strength.
The word 'focus' sounds like it is something we attain in our own strength.
Thankfully loving fellowship with God is available for everyone.

David grasped how inconsequential our lives are if we choose to do things in our own strength. He committed himself to the realistic goal of being led by God at every turn. No matter how impressive his deeds and his personal walk may have appeared to the people around him David understood that this does not benefit His heavenly Father's work on earth.
Very few Christian leaders walk in this truth.

David chose to first be grounded in the intimacy, guidance and necessary instruction of His Lord and King.

351

The elderly, the very young, the infirm in mind and body - the despot and the despicable.

Everyone may come to Jesus.

Jesus invites everyone to come to Him.
Once a person believes in Jesus and receives Him into their heart
they only need to make a place of fellowship with Him daily
for the rest of their life.

Consider this following verse in the light of God's commitment to you and His plan for your life.

"Do you not know? Have you not heard? The Lord is the everlasting God, the Creator of the ends of the earth. He will not grow tired or weary, and his understanding no one can fathom. He gives strength to the weary and increases the power of the weak. Even youths grow tired and weary, and young men stumble and fall; but those who hope in the Lord will renew their strength. They will soar on wings like eagles; they will run and not grow weary, they will walk and not be faint" (Isaiah 40:28-31).

Dear sincere reader, seeker of the Lord, is anything too hard for the Lord?

"Ah, Sovereign Lord, you have made the heavens and the earth by your great power and outstretched arm. Nothing is too hard for you." (Jeremiah 32:17).

You are most capable through your Jesus!

No one is disqualified from serving God due to personal limitations!
No one is too old,
nor sinned too greatly,
nor committed to Satan or demons to deeply,
nor too used up,
nor too young, nor too abused and damaged
nor too foolish, idealistic or too intelligent or too naïve.

You will walk with Him in a magnificent, powerful, faith-filled
love relationship.
You can make it through all things because He will perfect that which concerns you.

"Though the Lord is on high, he looks upon the lowly, but the proud he knows from afar. Though I walk in the midst of trouble, you preserve my life; you stretch out your hand against the anger of my foes, with your right hand you save me. The Lord will fulfill his purpose for me; your love, O Lord, endures forever - do not abandon the works of your hands" (Psalm 138:6-8).

There you have it! "The Lord will fulfill His purpose for me!" He will do it!

352

"For I know the plans I have for you," declares the Lord, "plans to prosper you and not to harm you, plans to give you hope and a future" (Jeremiah 29:11).

Seek Him and get alone with Him in order to listen
and the Lord will preserve your life
make a way for you
and the Lord will fulfill His purpose for you!

"Salvation comes from the Lord" (Jonah 2:9c).

The followers of Jesus are not hungry because He has given Himself
and has become their necessary food. He is Spiritual Food to be sure.
The followers rise up to God's call to listen.

Listen to the Son of God.
There is no other sacrifice He craves.

He is your friend and will walk with you as your friend.

353

Thank you for sharing these pages Dear Reader.

Our investigation is unfolding and I invite you to continue on.
You are greatly esteemed through His everlasting love for you. He is enamoured with all who believe in Him, focusing upon their every need. All believers are mighty through Him.

"But blessed is the man who trusts in the Lord, whose confidence is in him. He will be like a tree planted by the water that sends out its roots by the stream. It does not fear when heat comes; its leaves are always green. It has no worries in a year of drought and never fails to bear fruit" (Jeremiah 17:7-8).

"Blessed is the man who does not walk in the counsel of the wicked or stand in the way of sinners or sit in the seat of mockers. But his delight is in the law of the Lord, and on his law he meditates day and night. He is like a tree planted by streams of water, which yields its fruit in season and whose leaf does not wither. Whatever he does prospers" (Psalm 1:1-3).

354

Dear Reader, what will you do with this Jesus?

He named Himself 'the Bread of Life'.

What will you do with this Bread?

What do you typically do with good, fresh bread?
First you take it home.
Then you put it in a familiar place.
Then . . . you sit down and eat the bread.

You take it into your mouth and swallow it.
This is the only way bread can be useful.
It is why bread is made. It is the only way for bread to nourish you.

If someone else eats the bread it does not benefit you even if you sit together at the same table.
If the bread is passed to you and you decline to take the bread then you will not benefit from being present with it at the table.
You can't benefit from handling bread or buying it if you just give it away to someone else without partaking of it yourself.

Let the process of intimate fellowship with Jesus be more than a glimpse of Him.
Don't sit idly by while others go home and get alone with God to eat their fill.
Don't just look at the Bread of Life. Be filled.

He is the lover of your soul and you can only know Him if you receive Him as the Bread of Life.
Be still in His presence and He will become the Bread of Life to you.

Draw near to listen and you will be nourished.

355

"Guard your steps when you go to the house of God. <u>Go near to listen</u> rather than to offer the sacrifice of fools, who do not know that they do wrong. Do not be quick with your mouth, do not be hasty in your heart to utter anything before God. God is in heaven and you are on earth, so let your words be few. As a dream comes when there are many cares, so the speech of a fool when there are many words" (Ecclesiastes 5:1-3).

There is no joy in heaven when many words are spoken in Jesus name.

Ecclesiastes says many words in God's presence come from a fool.
Similarly, if you are in the presence of another person and speak without first listening
and continue to speak without allowing the other person an opportunity to communicate with you
- they might conclude you are not well, or you may be a fool.

You would be someone greatly pitied.

How could a person who doesn't listen cultivate a relationship with someone else?

Even with the best of intentions it will not be possible to begin an intimate relationship
when the other person is unable to convey their feelings, desires and a desire to love you in return.

356

The place of fellowship with our Lord and Saviour Jesus Christ is a place of kindness, peace, love,
forgiveness and joy.

The passage from Ecclesiastes 5:1 - 3 is given to help inform us.

When you go to spend time with Jesus remember that He has established a protocol -
or accepted procedure - for those who desire to seek Him.

Man tends to create 'a new thing' every once in a while.
But really, the process of relationship continues as it has all along.

Ecclesiastes 5:1 - 3 is a thorough understanding of our place in the presence of God.
It is meant to be followed from generation to generation.

Those in intimate relationship with Jesus
will find themselves unable to embrace the latest 'new thing'.
There is no substitute for the wisdom found in these faithful words of Ecclesiastes 5:1 - 3.

If you would know the Lord Jesus then you will spend time with Him.

He will be glad to help you listen.

He takes responsibility to furnish and equip you with understanding and guidance.

"The lions may grow weak and hungry, but those who seek the Lord lack no good thing"
(Psalm 34:10).

We abide in complete safety when it is the Shepherd's voice we follow and no one else.

Let Him draw near to your heart.

Let the Holy Spirit have His way within you.

"If you love me, you will obey what I command. And I will ask the Father, and he will give you another Counsellor to be with you forever - the Spirit of truth" (John 14:15-17).

The Holy Spirit is given to you by your Heavenly Father.
This means the Holy Spirit is a gift to you from the Giver of good gifts.

"Every good and perfect gift is from above, coming down from the Father of the heavenly lights, who does not change like shifting shadows" (James 1:17).

He is your very own counsellor.
The Holy Spirit is given to you to be with you.

He is a person like a family member is a person.
Or like the local policeman, the President or Prime Minister, your neighbour or a homeless person.
Together they are people, but each one individually is a 'person'.
The neighbour down the road is a person.

The Holy Spirit is a person and He will be with you forever
if you believe then receive Jesus Christ as your Saviour
and enjoy His fellowship for the rest of your life.

If you have rejected the Lord.
Turned from Him.
Or once accepted Him long ago but no longer humble yourself
that He might remain your friend - return to His loving arms.
He will receive you and answer your prayer for forgiveness.

Be safe.
Be saved.
Return to Jesus.

" - the Spirit of truth. The world cannot accept him, because it neither sees him nor knows him. But you know him, for he lives with you and will be in you" (John 14:17).

Jesus says the Person of the Holy Spirit - the Spirit of Truth - will be with you and will be in you.
Thank God, the Holy Spirit is a kind and loving Person.

He is completely in agreement with the good plan God has for your life.
This makes Him the best friend you could ever have.

God is three Persons in One.
God the Father
God the Son
God the Holy Spirit.

Jesus asked His Father to send the Spirit of Truth. Our heavenly Father answered every prayer
Jesus ever prayed while He was on earth. That is because Jesus is God and always prayed the will
of His Father. We see the evidence of this with the story of the fig tree.

"Seeing a fig tree by the road, he went up to it but found nothing on it except leaves. Then he said
to it, 'May you never bear fruit again!' Immediately the tree withered" (Matthew 21:19).
"When evening came, they went out of the city. In the morning, as they went along, they saw the
fig tree withered from the roots. Peter remembered and said to Jesus, 'Rabbi, look! The fig tree you
cursed has withered!' 'Have faith in God,' Jesus answered" (Mark 11:19-22).

359

"Every good and perfect gift is from above, coming down from the Father of the heavenly lights,
who does not change like shifting shadows" (James 1:17).

Jesus introduced us to an unusual love.
He has an everlasting love.

In all our time reading thus far it has always been about spending time with Jesus.
If you have been seeking Him each day then you will understand.
He fills that time with meaning and purpose.

Your time with Him can never be taken from you.
It is the only thing in your life that will always remain with you.

Your time spent with Jesus is safer even than jewels in a safe deposit box.
Jesus says those times of intimacy can never be taken from you.
It will now and always be your greatest treasure.
He freely gives the greatest of all gifts to any who will seek Him.

Yet in His eyes,
you are His greatest treasure.

"For what shall it profit a man, if he shall gain the whole world, and lose his own soul?"
(Mark 8:36).

You alone,
your ever living soul,
is worth more to Jesus than the whole world.
The wealth, the treasure, the money, the assets, the investments, the gold, silver and platinum
in the entire world - they all mean nothing to Jesus Christ compared to you Dear Reader.

"The Pharisees, who loved money, heard all this and were sneering at Jesus. He said to them, 'You
are the ones who justify yourselves in the eyes of men, but God knows your hearts. <u>What is highly
valued among men is detestable in God's sight</u>" (Luke 16:14-15).

You are grand beyond description in His eyes.
Precious,
precious,
precious.

You are so very precious.

360

All over the world today people are eating bread.

If someone offered you a loaf of bread you would want to know what kind it is.

White or wheat?
Multigrain or rye?

Right away you want to determine if it is fresh or stale.
You carefully check, turning it upside down,
just to make sure there is no mould.

You see,
these considerations stem from only one concern.
We associate bread with one thing -
our desire to eat it.

It doesn't enter our mind that there is another purpose for bread.

When Jesus said He is the bread of life He fully understood what He was saying.

'You need Me if you are going to survive.'
'I won't be able to sustain you if you don't take time alone with Me just as with a meal.'
'You will need to regularly stop what you are doing and devote your attention to Me
for I am spiritual food.'
'I am the bread of life. Apart from Me there is no spiritual food and you will starve.'

'I am your Saviour, you will need to meet with Me on a regular, daily basis
or as often as you are hungry.'
'You will grow in your passion for Me.'
'Your desire for other spiritual food will quickly disappear for I know exactly what you need
and you will feel great afterward.'
'You will see that our times alone are not optional.'
'Joy will overwhelm you as you live each day
in the freedom of My words 'only one thing is needed'.

"but only one thing is needed. Mary has chosen what is better, and it will not be taken away from
her" (Luke 10:42).

'Our fellowship will be fulfilling,
rewarding, intimate, personal,
loving and uplifting.'
'I will fill you with wisdom and understanding.'
'I will sustain you always for I am always available.'
'Whenever you want to meet with Me I am there completely with you.'
'Nothing is able to deprive you of your spiritual food. I am your spiritual food.'
'You are personally invited by Me, the creator of all things, to be My guest.'
'I will always give you exactly what you need, it will always be My very best.'
'No earthly love can take My place.'

'I am Perfect, Supreme and totally in love with you.'

"Why spend money on what is not bread, and your labour on what does not satisfy?
Listen, listen to me, and eat what is good, and your soul will delight in the richest of fare"
(Isaiah 55:2).

The scriptures are alive!
The scriptures are alive with the saving news of God's love for you!
You shall never be hungry again!

Jesus, Jesus, Jesus! King of the universe, friend of sinners.

"Can a mother forget the baby at her breast and have no compassion on the child she has borne?
Though she may forget, I will not forget you! See, I have engraved you on the palms of my hands;
your walls are ever before me" (Isaiah 49:15-16).

361

Walking through the kitchen and acknowledging your food does not feed you.

Preparing the food, setting the table and sitting in your chair will not feed you.

But if you take the bread,
put it in your mouth,
chew the bread,
swallow
and take time
to allow it to find its way to your stomach
the bread has fulfilled its intended purpose.

The point here is that you actively participate
when it comes to putting bread to good use.
Owning a loaf of bread doesn't mean you are fed.

The important aspects of digestion in your physical body happen unconsciously.
Though you aren't required to think through the breaking down and digesting of your food,
it is the most necessary part of eating.

Experiencing the love of God is like this!
In Ephesians it says His love, "surpasses knowledge!"
You will never experience the love of God by studying or offering mental ascent
to your church's doctrine.

Often of course, while you are reading the bible God will
pour out His love upon you!
That heavenly feeling is the love we are talking about.

But if God can only share His love in your soul when you read the bible
then past generations of people without a bible would have been shut out.
People without a bible in their own language
would miss the reason Jesus came to earth.
Little children who cannot read would be oblivious to His love.

God's intimate love for you surpasses knowledge.

No one else will ever know what you and your Saviour share when you are alone together.

362

Spending time with Jesus gives Him an opportunity to share His love within your soul.

You actually feel the love of Jesus Christ.

It surpasses knowledge just like the love a kind mother has for her children.
It isn't because she gives them candy. It isn't because they know where she lives.
A child does not merely look upon their mother and conclude, 'my mother loves me.'

No, it doesn't stop there. It is the expression of that dear love that furnishes
an acknowledgment in the mind of a child.

Believe me, if you are stripped of your worldly goods
and put into solitary confinement because of your faith
you will be sustained by the love of God!
It won't be because they have allowed you to have a bible to study!

There is a deep emotional expression of love
a mother pours out upon her little one.
Even she could not put it into words.
She just has to hug.
She just has to know what her child is doing.
She just has to know where they are.
She just has to know her child is safe.

She will never express this feeling for someone else's children.
She would have a love for other children and it is called 'compassion'.

Only her children will experience the profound and rare gift of nurture
which pours out her selfless devotion
hopeful optimism
kindness
steadfastness
sense of humour
and generosity of heart.

When you were hurt as a child
would you think of going anywhere else
but to your mother who loves you?

It's a different kind of love isn't it.

363

You do not need to determine the huge role the Lord plays when you sit in fellowship with Him.
It is a spiritual experience and you will be faithfully informed by the Holy Spirit in all
that you need to know.
He is the Potter and you are the clay.
Do you see a little more clearly why simply reading the bible
is not the fullness of entering into an intimate relationship?
Bible reading is clearly the most noble of all activities! But as long as you are withholding the ability
of your Saviour to communicate within your heart then the other side of the coin to bible reading -
that being the intimacy of your Lord - is missing.

Think of how long your precious spouse would be able to handle it if you did not stop, focus upon them and listen to what is upon their heart.

Jesus said listening is the singular key to knowing Him.

By the way, I love - absolutely love - to hear my wife's point of view on anything at all.
I count on the godly wisdom she seems effortlessly to possess.
She is the epitome of God's expression of love in my life, and also to our children.
I would miss out on everything if she did not have complete freedom to express herself.

There are books on marriage.

They will never enable me to be embraced with the wonder of being married to my sweetheart.

364

Intimate relationship.

Each person celebrates and respects the uniqueness of the other.

Each person is eager to listen to the other.
Each person delights in the discovery of the other.

Jesus is a Person. He has the freedom to do His own thing.
He is autonomous. He always chooses to do what His Father wants.
But He is here for you, and He has invited you to fellowship with Him.

You trust that He is there.
He is there to meet with you because Jesus is the good Shepherd.

He will do what is needed.

You are there waiting upon the Lord Jesus and being still in His presence because you believe you will end up nourished, sustained, encouraged and spiritually well fed.
And you will be!

Hallelujah!

365

Hello Dear Reader.

As you know, if you have invited the Lord Jesus to become an intimate friend
He is not meant to be a friend you acknowledge from a distance.

A. "I want to tell you about my friend Jesus."
B. "Do you ever spend time with Him?"
A. "Not regularly"
B. "I have deep needs. I don't need that kind of friend.
    I need someone I can count on night and day."
A. "Jesus is like that!"
B. "How do you know?"
A. ???

As our intimate friend He shares His life with us.
Go ahead, get up close to Jesus.

"Here I am! I stand at the door and knock. If anyone hears my voice and opens the door, I will come in and eat with him, and he with me" (Revelations 3:20).

He calls Himself the bread of life for this reason.
To know Him is to spend time with Him.

He becomes your spiritual food while you are quietly listening.
He shares His nurturing love with you because you are His child.
That is the kind of love He has for you.
How fortunate.

What a blessing.

366

It is the process of eating food that we are presently touching upon.

If a Christian is questioned about the passage where Jesus says He is our food it is nothing to be nervous about.

For the rest of today's devotional I hope it will be helpful to look at the passage in its entirety.

"Jesus said to them, "I tell you the truth, unless you eat the flesh of the Son of Man and drink his blood, you have no life in you. Whoever eats my flesh and drinks my blood has eternal life, and I will raise him up at the last day. For my flesh is real food and my blood is real drink. Whoever eats my flesh and drinks my blood remains in me, and I in him. Just as the living Father sent me and I live because of the Father, so the one who feeds on me will live because of me. This is the bread that came down from heaven.
Your forefathers ate manna and died, but he who feeds on this bread will live forever." He said this while teaching in the synagogue in Capernaum. On hearing it, many of his disciples said, "This is a hard teaching. Who can accept it?" Aware that his disciples were grumbling about this, Jesus said to them, "Does this offend you? What if you see the Son of Man ascend to where he was before!

The Spirit gives life; the flesh counts for nothing. The words I have spoken to you are spirit and they are life. Yet there are some of you who do not believe." For Jesus had known from the beginning which of them did not believe and who would betray him. He went on to say, "This is why I told you that no one can come to me unless the Father has enabled him." From this time many of his disciples turned back and no longer followed him. "You do not want to leave too, do you?" Jesus asked the Twelve. Simon Peter answered him, "Lord, to whom shall we go? You have the words of eternal life. We believe and know that you are the Holy One of God" (John 6:53-69).

Jesus spoke these words to all the people who came to hear Him speak.
Yet many stopped following Him after hearing it. The teaching was 'too hard' they said.

Who would stop following Jesus after being willing to be identified as His disciple?
They left work, friends, family and loved ones to walk around
and attend His sermons for days on end.
Following Jesus in our own strength and ability is one thing.
Drawing near to Jesus to become His intimate friend is an entirely a different thing.
Indeed, with chagrin and heartache on that day,
Jesus saw that He was left with only the original twelve.

With hurt in His heart and in His eyes He couldn't help but mention
that among the few He had left was a demon.

"Then Jesus replied, "Have I not chosen you, the Twelve? Yet one of you is a devil!" (John 6:70-71).

He referred to Judas, the son of Simon Iscariot, who, though he was one of the Twelve,
was later to betray him.

367

Only the original twelve stayed with Jesus after hearing about the cost of commitment.

How powerfully portrayed here is the army of the Lord!

The followers of Jesus who would 'know Him' are indeed few in number.
Once in a while
there may even be a deceiver in the midst.

Yet Jesus chose them all. There is a certain end for those who serve God outwardly
but in their heart they belong to the evil one.
In one place in the bible they are called 'tares'.

37 "He answered, "The one who sowed the good seed is the Son of Man.
38 The field is the world, and the good seed stands for the sons of the kingdom. The weeds are the sons of the evil one,

358

39 and the enemy who sows them is the devil. The harvest is the end of the age, and the harvesters are angels.

40 "As the weeds are pulled up and burned in the fire, so it will be at the end of the age.

41 The Son of Man will send out his angels, and they will weed out of <u>his kingdom</u> [not the kingdoms of this world, but out of 'His' kingdom] everything that causes sin and all who do evil.

42 They will throw them into the fiery furnace, where there will be weeping and gnashing of teeth.

43 Then the righteous will shine like the sun in the kingdom of their Father. He who has ears, let him hear." (Matthew 13:37-43).

[Verse 43] It is not possible for the church as God's people to fully shine like the sun at this present time, but we will one day all shine together like the sun.

[Verse 41] It says those who do evil will be removed from the midst of His kingdom!

How difficult it is for the unsaved around us
to accept the message of the gospel when they see hypocrisy, money loving, glory mongering, reputation seeking, sin and demonic carrying-on in the lives of some church goers.

Anyway, poor Judas the deceiver was of course not interested in a relationship with Jesus.
At the time He was following Jesus right alongside the true disciples
because he had access to the money.

"as keeper of the money bag, he used to help himself to what was put into it" (John 12:6b).

368

The eleven other disciples stayed with Jesus because 'He had the words of life."

The follower of Jesus listens to the words of Jesus.

He is become their only bread.
For your comfort dear reader after such a heated devotional yesterday, here is Luke 12:32

"Fear not, little flock; for it is your Father's good pleasure to give you the kingdom."

Remember what Jesus said dear reader,
He will not lose one that the Father has given to Him.
He knows all His sheep and calls each one by name.
Another they will not follow because they will not recognize the voice of a stranger.

While Jesus is calling
listen dear reader . . . listen.
For He is calling to you today.
He calls to you right now.

"The man who enters by the gate is the shepherd of his sheep. The watchman opens the gate for him, and the sheep listen to his voice. He calls his own sheep by name and leads them out. When he has brought out all this own, he goes on ahead of them, and his sheep follow him because they know his voice. But they will never follow a stranger; in fact, they will run away from him because they do not recognize a stranger's voice" (John 10:2-5).

The sheep listen for His voice.

369

His own sheep follow him because they know his voice.

Dear Reader, never let your salvation be based upon your ability to obey do's and don'ts, your form of dress, which church you attend and for how long, who the preacher is, how much money you give, who your friends are or how many people you tell about the Lord.

His sheep listen for His voice.

'His own sheep'
follow Him
because they know his voice.
He is so willing to teach.

He will literally give you
His kingdom.

Please, here is that verse again.

"Fear not, little flock; for it is your Father's good pleasure to give you the kingdom" (Luke 12:32).

370

"The Spirit gives life; the flesh counts for nothing. The words I have spoken to you are spirit and they are life" (John 6:63).

May you be comforted this day Dear Reader.

Jesus plans to give you the kingdom.
He is not an elusive friend.

He has plans to bring His very best into your life every day.

His love for you is the best gift He has to offer you
in this very short life.

Through the experience of being alone in His presence
you grow in freedom and thankfulness.
When things don't turn out the way you want them to
you are able to remain thankful.

He has not planned in any way to hide His love from you.
His perfect will is offered freely.
One of the ways we see this first hand is in the open and accessible instructions
He shared with those who would listen.

He said to Mary and Martha, 'only one thing is needed.'

What a comfort.

He came right out and told everybody what His followers would need to do. It is not a secret.
It is not just for a select few with an exceptional talent or the proper connections.
It is not for those who have lots of money to contribute.

Jesus felt comfortable enough to share it at a little house party
given by Mary and Martha. It was not a special meeting for the inner circle.
His important teachings are shared openly with everyone because He invites all people
into His deepest fellowship. He came to save the whole world.

It is the flesh, it is man who makes divisions.
In man's eyes some people are much more worthy than others.
But here we see Jesus telling his most important instruction to anyone who will listen.
In this house meeting He happened to be talking to two women.

Praise God!

371

He mentions also that the things He says are 'Spirit'.

The flesh 'counts for nothing.'

It is nice to get that settled right up front.
'The flesh counts for nothing' but when Jesus speaks it is Spirit.
If you want to follow Jesus why take time and energy and resources
to do things that 'count for nothing'.

All things done
without the personal instruction of Jesus
'count for nothing'.

'Let's go door to door and evangelise.'
Did Jesus indicate that you personally should go and do this at this time?
Do you know if there is a certain geographical area He wants to work in by His Holy Spirit?

'Let's have an all night prayer meeting.'
Did Jesus ask this of your group,
or did He ask it only of you
or is all of this just your flesh?

'I'm going to honour my pastor and support Him no matter what without questioning.'
Remember what God did the day they wanted to just go ahead and build the three shelters
to honour Jesus, Moses and Elijah? God spoke audibly from heaven clearly saying
His followers must listen only to His Son Jesus Christ and follow only Him.
Blind obedience to a leader is the flesh.
Just follow Jesus.

Anything else is the flesh.

372

Jesus said this.

He said His words are Spirit - and the flesh counts for nothing.

If you are to make a difference in this life and in this world you need the Spirit.
You need to hear from God yourself.

This is attainable by anyone and everyone who will wait upon the Lord
and listen for His teaching - this is what He openly told Martha.

He told it to someone who was not a member of a special group within a group.
He told it to the person who was showing a need. He made a point of drawing near
and sharing this important instruction with someone based upon their need for understanding.

He did not choose to talk to Mary because she was a Christian superstar.
She was an ordinary person that Jesus loved.
A person He planned to prosper and provide a future.
Jesus loves His sheep.
Jesus is always helping those who need a Shepherd.

Today Jesus knows your need.
He will be with you just as He chose to visit the house of Mary and her sister Martha.
Jesus will tell you what you need to know.
He will do it through the bible as you sit and fellowship with Him.

He will also speak to your heart by His Holy Spirit who lives in you.
Jesus said that would be the role of His Holy Spirit.

The Holy Spirit's voice actually sounds like something!

"After the earthquake came a fire, but the Lord was not in the fire. And after the fire came
a gentle whisper" (1 Kings 19:12 New International Version).
"And after the earthquake a fire; but the Lord was not in the fire: and after the fire
a still small voice" (1 Kings 19:12 King James Version).

How precious that the bible has given us a solid understanding about the existence of God's voice,
and what His voice sounds like! God wants to speak to His people.
Not as He did to the High Priests of old -
once a year, allowing only one person in the Holy of Holies at a time.
God wants to speak to all of His people,
because we are all now become High Priests of this wonderful and awesome new covenant
established with the precious blood of Jesus.

"To him who loves us and has freed us from our sins by his blood, and has made us to be a
kingdom and priests to serve his God and Father - to him be glory and power for ever and ever!
Amen" (Revelation 1:5c-6 New International Version).
"But you are a chosen people, a royal priesthood, a holy nation, a people belonging to God, that
you may declare the praises of him who called you out of darkness into his wonderful light"
(1 Peter 2:9).

His deepest truths are for you.
God didn't choose to share them with another person
and hope you would find out what He told them!
His deepest love is yours right now.
Just get started.
He is waiting with all the love in His heart.

You are the apple of His eye and He treasures you.

373

Dear Reader, let's look at these verses again.
"Jesus said to them, "I tell you the truth, unless you eat the flesh of the Son of Man and drink his
blood, you have no life in you. Whoever eats my flesh and drinks my blood has eternal life, and I
will raise him up at the last day. For my flesh is real food and my blood is real drink. Whoever eats
my flesh and drinks my blood remains in me, and I in him. Just as the living Father sent me and I
live because of the Father, so the one who feeds on me will live because of me. This is the bread
that came down from heaven. Your forefathers ate manna and died, but he who feeds on this
bread will live forever." He said this while teaching in the synagogue in Capernaum" (John 6:53-59).

Out of the great love of His heart Jesus gives distinct instructions.
Parents who truly love their children do this all the time.

'Don't touch that stove - it is hot.'
'Try to get a good night's sleep, you'll feel better.'
'Don't play on the road where there is traffic.'
'That food is good for you.'
'Be careful to choose the right friends.'

'I will always be there for you.'
'If you need me just ask for help.'
'You can count on me.'

Isn't that a kind and loving thing for a parent to say?
It is great joy when a kind and loving parent has opportunity to act upon those precious words.

Dear Reader, If you have never heard these words spoken to you please take heart
for you are not forsaken.

"Though my father and mother forsake me, the Lord will receive me" (Psalm 27:10).

374

Direct and concise instructions come from someone who loves you.

Every once in a while Jesus spoke this way.

'He who feeds on this bread will live forever.'
These words are spoken out of love.
Jesus is not willing that any should perish.

"The Lord is not slow in keeping his promise, as some understand slowness. He is patient with you,
not wanting anyone to perish, but everyone to come to repentance" (2 Peter 3:9).

Jesus said,
'whoever eats my flesh and drinks my blood remains in me and I in him.'

A word of comfort and reassurance.
That is because the word, 'whoever'
includes you and me.

There is no hierarchy of blessing with the intimate love of Jesus.
There is no inner circle in the midst of God's people.
It means we are all the sheep of His pasture.

God uses spiritual leaders
who humble themselves
and honour Him with their surrender in intimate fellowship.
As a consequence of having 'been with Jesus' they are given grace to serve and honour others.

A leader who has been in the presence of the Lord in intimate relationship has the nature
of a servant. They make people feel loved, acceptable to God, full of hope for their future.

They are waiting to receive their reward in heaven, safely stored there for them by God.

375

"Enter through the narrow gate. For wide is the gate and broad is the road that leads to
destruction, and many enter through it. But small is the gate and narrow the road that leads to life,
and only a few find it" (Matthew 7:13-14).

A man or woman whom God is using will leave you with a growing esteem for Jesus Christ
and how great He is.

Sadly in the eyes of God, some leaders find a way to leave people with the impression
of how great they are.

The Lord does not want His sheep
to feel they are inferior
to anyone.

The flesh loves to be lifted up.
This happens in church all the time.

Be careful, be on your guard against those who labour their whole ministry career
just to receive the praise of men.
They have their reward now.
They have not elected to wait
and receive it later . . .
from the hand of Jesus Himself.

"Humble yourselves, therefore, under God's mighty hand, that he may lift you up in due time"
(1 Peter 5:6).
"Then we your people, the sheep of your pasture, will praise you forever; from generation to
generation we will recount your praise" (Psalm 79:13).

One and all can enter into this sacred and marvellous privilege of praising God.

Jesus knows all of His sheep by name.

He calls each one and they all follow Him out.
There is no mention of a differentiation between the sheep.
All are called by name - there is no indication that He will do it in a certain order
or designation of accomplishment. That is the flesh.
It counts for nothing. That's what Jesus says.

"You will seek me and find me when you seek me with all your heart" (Jeremiah 29:13).

376

He is interested in all of His sheep.

He speaks with utmost regard to each one.

The Father of Jesus Christ gave but one flock in which Jesus is the sole Shepherd.
It is the only flock His Father will ever ask Him to care for.
And remember, He does all things well! Hallelujah!

He desires for each sheep to be safe
and kept by His care.
He has not selected out sheep that are somehow in a higher state of privilege.
That is how the flesh sees it.
There are leaders in church who see it this way.
This is one reason it is all the more important
for God's tender hearted followers
to seek Him daily.

Only there with the Master is the love you crave.

"The Lord does not look at the things man looks at. Man looks at the outward appearance, but the Lord looks at the heart" (1 Samuel 16:7b).

377

God is overflowing affirmation in spite of your insurmountable weakness.

He is your reassurance . . . that all is well, all continues as it should.

You continue as always
to be held in absolutely the highest regard
by your great, All-powerful God.

God sets a table of abundance for all who would spend time with Him.
Meeting with God takes on the reality and importance of a necessary meal.

All who seek Jesus are served by the Most High
exactly according to their needs.
Oh the precious unity for those who make the Lord their meat, their drink and their bread.
Jesus is not their rule maker he is the One who feeds their soul.

"You prepare a table before me in the presence of my enemies. You anoint my head with oil; my cup overflows" (Psalm 23:5).

You see, God refers to intimate fellowship as a 'table'.
He considers intimate fellowship
to be just as important as our necessary food.

If you have served the Lord,
gone to church
and done everything you were supposed to
- but have not established a place for the Lord's table in your life -
simply start now!

How keenly the Lord has looked forward to this next step in your growing relationship with Him.

Bless you!

378

You will grow to desire this Bread above all else.

The Bread will become your life.
And of course - it is Jesus of whom we speak.
Wonderful Jesus who asked you to think of Him as 'the Bread of life.'
Oh the wondrous glory of the grace and love of God!

Is the Bread sufficient for your every need?
It is true. Jesus was correct. Time and experience in His presence confirms
that His love becomes the very source of your life - and He is all you need.

Time with the Son of God becomes a visceral experience.
We have experienced the blessing of God's fellowship along with our young and now growing children. We have spent time with Jesus together most days. Even young children can accurately acknowledge the presence and leading of the invisible Holy Spirit. They comment after being with Jesus something precious has taken place. They feel changed. It felt it is the very thing they needed to do at that moment. They always enjoy our prayer times when we are finished. They consider it time well spent and better than any other activity they could choose to do in that moment. This would speak of the wondrous experience of being right with their creator. Nothing else compares. It was healthy, wholesome, meaningful and uplifting for their little souls.

"you will fill me with joy in your presence," (Psalm 16:11b).

God refers to the experience of His fellowship as altogether satisfying.
A reality surpassing any other.
He is not just the bread. He is the meat and drink.
He is all the sustenance you need.

He is life to you spiritually.

"Jesus answered, "I am the way and the truth and the life. No one comes to the Father except through me" (John 14:6).

Jesus is being very loving here.
He is being very specific because He doesn't want to anyone to miss out
on how important He is.

"Salvation is found in no one else, for there is no other name under heaven given to men by which we must be saved" (Acts 4:12).

"Thank you Jesus for telling it like it is."

379

Now, there is another aspect to this spiritual reality that relates to eating.

It has to do with the diversity of steps that take place to prepare your meal.

As you wait upon the Lord with your bible
and your journal for keeping notes,
in the early moments and minutes there is a lot going on in the spiritual realm directed by
the Holy Spirit on your behalf.
God is wiping out activities directed by the enemy
meant to thwart your time of intimate fellowship with God.

"but I want you to be wise about what is good, and innocent about what is evil" (Romans 16:19b).
"For our struggle is not against flesh and blood, but against the rulers, against the authorities,
against the powers of this dark world and against the spiritual forces of evil in the heavenly realms"
(Ephesians 6:12).

God wants you to be innocent about what is evil.

Often He will do 99% of the spiritual warfare without letting you know
what He has taken care of.

If He does reveal something then it is because your prayers
will be a part of His plan to resolve the issue!
Usually if God reveals something the enemy is doing then it means
He is going to DEAL WITH IT by the blood of Jesus and in the name of Jesus!

380

Often in these initial stages of sitting with Jesus it will feel like you are restless.

You will think you are 'unspiritual' because your mind may wander.

You will figure it best to walk away.
But wait!
Be still!
You will be amazed as the Lord will suddenly calm your heart and mind!
Sometimes it may take up to twenty minutes or more. Sometimes only a minute or two!
That is intimacy Dear Reader! You are meeting with God.
He has all the power - not you!

Give Him the time He needs to set things up for you,
to prepare the table for your intimate time together.

While you feel restless you are most definitely in the guidance and care of the Shepherd.
He is working in the unseen realm
to open up the way entirely for you to be in fellowship.
It will be the delight of the Lord to guide you.

"Who shall separate us from the love of Christ? Shall trouble or hardship or persecution or famine
or nakedness or danger or sword? As it is written: 'For your sake we face death all day long; we are
considered as sheep to be slaughtered.' No, in all these things we are more than conquerors
through him who loved us" (Romans 8:35-37).

381

You will be made aware of the inflections and nuances - the sense of the moving of His Spirit -
when you sit with your Master.

He will direct you to where you should be reading in the bible.

He will indicate the content you should dwell upon.
Though there may be many pressing issues
Jesus will bring your attention to the area He wants to shed His Light upon.

Sometimes He will invite you to sing a worship song.

Maybe you will feel to raise a hand or both hands in the air in worship.
Usually the Lord will draw you near to listen.
Most often your times together begin with listening unto Him.
A time that might be characterized as 'restless' or feeling 'unspiritual'.

Yet life can be very difficult
and there will be times when you are tearful with grief or anger
or a lack of understanding about what is going on in daily life.
You may be heartbroken
and can't help but pour out your feelings before the Lord!

"I cry aloud to the Lord; I lift up my voice to the Lord for mercy. I pour out before him my complaint; before him I tell my trouble" (Psalm 142:1-2).

Do you remember a time when you 'poured out' say, a glass of water?
Did it like, go everywhere and anywhere?

Jesus can handle it
when you pour out your feelings.
Even if it is a complaint!
Pour it out!

You are with your best forever friend.

382

What a wonderful friend.

Someone you can go to with all your troubles.

Jesus establishes loving relationship
with each of His sheep.

Jesus does this.

It is not by your might or power but by His Spirit.
He is the stronger One in your relationship!
He is the Potter you are the clay.

He says He is your Shepherd.
What an awesome Shepherd to have walking around with you everywhere you go!
The King of Kings, the One who crushed Satan and death!

He says, 'I am the Good Shepherd.'

I am happy to be seen anywhere with this Shepherd.
"Yah, that's Jesus! The One you've heard about.
Check it out - Satan *was* no match and *is* no match for my Shepherd!"

Oh, I love Jesus Dear Reader. Does Jesus go with you everywhere you go?
Is the Son of God with you at school? On the bus or train? Standing quietly with you at work?

Go ahead and invite Jesus Christ to be with you!
As a friend, He is awesome!
Never be alone again Dear Reader. Choose Jesus, choose life.

Each person has a unique relationship with Jesus because each person is unique.

383

If you are feeding upon the Bread of Life then you belong to Jesus.

You are alive in the Spirit and walk in great privilege.

Just like the believing thief on the cross who could see Jesus
in the midst of his suffering.
Just to see Jesus overshadows all else.

This privilege of needing the Bread of Life gives you the right of access to God at any time.
This is your most significant blessing.

That is why the thief that got saved while on a cross
didn't mention a need for more faith.
Nor did He pray to be taken down from that cross and escape death.
The other thief . . . the profane thief
was the one crying out to God
for escape from His cross.

"One of the criminals who hung there hurled insults at him: 'Aren't you the Christ? Save yourself and us!' " (Luke 23:39).
"Whoever believes in the Son has eternal life, but whoever rejects the Son will not see life, for God's wrath remains on him" (John 3:36).

384

For the believing thief.

Jesus was right there beside him going through everything he was going through and more.

The thief who was now a friend of God said it this way:

"We are punished justly, for we are getting what our deeds deserve. But this man has done nothing wrong" (Luke 23:41).

Jesus said, 'this day you will be with Me in paradise.'
The thief was good with that.

Though it doesn't mention what the thief did before death,
I would think he was overwhelmed
that he had been forgiven by God.
The salvation of his soul was the goal of his faith.

He would die with a peace that passes all understanding.

"And the peace of God, which transcends all understanding, will guard your hearts and your minds in Christ Jesus" (Philippians 4:7).
"Blessed is he whose transgressions are forgiven, whose sins are covered. Blessed is the man whose sin the Lord does not count against him and in whose spirit is no deceit" (Psalm 32:1-2).

385

Your belief in Jesus has given God permission to take care of you also, just as He did the thief on the cross, with all of His power and resources!

This did not get the righteous thief off of his cross.

It did mean
that the power of Satan would never again
be able to separate this sheep from the sweet love of God.
The thief gained eternal life by believing in Jesus.
This is the greatest of all blessings.

When the thief was looking into the eyes of Jesus Christ behind the matted hair, the blood and bodily fluids of a man about to die - he knew they would be together forever.
That was good enough for him.

"Now this is eternal life: that they may know you, the only true God, and Jesus Christ, whom you have sent" (John 17:3).
"Never will I leave you; never will I forsake you" (Hebrews 13:5b).
"For I am convinced that neither death nor life, neither angels nor demons, neither the present nor the future, nor any powers, neither height nor depth, nor anything else in all creation, will be able to separate us from the love of God that is in Christ Jesus our Lord" (Romans 8:28-39).

386

'The one who feeds on Me will live because of Me,' Jesus said.

Clear and concise.

He repeats this again in the same passage.
'He who feeds on this bread will live forever.'
Ok, this is when it gets even more exciting! If you are enjoying the Bread of Life
then you are giving Jesus an opportunity to give you His most personal gift
besides the gift of salvation.

Do you know what this gift is?

It is the gift of your individuality.

You are created by God to be just the way you are.
Transformed by His own hand as clay is transformed - yet a person unique from all others
at the same time. As the Master Potter, He alone knows how to shape you and mould you
in your times of fellowship with Him.

He is able
to use every possible experience in life
to develop the most unique person on earth.
That is you Dear Reader.

All the love, creativity and power of His Holy Spirit is with you and in you.

"But you know him, for he lives with you and will be in you" (John 14:17b).

This is you when you are in God's fellowship.

387

"Unless the Lord builds the house, its builders labour in vain" (Psalm 127:1a).

Be careful dear reader. Let the Lord be your one builder.

If you do not commit your life entirely unto Him you will not escape
the 'work' of many builders
in your life.

To forsake a walk in which you serve God with your whole heart
leaves you open to the influence of many others.

You will not have the freedom you might imagine.

Only Jesus is able to bring out all the amazing qualities you already possess.
Lots of people become directly involved in your life when you distance yourself from God.
People are just that way.
They love to influence others and even get them to do their bidding -
whether it is good for the other person or not.
A loving relationship with God brings you the freedom, faith and power to grow spiritually.
God says it is a slow but determined process.

He says it is like the growth of a tree, but not just any tree!

"He (or she) is like a tree planted by streams of water, which yields its fruit in season and whose leaf does not wither. Whatever he does prospers" (Psalm 1:3).
"He (or she!) will be like a tree planted by the water that sends out its roots by the stream. It does not fear when heat comes; its leaves are always green. It has no worries in a year of drought and never fails to bear fruit" (Jeremiah 17:8).

388

"Then Jesus asked, "What is the kingdom of God like? What shall I compare it to? It is like a mustard seed, which a man took and planted in his garden. <u>It grew and became a tree</u>, and the birds of the air perched in its branches" (Luke 13:18-19).

Right, ok now.

Jesus said, "What is the kingdom of God like?"

He said it is like the grandest of trees that He plants 'in his own garden.'
When He plants you in his own garden
he will be the only person to tend you.

The only builder.

The only Shepherd.

(Ahhhh. Isn't it nice to be there!)

In another reference His follower is like a tree
planted by streams of water.
Because a tree starts with just a small seed He takes care of the tree every step of the way.
All the while you are putting down a tremendous root system.
This takes place underground. It doesn't matter what is going on above the ground.
Fair weather or not - your roots continue to develop.

Isn't the root system the most important part of a tree? When a strong wind comes along an entire tree can be upended! All those years of growth terminated suddenly just because the root system was not sufficient for the tree.

God continually works all things out for your good so that your roots will be sufficient and He will get great glory to His name.

389

Where is the Kingdom of God?

Remember when we discovered that God has chosen to be on this planet as closely as He could with mankind by placing His Holy Spirit inside of His believers?

You are a member of a special group of people that have become a temple of the Holy Spirit. Jesus has other kind words to describe your new status.

"But you are a chosen people, a royal priesthood, a holy nation, a people belonging to God, that you may declare the praises of him who called you out of darkness into his wonderful light" (1 Peter 2:9).

This all comes together nicely when you consider these words of Jesus.

"Once, having been asked by the Pharisees when the kingdom of God would come, Jesus replied, "The kingdom of God does not come with your careful observation, nor will people say, 'Here it is,' or 'There it is,' because the kingdom of God is within you' " (Luke 17:20-21).

Dear Reader, we are not likened unto trees
because we are exactly the same as all the other followers of Jesus.
God does not see you like a blur of identical trees, row after row.

You are likened unto trees in your growth
because He has planted you in His garden
to be cared for by Him alone.

He is the stream by which you are continually fed.
His kingdom is in you because you grow
in an assured,
steadfast
and stately manner.

Your growth,
though slow and seemingly uneventful at times,
also produces vast roots that hold you fast
in the face of inclement conditions.

Jesus is not looking for a 'row of trees'.
People that all look the same, sound the same.
Pray the same and speak the same.
Jesus is looking for friends who grow over time as unique individuals in the shelter of His love.
Friends who discover how precious they are in the hand of a loving God.

Though we are likened unto the majestic growth of trees,
each one is an individual person unto God.
Each one is unique.

He knows each one by name.

"And even the very hairs of your head are all numbered" (Matthew 10:30).
"I praise you because I am fearfully and wonderfully made; your works are wonderful, I know that full well" (Psalm 139:14).

390

Dear Reader, let's do it.

Will you repeat those divinely inspired words about yourself?
Ok, here we go.

Please say this true statement about yourself
out loud.

"I am fearfully and wonderfully made.
Praise you Jesus.
I am fearfully and I am wonderfully made."

Don't aspire to be like anyone else in the church you go to.
Seek to be like Jesus.
If someone prophecies to you that God is going
to raise you up like 'so-and-so'
you deserve to be disappointed.

If someone prophecies to you that God is going to raise you up to walk with Jesus,
to be like Jesus, raise you up to love with God's love then rejoice.
You will also have an inheritance to look forward to in the next life.

"Before I formed you in the womb I knew you, before you were born I set you apart; I appointed you as a prophet to the nations" (Jeremiah 1:5a).

You see, it is God who will shape you and mould you.

Not to be like someone else.
You are going to become the person He loved
before you were even formed in the womb.
He will not fail you.
He knows exactly who you are
and will bring all good things to pass.
You don't need to try to become like anyone else.

Let the Master finish the good work He began in you at the time you first believed.

"being confident of this, that he who began a good work in you will carry it on to completion until the day of Christ Jesus" (Philippians 1:6).

391

Jesus only had a short time to minister on earth.

When He repeats certain instructions it is good to consider what He has said.

He is clear that we should walk in the Spirit of His word.
He is clear that doing things for Him without first hearing from Him - 'counts for nothing'.
No matter how successful it looks, to Jesus it counts for nothing.

Once you begin to take time with Him you will anticipate the simplicity
in which He asks -
"just come and listen".

"Just come and wait upon Me."
"Just come and be still."
"Be still and know that I am God."

He will do the rest.
After all
He is the potter
and you are the clay
            in His hand.

He is faithful.

392

"Enoch walked with God; then he was no more because God took him away" (Genesis 5:24).

Enoch was a man who walked with God.

What does this mean,
'he walked with God?'

Well first of all,
a person who walks with God
is one who brings great pleasure
to the Almighty.

Ah, but the pleasure is mutual for the privilege of walking with God is our 'fullness of being'.
It is the highest order in what we are created for.
We are created to be loved and to love in return.
Though mankind initiates many plans and purposes during their short sojourn on this earth
it still remains that all people were created by God
to 'walk with Him'!

We are ever-living beings,
human souls who will need to prepare for an endless eternity.
One way or another it is certain that we will face eternity.
When and how we go for the most part remains a mystery
to every person alive.

Will you be alone in eternity
or with God?

In heaven or in hell?

393

It is a misconception held by many that a godless eternity still holds the benefits of fellowship,
friendship, re-acquaintance with old pals and affable hanging out.

Some people hold out a hope that all is benign on the other side.

More than just a release from the daily struggles of existence in this life
they really, really hope it holds the last ultimate escape
from accountability.

A place where - low and behold - no one will have to account for anything, ever.
A place where everyone will share a general sense of well being
because no one will ever have to answer for anything they have ever done.
A place where there will never be accountability ever again.

This is a most whimsical speculation. Even on a children's playground there is accountability.

Please consider this my friend.

The enemy of your soul will not be up front about your future or about his.
Did you know for instance,
that Satan will initially be bound in chains for one thousand years and cast into a pit?
He is certainly not to be admired or held in awe.
He and his demons - consisting of only 1/3 of the angels - cannot be trusted.
Let's hear it from the Truth Himself.

Precious Jesus Christ the Righteous.

"Jesus said to them," If God were your Father, you would love me, for I came from God and now am here. I have not come on my own; but he sent me. Why is my language not clear to you? Because you are unable to hear what I say. You belong to your father, the devil, and you want to carry out your father's desire. He was a murderer from the beginning, not holding to the truth, for there is no truth in him. When he lies, he speaks his native language, for he is a liar and the father of lies. Yet because I tell the truth, you do not believe me!" (John 8:42-45).
Jesus said, "The thief comes only to steal and kill and destroy; I have come that they may have life, and have it to the full" (John 10:10).

That is just a bit of the information the devil attempts to withhold from mankind.
Later in this devotional you will be able to read about the fate
of the many who reject the invitation to walk in fellowship with God.
They choose instead a life of self-will, sin, rebellion
and a wide path of resistance to God.
Even if they purpose in their heart not to hurt others and be the best they can be
it is still not good enough. It is still their own self-effort to gain righteousness.

There is no cleansing of sin apart from Jesus Christ.

"All of us have become like one who is unclean, and all our righteous acts are like filthy rags; we all shrivel up like a leaf, and like the wind our sins sweep us away" (Isaiah 64:6).

394

I realize the devotional book of ours is fast drawing to a close.
I will continue to look to the Lord to bring
all that is helpful for you.

God mercifully provides opportunity for each person to repent.

Repentance is good.
It is pure.
It is clean.

Repentance before God washes clean from all sin.

Don't wait. If you know in your heart you are not a friend of God,
if you are unsure about your eternity
then repent.

Get right with Jesus Christ, God's Son.

"You believe that there is one God. Good! Even the demons believe that - and shudder."
(James 2:19).

If you are a full time church attendee
who started out a long time ago with a decision for Jesus Christ
you might not know Him as an intimate friend.
It is not rightly emphasized in many church circles.

Jesus refers to people who believe in Him by name without an intimate relationship
as 'such branches'.

"Remain in me, and I will remain in you. No branch can bear fruit by itself; it must remain in the vine. Neither can you bear fruit unless you remain in me. "I am the vine; you are the branches. If a man remains in me and I in him, he will bear much fruit; apart from me you can do nothing. If anyone does not remain in me, he is like a branch that is thrown away and withers; <u>such branches</u> are picked up, thrown into the fire and burned. If you remain in me and my words remain in you, ask whatever you wish, and it will be given you. This is to my Father's glory, that you bear much fruit, showing yourselves to be my disciples. "As the Father has loved me, so have I loved you. Now remain in my love. If you obey my commands, you will remain in my love, just as I have obeyed my Father's commands and remain in his love" (John 15:4-10).

You alone have the power to establish your fate and your destiny.
Jesus has prepared all things just for you.
If only you will come to Him
and accept what He has done for you.

He offers an intimate relationship to any person who receives Him.

God is love and God is truth.
The fullness of His personal disclosure to you
is all there for you in the bible.
The bible
is your source of truth,
the written word of God.

No other book written by the hand of a man compares nor surpasses nor replaces it.

Hell is a place you do not want to be part of.

There is nothing on earth that compares to the endless reality of hell.

The worst person, place or thing you can think of
is nowhere near as bad as hell.
Later on we will touch on what hell holds for the many who will go there.
Remember,
it says many shall go into eternity freely choosing to reject or forsake the narrow path.
They choose instead to take the wide road
leading them to destruction.

Please Dear Reader, meet with me
in heaven someday
where Jesus awaits you and me.

Jesus is the door you must go through to get to heaven.
Will you receive Him right now, and hold tightly to Him for the rest of your life?
Jesus will never let you down.

"Trust in the Lord with all your heart and lean not on your own understanding; in all your ways acknowledge him, and he will make your paths straight" (Proverbs 3:5-6).
"The days of the blameless are known to the Lord, and their inheritance will endure forever. In times of disaster they will not wither; in days of famine they will enjoy plenty. But the wicked will perish: The Lord's enemies will be like the beauty of the fields, they will vanish - vanish like smoke. The wicked borrow and do not repay, but the righteous give generously; those the Lord blesses will inherit the land, but those he curses will be cut off. If the Lord delights in a man's way, he makes his steps firm; though he stumble, he will not fall, for the Lord upholds him with his hand" (Psalm 37:18-24).

Meeting you Dear Reader in eternity would be a great high point in my life.
How wonderful to behold the Lord Jesus together!
He is our friend and keeper! It is because of Him that we would be brought together!
It would be a rare treat to trade stories and share together in the joy of the Lord!

We enter into this eternal state of bliss when we die with faith in Christ.

"Precious in the sight of the Lord is the death of his saints" (Psalm 116:15).
"He will wipe every tear from their eyes. There will be no more death or mourning or crying or pain, for the old order of things has passed away" (Revelation 21:4).

Eternity past is the place where God thought of you and prepared for your creation.

You are His most magnificent creation because He chose to create you in His image.
He craves to love you and to be loved by you in return.
He created you to share fellowship with Him.
His intent was for you to walk with Him and have dominion over all the earth.
It is the freedom to love or not
that makes it a true love.

It is your incalculable privilege and spiritual destiny to commune with God Almighty
in the short time you live on this earth!

396

Spiritual fullness has nothing to do with being good at a task or how important it is.

This is actually good news because there is little assurance with a job.

One thing a person knows for sure,
one day they won't have that job
for one reason or another.

Your deep spiritual fellowship with God
has nothing to do with anything you 'do'
because it can't originate
in your humanity!

If your spiritual fulfillment was a result of your insight or ability
then what of those robbed of the opportunity
to develop their gifts and skills?
What if you lack the outer appearance or social graces
that are esteemed and coveted in the marketplace?
What would become of a person falsely arrested and imprisoned?

A little person who has been sexually, physically, psychologically, emotionally or spiritually abused
and will suffer
for the rest of their life?

What if a person didn't get a copy of a certain self-help book
or misses a decisive TV talk show because they don't own a TV.
What if a car accident or vehicle wreck robs someone of their sight
who once flew a plane
or painted beautiful pictures
or participated in an athletic sport
or was an awesome movie director
or actor?

Spiritual fullness is not found in great sex.
It is not about having things go your way
or because others do what you want them to.
It is not found in helping the environment
(although this is an important thing for all mankind to do)
nor in helping others
(thank God for people who care enough to help others).
It is not found in helping animals
(this is also an excellent thing for people to do).

True spiritual fullness originates with God.
That is why it is impossible to fail at it!

God has made it possible for any person to live in their spiritual fullness!

If any person will humble themselves,
accept the free gift of grace from Jesus Christ - which is the forgiveness of sin - and walk daily
with Him in intimate relationship
then they will be as spiritual as they can possibly be!

"if my people, who are called by my name, will humble themselves and pray and seek my face and
turn from their wicked ways, then I will hear from heaven and will forgive their sin and will heal
their land" (2 Chronicles 7:14).

397

Spiritual fulfillment.

Spiritual fullness.

It is a gift that God gives you
the moment you believe in His Son
Jesus Christ.

This fullness grows over time as you walk with God and His Spirit brings about maturity
within you - like roots on a tree that are continually growing.

We are all created in the image of God.

In an intimate relationship with your Creator everything
in your own personal universe
will be just as it should be.
You will have His grace in both good times and hard times.
His love and His fellowship will be your everything.

"So God created man in his own image, in the image of God he created him; male and female he created them" (Genesis 1:27).

"If you make the Most High your dwelling - even the Lord, who is my refuge - then no harm will befall you, no disaster well come near your tent. For he will command his angels concerning you to guard you in all your ways; they will lift you up in their hands, so that you will not strike your foot against a stone. You will tread upon the lion and the cobra; you will trample the great lion and the serpent. "Because he loves me," says the Lord, "I will rescue him; I will protect him, for he acknowledges my name. He will call upon me, and I will answer him; I will be with him in trouble, I will deliver him and honour him. With long life will I satisfy him and show him my salvation" (Psalm 91:9-20).

398

Getting into a relationship with God makes you in tune with the unseen things
that pertain to eternity!

That is why when you are saved you know that you will go to heaven.

You are not afraid of death
or the concept of what will become of you
in the afterlife.

"Even though I walk through the valley of the shadow of death, I will fear no evil,
for you are with me; your rod and your staff, they comfort me" (Psalm 23:4).

Praise God, somehow you just know that you will go to heaven!
Notice it is not how great is the faith of the one who faces death.
It is not how long they have walked with God.
It is not even whether they are male or female.

"Even though I walk through the valley of the shadow of death, I will fear no evil,
for you are with me;" (Psalm 23:4ab).

Now that is love.
It is the blessing of an intimate relationship.

Jesus said to the thief on the cross,
'this day you will be with me in paradise.'
He believed and followed Jesus for only a few hours!
How precious is the cornerstone of sincerity and complete surrender
in an intimate relationship.

Romantic relationships very early in life are like that aren't they?
Do you remember a first love? Overwhelming surrender.

Being swallowed up with the whole idea of that special person.
The way they were continually in your thoughts
and made everything seem a little more special.

To know Jesus
is to know Him in this way.

He is the Way and the Truth and the Life.

He said in John 14:19, "Before long, the world will not see me anymore, but you will see me.
Because I live, you also will live."

Is it because His loving arms uphold you
that death no longer scares you?
That would be part of the reason for sure.

"The eternal God is your refuge and underneath are the everlasting arms" (Deuteronomy 33:27).

399

It makes a big difference when you have 'everlasting arms' underneath you.

Ultimately, you know there is hope in death.

You see,
Jesus Christ conquered death!
And Sin!
And Hell!
Jesus Christ has overcome and conquered
all the powers of the devil and demons and all evil!

That is what Psalm 91:9 - 20 reveals to us.

"If you make the Most High your dwelling - even the Lord, who is my refuge - then no harm will
befall you, no disaster will come near you tent. For he will command his angels concerning you to
guard you in all your ways; they will lift you up in their hands, so that you will not strike your foot
against a stone. You will tread upon the lion or the cobra; you will trample the great lion and the
serpent. "Because he loves me," says the Lord, "I will rescue him; I will protect him, for he
acknowledges my name. He will call upon me, and I will answer him; I will be with him in trouble,
I will deliver him and honour him. With long life will I satisfy him and show him my salvation."

Any evil spiritual power - though it be as fierce as a lion or a serpent or a cobra -
is no longer a threat to your safe keeping
in the light of eternity.

"I have given you authority to trample on snakes and scorpions and to overcome all the power of the enemy; nothing will harm you" (Luke 10:19).

Even though you will go through difficulties and trials you have hope.
You know God has a great plan unfolding for you even if it is not seen
while in difficult circumstances.

"When you pass through the waters, I will be with you; and when you pass through the rivers, they will not sweep over you. When you walk through the fire, you will not be burned; the flames will not set you ablaze" (Isaiah 43:2).

When circumstances of life are like passing through waters.
Trying to wade through a raging river.
Or like you are being made to walk - not run or tip toe - through a fire.
You will be kept from eternal harm.
You will have God right there with you.

"And I am with you always, to the very end of the age" (Matthew 28:20b).
"Never will I leave you; never will I forsake you" (Hebrews 13:5b).

This should be on the front page of every newspaper, every internet site and every signpost on this planet!

YOU DO NOT HAVE TO FACE DEATH ALONE!
Jesus Christ has conquered death!

With certainty there is One who awaits you. Jesus Christ the Righteous.
The ultimate superhero. He conquered Satan, death and hell.
Don't mess with the Good Shepherd when it involves one of His sheep.
Last we heard Jesus speak on the subject of your eternity
He was going to prepare a place for you Dear Reader!
No one can set things up like Jesus. The place He is preparing for you
will be far beyond what you can imagine.
Jesus does all things well.

Let us spread the news here. Far and wide as it should be!

"When the perishable has been clothed with the imperishable, and the mortal with immortality, then the saying that is written will come true: "Death has been swallowed up in victory." "Where, O death, is your victory? Where, O death, is your sting?" The sting of death is sin, and the power of sin is the law. But thanks be to God! He gives us the victory through our Lord Jesus Christ" (1 Corinthians 15:54-57).

In Enoch's situation His relationship with God was intense in an amazing way.

We will not understand the love between them.

Of course not.
When intimate friends share with one another it is private.
Relevant only for the two parties involved.

How they talk.
The topics they discuss.
The thrill they share in the trust and safety of their rapport.

No one will know about that special nuance and affection.
No one will see when comfort is poured out
upon tears of frustration, guilt or shame.
No one will see the patience and struggle as trust is growing with a friend
who will not stop loving you.

With God the intimacy starts now
and lasts for all time.
There is no end in His ability to love you or to the adventure
in getting to know someone
able to love you perfectly.
His relationship is all you need.

I could grow close to someone like that,
couldn't you?

I love Jesus Christ.

"By faith Enoch was taken from this life, so that he did not experience death; he could not be found, because God had taken him away. For before he was taken, he was commended as one who pleased God" (Hebrews 11:5).

Anyway, Enoch is seen as a unique follower of God.
That is because God did not let him experience physical death.
God just 'took him away'
and Enoch went to heaven.
Is that awesome or what?!
That is what it means when it says,
'then he was no more because God took him away.'
Enoch was just gone.

The day was going along with Enoch spending time with God as he usually did.
Then God just 'took him'.

If Enoch happened to be going somewhere,
suddenly with the next step he was in another place! He was gone!
They were no longer communing together with Enoch in his physical body
and God as an invisible Creator. Enoch was now with God.

His race was finished. He was on the other side.

401

Walking with God means you acknowledge His great supremacy and wisely seek His direction in everything.

You seek for His guidance in every decision and you surrender all earthly belongings to His use.

All relationships are submitted to Him.
You seek His will in the use of your finances
and even the place where you choose to live.

The gifts and talents you develop are sheltered by the guidance,
wisdom and understanding freely given to you by God.
As you use them people come away marvelling
at the reality of God and His love.

This total surrender is sustained through intimate fellowship.

Walking with God means you have made the choice
to be in intimate fellowship with Him.

Dear Reader, how carefully you are tended to!

The development of your walk
is your heavenly Father's responsibility!

He tends unto you like someone owning a vineyard into which they invest
every ounce of their life's worth.

Remember it said His kingdom is like a seed He plants in His garden? Hallelujah!
So much is changed when you first believe!

You are planted in His garden.

As with anyone who likes to garden, it is a joy to prune your vines and branches because you know how well they grow afterward.

"I am the true vine, and my Father is the gardener. He cuts off every branch in me that bears no fruit, while every branch that does bear fruit he prunes so that it will be even more fruitful. You are already clean because of the word I have spoken to you. Remain in me, and I will remain in you. No branch can bear fruit by itself; it must remain in the vine. Neither can you bear fruit unless you remain in me" (John 15:1-4).
Verse 5. "I am the vine; you are the branches. If a man remains in me and I in him, he will bear much fruit; apart from me you can do nothing."

Hence, when you are walking with someone you move along with them step by step.
You are side by side.
You are on the same path going in the same direction
and you are ultimately going to arrive exactly where you should.
That is how it is with God.

Jesus said it is called 'remaining in Him.'
He knows how much you need the care of a great Shepherd.

"Nevertheless, the righteous will hold to their ways, and those with clean hands will grow stronger" (Job 17:9).

Remaining in Him is all about having His point of view on what is going on.
As you spend time with Him you will discover
that He generously shares His outlook with you.
This has a lot to do with your desire to seek His point of view.

He doesn't want you to be nervously looking around for Him
because you don't know what He is thinking.
This happens when we do not permit Him to become our friend.

Busy doing things your own way.
Or failing to wait upon the Lord and enquire of Him.

But a slow and steady pace with constant reassurance from your best friend
is preferable even to great riches,
the esteem of others
or the fleeting reality of worldly success.

Remember dear friend,
intimacy is not established by how our walk looks outwardly.

This is good because it means people of all walks of life, temperaments,
means of expression and quirks
are eligible.

The bible says many who have the best outward show for their faith
will be told by Jesus, 'I never knew you,' and send them straight to hell.
Don't follow man. Don't seek man's advice above the Lord's.

Gaze

just gaze upon the beauty of the Lord.

403

The term describing relationship with God is called someone's 'walk with God.'

It refers to their life in its entirety.

In truth, God powerfully influences all aspects of your life in your best interest
when Jesus Christ forgives and the Holy Spirit lives inside you.

This goal of 'pleasing God' resides in every person who is saved. After being washed with the
precious blood of Jesus Christ you become a new person.

"Therefore, if anyone is in Christ, he is a new creation; the old has gone, the new has come!"
(2 Corinthians 5:17).
Now, when God is pleased you are intensely aware.
His Holy Spirit radiates this awareness inside of you.
As time goes on you will find this more meaningful unto you than anything else.

Since God is your heavenly Father,
there is a deep meaning to pleasing Him.

When you please a parent you share a sweet joy with them.
It is empowering.
For those blessed with a supportive, loving earthly father or mother this dynamic is often the root
of your greatest accomplishments and the uncanny ability to recover from the setbacks of life.
It is a real source of strength when a parent believes in you.
Children will do anything
to please a loving parent.

If you have been a loving parent
you are to be commended for investing in your precious child.

It means everything to that one little person.
You have given your child the greatest gift possible.
If you have also shared your faith it brings the relationship
into another dimension entirely.

Step up and be commended dear mother or father, whoever you may be!

All a child really wants is to be loved.

Oh the things a daughter or son can accomplish
when they have the love of one or of both parents!
Similarly
with your heavenly Father
you will go on to true success. Living your life to please Him!

"And we know that in all things God works for the good of those who love him, who have been
called according to his purpose" (Romans 8:28).
"For I know the plans I have for you," declares the Lord, "plans to prosper you and not to harm
you, plans to give you hope and a future" (Jeremiah 29:11).

For this next verse especially remember when there is a reference to 'him'
it means to both male and female.

"Because he loves me," says the Lord, "I will rescue him; I will protect him, for he acknowledges my
name. He will call upon me, and I will answer him; I will be with him in trouble, I will deliver him
and honour him. With long life will I satisfy him and show him my salvation"
(Psalms 91:14-16).

404

This is a good time to provide a better understanding of hell.

Hell exists at this very moment.

As you are reading this book
Hell and heaven are real places simultaneously existing
in the spiritual realm.

People presently live
in both destinations
as they will for all eternity without end.
I realize it is a sharp contrast from our last devotional Dear Reader.
How could this book share the full revelation of God's love for you
yet withhold portions of the truth.

God is faithful and just.

Everything pertaining
to the consequences of receiving or rejecting Jesus Christ the Son of God
is carefully laid out in detail
in the Holy Bible.

It is a huge truth to find out that there is a certain future for every person who will ever live.
The eternal existence of all human souls is based upon
the freedom an individual has to accept or reject Jesus Christ.

Those who decide to reject Christ and surrender all to Him
are certain to abide forever in hell.

The certain end for church people who know 'about' God
but do not 'know' God it is written in Revelations 3:14 - 16.

"To the angel of the church in Laodicea write: These are the words of the Amen, the faithful and
true witness, the ruler of God's creation. I know your deeds, that you are neither cold nor hot. I
wish you were either one or the other! So, because you are lukewarm - neither hot nor cold - I am
about to spit you out of my mouth."

Is there any better time to decide to have an intimate relationship with God
than right now?
Why wait? Why hold off?

Would you run your car engine without a drop of oil because it is convenient to do so?
Would you swim across a piranha infested river because it is convenient to do so?
Would you leave your little child in the hands of a pedophile family member
because it is convenient to do so?

Plainly, there is a cause and effect reality
in life
and in death.
Your own personal gift of salvation is free.
In the long and short term there is no convenience in setting it aside.
None
whatsoever.

Dear Reader, hell is much more than just a great inconvenience.

To say eternity without Christ will be whatever we decide is a breakneck assumption.

Is there ever an instance where we base a life and death decision on this kind of thinking?

A child's car seat. Do you decide which model will suit your youngster without first checking with the manufacturer? Do you place a little child into the seat because you 'believe' they are the correct weight and height?
Do you have the freedom to waive criminal law, the regulations and government legislation when you decide not to put your baby in a car seat?
Is that how to define true 'freedom'? Or would a person say it is an exercise of 'freedom of choice'?

In short, parents put children in a car seat because they are informed,
because they care
and because they choose to act upon the information experts freely provide on the matter.
The decision to use a car seat is a well informed choice with a splendid outcome.
There are occasions when a child properly seated is the only survivor in a wreck.

We wouldn't buy an automobile or life insurance based upon what we 'think' the outcome will be.
These decisions follow an investment of time, investigation, research into the information
made available by friends and other informed people.
"This is how my car is going to be used."
"This is how my insurance company will look after me."

Few people make travel arrangements because they have decided in advance how things
will turn out for them without first checking into it.

Someone that decides they know what will happen after they are dead
without reading about it in the New Testament of the Bible and making peace with God
through Jesus Christ our Lord is making an all important decision based upon assumption.

I assume I will be safe without a seatbelt.
I assume my baby will be safe on my lap as I drive because I will hold her close
at the time of impact.
I am a careful driver.
I don't drive very often.
There aren't many people on the road this time of night.

Assumption in some cases may result in death.

Assumption about the afterlife will mean hell.

Dear Reader, if this talk of hell turns you off, I ask that you might continue reading regardless.

If you have found this book encouraging, curious and insightful up until this point then by all means, continue - as there are significant nuggets of truth yet to come for you in these pages.

406

I know it is very challenging to ponder the afterlife.

There are many people trying to get us to believe their interpretation of who gets to go to heaven, and who gets thrown into hell.

It is very confusing when it comes to spiritual truth with so many 'voices' out there.

"First of all, you must understand that in the last days scoffers will come, scoffing and following their own evil desires. They will say, "Where is this 'coming' he promised? Ever since our fathers died, everything goes on as it has since the beginning of creation" (2 Peter 3:3-4).
"At that time if anyone says to you, 'Look, here is the Christ!' or, 'Look, there he is!' do not believe it. For false Christ's and false prophets will appear and perform signs and miracles to deceive the elect - if that were possible. So be on your guard; I have told you everything ahead of time" (Mark 13:21-23).

Please take note it affirms the safe keeping power of Jesus in His mission
as your Good Shepherd. The 'elect' will not be deceived and taken from Him. It is not possible.
Jesus has already prayed that He has not lost one the Father has given to Him.

There is one true spiritual road map for all mankind.

It is in one book called the Holy Bible.

There is no additional sacred text required
nor will God give an additional text needed to unlock the truths of the Holy Bible.
That will forever be the job of the Holy Spirit who comes to live within you.

Read that one book for yourself.
Be on your guard
and don't accept someone else's interpretation
or 'new revelation' held up to supersede the Holy Bible.
When someone says "everyone else is going to hell except for our singular group"
- just walk away. Show love, but walk away.

Here is our headline at this important time in our devotionals.

THIS GROUP SAYS THEY ARE THE ONLY ONES GOING TO HEAVEN AND THEY EXCLUDE ALL OTHER CHURCHES!
Different Group Down The Street Claims The Same Thing.

Salvation is found in Jesus not in group membership!
In depth report from the thief on the cross in tomorrow's edition!

The Holy Spirit is with you to bring God's understanding to your heart and mind.
The freedom Jesus gave to all people is that each of us is taught by His Holy Spirit.

"No longer will a man teach his neighbour, or a man his brother, saying, 'Know the Lord,' because they will all know me, from the least of them to the greatest," declares the Lord. "for I will forgive their wickedness and will remember their sins no more" (Jeremiah 31:34).

407

The Holy Spirit will guide you in the truth and the fellowship God has for you to walk in.

There are basic tenants of faith that apply to all Christendom.
The Nicene creed covers the essential, fundamental truths.

All Christian churches contain these core beliefs. It is not for one group but for all who would follow Jesus in God's plan of salvation for all mankind.

We believe in one God the Father Almighty, Maker of heaven and earth, and of all things visible and invisible. And in one Lord Jesus Christ, the only-begotten Son of God, begotten of the Father before all worlds, God of God, Light of Light, Very God of Very God, begotten, not made, being of one substance with the Father by whom all things were made; who for us men, and for our salvation, came down from heaven, and was incarnate by the Holy Spirit of the Virgin Mary, and was made man, and was crucified also for us under Pontius Pilate. He suffered and was buried, and the third day he rose again according to the Scriptures, and ascended into heaven, and sitteth on the right hand of the Father. And he shall come again with glory to judge both the quick and the dead, whose kingdom shall have no end. And we believe in the Holy Spirit, the Lord and Giver of Life, who proceedeth from the Father and the Son, who with the Father and the Son together is worshipped and glorified, who spoke by the prophets. And we believe one holy catholic and apostolic Church. We acknowledge one baptism for the remission of sins. And we look for the resurrection of the dead, and the life of the world to come.

"Salvation is found in no one else, for there is no other name under heaven given to men by which we must be saved" (Acts 4:12).
"Once again, the kingdom of heaven is like a net that was let down into the lake and caught all kinds of fish. When it was full, the fishermen pulled it up on the shore. Then they sat down and collected the good fish in baskets, but threw the bad away. This is how it will be at the end of the age. The angels will come and separate the wicked from the righteous and throw them into the fiery furnace, where there will be weeping and gnashing of teeth" (Matthew 13:47-50).

The reality and consequence of extreme heat
is the essence of this devotional.
The following references are included only to help focus a little on this uncomfortable truth.

"If anyone's name was not found written in the book of life, he was thrown into the lake of fire" (Revelation 20:15).

"The time came when the beggar died and the angels carried him to Abraham's side. The rich man also died and was buried. In hell, where he was in torment, he looked up and saw Abraham far away, with Lazarus by his side. So he called to him, 'Father Abraham, have pity on me and send Lazarus to dip the tip of his finger in water and cool my tongue, because I am in agony in this fire.' "But Abraham replied, 'Son remember that in your lifetime you received your good things, while Lazarus received bad things, but now he is comforted here and you are in agony. And besides all this, between us and you a great chasm has been fixed, so that those who want to go from here to you cannot, nor can anyone cross over from there to us.' "He answered, 'Then I beg you, father, send Lazarus to my father's house, for I have five brothers. Let him warn them, so that they will not also come to this place of torment' "(Luke 16:22-28).

"As the weeds are pulled up and burned in the fire, so it will be at the end of the age. The Son of Man will send out his angels, and they will weed out of his kingdom everything that causes sin and all who do evil. They will throw them into the fiery furnace, where there will be weeping and gnashing of teeth" (Matthew 13:40-43).

408

In death without Jesus you will be forced to live with two very intimate, very personal realities.

You are still very much alive and you are very much alone.

You no longer have your friends, family members,
supporters, well wishers, admirers, lovers and social infrastructure.
All have vanished the moment you die.
Never to return again.
Never again will you see these people
when you are in hell.

There are no good times in hell.

No beer, liquor, drugs, promiscuity, pornography, enticing nudity,
musical instruments, computers, sporting events or sports of any kind, no great hit songs
and no laughter.
There is only weeping and wailing and gnashing of teeth.

Think about it.
Satan and the forces of evil are all about getting you to sin and messing up your life now.
They are strangely silent when it comes to spelling out what will happen after you sin,
or what will happen to you after you die.

You are choked, gripped in an entirely foreign state of being.

It is the beginning of a new life.
You will never again determine anything about yourself
and that is just the intellectual part.

It's too hot - I want out of here.
I'm going to leave now.
I'm burning up!
All my bodily hair is gone.
My clothes are burnt off my skin is burnt and I stink from the smell of it.
Ok. I'm willing to believe now.
Let me out of here.

Whatever you express out loud
will actually sound like weeping, wailing and gnashing of teeth.
I guess gnashing is neither necessarily loud nor coherent.
Gnashing is more about a state of mind.
Regret.
Fear.
Torment.
Pain.
Agony.
You will find out soon
that your pleas, no 'commands' for any possible assistance have come to no avail.

What will you do then?
What will you do for the rest of eternity?

You are robbed completely of your right to self determination.
The freedom of personal choice has abruptly ended.

Your ideas, beliefs and point of view are not heeded
nor listened to nor even solicited.

As surely as the force in a railroad unerringly propels a train on its trajectory
so it will be for the damned.
Once you slip into eternity there will never be a change in your existence.
No matter what your profession, religious affiliation, beliefs, accomplishments and achievements -
whether you felt you were good or bad -
all people without Christ are the 'damned'.

Without Christ you are damned.

Once you are dead
the opportunity to choose God
will never again be available.

There is belief in hell.

The belief you will have in common with others in hell is that you are in unimaginable torment without remedy and without end.

409

It is the heat, the fire, the consuming fire of hell that we consider today.

We are aware to some degree of what burning heat does to our flesh and mind.
It consumes the life force of both
immediately
on contact.
It creates a focus pulling our consciousness into the realm of torment.

So it will be for those who reject the forgiveness and mercy of our precious Christ.
Everything will be lost. Everything includes material goods - for we already know
we can't take our possessions over into eternity.
We go there naked
without them.

Without Jesus to welcome you into the eternal joy of being in His presence forever,
the first death in your physical body will not be the true death.
The feeling and impact of death is yet to come though the damned soul is already
beyond this present life.
Oh the loss.
Oh the loss.
This first death which man so greatly fears is but a gateway
to the second death awaiting the non-believer
in the godless eternity they have foolishly chosen.

"The fool says in his heart, 'There is no God.' They are corrupt, their deeds are vile; there is no one who does good" (Psalm 14:1).

"Then Jesus said to his disciples, "If anyone would come after me, he must deny himself and take up his cross and follow me. For whoever wants to save his life will lose it, but whoever loses his life for me will find it. What good will it be for a man if he gains the whole world, yet forfeits his soul? Or what can a man give in exchange for his soul? For the Son of Man is going to come in his Father's glory with his angels, and then he will reward each person according to what he has done. I tell you the truth, <u>some who are standing here will not taste death before they see the Son of Man coming in his kingdom</u>" (Matthew 16:24-28).

Since the Son of Man has not yet come in His kingdom, all who have died without Him have yet to be assigned with the truly dead. Please read on Dear Reader.

There is a far greater loss.

A loss worth more than all the treasures of the earth combined.

The eternal loss
of one
soul.
I cannot bear almost to write such sorrowful content...
'The loss of a single soul.'

And Jesus weeps.

"As he approached Jerusalem and saw the city, he wept over it" (Luke 19:41).
'O Jerusalem, Jerusalem, you who kill the prophets and stone those sent to you, how often I have longed to gather your children together, as a hen gathers her chicks under her wings, but you were not willing' (Matthew 23:37).

Consider the snowflakes that fall.
Each one is unique.
No two anywhere in the world are identical.
In a blizzard
it is wondrous
to see their myriad numbers
swirling ever downward.
There are so many and each one is different from every other.
People are like that.
No two are the same.
It is like a picture of the many that lose their life each and every day.
Scores and scores slip off the treadmill of existence.
Dropping off into their death because they have come to their appointed time.
There is no discriminating here.
All ages,
male and female,
good and evil,
healthy and unfit.
Politically connected
or not.

The appointment to die arrives and all mankind are most prompt in keeping it.

"And as it is appointed unto men once to die," (Hebrews 9:27a).

Sometimes we meet someone who looks like another person but the similarity stops with their outer appearance.

Their upbringing, marital status, childhood, likes and dislikes and the state of their physical and emotional health are but a few differences.

Their fingerprints and DNA reveal a drastic difference.

Each day people physically die in the tens of thousands.
Suddenly they swirl outward into their own personal eternity.
For some it is an anticipated death due to illness
but for others it is unexpected and tragic.

For all there is an immediate awakening.
It is the discovery of something called
'life after death'.

They leave behind
their beliefs about heaven and hell.
What do beliefs matter now?
Reality is a thug. The truth is crude. Unseemly. Unsightly.
No, sickening.
They are not in shock. They are in the fire that never ends.
What do beliefs matter now?

All their earthly possessions, friends and loved ones, accomplishments and deeds,
the acclaim or ignominy and the relentless race of life they have run
has all vanished.
The false belief that death is akin to peace or rest will be shattered
for the unrighteous dead.

"Just as man is destined to die once, and after that to face judgment," (Hebrews 9:27).

Please count the cost with a decision for Christ.
It doesn't matter if you are disowned or laughed at.
If you lose your life or lose your job.
Your family your spouse your bank account.

What would you give in exchange for your soul?
The only other thing you have waiting for you are loving arms, forgiveness and heaven.

You are on the right track Dear Reader as you keep looking to God!

As surely as snowflakes fall each one an individual so do the people of this earth move into eternity.

But once on the other side their individuality is lost.

The person you once were, and existed in the minds of others will evaporate.
You will vanish in their thoughts.
All who die without Christ are immediately preoccupied with their own suffering.

Just as you physically vanish so will recollection of your existence
predictably fade.

Vanish like smoke vanishes.

There will be unbearable heat,
burning fire into which the unbeliever will be cast.
The pain will banish any other conscious consideration.

I am burning. I am in pain. There is no escape.
These will be your only thoughts.
It won't be your worldly accomplishments
or personal beliefs about God and the afterlife.
It won't be about how much is in
your bank account.

Individuality has already begun to dim,
for who among the tormented will have the ability to spare consideration
for the state of others in the fire.
Each will be involuntarily governed by the immediate concern
to alleviate their own suffering.

Don't perform this next illustration at home! It is simply a story
told to me by a faithful street evangelist trying to illustrate hell.

It is similar to turning a water tap on full hot and letting it run for a minute
then holding your hand under it for 20 minutes. How long would it take you to cease
thinking about all things except the burning pain of your hand?

What would occupy your mind?

The latest hit song,
the lead singer in a successful band,

how your investments are doing without you there to look after them,
whether your love interest is available,
the person who broke your heart?
As the painful seconds accrue,
little by little your struggle
will annihilate other thoughts.
As minutes pass it will be less possible to 'know' anything else.
Aside from inescapable pain, unable to pull your own life into the arena of thought,
an awareness of who you were will begin to dim.
The others who thought well of you and your good qualities will be similarly self-absorbed.
The only thing that remains of your life is your memory along with the memories
held in the minds of others.

Probably within 20 minutes in the burning fires of hell
your prior existence - all that you once were - will begin to vanish
forever.
On earth you will still be remembered. The living will cherish your memory in varying degrees.
But the godless damned in hell for all eternity
will be unable to remember that you even existed.

"But the wicked will perish: The Lord's enemies will be like the beauty of the fields, they will vanish
- vanish like smoke" (Psalm 37:20).

Dear Reader it doesn't have to be this way.

Let the Lord save you and preserve the wonder of who you are.
You truly are a wonder. It doesn't matter to what degree you have sinned.
It doesn't matter to what degree you feel unworthy.
Your wonder is reflected in what Jesus was willing to do to offer you salvation.

This wonder is seen when you accept His saving grace.
All people need the precious blood of Jesus to wash away their sins.
The time is now.

"I tell you, now is the time of God's favour, now is the day of salvation" (2 Cor. 6:2b).

Dear Reader there is hope!
Jesus said anyone who wants to walk with Him will be able to do so.
That means you.

This is because of the transformation that instantaneously takes place
when you believe in Him
and receive His forgiveness.
Jesus' love for you and obedience to His Father established a gift of salvation.

Once saved
Jesus is completely intimate with you right away.
You will know Him and He will know you
just as the Father knows Jesus
and Jesus knows the Father.

Can this be possible?

Will your background, those who oppose you or your own weakness get in the way?

"I am the good shepherd; I know my sheep and my sheep know me - just as the Father knows me
and I know the Father - and I lay down my life for the sheep" (John 10:14-15).

413

Jesus has laid down His life for the sheep.

That means you dear reader.

May you receive Him this day. Only an intimate relationship with God
will enable you to escape the endless flames of hell.
Jesus stands at the door of your heart just waiting to save your soul.

You will not have to prove anything to Him or get good enough for Him
to accept you and take notice of your deep need.
It is a gift.
It is the only important thing you need to do in this life.

"For it is by grace you have been saved, through faith - and this is not from yourselves, it is the gift
of God - not by works, so that no one can boast. For we are God's handiwork, created in Christ
Jesus to do good works, which God prepared in advance for us to do" (Ephesians 2:8-10).

Here is a prayer to help guide you, if you feel ready and desire some assistance.
"I am ready Lord Jesus.
If you really exist and can save me,
please forgive me of my sins.
You know what I have done.
Let your blood cleanse me.
I surrender my life entirely to You Dear Jesus.
I want to know that I will go to heaven.
Please save me."

God bless you dear reader.

If you are still seeking to know the Lord
and honestly don't feel ready for a decision to receive Him please read on.

I offer this prayer for you.

"I am not ready to believe in you Jesus.
I hurt too much and have seen too much harm done in your name.
If you love me I need you to show me.
Heaven and hell are just a concept to me at this point.
I need to know that I am not doing something wrong or false.
I ask sincerely for you to introduce yourself to me that I may know who you are.
Since I am praying on my own I do not need to fear your answer
as it is just between you and me.
If you are real, just show me.
If heaven is real, then that is where I want to be someday. Amen"

414

Rest.

Rest in the Lord.

"Come to me, all you who are weary and burdened, and I will give you rest" (Matthew 11:28).

Rest is free.
Jesus gives you rest freely.

What does this mean dear Reader?
Jesus will show you what resting means in your day to day life.

"When they saw the courage of Peter and John and realized that they were unschooled, ordinary men, they were astonished and they took note that these men had been with Jesus" (Acts 4:13).

Could it be any other way?

You could sit with a wise man or woman
or attend a multitude of meetings,
watch TV
or listen to great CD's
or DVD's
or streaming internet.

In the end it all comes down to the trustworthy reality,
'they have been with Jesus.'

They are ordinary but now they are astonishing.
This is how we are changed from the inside out.
Thank God it is not based upon our human effort.

So many people would be unable to even begin to make the effort.
There are so many wounded, so many abused.
So many counted out by their family, peers and friends. Others robbed of their future
due to ill health. There are many things that directly affect our life which we have no control over.
Consider the tragedy of a natural disaster like a tsunami, mud slide or flood.
There are so many who need relationship with God because they do not have
the might nor power to serve Him any other way.

Because our Saviour has asked for nothing but our love there is hope for everyone.

415

Without schooling.

Ordinary men.

The original disciples were astonishing
and not because they were busy
telling others about Jesus.

They were not exceptional
because of the 'way' they went on talking about Jesus.
They were not even astonishing
because of how many years they had been talking about Jesus
nor because of who said they were being really good at it!

These men
had been with Jesus.
The kingdom had been given to them with pleasure.

'Do not be afraid, little flock, for your Father has been pleased to give you the kingdom'
(Luke 12:32).

Wisdom is given generously. Just go to Jesus and ask Him for it.

"If any of you lacks wisdom, he should ask God, who gives generously to all without finding fault,
and it will be given to him" (James 1:5).

Thank God it is for all of us and not just for a chosen few.
Not just for the inner circle.

It isn't for those
who get a special invitation to separate themselves
from the rest of the sheep of God and sit in a room around a table.

It is for any person who comes to God.

"Whoever is thirsty, let him come; and whoever wishes, let him take the free gift of the water
of life" (Revelations 22:7b).

Everything that God has is yours for free.
A leader who loves His people will in all things encourage them to 'be with Jesus.'

The water of life is the answer.
Drink freely.

Rest in the Lord.

416

It is His pleasure to give you all you need.

It is an intimate relationship.

In the times of private sharing you will understand Him.
He promises to immediately and abundantly help
whenever you ask Him.

"If any of you lacks wisdom, he should ask God, who gives generously to all without finding fault,
and it will be given to him" (James 1:5).

There is no special way to receive wisdom. No person has more wisdom than anyone else.

Jesus has all the wisdom.

When His sheep need wisdom He gives it to them.
Let Jesus receive all the praise. Let Jesus receive all the glory.

We help one another with what the Lord has shown us,
encouraging one another and lifting one another up in love.
But, there is no special pool of wisdom found by the chosen few.
Wisdom is the birthright of every Christian.
Thank God for those who have received freely the water of life for many years and now freely
share with others. Thank God for the older men and women who continue to be steadfast
in their walk with Jesus Christ.

It isn't how many years.
It is how often they have been with Jesus
that makes them astonishing!

Those ordinary men and women have been with Jesus!

417

A shepherd who loves his people will encourage them one and all to seek the Lord.

He or she will clearly understand that every follower of Jesus
must have God's wisdom and know where to find it.
If that pastor/leader gives Jesus the 'one thing that is needed' then they will
most certainly lead their people to do likewise.

Don't wait for any man or woman to give you permission to be filled
with God's wisdom and understanding. Neither is it the plan of God for your life
to wait for permission to love God passionately with all your heart.
Doing so naturally flows with quiet times alone with Him.

He gives wisdom generously to everyone that asks
without finding fault.
Anyone at anytime can ask God for wisdom and understanding
and they will receive from Him.

May you be filled with the Spirit
and walk in the pleasure of God.

He chose wisely
when He chose to give you
His kingdom.
Don't wait to inherit it.

It has already been given to you with great pleasure.

418

"Only one thing is needed" (Luke 10:42a).

In that 'one thing' is all wisdom, understanding
and the most important friendship you will ever have in this lifetime.
It is given freely to those who choose.

"Mary has chosen what is better." (Luke 10:42b).

It is the most blessed thing you could pray for God to give your friends or enemies.
Bless them even as you would have them bless you in return.

We know where an experience with God unfolds.
In all matters related to serving God Jesus has given those who seek Him this instruction.

'Only one thing is needed.'

That 'one thing' is a good thing. 'One thing' brings fruitfulness in everything you will do for God.
By giving Jesus the opportunity to build a friendship with you
He is free to bring His will to pass in your life.

He has already given you His kingdom. Why not be His friend in return?

Friendship will take time. Getting to know one another is most certainly a process.
With God it is likened to shaping a piece of clay on a potter's wheel.
God is the potter.
When we are busy for God and not spending time with Him
it keeps Him from working with us as we need.

When we are still
and choosing to walk in friendship with Him
He is leading,
guiding
and directing all things
according to our exact needs!
It is a blessed thing. Jesus has come to teach mankind about friendship.

He has not come to look for the mighty to bear His name.
Instead,
He invites the humble to follow Him through the simplest activity possible
and along with it He gives each one His entire kingdom.
That activity was shown to us by Mary the sister of Martha.

Mary spent time with Jesus and desired above all things to listen unto Him.

"Do not be afraid, little flock, for your Father has been pleased to give you the kingdom"
(Luke 12:32).

How kind and loving you're Father has been, for He has been 'pleased to give you the kingdom'.

Doesn't that feel good!
God is already pleased with you.

With pleasure He has already given you the kingdom.

It is the place of wisdom that means most to God in your walk.

It brings Him great pleasure for you to walk in wisdom even though He has freely given it to you.

He just loves to give good things to you!

Here is the mystery in salvation.
Jesus Christ has become your salvation.
It is found in no other.
Everything to do with your salvation
is found in Christ Jesus.

"It is because of him [God the Father] that you are in Christ Jesus, who has become for us wisdom from God - that is, our righteousness, holiness and redemption" (1 Corinthians 1:30).

Jesus Christ fulfilled all of the righteous requirements of His Father.
He became the offering,
the sacrifice on your behalf.
There had to be 'atonement' for the sin of each and every person.
It is this way in normal, daily life all over the world.
There is a system of justice.
It is in place to protect the citizens.

But friend, there is a higher Judge than any judge on earth.
It is God who judges all mankind.
There will be an accounting for our lives.

Without the forgiveness of Jesus and the washing away of sin by His blood,
we will be guilty before God.
Our punishment in the afterlife will be a 'forever' in hell.
The sinner will vanish even though he once flourished as a field flourishes in its season.
That same field is barren in winter where once it was greatly alive and on display.

"The senseless man does not know, fools do not understand, that though the wicked spring up like grass and all evil doers flourish, they will be forever destroyed." (Psalm 92:6-7).

Wisdom?
Jesus has become wisdom in you! It is true.
Seek the Lord and somehow in His fellowship of love and mercy He is your wisdom.
Ask of Him.

He is all and has all things you have need of.

"It is because of him [God the Father] that you are in Christ Jesus, who has become for us wisdom from God - that is, our righteousness, holiness and redemption" (1 Corinthians 1:30).
"You want something but don't get it. You kill and covet, but you cannot have what you want. You quarrel and fight. You do not have, because you do not ask God" (James 4:2).

420

There once was a man named Solomon.

He was the son of David.

God said to Solomon in a dream, 'ask for anything you want from Me.'
Solomon could have asked God to wipe out his enemies.
He could have asked for long life and great riches.
Instead, he opened up
and shared his heart with God who was his Friend.

Solomon was transparent before God and that is intimacy.
God is only looking for you to be authentic with Him.
God had no problem with Solomon's shortcomings and weaknesses.
God already knew what they were.
They were not a stumbling block to Solomon's faith in God.

Solomon exercised his faith in God by coming to Him in intimate fellowship.

Solomon talked things through with his Friend.
This is what happens with people who are friends on earth.
It is especially true in a marriage
that has God's blessing upon it.

So he mentioned he was still very young
and lacking in experience to be king over his people
who were now too numerous to count.
This was honesty. This was Solomon being real with God.
God can handle anything you are dealing with!

Do you see what was happening between Solomon and God?
God is not like a bank machine. Impersonal. Unknowable.
Push the right buttons and you will get what you want!
That is not at all equivalent to knowing God.

Solomon was in a comfortable, honest conversation with God!
He was free to express his feelings to an all knowing God.

It was in this process of communication between two friends
that Solomon reached his conclusion.
Solomon did not approach his time with God that day with 'the right answer.'
Offering God 'the right thing to pray.'

To be honest with you, that is how I had always seen it until now. I thought that Solomon was
commended of God because he asked for wisdom. As if this one petition was all there was to it.
In the light of intimacy and fellowship there became a new perspective.

I saw that a long conversation took place
before Solomon even got around to asking for wisdom.
Having a friend to listen to all the issues enabled Solomon to come to the conclusion
that he could really use wisdom above all other things.
God guided Solomon.
Solomon was talking with God after all.

God is the higher power. The stronger partner in the relationship bringing benevolence and mercy
toward the weaker partner. This is the definition of agape love.
Do you see how much good
comes from spending time with God
and communicating with Him?

It was only in the face of God that Solomon processed
the awareness of a need for wisdom above all things.
He did not need to consult with any other.

Why not confide in
and seek solace, comfort and wisdom
from the greatest friend of all friends.

God went ahead and freely gave Him the wisdom he needed!

421

Solomon was attending to fellowship with God just as Mary had.

Solomon was listening.

It was now God's turn to talk to Solomon
about His own feelings on the matter.
He said to Solomon, 'you could have asked for a lot of other things that are practical and helpful
and of great value. Because you asked me to give you a wise and discerning heart
you will also receive from Me every other blessing.
If you remain faithful to Me I will even bless you with a long life.'

So Dear Reader,
this is why we conclude that nothing means more
in an intimate relationship with God
than wisdom.

"At Gibeon the Lord appeared to Solomon during the night in a dream, and God said, "Ask for whatever you want me to give you." Solomon answered, "You have shown great kindness to your servant, my father David, because he was faithful to you and righteous and upright in heart. You have continued this great kindness to him and have given him a son to sit on his throne this very day. "Now, O Lord my God, you have made your servant king in place of my father David. But I am only a little child and do not know how to carry out my duties. Your servant is here among the people you have chosen, a great people, too numerous to count or number. So give your servant a discerning heart to govern your people and to distinguish between right and wrong. For who is able to govern this great people of yours?" The Lord was pleased that Solomon had asked for this. So God said to him, "Since you have asked for this and not for long life or wealth for yourself, nor have asked for the death of your enemies but for discernment in administering justice, I will do what you have asked. I will give you a wise and discerning heart, so that there will never have been anyone like you, nor will there ever be" (1 Kings 3:5-12).

Nothing means more to a follower of Jesus
than to receive wisdom through the intimate friendship of their God.
God will add all manner of blessing and you will have that great feeling inside
from pleasing your heavenly Father.

422

There is a sweetness to the word.

There is a refuge in the word.

A sense of safety that goes beyond feeling.
Hearing from God
is the apex of human experience.
The benefits defy human intellect
because it is an eternal reality.

As you listen and obey the creator you will be walking in love.
How wonderful to be under the influence of Love
and see the love of God influence the world around you!

"He sent forth his word and healed them; he rescued them from the grave" (Psalm 107:20).
"The world and its desires pass away, but the man who does the will of God lives forever"
(1 John 2:17).

Oh yes dear brother, dear sister, when you receive His word of forgiveness
it isn't about your ability to be 'spiritual'.
It isn't a fad nor is it a lifestyle choice
like painting your house
or enrolling in school.

It hasn't been the result of your own strength,
talent or religious exertion.

He sent His word and freely delivered you from the grave!
How astounding!

I ask you, of all the detractors of our precious Jesus, who among them can refer you to someone
who is able to deliver from death, sin and the grave?

423

Who can save your soul?

Who has stood up in history and given His life for all mankind?

Jesus did and He is the Way,
the Truth
and the Life!

After receiving Him, there is no fear of death.
Now that is power!

It is called resurrection power!

Jesus said in John 14:6,
"I am the way and the truth and the life. No one comes to the Father except through me."

Jesus is the Life. Jesus is the Word.
He hid nothing from the people of His day.
No good thing will be hidden from anyone who sincerely enquires of Him.

He is prepared to share everything with any person who desires to get to know Him.

"And if the Spirit of him who raised Jesus from the dead is living in you, he who raised Christ from
the dead will also give life to your mortal bodies through his Spirit, who lives in you"
(Romans 8:11).

Do you want the same Spirit who raised Jesus from the dead to be your Counsellor?

Then humble yourself.
Ask Him.
And He will freely forgive you.
A Person named the Holy Spirit will quicken (give life) to your mortal body.
The Holy Spirit was present long ago. Before, during and after the dreadful crucifixion
of our Lord Jesus Christ. This same Holy Spirit will also quicken your mortal body
exactly like He did in the very body of the Lord Jesus Christ.

The same Spirit will live in you and keep you for all time.

It doesn't get any better than that.

424

The word given to your heart by the Holy Spirit thrills like nothing else.

He brings the end of the matter for He is Truth.

When He speaks you are delivered from all that opposes you.
His word is the Light and the sword that brings an end to the deception of the enemy.
The lies of Satan are no match for any follower of Jesus once they receive His word!
The word of the Lord is given to all who seek Him.

"If you belonged to the world, it would love you as its own. As it is, you do not belong to the world,
but I have chosen you out of the world. That is why the world hates you. Remember the words I
spoke to you: 'No servant is greater than his master.' If they persecuted me, they will persecute you
also. If they obeyed my teaching, they will obey yours also. They will treat you this way because of
my name, for they do not know the One who sent me" (John 15:19-21).

He brings His light upon your situation and determines who is just.
He says it like this. 'I have decided in your favour.'
God decides who is right.
God settles it.
It is Almighty God who settles it

with
His
word.

It is God who has the final say.

He called Himself, 'the Truth'.
There is magnificent comfort in that.
There is also kindness and endearment.

414

You will love your Father all the more when He quietly says He is with you.
This means He is against your accuser.
Their railing, gossiping and lying -
it means He is not having it.
His word is the end of the matter.

You are never so safe as to trust in the Lord
and remain faithful unto Him alone.
No matter what people say about you to others.

On account of your obedience to God and fellowship with the Holy Spirit the reward of being able to walk with Him will only grow all the sweeter.

"Therefore he is able to save completely those who come to God through him, because he always lives to intercede for them" (Hebrews 7:25).

425

The Father, the Son and the Spirit are One.

When the Holy Spirit brings a word to your heart you are enjoying the fellowship of the Trinity.

Are they not bringing you into their confidence at that very moment?
Jesus Christ is the word made flesh.
Jesus Christ is the Word.

The word spoken to your heart is a wondrous thing.
Each word is your lifeline of Love.

"<u>In the beginning was the Word, and the Word was with God, and the Word was God.</u> He was with God in the beginning. Through him all things were made; without him nothing was made that has been made. In him was life, and that life was the light of men. The light shines in the darkness, but the darkness has not understood it. There came a man who was sent from God; his name was John. He came as a witness to testify concerning that light, so that through him all men might believe. He himself was not the light; he came only as a witness to the light. The true light that gives light to every man was coming into the world. He was in the world, and though the world was made through him, the world did not recognize him. He came to that which was his own, but his own did not receive him. Yet to all who received him, to those who believed in his name, he gave the right to become children of God - children born of natural descent, nor of human decision or a husband's will, but born of God.

The Word became flesh and made his dwelling among us. We have seen his glory, the glory of the One and Only, who came from the Father, full of grace and truth" (John 1:1-14).

Each word God sends to your heart is full of grace and truth.
It is a highly favoured 'state of being' to resonate
with the thoughts of the Divine.
As you agree with the word He sends to your heart
you enter into His work. His will being done on earth as it is in heaven.
When you agree with Him you will be watching Him fulfill His plan and purpose.
These plans were prepared before He made the world.

Since nobody is smarter than God this is the best way to walk with God.

"your kingdom come, your will be done on earth as it is in heaven" (Matthew 6:10).

You are watching Him work.

That is what it is like to be in agreement with the Holy Spirit of God.

426

I ask God on your behalf: "may you continue to be guided with each daily reading. Let your time reading bring His perfect will on your behalf and His sweet desire to share with you in an intimate relationship. May the precious and wonderful Holy Spirit share with you the depths of God's fellowship."

Have you been apprehended by the love of the Lord?

Do you really know
how important you are?
How special you are in His eyes?

This is a part of the understanding of what it means to be apprehended by the Lord!
To know you have such incredible value in His eyes.
Mainly to be apprehended by the Lord is to have the grace to seek Him every day
just like you do when you consider your next meal.
You just do it.
No book you read will ever bring this experience to your heart.
Remember,
the knowledge of God's love for you grows
ever deeper
higher
ever longer and wider
and His love surpasses knowledge when you share time with Him.
This ever growing experience is only shared
in the intimacy
of two people in love.

Listening
is the dynamic
that unites heart and mind.

Each friend listening to the other.

427

His love has the power to transform.

In every way His intention is to influence your life just as a Master Potter
skilfully shapes the clay
on His own wheel.

Moulding and shaping. The experience of being touched by the very hand of the Potter Himself.

Don't look for things to do for God.
Look for God.

Don't show Him how much you've done for Him.
Show Him how much you love Him
by waiting quietly upon Him
and ministering to Him in your silence.

Don't compare yourself to others.
While spending time with God let Him reflect back to you
that you are fearfully and wonderfully made - by Him!

Marvel
as He truthfully shares
how much He loves you.
He knows you like no other
for He looks upon your heart.

"The Lord does not look at the things man looks at. Man looks at the outward appearance, but the Lord looks at the heart" (1 Samuel 16:7b).

You will never study your way into the love of God.
You have to take the step to be alone with God yourself.

Be enthralled.
Overwhelmed at times.
Weep, worship and raise your hands in response to His presence and love.

You might dance,
speak in tongues, prophecy,
write music or create a work of art.
You may help the poor, travel to another country or visit the aged or sick.
With all that said,
it remains that the only thing the Lord is looking for
is to spend some time with you
every day.

Only one thing is needed.
After giving Him that 'one thing', in His timing He may open up some doors
for you to share His love in your own unique way with others.

You have to come to God
on your own
to enter into an intimate sharing with Him.
Open up the door of your heart and let Him in.

428

I have written a few prayers in the devotional thus far, but only a few.

It is a fellowship God invites you to join - so I didn't want you to feel a prayer in this book
is some how a substitute for your own worthy prayer.

It isn't about do's and don'ts.
It isn't about mustering up something in His name.
God is a loving, compassionate, caring individual.
He sees you as His only true love.

That is one of the great things about unconditional love.
After giving His life
He keeps you safely as a sheep
in His pasture.

There is suffering in the world.

I know that.

Once you are alive with God through Jesus Christ,
you will become a part of the solution
for the ills of mankind.
Your heart will ache along with God's.
He will share His concern for other people and difficult situations with you.

With a free will man can choose to serve God.

With a free will man can choose to do what he wants.

Even if it is to sin against himself or others.

429

The riches of intimacy begin when two people see each other for the first time.

Their relationship grows through honesty and vulnerability.

Seeing one another,
getting to know each other -
one day,
trusting one another.
A process that can't be scripted.

I can't write down here the prayers that I have prayed.
Like 'help me God' when I thought I was going to die one night with complications
from abdominal pain. There had been four major operations leading up to that night.
Or when I said 'I am no longer of any use to You' after a car accident destroyed my back and neck.

How will intimate things I've said while alone with God benefit you?
In that private place I have only been able to offer God a conversation
best described as very plain, common and uncomplicated.
I am only a human with weakness, frailty and self-centeredness.
Without His help
my communication would only be about myself and my own troubles.
Without His help I could not be thankful.
Though I am a flawed human being - and here is the wonderful thing -
He has never once made me feel He would be happier to talk with someone else.
Or that He is half-listened to me.
He has never made me feel I am bothering Him.
He has never made me feel inadequate as a spiritual person.
That He has better servants than me.
That I don't matter that much.

I don't deserve this through anything I have done, but I have a friend named Jesus.

Ah Dear Reader, Jesus is true and loving.
Forgiving and faithful.
He determined in advance to give me His kingdom
before I even knew how good He is.

Along with the kingdom He has given
to me and my lovely wife and children
every good thing we need.

I have never deserved it but He continues to take care of me.
Because He has been able to do this with a common, ordinary soul like mine
I enthusiastically recommend this friendship to you!

Open up your heart to the Son of God. God is faithful.

He
loves
you
too.

"The one who calls you is faithful and he will do it" (1 Thessalonians 5:24).
"To him who is able to keep you from falling and to present you before his glorious presence without fault and with great joy - " (Jude 1:24).
"Therefore he is able to save completely those who come to God through him, because he always lives to interceded for them" (Hebrews 7:25).

430

There is a tension in the relationship.

A tension that has always been there when God is reaching someone.

Remember John 14 when Jesus told His true disciples they already trust in God?
Trust in Him, and know the place He is going?
Right away they said they didn't.

There is a tension there.

"But there is a place where someone has testified: "What is man that you are mindful of him, the son of man that you care for him?" (Hebrews 2:6).

'Why God, do you even think about mankind?'
'Why do You bother with me?' you may ask sometimes as I have.
'Why do you care for us when we are so prone to sin?'
Ah, but don't you see?
Jesus Christ came to earth
in
our
form.

When God revealed Himself He was the Spirit made flesh.
He was in like-form as we are. There must be something about being a human
since the manifestation of the Spirit of God was in our human form.

"The Word became flesh and made his dwelling among us. We have seen his glory, the glory of the
One and Only, who came from the Father, full of grace and truth" (John 1:14).

There is something really important
about each
and every person.
God knows how important you are because He made you.
Carefully,
thoughtfully creating you just the way you are
with the genius of His limitless insight.
You may have done things that keep you from accepting this.
But remember, when Jesus came to earth he was in the same form as you are!
There is something eternally precious about you.

The devil fights to keep you from knowing this.
He will use flattery and pride to inflate how important and special you are
but it ends with hurt.
His plan is to oppress you, use you and ruin you.
He is lurking behind every selfish temptation.
He always takes God out of the picture. That is because he wants you to serve him and his demons.
He is a liar and will never focus your attention upon the consequences of your sinful behaviour.
Let me say that again, the devil will never focus your attention upon nor disclose to you
the consequences of a decision to sin.

Jesus said in John 10:10,
"The thief comes only to steal and kill and destroy; I have come that they may have life, and have it
to the full."

Jesus is talking the truth!
Satan is a liar and the father of lies. He is out to take your soul.
Do not ever listen to the devil or demons nor give them one bit of room in your life.

Plead the blood of Jesus against them saying, "I plead the blood of Jesus against
all forces of darkness. In the name of Jesus GO! Jesus help me!"
But only do so if you are in a committed relationship with Jesus Christ the King of Kings.

"Paul entered the synagogue and spoke boldly there for three months, arguing persuasively about
the kingdom of God. But some of them became obstinate; they refused to believe and publicly
maligned the Way. So Paul left them. He took the disciples with him and had discussions daily in
the lecture hall of Tyrannus. This went on for two years, so that all the Jews and Greeks who lived
in the province of Asia heard the word of the Lord.

God did extraordinary miracles through Paul, so that even handkerchiefs and aprons that had touched him were taken to the sick, and their illnesses were cured and the evil spirits left them. Some Jews who went around driving out evil spirits tried to invoke the name of the Lord Jesus over those who were demon-possessed. They would say, "In the name of Jesus, whom Paul preaches, I command you to come out." Seven sons of Sceva, a Jewish chief priest, were doing this. One day the evil spirit answered them, "Jesus I know, and I know about Paul, but who are you?" Then the man who had the evil spirit jumped on them and overpowered them all. He gave them such a beating that they ran out of the house naked and bleeding. When this became known to the Jews and Greeks living in Ephesus, they were all seized with fear, and the name of the Lord Jesus was held in high honour. Many of those who believed now came and openly confessed their evil deeds. A number who had practiced sorcery brought their scrolls together and burned them publicly. When they calculated the value of the scrolls, the total came to fifty thousand drachmas. In this way the word of the Lord spread widely and grew in power" (Acts 19:8-20).

"You, dear children, are from God and have overcome them, because the one who is in you is greater than the one who is in the world" (1 John 4:4).

"I have given you authority to trample on snakes and scorpions and to overcome all the power of the enemy; nothing will harm you" (Luke 10:19).

"They overcame him by the blood of the Lamb and by the word of their testimony; they did not love their lives so much as to shrink from death" (Revelation 12:11).

431

Dear Reader, Christianity is not a lifestyle choice.

It is power over the evil one.

The kindness of Jesus in your intimate fellowship will crush the devil's plan to destroy your life. Jesus is the door and your escape from hell and it's infernal damnation.
Keeping fellowship with Jesus means eternity in heaven one day.

"I am the true vine, and my Father is the gardener. He cuts off every branch in me that bears no fruit, while every branch that does bear fruit he prunes so that it will be even more fruitful. You are already clean because of the word I have spoken to you. Remain in me, I will remain in you. No branch can bear fruit by itself; it must remain in the vine. Neither can you bear fruit unless you remain in me. "I am the vine; you are the branches. If a man remains in me and I in him, he will bear much fruit; apart from me you can do nothing. If anyone does not remain in me, he is like a branch that is thrown away and withers; such branches are picked up, thrown into the fire and burned. If you remain in me and my words remain in you, ask whatever you wish, and it will be given you. This is to my Father's glory, that you bear much fruit, showing yourselves to be my disciples" (John 15:1-8).

The blood of Jesus gives restoration to fellowship through the forgiveness of your sins.

And Dear Reader it is your only hope.

"For the Son of Man came to seek and to save what was lost" (Luke 19:10).
"The reason the Son of God appeared was to destroy the devil's work" (1 John 3:8b).
"For this purpose the Son of God was manifested, that he might destroy the works of the devil" (1 John 3:8b King James Version).

Jesus is by no means on the side of the abuser.
Those who abuse others are doing Satan's work on earth.
They are evil ambassadors who's father is the devil.

The lake of fire is prepared for those who abuse others and do not repent.
There is peace one day for every victim. God is just. He has not forgotten you.
Nobody gets past the justice of our God.
The Lake of Fire.
There is justice.

Do not let what has been done to you in your life
prevent you from being saved yourself.
Neither let it be an obstacle when your abuser
has not been brought to justice
for what they have done to you.

Save yourself.
Come to Jesus.

Jesus knows and cares.

Be healed and saved in Jesus Holy name.

432

Greetings Dear Reader.

May God's blessings abound to you on this new day.

"Praise be to the Lord, to God our Saviour, who daily bears our burdens"
(Psalm 68:19 New International Version).
"Blessed be the Lord, who daily loadeth us with benefits, even the God of our salvation"
(Psalm 68:19 King James Version).

Where is God in your life today?

Here in the Psalms it says He is once again bearing your burdens
and loading you with benefits.

There are times when we really feel burdened.
Mean people, the loss of a friend or loved one.

The loss of a friend is life-changing.
It hurts
and generally brings complications
and sadness that can last for the rest of your life.

Misunderstanding with your spouse.
Disappointments or complications in a marriage.
Being alone and being lonely.
Being with someone and being lonely.
Setbacks in your career
or lack of a career.
Unexpected health complications.
Money woes that seem very large when you think about them.

Why would God say He daily bears our burdens
if the faithful sheep are supposed to be the ones
with enough faith to escape trouble?

Some people think doing
the Christian thing correctly
means you don't have troubles.
Does that mean if you have a burden that you are out of God's will?
Do troubles reveal that there is something wrong with you? God forbid!

"A righteous man may have many troubles, but the Lord delivers him from them all"
(Psalm 34:19 New International Version).

Consider God's perspective on the role of an earthly friend.
It is a friend who helps you when you fall down! That is what a friend will do.

We all need help once in a while.

God plans for you to have troubles that are too big for you sometimes.
God plans for you to have someone to help you at times like that.

"Two are better than one, because they have a good return for their work: If one falls down,
his friend can help him up. But pity the man who falls and has no one to help him up!"
(Ecclesiastes 4:9-10).
"A friend loves at all times, and a brother is born for adversity" (Proverbs 17:17).

Consider the burden shared by Shadrach, Meshach and Abednego.

Those fellows ended up in all kinds of trouble
and they were in the perfect will of God!

It is a story found in Daniel 3:13 - 30.
"Furious with rage, Nebuchadnezzar summoned Shadrach, Meshach and Abednego. So these men
were brought before the king, and Nebuchadnezzar said to them, "Is it true, Shadrach, Meshach
and Abednego, that you do not serve my gods or worship the image of gold I have set up? Now
when you hear the sound of the horn, flute, zither, lyre, harp, pipes and all kinds of music, if you
are ready to fall down and worship the image I made, very good. But if you do not worship it, you
will be thrown immediately into a blazing furnace. Then what god will be able to rescue you from
my hand? Shadrach, Meshach and Abednego replied to the king, "O Nebuchadnezzar, we do not
need to defend ourselves before you in this matter. If we are thrown into the blazing furnace, the
God we serve is able to save us from it, and he will rescue us from your hand, O king. But even if
he does not, we want you to know, O king, that we will not serve your gods or worship the image of
gold you have set up."
Then Nebuchadnezzar was furious with Shadrach, Meshach and Abednego, and his attitude toward
them changed. He ordered the furnace heated seven times hotter than usual and commanded
some of the strongest soldiers in his army to tie up Shadrach, Meshach and Abednego and throw
them into the blazing furnace. So these men, wearing their robes, trousers, turbans and other
clothes, were bound and thrown into the blazing furnace. The king's command was to urgent and
the furnace so hot that the flames of the fire killed the soldiers who took up Shadrach, Meshach
and Abednego, and these three men, firmly tied, fell into the blazing furnace. Then King
Nebuchadnezzar leaped to his feet in amazement and asked his advisers, "Weren't there three men
that we tied up and threw into the fire?" They replied, "Certainly, O king." He said, "Look! I see
four men walking around in the fire, unbound and unharmed, and the fourth looks like a son of
the gods." Nebuchadnezzar then approached the opening of the blazing furnace and shouted,
"Shadrach, Meshach and Abednego, servants of the Most High God, come out! Come here!" So
Shadrach, Meshach and Abednego came out of the fire, and the satraps, prefects, governors and
royal advisers crowded around them. They saw that the fire had not harmed their bodies, nor was a
hair of their heads singed; their robes were not scorched, and there was no smell of fire on them.
Then Nebuchadnezzar said, "Praise be to the God of Shadrach, Meshach and Abednego, who has
sent his angel and rescued his servants! They trusted in him and defied the king's command and
were willing to give up their lives rather than serve or worship any god except their own God.
Therefore I decree that the people of any nation or language who say anything against the God of
Shadrach, Meshach and Abednego be cut into pieces and their houses be turned into piles of
rubble, for no other god can save in this way." Then the king promoted Shadrach, Meshach and
Abednego in the province of Babylon."

These three dear fellows were serving God with all faithfulness.
Faithful because they walked in obedience to what God had told them.

They had an intimate relationship with God.
Faithfulness = obedience to God.

Can you see the difference here?
Faithfully practicing a belief system,
a doctrine,
a lifestyle based upon religious practices,
pronouncing a creed,
wearing certain clothes
and making the effort to obey a list of do's and don'ts
are religious observances.

Some people naturally have the strength within themselves to do quite well at this.
They are able to follow the rules and have the appearance of godliness far better than others.
Pity the poor folks who have been damaged in life and can't keep up with other church going folks
in acting the 'right way', saying the 'right things' at the 'right time' and exhibiting all
the 'right' social graces!

It would 'seem' if one keeps these observances it is due to a love for God.
Outwardly anyways.
It is a sliding scale however
since some people will be able to keep the rules better than others.

Activities reflecting moral goodness
are practiced by people who know the Lord
and by people who have no idea
who Jesus Christ is.

In fact charitable acts and social finesse is practiced by all manner of religions all over the world
all the time. Kind, thoughtful, gracious and caring people who are a great example to those around
them. Some of these people are not saved. Some are.
Dear Reader, the outward show
is not what the Lord is looking for.

Shadrach, Meshach and Abednego were in love with God.
They spent time with Him and God directed them personally
in how they were to honour and serve Him.
They conducted themselves in a certain manner as a consequence of having been with God.
You can call this obedience or the outcome of being in a loving relationship.

The anger directed toward them was due to the true righteousness of God in their lives.
People get very upset with those who spend time with Jesus.

Church people who only know about God get very upset
with those who have been with Jesus.

426

But this wonderful intimacy is reflected in the light of eternity.
This is a love that surpasses knowledge and means everything to our heavenly Father.

"Greater love has no one than this, that he lay down his life for his friends" (John 15:13).

Jesus did it all for love.

He was manifest upon the earth.
He came to get you.

He wants to save you.

434

Outwardly we are able to do incredibly noble and pious deeds.

Attending church, giving money for the poor, telling others about Jesus and His love for the lost.

Even preaching the gospel with all boldness can be done
with all appearance of godliness and consecration.

"The Lord says: 'These people come near to me with their mouth and honour me with their lips,
but their hearts are far from me. Their worship of me is made up only of rules taught by men"
(Isaiah 29:13).
'These people honour me with their lips, but their hearts are far from me' (Matthew 15:8).

If your deeds spring forth from your own family name,
history in or length of service in your denomination, your strength, you were unscathed by abuse,
your own imagination, social connections or ingenuity - then your deeds lack eternal value.

The need to listen to the God of Power in an intimate relationship
permeates the bible from cover to cover.

'Therefore everyone who hears these words of mine and puts them into practice is like a wise man
who built his house on the rock' (Matthew 7:24).

"Guard your steps when you go to the house of God. Go near to listen rather than to offer the
sacrifice of fools, who do not know that they do wrong" (Ecclesiastes 5:1).

Only deeds done in love abide forever.

"If I give all I possess to the poor and surrender my body to the flames, but have not love, I gain
nothing" (1 Corinthians 13:3).

Many pastors and ministers of the gospel talk about Jesus and don't personally know Him.

They don't spend time with Him.

They are held aloft by the latest gospel trend
and go from mindset to mindset on whatever is popular at the moment.
They sound, act, look and appear quite committed.
That is the problem.

They don't sound, act, look and appear like Jesus.

As a consequence the majority of their followers never get around
to spending time with Jesus and getting to know Him either.

The adherents are slowly caught up in how tremendous the messenger is.
It erodes the trust in the timely word God brings to their own hearts.
Listening to the word quietly whispered to their hearts by Jesus takes a second place to the latest
articulations and bombast of the 'man or woman of God'.

If your conclusion through the teaching of an individual
is how great they are

instead of a deepening grasp of how great Jesus is
and a deeper persuasion of His love for you,
then you are wasting your time
with a career minister.

This is a person who is not in step with Jesus Christ.
They are living to fulfill the goals that satisfy their own flesh.
It is an easier path.
They will not suffer as the faithful always have.

"In fact, everyone who wants to live a godly life in Christ Jesus will be persecuted" (2 Timothy 3:12).

But those who will walk in step with God
like Shadrach, Meshach and Abednego did so long ago -
they will one day receive a magnificent inheritance in heaven.

"Do not be deceived: God cannot be mocked. A man reaps what he sows. The one who sows to
please his sinful nature, from that nature will reap destruction; the one who sows to please the
Spirit, from the Spirit will reap eternal life" (Galatians 6:7-8).

No one in heaven is disappointed for having prayed,
"Lord, let me live to please the precious Holy Spirit."

Amen.

"The one who calls you is faithful and he will do it" (1 Thessalonians 5:24).
"To them God has chosen to make known among the Gentiles the glorious riches of this mystery, which is Christ in you, the hope of glory" (Colossians 1:27).
"Since, then, you have been raised with Christ, set your hearts on things above, where Christ is seated at the right hand of God. Set your minds on things above, not on earthly things. For you died, and your life is now hidden with Christ in God. When Christ, who is your life, appears, then you also will appear with him in glory" (Colossians 3:1-3).

436

Christ is your life.

Don't leave Him outside the door of your heart.

He is also the One and only
Son of God.
Is it a good idea to put Him off?

"Here I am! I stand at the door and knock. If anyone hears my voice and opens the door, I will come in and eat with him, and he with me" (Revelation 3:20).

Let the Lord turn your experience with carnal church leaders for His good.
May the cliché and tactics
of a lukewarm church leader
challenge your heart to discover for yourself
that God gave His Son for the express purpose
to speak personally with you.

Let the experience drive you to seek God on your own.

You may have very likely given up going to church.
You may have lost out on really great relationship
with sincere people seeking God just as you are.
People who knew and loved you.

God will pick up what appears to be the pieces of your spiritual life.
He will inspire you with a love for His word.
You will not regret leaving a lukewarm church
for the shelter of a quiet place reserved just for you by Jesus Christ Himself.

Carnal preaching from someone who does not spend time with Jesus
will always compete with the voice of the Holy Spirit
for pre-eminence in your heart.

I have seen first hand the effects of erosion in a heart that was once on fire for God. It happened when they started attending a big, successful, prosperous, lukewarm Christian church. It was all a good time with lots of preaching and teaching and all the things people do in a church. But they slowly lost the desire for intimacy with Jesus. It imperceptibly slipped away. Daily prayer, the time spent with Jesus, became a form. At length they walked in a self-sufficient religious mindset. One day when they became aware of this great loss, they returned to the Lord with their whole heart. In the quiet place God told them to withdraw from that religious setting. The fire returned to their heart. They have walked in intimacy ever since. They are wonderfully in love with God. They are continuing to get to know the Lord. They are no longer numbered among the ranks of those who are getting together to talk about God. He made the courageous and humble choice instead to personally meet with God. This soul is wrapped up in a passionate fellowship with Jesus. He made this choice, and gained his own soul. Only after submitting his entire life back to God was he able to receive the instruction to no longer attend this church.

"Be careful," Jesus said to them. "Be on your guard against the yeast of the Pharisees and Sadducees."
"How is it you don't understand that I was talking to you about bread? But be on your guard against the yeast of the Pharisees and Sadducees." Then they understood that he was not telling them to guard against the yeast used in bread, but against the teaching of the Pharisees and Sadducees" (Matthew 6:6,11-12).

Be careful, be on your guard if your place of fellowship is not fostering a burning desire to know and get alone with God. You are in danger of losing the only valuable thing you have.
Your love for Jesus Christ.

I am not talking about going through the motions if that is what you are seeking.
Like I said earlier, you don't need the Holy Spirit for that.

The bible says in the reference to the Laodician church that this love is 'hot' - not lukewarm or cold. Make a decision first to get alone with God everyday. Then let Him tell you whether He has a purpose for you in your lukewarm church. Follow the instructions God provides within your heart. He will send you confirmation. He will speak to you through the Bible. You will be led by His Spirit about continuing to attend one way or the other.

"Because those who are led by the Spirit of God are sons of God" (Romans 8:14).

This will bode well for you when you will have to give an account for your life.
There are others who are on fire for God. God has always had a people!
God always has a people!
The pastor of a lukewarm church will not be their to stand with you and offer an account
of your Christian service because he or she won't know who Jesus is in the first place.

You will be on your own.

"He replied, "I have been very zealous for the Lord God Almighty. The Israelites have rejected your covenant, broken down your altars, and put your prophets to death with the sword. I am the only one left, and now they are trying to kill me too. [God replies] Yet I reserve seven thousand in Israel - all whose knees have not bowed down to Baal and all whose mouths have not kissed him"
(1 Kings 19:10,18).

437

If church work has you too busy to spend time alone with Jesus please consider this verse.

"That servant who knows his master's will and does not get ready or does not do what his master wants will be beaten with many blows" (Luke 12:47).

What does your Master want you to do? It is a mercifully simple question.

This is different than making the decision to do what you want to do.
Different than your spouse wants you to do, your parents or your overseer or head office.
Maybe you will differ a little from your peers.
The men, women, boys and girls of your church
need to know what is on the heart and mind
of Jesus Christ.
They belong to Him.

Men or women in the ministry - what in God's name are you doing
with these sheep
that are the property of the Lord Jesus Christ?

If you are a church leader who is paying the price to walk with God
and your work does not bring in a lot of money please take heart!
It will abide forever because you will be doing it in love.
You will please God
and you will have much
to look forward to
in the next life.

Not knowing what the Lord wanted from you
will not hold up as an excuse.
Don't be lukewarm.

If you are busy with church but don't have time for your kind and loving Jesus
then you are only lukewarm
and a robber

of poor
weak
helpless
sheep
whom Jesus died for.
You will one day face serious consequences from someone higher up than the head office.
Jesus will think nothing of spewing you out of His mouth. He is just. He already told you
what He will do with lukewarm church people.

Even if you wear a suit.
Even if you have your name on the door.

Even if you get to tell people what to do - for awhile.

438

This book is meant to encourage you in your preparations for a fruitful outcome in your faith.

Let your faith be in Jesus Christ and His relationship with you.
In the things He lovingly shares with you
when you are alone together.

He will always share in perfect timing the things that you need to know.
Keep a journal with you to write them down if it helps.

Even if you don't make a practice of returning
to what you have written,
it is a soothing practice
to record God's loving, kind, helpful and insightful thoughts.
It makes His words to you more real somehow.

"We have not received the spirit of the world but the Spirit who is from God, that we may
understand what God has freely given us. This is what we speak, not in words taught us by human
wisdom but <u>in words taught by the Spirit expressing spiritual truths in spiritual words</u>"
(1 Corinthians 2:12-13).

Inevitably, when I get to the end of a journal I just shred it.
I go through journal after journal. Each day God brings new manna for me.
Every so often my dear wife picks up a few coiled notebooks for me to write in.
I have never found a use afterward for the intimate conversations shared together
with my friend Jesus. Only if I feel to write down the date and later it fits in providentially
with how things are turning out. It is very encouraging when God answers prayer or tells you of
things to come and you can refer back to the time Jesus told you about it.

"But when he, the Spirit of truth, comes, he will guide you into all truth. He will not speak on his own; he will speak only what he hears, and he will tell you what is yet to come" (John 16:13).

Writing things down,
drawing diagrams and pictures He gives me - these were essential at the time.
I guess I wouldn't find a reason to use them anywhere else.

This would be similar to the intimate but ordinary conversations that go on all the time
with my wife. They would serve no purpose beyond the time they are spoken.
It's just the stuff of life between precious Kathy and me.

Anyone can walk in a relationship with God.
God has made it possible for everyone to be able to live in a deep, intimate relationship with Him.
Sheep are so very apt to respond appropriately to a kind, faithful, good, strong, protective
and loving shepherd.

"You will seek me and find me when you seek me with all your heart" (Jeremiah 29:13).
"My sheep listen to my voice; I know them, and they follow me. But they will never follow a
stranger; in fact, they will run away from him because they do not recognize a stranger's voice"
(John 10:27,5).

439

Because of their faithfulness to God their earthly king had become very angry
with Meshach, Shadrach and Abednego.

They would be unable to honour God if they obeyed the king's latest decree.

Shadrach, Meshach and Abednego had a tremendous burden now.
They were under the threat of the loss of their lives
because they did what God wanted them to do.
They were now in trouble but is wasn't because there was something wrong in their lives.
There was something very right in their lives.

How important was it to them to hear and obey God?
They spoke up to the authorities about it. They said it was more important to have a relationship
with God than anything else. They were willing for their lives to end rather than disobey what God
had asked of them. This brings light upon the reference to attending a lukewarm church.
The matters that pertain to the kingdom of God really do pertain to life and death issues.
All the time.

To be obedient is to be red hot for God. On fire for God.
There is no race to run for those who go through the motions and lack commitment to our loving
Jesus. It isn't a race. It is hypocrisy.

It is a daily slap in the face of an already weeping and broken Saviour.

Obedience is better than sacrifice.

If Shadrach, Meshach and Abednego were just keeping up with the crowd
and going through the motions with their faith this wouldn't have happened to them.
That is why nobody else was getting into trouble. These fellows were giving God what He wanted.
Since God asks the same (that being, obedience and fidelity of heart) from all of His people
it is fair to assume that no one else was listening to God. This is graciously outlined
in Deuteronomy 30. Our merciful God remains the same to this day.

"Shadrach, Meshach and Abednego replied to the king, "O Nebuchadnezzar, we do not need to
defend ourselves before you in this matter. If we are thrown into the blazing furnace, the God we
serve is able to save us from it, and he will rescue us from your hand, O king. But even if he does
not, we want you to know, O king, that we will not serve your gods or worship the image of gold
you have set up" (Daniel 3:16-18).

They realized that fellowship with God was everything. Better than life itself.

"Because your love is better than life, my lips will glorify you" (Psalm 63:3).
"Though he slay me, yet will I hope in him;" (Job 13:15a).

440

Is He the kind of Shepherd that excludes everything in your life that would upset you?

In truth, a faithful walk with God has you share in His burden.

You enter into identification with His love for mankind.
Intimate relationship with God introduces you to His perceptions.
This is included when you walk in His perfect will for your life.

"For we are God's workmanship, created in Christ Jesus to do good works, which God prepared in
advance for us to do" (Ephesians 2:10).

It is your own path. Getting to know Jesus includes learning how He feels about people
and how He still suffers for those around you.

"I want to know Christ and the power of his resurrection and the fellowship of sharing in his
sufferings, becoming like him in his death," (Philippians 3:10).

"For just as the sufferings of Christ flow over into our lives, so also through Christ our comfort
overflows" (2 Corinthians 1:5).

"Praise be to the God and Father of our Lord Jesus Christ, the Father of compassion and the God of all comfort, who comforts us in all our troubles, so that we can comfort those in any trouble with the comfort we ourselves have received from God. For just as the sufferings of Christ flow over into our lives, so also through Christ our comfort overflows" (2 Corinthians 1:3-5).

441

Your loving Saviour continues to suffer as He intercedes for mankind.

Intercession is the deepest form of prayer.

By definition it is to identify with a person or situation,
experiencing a small measure first hand as a tangible,
visceral identification or introduction to that suffering or need.

"Therefore he is able to save completely those who come to God through him, because he always lives to intercede for them" (Hebrews 7:25).

Jesus 'ever lives' to make intercession for the sheep of His flock (King James Version).
He always lives to intercede for them.

A caring

compassionate

committed

victorious

Saviour of the world.

442

Your Shepherd is ever watching on your behalf.

He began once again to bear your burden this morning before
you had opened your eyes to a new day.
And what a wonderful new day it is for you!

"This the day the Lord has made; let us rejoice and be glad in it" (Psalm 118:24).
"And my God will meet all your needs according to his glorious riches in Christ Jesus"
(Philippians 4:19).
"The Lord himself goes before you and will be with you; he will never leave you nor forsake you.
Do not be afraid; do not be discouraged" (Deuteronomy 31:8).

"For it is God who works in you to will and to act according to his good purpose" (Philippians 2:13).

It is God who greets you in the new day Dear Reader!
Have no fear!
It is God who works in you as you seek Him.
Oh how He loves you Dear Reader.
Do not fear the fiery trial.

He will bring only good to pass in your life.

"Consider it pure joy my brothers, whenever you face trials of many kinds, because you know that the testing of your faith develops perseverance. Perseverance must finish its work so that you may be mature and complete, not lacking anything" (James 1:2-4).
"Praise be to the God and Father of our Lord Jesus Christ! In his great mercy he has given us new birth into a living hope through the resurrection of Jesus Christ from the dead, and into an inheritance that can never perish, spoil or fade - kept in heaven for you, who through faith are shielded by God's power until the coming of the salvation that is ready to be revealed in the last time. In this you greatly rejoice, though now for a little while you may have had to suffer grief in all kinds of trials. These have come so that your faith - of greater worth than gold, which perishes even though refined by fire - may be proved genuine and may result in praise, glory and honour when Jesus Christ is revealed" (1 Peter 1:3-7).

443

Daniel chapter 2 tells of King Nebuchadnezzar having trouble sleeping because of his dreams.

This caused him to live with a troubled mind. It turned his life upside down.

Though he was the most powerful person around,
he could not help himself nor did he have a way
to find someone who could.

He did not serve the One True God.

He was stuck.

"Humble yourselves, therefore, under God's mighty hand, that he may lift you up in due time" (1 Peter 5:6).

Because he did not have a spiritual foundation
he was under the influence of flawed and inconsistent forces.
His advisers were self-serving. Their response to the king typifies the sad consequence of lacking faith in God and 'leaning upon' or taking refuge in other people at the time of your greatest need.

With God as your refuge or hiding place you will have One builder
both great and true. Along with His refuge is the wonderful fellowship
of others whom God will send to comfort you
and meet your good need.

"You are my hiding place; you will protect me from trouble and surround me with songs of
deliverance" (Psalm 32:7).

In His loving care there is no regret
for He does all things well.
Without God you are stuck with many builders.

How could an ordinary person possibly have a prosperous vision for your life like God?

God will plant you in His garden.

"For I know the plans I have for you," declares the Lord, "plans to prosper you and not to harm
you, plans to give you hope and a future" (Jeremiah 29:11).
"Unless the Lord builds the house, its builders labour in vain" (Psalm 127:1a).

444

Nebuchadnezzar is an example of the helpless estate of a spiritually sensitive person without
a refuge in God.

When you desire to live with a sense of personal freedom from God you are actually under the
influence of other people!

In this heart-wrenching example Nebuchadnezzar is asking for help from those wicked spiritual
builders - the magicians, enchanters, sorcerers and astrologers (Daniel 2:2).

Pity him in his troubled state of mind.

Having no help,
no hope
and the absence
of mental healthcare widely available in our world today.

Those who seek answers without the guidance of the Spirit of God
live without the loving foundation of God.

Sheep without the benefit and care of a loving Shepherd are lost sheep.

"They sow to the wind and reap the whirlwind" (Hosea 8:7a).

445

Do you know a poor soul who is troubled and vexed?

Someone who doesn't know if they are coming or going?

Is there someone in your life who is under the influence of others
who do not esteem them as precious and irreplaceable?
Someone being humiliated,
abused and kept from the freedom God has for them?
Be still before the Lord and see if the Holy Spirit would lift them up through your prayers.
Jesus Christ is all-powerful.

Praise God!
There is a Saviour!
There is a King who is King above all Kings.

If the Holy Spirit leads you, call on Him today on behalf of those who are lost and suffering.
God will SURELY hear your prayer.
God will SURELY reward you for your willingness to reach out with your heart.
But first, be still.
See if you are in step with your Master for the specific needs of dear people you are thinking of.

God is near to those who cry unto Him for help.

"The Lord is near to all who call on him, to all who call on him in truth" (Psalm 145:18).
"The Lord is close to the broken hearted and saves those who are crushed in spirit" (Psalm 34:18).
"But as for me, I watch in hope for the Lord, I wait for God my Saviour; my God will hear me"
(Micah 7:7).

446

Dear Reader, with but a moment of repentance this next passage from Hosea could have been
Nebuchadnezzar - right there in the midst of his deepest troubles!

This is miraculous! This is glorious! Oh the glorious riches that belong to the people who's God is
the Lord! Hosea 2:19 - 21.

"I will betroth you to me forever; I will betroth you in righteousness and justice, in love and
compassion. I will betroth you in faithfulness, and you will acknowledge the Lord. "In that day I
will respond declares the Lord - "I will respond to the skies, and they will respond to the earth; and
the earth will respond to the grain, the new wine and oil, and they will respond to Jezreel. I will
plant her for myself in the land; I will show my love to the one I called 'Not my loved one.' I will
say to those called 'Not my people,' 'You are my people'; and they will say, 'You are my God.' "

God's response to the repentant and troubled heart
that calls out to Him

is immediate betrothal!

That is how precious you already are in His sight.
There is no deeper response of love given between two people.

God responds with all He has.

447

God, your God, is so transparent with His feelings.

He comes right out and says in the bible
He desires betrothal to you
before you even express an interest in Him!

How magnificent is that.

It is only a matter of time until you get around to responding to Him.
All of that love has always been there

for you.

"Before I formed you in the womb I knew you," (Jeremiah 1:5a).

Here is a wonder.
He attends to you with this same heart
every single time you call upon Him.

He is there with fullness of commitment as unto His betrothed.

Though you feel less than perfect
it does not change the deep love
in which He attends to your needy heart.

How great is our God.

How great is His love.

"How great is the love the Father has lavished on us, that we should be called children of God! And that is what we are! The reason the world does not know us is that it did not know him"
(1 John 3:1).

If Nebuchadnezzar had only repented - through the betrothal love of God he would have instantly inherited everything belonging to God.

This happened with the thief on the cross.

Nebuchadnezzar didn't turn to God.
Later on God arranged for Daniel to interpret a dream that was troubling Nebuchadnezzar.

Daniel did what Nebuchadnezzar could have done.
Daniel humbled himself to seek God and wait upon Him for the answer.
God would have freely helped and explained the dream to Nebuchadnezzar because God
is no respecter of persons. He gives love and help to all who seek Him.

"Then Peter began to speak: 'I now realize how true it is that God does not show favouritism but accepts men from every nation who fear him and do what is right' " (Acts 10:34-35).

If you already belong to God
can you see that all He has
belongs to you?

Is this due to great faith on your part?
No,
it is true
through the greatest of all Loves.
Everlasting love.

He has betrothed Himself to you.

His deep, everlasting bond with you is forever.

Here is King Nebuchadnezzar in a troubled state of mind seeking help from his special servants.

He firmly decided to withhold information from them about the dream.
It was the king's way of seeing if they truly had a unique power
or were just using their position to benefit from his money
and special care he provided.

It appears the magicians, enchanters, sorcerers and astrologers
did not live to offer humble service to the King
but rather to benefit from his wealth.

They were selfish in their position of privilege.
They had such privilege as to be sought out
by the most important person in the land.

Through past experience the King was now wary of his advisors.
He had learned he could not trust them despite
the privilege he afforded them.

"If you do not tell me the dream, there is just one penalty for you. You have conspired to tell me misleading and wicked things, hoping the situation will change" (Daniel 2:9a,b).

The uncaring, unfeeling attitude of the King's advisers
must have been a pattern with their conduct.

As capable as he was as King of the land, Nebuchadnezzar was no match
for the challenge presented to him by his dream.
He was unable to cope and the poor guy was in anguish.

I pity the man for he was mentally in a state of anguish.
Just one heartfelt prayer of repentance and God could have helped him.
The King was so close to deliverance and wholeness of mind!
If only the King had cried out to God his Father.

"For you did not receive a spirit that makes you a slave again to fear, but you received the Spirit of sonship. And by him we cry, 'Abba, Father' " (Romans 8:15).
"For God hath not given us the spirit of fear; but of power, and of love, and of a sound mind"
(2 Timothy 1:7 King James Version).

He was pushed to the limit of his ability to endure.
His advisers would have to come through with real answers.
Their typical conduct would simply not do.
It was the last time the King would be able to bear their apparent lack of true power.

Seeing their King and benefactor in great mental anguish should have elicited
an empathetic response.

They had no empathy to give.

This is a most sad state of affairs. I realise the King was not serving God.
But to be so alone in a state of despair . . .
Do you know someone like this right now? Are you in this state right now?
Please, ask God to guide you if you feel it is appropriate at this time.
Does He want you to pray for someone? Does someone come to mind?

Are you alright? Can you use some love and reassurance?

Wait upon the Lord. Let Him love you. Call upon the precious name of Jesus.
You can come back to this book later on, ok Dear Reader?

You are loved. God loves you just as you are.
How sad for this afflicted man.
With all his success he still had no assurance that his advisors would stop exploiting him.
He was desperate and there was no one else to reach out to.
He had come to know their hearts through their behaviour leading up to this awful episode.

Evidently it had become their code of conduct
to focus upon what they would get
out of the king's misfortune.

It is true that people can be misled even when there are so called 'red flags' to warn
that something isn't right. Even if there is evidence not to trust someone or a situation.
Without a Shepherd there is no 'higher power' to pull you out of a bad situation.
And no 'higher power' to turn all things for good when there is a bad situation.
Oh the sorrow for those without the goodness of the Lord.

Yes Dear Reader,
Jesus Christ is the only Son of God.
Oh how He weeps for the lost.
For those beyond His reach.

"No temptation has seized you except what is common to man. And God is faithful; he will not let
you be tempted beyond what you can bear. But when you are tempted, he will also provide a way
out so that you can stand up under it" (1 Corinthians 10:13).

450

"The king replied to the astrologers, "This is what I have firmly decided: If you do not tell me what
my dream was and interpret it, I will have you cut into pieces and your houses turned into piles of
rubble. But if you tell me the dream and explain it, you will receive from me gifts and rewards and
great honour [the astrologers were not motivated by love or respect or gratitude, the King knew this
and offered them what their hearts craved]. So tell me the dream and interpret it for me. Then the
king answered, "I am certain that you are trying to gain time, because you realize that this is what I
have firmly decided: If you do not tell me the dream, there is just one penalty for you. You have
conspired to tell me misleading and wicked things, hoping the situation will change. So then, tell
me the dream, and I will know that you can interpret it for me" (Daniel 2:5-9).

Here is the King.

Troubled in mind.

Sleep deprived and emotionally unstable.
So desperate as to even try and coax the compassion from his entourage.
All he gets in return is more of their artful deceit.
Having many friends to surround you is no assurance of success in this life.

"A man of many companions may come to ruin" (Proverbs 18:24).
"This is what the Lord says: "Cursed is the one who trusts in man, who depends on flesh for his strength and whose heart turns away from the Lord" (Jeremiah 17:5).

They play him.
Right there in midst of his terrible struggle
he can still see right through them.

Oh the pathos
as this scene unfolds
in each humiliating,
degrading moment.

If only,

if only Nebuchadnezzar had turned to God
and not to those who presume to speak the mysteries of heaven
and the spirit realm.

The King was desperate. If only he had humbled himself and turned to God.

The answers he was seeking were there if only he were to ask.

'Call to me and I will answer you and tell you great and unsearchable things you do not know'
(Jeremiah 33:3).

451

"Come to me, all you who are weary and burdened, and I will give you rest" (Matthew 11:28).

God is not waiting for us to be perfect or 'good enough' to come to Him.
He invites all people to freely and quickly respond.

Really,
He is just waiting now for you to take Him up on His offer.
To be clear,
it is an offer to do something for you
that you can't do for yourself.
One day you will need to call upon Him.

What crisis would bring you to your knees?
The tragic death of a friend or loved one comes to mind.
I have been there.

There are friends that loved me and I loved them.
They have died and all I could do is go to God for myself and for their sweet loved ones. I don't know what I would have done otherwise. I am so thankful God has provided the opportunity to love and to be loved in return through the death of His own dear Son.

There is no One else able to make the offer that your Jesus is making today.
Talk about bold! Here is real authority in the spirit realm.
Here is a statement from Jesus Christ the Lord of Lords.

'As surely as I live,' says the Lord, 'every knee will bow before me; every tongue will confess to God' (Romans 14:11).

Dear Reader you are reading something about yourself that is written in the bible. Jesus has said the time will come when all will have to declare Him Lord because that is who He is. You are included in this future event. You are going to declare Him Lord! You will do it in this present life of your own free will. Or in the next life as an unbeliever on bended knee before you are thrown into hell where you will vanish for all eternity.

He has no favourites. He is ready to forgive and receive anyone.

"Then Peter began to speak: "I now realize how true it is that God does not show favouritism" (Acts 10:34).
"If any of you lacks wisdom, he should ask God, who gives generously to all without finding fault, and it will be given to him" (James 1:5).

If only King Nebuchadnezzar had gone to God,
repented of worshiping idols and other gods.
God would immediately forgive and wash his sins spotless white.

God will do the same for you. Let Him spare you from other loves
that will never really save nor satisfy you.

"If we confess our sins, he is faithful and just and will forgive us our sins and purify us from all unrighteousness" (1 John 1:19).

452

"Come now, let us reason together," says the Lord. "Though your sins are like scarlet, they shall be as white as snow; though they are red as crimson, they shall be like wool" (Isaiah 1:18).

"I love the Lord, for he heard my voice; he heard my cry for mercy. Because he turned his ear to me, I will call on him as long as I live. The cords of death entangled me, the anguish of the grave came upon me; I was overcome by trouble and sorrow. Then I called on the name of the Lord; "O Lord, save me!" The Lord is gracious and righteous; our God is full of compassion. The Lord protects the simple-hearted; when I was in great need, he saved me. Be at rest once more, O my soul, for the Lord has been good to you. For you, O Lord, have delivered my soul from death, my eyes from tears, my feet from stumbling, that I may walk before the Lord in the land of the living. I believed; therefore I said, "I am greatly afflicted." And in my dismay I said, "All men are liars." How can I repay the Lord for all his goodness to me? I will lift up the cup of salvation and call on the name of the Lord. I will fulfill my vows to the Lord in the presence of all his people"
(Psalm 116:1-14).

This could have been 'the great story' of King Nebuchadnezzar.

Everything he needed would have been freely given to him.
The lowest person in his kingdom could have received the same blessing.
The blessing of God is without limit to them that ask.
Our God is the Prince of Peace.

What a Prince He is to care about us in our need.

"And he will be called Wonderful Counsellor, Mighty God, Everlasting Father, Prince of Peace"
(Isaiah 9:6b).

453

Twice the King's advisers asked him to explain the contents of the dream.

Each time the King stood firm.

If they were legitimately spiritual they would have known the dream before being told.
When the King could see they were just trying to buy themselves some time
he wanted to have them executed.
This was a King who would no longer mess around with charlatans.

Anyone who claims spiritual knowledge without the precious Holy Spirit
is deceived and a deceiver.
Again, there will be 'red flags' go up with the things they do and say.

A red flag may be the desire to control or manipulate.
Inappropriate sexual involvement.
An emphasis on money is also an indication that a charlatan is at work.
The absence of real love or compassion is also a red flag.
Warnings from loved ones who care about us that we are in an inappropriate relationship.

The King sent out Arioch, the commander of the King's guard to seek out and put to death all of the other wise men in the kingdom. The King was not thinking straight by now, wanting to put all of the wise men in the kingdom to death, not just the men before him. Daniel was about to get into trouble through no fault of his own. He was implicated through the unrelated shenanigans of the counterfeit wise men. Suddenly Daniel is lumped in with the phoney, disreputable spiritual leaders. They were counterfeit because they sought wisdom outside of a relationship with God.

Now, this wisdom we are speaking of is not the wisdom you get from a kind mom or dad.
A kind mom or dad would tell you to wear your boots in the rain.
Or, 'wait for me to come and pick you up after school'.
That would be a 'general wisdom'. Suitable for anyone at any time.

Wisdom from God is huge because it is part of the experience of being saved.
Every time God speaks to you and shares His wisdom it is your lifeline. As soon as God revealed wisdom to Daniel about Nebuchadnezzar the situation was resolved.

With truth comes the end of the prattling of the enemy. The accuser is silenced.
The Word has arrived. And nobody messes with the Lion of the Tribe of Judah.
The trouble of mind was arrested. Truth arrived through the words God spoke to Daniel and it settled everything. That is how close the King got to the King of Kings.

His heart did not change for later on he built an idol for his people to bow down to.
Everyone will have the opportunity to accept or reject God in this lifetime.

Ask God for His wisdom today.
Ask God for His wisdom in all of your circumstances.
The last thing your betrothed would have you do is to seek shelter in another.
God is your betrothed.
Rest not in any other.

454

Nebuchadnezzar was a sinner whom God loved.

God loves the whole world.

It's hard to fathom that much love,
but He loves every person in every nation of this world.

"For God so loved the world" (John 3:16).

When it comes to being separated from God
it doesn't matter to Him how big your sin is.
Big or small is not how He sees it.

When a helpless child is heading away from his or her parents on shore
it doesn't matter if the child in a large boat or a small boat.
They are slowly drifting away from all that is important.
Their parents and the place they call home is their whole world.
As soon as the journey away from land begins all is lost for that child.
Whether it is a fishing boat,
a cruise ship
or even a submarine
it is all the same

to *that* child.

Separation from fundamental, essential saving love is the common thread in this little story and the
age old story of man's separation from God. This is how God sees lost humanity.
Without His intimacy and shelter each individual is separated from Him.
It is the true state of the soul without God.
There is the appearance of life yet the soul remains separated from God.
They are lost because they are not reborn.

Separation from God is all the same no matter how great or small
the condition of the sin. Those who don't know the Lord are lost.

How lost are you?
The sin that separates you can be instantaneously washed away and forgiven
by your Father in heaven. He really just wants you back.
You see, you are separated from Him and like a parent with a little child,
getting you back is all He cares about!

You were His when you were in the womb. You remained His
until you were old enough
to reach the age of accountability.
When you are able to consciously decide to act upon your desire to sin (with your free will)
you are no longer young enough to be in His state of grace.

Once you reach this age you are in need of salvation. My wife and son were aged three
when they believed and received Jesus into their hearts. I was ten and my daughter was five.
Later on I turned away from God out of bitterness but He mercifully brought me back later on.
When it comes to forgiveness from God it doesn't matter how far you have journeyed from Him
or how much you've done in your separation from Him. God's love through Jesus Christ
is available to immediately forgive and cleanse from all sin.
He is ready to receive the whole world if each one were to repent.
God does the saving. So come to Him as you are.

"For God so loved the world that he gave his one and only Son, that whoever believes in him shall
not perish but have eternal life" (John 3:16).

So when we think of Nebuchadnezzar
and the power of God to save and forgive
it can cause us to love,
worship,
glorify and magnify God when we see what was possible for a man so afflicted and lost.
In God's sight he was no more lost than the next man.
God is a refuge for all mankind.

If you are willing then He is able.

455

"The eternal God is **your** refuge," (Deuteronomy 33:27a).

No one is meant to be left behind in eternity.

Are you old?
Are you a rank sinner?

Do you consider yourself unreachable
or have been told you are unreachable?

Have you seen friends and loved ones slip into a godless eternity
maybe cursing God in their last breath?

Don't follow those who are lost like one sheep follows another.
You were created for more than that.

If your plan is to choose an eternity with lost people
you will be sorely disappointed.
They are going to vanish on the other side.
So will you if you won't acknowledge God - until after your physical death.
Of a certainty, one way or the other you are going to acknowledge God.

It is written: 'As surely as I live,' says the Lord, 'every knee will bow before me; every tongue will
confess to God' (Romans 14:11).

After this life He will be your supreme friend.
You will behold Him with all joy.

Or He will be the unyielding Truth before whom you bow with a regret
that beggars the imagination.

God is asking to become your refuge and God is love.

456

"The eternal God is your refuge, and underneath are the everlasting arms" (Deuteronomy 33:27a,b).

If you choose to, you will be held there in His arms as His precious treasure.
He becomes your safe place and proves Himself in every trial you will face!
The resting place of your soul.
The One who faithfully provides the desire of your heart in perfect timing.

"Delight yourself in the Lord and he will give you the desires of your heart" (Psalm 37:4).

Dear Reader, neither material blessing nor possession
can ever satisfy this craving inside.
You might identify the craving
as a longing for the truth.
It may feel like you are consumed at times with a loneliness or longing for love though you are surrounded by those who think well of you. Or you may dwell in the midst of ambivalence or a real threat of evil upon you and your children.

"The eternal God is your refuge and underneath are the everlasting arms. He will drive out your enemy before you, saying 'Destroy him!' " (Deuteronomy 33:27).

457

Your Saviour is a realist.

He knows for the time being while mankind has a free-will they will lay claim to the entitlement to wrong their fellow man. Man is prone to harm others and to harm themselves.

Do you have someone to take care of you
or are you working hard on taking care of yourself?
How wonderful it is if you have an All Powerful God to keep you.
What a blessing it is to entrust yourself,
your family members and friends
to a compassionate God.

"The Lord himself goes before you and will be with you; he will never leave you nor forsake you. Do not be afraid; do not be discouraged." (Deuteronomy 31:8).

In the midst of your trials you will have a friend alongside.

His name is Jesus.

"Then Nebuchadnezzar said, "Praise be to the God of Shadrach, Meshach and Abednego, who has sent his angel and rescued his servants! They trusted in him and defied the king's command and were willing to give up their lives rather than serve or worship any god except their own God." (Daniel 3:28).

Shadrach Meshach and Abednego each had their own relationship with God!

With faithful people God is able and He responds to their need in supernatural ways.
In this verse we see that God sent his angel to rescue His servants.

He is so invested in His people that each sheep in His care can say with utmost confidence,

He is my God
I belong to Him
He will take care of me.

"But the Lord is faithful, and he will strengthen and protect you from the evil one," (2 Thessalonians 3:3).

When you accept Jesus Christ as your Saviour He is your 'own' God.
He is so invested in you that you may call Him 'your own'.

This God is able to take care of you on every level.

At times do you feel incapable of serving Him or walking with Him?

Dear Reader - He is able.

He is greater than the sum of all of your weakness.

"if we are faithless, he will remain faithful, for he cannot disown himself" (2 Timothy 2:13).

He will not lose you Dear Reader!
Do you think it is possible for you to wander off
and prevent Him from caring for you?

"So He told them this parable, saying, "What man among you, if he has a hundred sheep and has lost one of them, does not leave the ninety-nine in the open pasture and go after the one which is lost until he finds it? "When he has found it, he lays it on his shoulders, rejoicing. "And when he comes home, he calls together his friends and his neighbours, saying to them 'Rejoice with me, for I have found my sheep which was lost!' "I tell you that in the same way, there will be more joy in heaven over one sinner who repents than over ninety-nine righteous persons who need no repentance." (Luke 15:3-7).

Oh Dear Reader,
Jesus says 'Rejoice with me, for I have found MY sheep!'

How He boasts over you!
It says He will pick you up with strength and joy and love
to lay you over His shoulders and bring you home to safety!
This is not the picture of a vengeful, nasty God out to squash people
who suffer with the consequences of sin and human weakness.
He already knows what we are capable of in our treatment of others and of ourselves.
He came to seek and to save that which was lost!

"Yet man is born to trouble as surely as sparks fly upward." (Job 5:7).
"For the Son of Man came to seek and to save what was lost." (Luke 19:10).

He goes after you.

He stays faithful to you
beyond your human understanding of what faithfulness is.
He pulls you out of all harm.

He pursues every person with only a heart of love and concern.

460

If you are confronted in your path of life by Jesus Christ consider the effort He has made to find you.

Consider also how graciously He approaches you. He has a gift to give you.
Reflect for a moment or longer even,
the timing and peril that has compelled Him to search you out!
You have not found Him. Rather, He has sought you out and has found you.

"For this is what the Sovereign Lord says: I myself will search for my sheep and look after them. As a shepherd looks after his scattered flock when he is with them, so will I look after my sheep. I will rescue them from all the places where they were scattered on a day of clouds and darkness" (Ezekiel 34:11-12).

Now then, I beg of you
do not turn away Someone
who has so much love for you.

He has left all others to pursue you.
Think of the power of God's love able to break through all manner of evil so that you are free to choose Light instead of darkness.
You are that important to Him.

You are important.

If you have started your journey with Him
He is the One to bring you through all
that lay ahead!

"The one who calls you is faithful and he will do it." (1 Thessalonians 5:24).
"being confident of this, that he who began a good work in you [He] will carry it on to completion until the day of Christ Jesus." (Philippians 1:6).

You will make it and your loving God will always be with you.

So great is His love for you Dear Reader!

461

This devotional has been a journey sharing many special moments of discovery.

Woven through bible verses and thoughts is the wondrous truth
that you are already loved very deeply.

Yes, that means you sitting there in prison.

It means you with a bottle of liquor half empty.
It means you precious young girl after being used in your innocence.
It means you serious church person working so hard
to be good enough for God to love you
and notice you.

You need to accept so completely
the invitation Jesus gives you.
Jesus shows you your true value.
Your value is so great it cannot be measured against all the riches of this earth.
Jesus is able to restore your innocence.
We have all lost our innocence somehow.

The purpose of these daily writings has been to invite you, implore you to discover these truths directly from the Truth Himself!
Don't be satisfied any longer with what others have told you about Jesus.

Don't be turned off by what others are doing in His holy name.
A lot of these folks don't know the Lord. In their own strength they are trying
to get to know Him but they still only know 'about' Him.

Experience Him for yourself!

Are you in a prison right now? This is the perfect time to open your heart to the reality of God's
love and forgiveness in your life. The work that God will do each moment in your heart cannot
be taken away from you by any person or spiritual power. Your walk with Jesus will redeem
every second you are on the inside. When God establishes something in your life as the builder,
He then becomes the watchman over it to preserve and keep it.

This is your opportunity to grow in grace each day.
Consider this time to be the richest of your entire life!

A spiritual gold mine in Christ Jesus.

462

Have you been searching for a greater reality of God in your life?

You already believe and are saved.

Yet you feel like you have been in a spiritual whirlpool
going round and round for years.
You have always had lots of good things to do.
You are blessed with all the right friends.

You take in great teaching and meetings but it occurs to you
there is no consuming personal touch from God.

Dear Reader, He is your bridegroom.
With the approaching marriage supper of the Lamb,
it is an important time to draw near to your betrothed!
You are meant to be enthralled with Him just as you would
the wonderful person you are to be joined with in marriage.

When you stand face to face with Him what a relief to exclaim,
'Thank you dear Jesus my Friend. We are finally together'.

The Holy Spirit is preparing you for this.
He is the One to prevent you from sinking exasperation after this life
should you look into Jesus eyes with hopeless despair thinking,
'I don't know you, I only know about you. Where did my life go?'

Dear Reader, you are on the right track.
Your persistence to read this book through to the end has helped
examine the deep need for God we all have in common.
There is a reason God had you select or receive this book.
It is all about the promise of relationship held out for you
in our marvellous Saviour Jesus Christ.
It will never
be too late at any time in this life
for you to turn to Him.

It will always be His perfect timing for you to take His hand right now.

463

Jesus scooped up little children into His arms.

When He walked upon the earth He loved and focused upon people one at a time.

Children know when someone is just putting up with them.
Children ran to Jesus.
He celebrated their uniqueness and invited them to experience His love first hand.
Those little children did not have to sit quietly in rows.
They did not need a special expertise nor be in the right denomination
or have a special religious zeal!
He did not favour or select out a certain individual, gifting, talent or ability with a particular child.
Jesus instructed that they be immediately brought to Him.
There were no conditions to fulfill.

God began a new experience of relationship with mankind with the arrival of Jesus upon the earth.
It was a new time of forgiveness and new life
in this precious Son of God.

"Jesus said, 'Let the little children come to me, and do not hinder them, for the kingdom of heaven belongs to such as these.' " (Matthew 19:14).

Jesus Christ receives all who come to Him. When He received the children He saw a perfect time to teach those around Him who were watching. The children were His example of how uncomplicated it is to inherit the kingdom of God.
Each and every child is special.

It would be impossible to separate out one child from the next
as the better,
or more exemplary,
or more deserving of God's loving attention.

God will always love *you* Dear Reader.

The measure of His love for you is stated as such:
God the Father loves you the same as He loves His own Son Jesus Christ the Lord.
Jesus prayed to His Father,

"you sent me and have loved them even as you have loved me" (John 17:23c).

464

Then they asked him, "What must we do to do the works God requires?" Jesus answered,
"The work of God is this: to believe in the one he has sent." (John 6:28-29).

'What must we do to do the works God requires?'

Jesus answers with a declaration. 'Believe in Me!'
Spiritual freedom is now possible
for all mankind!

Jesus Christ. Your true-to-life superhero.
He conquered.
He rescues.
He saves.
He delivers from sin and the power of hell and He has come for you!

"Therefore God exalted him to the highest place and gave him the name that is above every name,
that at the name of Jesus every knee should bow, in heaven and on earth and under the earth, and
every tongue confess that Jesus Christ is Lord, to the glory of God the Father" (Philippians 2:9-11).

The blind man asks Jesus, 'how shall I do the works of God?'
The paraplegic asks as well.
So does the mute person.

How about the old man or woman with small resources, little strength,
no one who understands them
and no friends?

"let the weak say, I am strong." (Joel 3:10b).

Most old people have no visitors or someone who cares enough to check in on them to see how they are doing.

Many women in our world would ask Jesus the question, 'What do I do to do the works of God?'
Her culture, family or community may forbid her from exercising her rights
without the correct approval.

What of those who started following Jesus ten, twenty, thirty years ago?
What work does Jesus require of them?
Do they have 'different' more privileged works?

Are some disqualified from the 'works of God' because they don't have a favourable appearance
or present themselves in the prescribed manner?

Many folks live in a place where Christianity is forbidden.
They have to hide when they assemble and they live their faith secretly.
Do they cease to 'let their light shine' as a result?
Do they miss out on a whole range of God's 'works' if they are put to death because of their faith?
Some of our brothers and sisters in the faith have a short life span as result.

If a follower of Jesus is hanged, shot or tortured to death within two weeks of being born again
have they seriously missed out on 'the works of God?'

Jesus has declared that all are saved who believe in Him.
Your works or Christian service is not applied to your debt of sin.
Nor do your works - no matter how great - enhance His estimation of your worth in His sight.

The blood of Jesus has obliterated the power of sin and you are set free through faith in Jesus Christ.

"For Christ died for sins once for all, the righteous for the unrighteous, to bring you to God"
(1 Peter 3:18a).

Dear Reader, Jesus Christ has earned for you a position of great privilege.

You have liberty to go to Him yourself and ask, 'what are God's works for me?'
This is an intelligent and supremely well informed question.

That is because the enquiry is directed straight to the Author and Finisher of faith.

Jesus Christ is presently seated at the right hand of the Father in heaven
and is always interceding for you. He is the One to speak to.
He is the author and perfecter of your faith
and no one else.
There isn't an organization on earth that is worthy of the trust that rightfully belongs to Jesus.

Your love and support, 'yes.'

But not the trust deserved only by Jesus.

"Let God be true, and every man a liar" (Romans 3:4a).

"And God placed all things under his feet and appointed him to be head over everything for the
church, which is his body, the fullness of him who fills everything in every way"
(Ephesians 1:22-23).
"Trust in the Lord with all your heart and lean not on your own understanding; in ALL your ways
acknowledge him, and he will make your paths straight" (Proverbs 3:5,6).

It does not matter what title the ruling members of a church assign themselves.
Even if it sounds like:
The Super Extreme Counsel and Assembly of the Apostolic Prophetic Wise and Learned
Specially Convened Group of Men Totally Direct From GOD.
In spite of the window dressing
no one is entitled to tell you what God's plan is for your life.
A true man or woman of God will serve you,
love you,
and encourage you to exercise your own franchise of faith.
They will compel you to get alone with God and hear from Him
just as they should be doing!

You get the idea,
don't be deceived by window dressing.
Let no assembly on earth take the place of Jesus in your life.

It is critical to read the New Testament yourself, ask Jesus to save you and invite Him to guide you
with the bible and with the word He sends to your heart.

467

So you go ahead.

Talk to Jesus yourself and let the Holy Spirit work through the bible to speak to you.

That is exactly where one should seek for wisdom and understanding.

Here is a beautiful boast from the book called Hebrews in the bible.

"Let us fix our eyes on Jesus, the author and perfecter [or 'finisher'] of our faith" (Hebrews 12:2a).

Your need to depend upon God is the same now as it was when you first believed.
Only Jesus can bring to you the blessing of new life.

When you read the following scripture please ask yourself,
'which great leader in my organisation can take the place of Jesus in my life?'

Has your leadership demanded you look to them for your instruction thereby taking upon them the stature only Jesus should have? Who has died for your sin and then been raised from the dead?

Do you see why no ordinary human being can take the place of God's only Son
Jesus Christ the Righteous?

Have they written additional texts and held them up as equivalent to the Holy Bible?
If your leadership does not encourage you to read the New Testament for yourself and to receive salvation by grace through faith in our precious Jesus Christ alone without the need for works - then seek for fellowship with those who do.

You have permission to leave.

"David said about him: 'I saw the Lord always before me. Because he is at my right hand, I will not be shaken. Therefore my heart is glad and my tongue rejoices; my body also will live in hope, because you will not abandon me to the grave, nor will you let your Holy One see decay. You have made known to me the paths of life; you will fill me with joy in your presence' " (Acts 2:25-28).

I ask you, who will fill you with joy in God's presence?
Who will make known to you the paths of life?
Who will not abandon you to the grave?

Jesus!
That's who!
Neither man nor earthly organisation can do these things.

Abandon your faith in all others for your salvation.

"Salvation is found in no one else, for there is no other name under heaven given to men by which we must be saved." (Acts 4:12).

When asked, 'what must we do to do the works of God?,' Jesus answers with a wonderful, liberating truth!

The answer is the very cornerstone of your walk with God.

He told them their 'work' was to believe in the one God has sent.
Believe in Him.
The Truth is available to all who will come to God through Jesus Christ.

"In the beginning was the Word, and the Word was with God, and the Word was God" (John 1:1).
"Beyond all question, the mystery of godliness is great: He appeared in a body, was vindicated by the Spirit, was seen by angels, was preached among the nations, was believed on in the world, was taken up in glory" (1 Timothy 3:16).

The works of God do not refer to physical works at all!

Your work is that you come near to God yourself.
It is the manner in which a bride fulfills the desire of her heart.
Her longing is only satisfied when with her bridegroom.
Whiling away the hours.
Delighting in one another.
Getting to know each other more intimately.
In their hearts they know there will be so much more to share once they are wed.

"You yourselves can testify that I said, 'I am not the Christ but am sent ahead of him. The bride belongs to the bridegroom. The friend who attends the bridegroom waits and listens for him, and is full of joy when he hears the bridegroom's voice. That joy is mine, and it is now complete" (John 3:28-29).

Those words were spoken by John the Baptist.
Jesus, the bridegroom, had arrived.
John no longer had to wait and the joy was his.

This joy can also be yours Dear Reader!

Jesus is the only source of true spiritual food.

This is the same as a branch receiving life from the vine. It is a Good Shepherd living there in the midst of His flock day and night recognizing that He alone is the source of safety, provision and life for His sheep.

"Our forefathers ate the manna in the desert; as it is written: 'He gave them bread from heaven to eat.'" Jesus said to them, "I tell you the truth, it is not Moses who has given you the bread from heaven, but it is my Father who gives you the true bread from heaven. For the bread of God is he who comes down from heaven and gives life to the world." "Sir," they said, "from now on give us this bread." Then Jesus declared, "I am the bread of life. He who comes to me will never go hungry, and he who believes in me will never be thirsty" (John 6:31-35).

Jesus named His heavenly Father as the One who gives unto mankind the bread of life.
Similarly, it is clearly stated that even Moses did not have the means, stature, power,
glory or favour to be the source of the Bread of Life.
This remains true today ever since that time. Any man or woman would be a fool
to lay claim to a position even Moses dared not aspire to.
Moses and Elijah spoke with Jesus on the mount of Transfiguration.
Even this profound event did not make them equal to God.
There is no one outside of Jesus who has the words of life.
If even Moses is not worthy, how could any person be foolish enough
to commend themselves to provide a new dispensation
of God's word for the entire human race?

No man is God. No man is equal to Jesus Christ.
Only Jesus was and is eternally God.
Do not seek the Bread of Life through any religion or cult or person.
Man cannot give you this Bread.

'I am the vine; you are the branches. If a man remains in me and I in him, he will bear much fruit; apart from me you can do nothing. If anyone does not remain in me, he is like a branch that is thrown away and withers; such branches are picked up, thrown into the fire and burned. If you remain in me and my words remain in you, ask whatever you wish, and it will be given you. This is to my Father's glory, that you bear much fruit, showing yourselves to be my disciples' (John 15:5-8).

Jesus said, 'I am the vine.' There is no one else to abide in.
And no one else will ever, ever be assigned to take His place.

470

Jesus said, 'I am the Bread of Life.'

When the people heard this they immediately associated Him with the manna provided by God in the wilderness.

They linked 'the works of God' with the manner God kept their forefathers alive.

They saw immediately that 'manna' and the 'works of God'
were one in the same.

In the wilderness
all
they
could
do
was
wander.

There were no works to be done.

There were no 'works of God.'
All they did was walk, walk, and walk.
There was only wandering and wandering all day long for 40 years.

Since that time Jesus Christ has been sent by God to solve the spiritual needs
of His beloved Jewish people along with all the rest of mankind.

"There is neither Jew nor Greek, slave nor free, male nor female, for you are all one in Christ Jesus.
If you belong to Christ, then you are Abraham's seed, and heirs according to the promise"
(Galatians 3:28-29).
And so all Israel will be saved, as it is written: 'The deliverer will come from Zion; he will turn
godlessness away from Jacob. And this is my covenant with them when I take away their sins'
(Romans 11:26-27).

When the people heard God the Son say this about being the Bread of Life
there would no longer be a 'wandering in the wilderness'.

They could be in a position to do whatever God would ask of them.
Jesus said mankind only had to 'believe in Him.'

They said, 'ok, in the past God gave manna to sustain us.
How will believing in You sustain us now?'

Here is the wisdom of God Dear Believer.
There are no 'works of God' that make you saved.

Jesus has completed this once and for all time for only one reason - to save you.

"But when this priest [Jesus] had offered for all time one sacrifice for sins, he sat down at the right
hand of God. Since that time he waits for his enemies to be made his footstool, because by one
sacrifice he has made perfect forever those who are being made holy" (Hebrews 10:12-14).

You are not in favour with God ever, based upon how well you perform.

He does not love you based upon what you do,
how much you do,
how big your work is,
how many friends you have,
how long you have had your friends,
what church you belong to,
you go to church faithfully or not,
how many people say you are a great man or woman of God,
whether you are in debt or not,
healthy or not,
rich or not,
traveled or not,
done missions or not,
done street witnessing or not,
'feel' saved or not,
succeed in business or not,
give a lot of money to your church or not,
served God a long time or not,
people think well of you or not,
have the right family name or not,
your family helped establish the church you attend,
your dad is in the ministry or not
or can afford to dress the right way or not.
I have had to sort through all of these religious things in my short life.

Dear Reader, there is no boasting about anything.
Jesus calls all the sheep by name but not on the basis of their importance assigned to them
by others. 'Importance' is a human thing. We attribute importance to people, places, things and
situations. We can't see the human heart like God does.
God justifies freely and receives all people equally. All are loved the same.
It is unconditional love and you are included!
Your salvation will never depend upon you doing any sort of act of service for God.
How blessed it is to live your life as God's friend.

Here is a prayer from the book of Ephesians requesting the greatest blessing of God.
It is meant for you.
You can also pray it for other people - that they may know Him better.

"I keep asking that the God of our Lord Jesus Christ, the glorious Father, may give you the Spirit of
wisdom and revelation, so that you may know him better" (Ephesians 1:17).

The gift of God is available to all who desire it. It is unconditionally given.

God sees such great value in all people and will freely save anyone.

All they have to do is come to Him and ask. There is no need to sign anything.
The thief on the cross beside Jesus didn't sign anything.
There is no need to acknowledge any other man.
Only Jesus.

There are no 'levels' once you are saved.
It is a scourge to the family of God to set up one above another
as being more entitled or superior spiritually.
A nasty scourge upon the sheep of God.
Therefore it is a nasty scourge upon Jesus, for what is done to the least of these is done to Jesus.

"Jesus called them together and said, "You know that those who are regarded as rulers of the Gentiles lord it over them, and their high officials exercise authority over them. Not so with you. Instead, whoever wants to become great among you must be your servant, and whoever wants to be first must be slave of all. For even the Son of Man did not come to be served but to serve, and to give his life as a ransom for many" (Mark 10:42-45).

"For the kingdom of heaven is like a landowner who went out early in the morning to hire men to work in his vineyard. He agreed to pay them a denarius for the day and sent them into his vineyard. "About the third hour he went out and saw others standing in the marketplace doing nothing. He told them, 'You also go and work in my vineyard, and I will pay you whatever is right.' So they went. "He went out again about the sixth hour and the ninth hour and did the same thing. About the eleventh hour he went out and found still others standing around. He asked them, 'Why have you been standing here all day long doing nothing?' "'Because no one has hired us,' they answered. "He said to them, 'You also go and work in my vineyard.' "When evening came, the owner of the vineyard said to his foreman, 'Call the workers and pay them their wages, beginning with the last ones hired and going on to the first.' "The workers who were hired about the eleventh hour came and each received a denarius. So when those came who were hired first, they expected to receive more. But each one of them also received a denarius.
When they received it, they began to grumble against the landowner. 'These men who were hired last worked only one hour,' they said, 'and you have made them equal to us who have borne the burden of the work and the heat of the day.' "But he answered one of them, 'Friend, I am not being unfair to you. Didn't you agree to work for a denarius? Take your pay and go. I want to give the man who was hired last the same as I gave you. Don't I have the right to do what I want with my own money? Or are you envious because I am generous?' "So the last will be first, and the first will be last." "What you have done to the least you have done unto Me" (Matthew 20:1-20).

Oh my God,
there will be an accounting one day for the leaders who pushed aside
the weak, humble ambassadors of the King of Kings imagining themselves to be
more informed, knowledgeable, superior and entitled.
I tell those in leadership who don't have time for Jesus,
if you don't repent you will reap judgement
and the money of your wage will burn in your pockets one day when you stand before Him.
The judgement for your empty sermons awaits you.
You knew about Jesus. You did not pay the price to 'know' Jesus.

" 'Make a tree good and its fruit will be good, or make a tree bad and its fruit will be bad, for a tree is recognized by its fruit. You brood of vipers, how can you who are evil say anything good? For the mouth speaks what the heart is full of. A good man brings good things out of the good stored up in him, and an evil man brings evil thing out of the evil stored up in him. But I tell you that everyone will have to give account on the day of judgment for every empty word they have spoken. For by your words you will be acquitted, and by your words you will be condemned' " (Matthew 12:33-37).

You took a wage on the backs of the sheep of God. You rode those dear sheep as your paycheque thinking your mess would hold up as the 'works of God.'

"That servant who knows his master's will and does not get ready or does not do what his master wants will be beaten with many blows. But the one who does not know and does the things deserving punishment will be beaten with few blows. From everyone who has been given much, much will be demanded; and from the one who has been entrusted with much, much more will be asked." (Luke 12:47-48).

Precious Reader, does this verse help you to see why I have written in most uncompromising terms about leaders in the church?

Even if they go to heaven, what a miserable way to start your eternity, being disciplined in front of all mankind. Shown for what they are - an unfit leader who has done so much harm to the Lord Jesus that they deserve to be 'beaten with blows.' Punished for wilfully afflicting God and His people. In the King James Version it says these individuals will be "worthy of stripes" - which is like getting the strap when you have been disobedient as a child.

In His mercy God gives everyone an opportunity to repent while there is still time.

God loves and receives all sinners, even a vile sinner like the career minister of the Gospel who makes merchandise of God's people.

"For it is by grace you have been saved, through faith - and this not from yourselves, it is the gift of God - not by works, so that no one can boast. For we are God's workmanship, created in Christ Jesus to do good works, which God prepared in advance for us to do" (Ephesians 2:8-10).

"Because of the Lord's great love we are not consumed, for his compassions never fail" (Lamentations 3:22).

Jesus calls you to a lifetime of loving relationship.

The span of your life on this earth is only a beginning.

It is a time of beginnings.

Getting to know one another will bring you through many trials in this short life.
After this life you will finally be united with your God in intimacy of heart
like a man and woman fulfill their betrothal
to finally become husband and wife!

"Then a voice came from the throne, saying: "Praise our God, all you his servants, you who fear him, both small and great!" Then I heard what sounded like a great multitude, like the roar of rushing waters and like loud peals of thunder, shouting: "Hallelujah! For our Lord God Almighty reigns. Let us rejoice and be glad and give him glory! For the wedding of the Lamb has come, and his bride has made herself ready. Fine linen, bright and clean, was <u>given</u> her to wear." Then the angel said to me, "Write: 'Blessed are those who are invited to the wedding supper of the Lamb!'" And he added, "these are the true words of God" (Revelations 19:5-9).

There is no need to hurry
when you are walking with God.

In the end your fine linen, bright and clean, will be *given* to you!
You neither have to earn nor bring this important part of your preparations with you!
It will be given to you!
There is no need to hurry because your wedding date is already set!
You are going to be there because of His grace.

Get to know the bridegroom now before the blessed marriage supper.
Just as it is with a human betrothal
you enjoy the presence of your intended
in the sweet time that leads to marriage.
That time of being engaged,
of having a fiancé,
is unlike any other time in your life.
It is filled with the great wonder of your betrothed leading up to a marriage supper
of celebration and new beginnings.

After the wedding date you will be together forever!

Jesus Christ reaches out to you because He has an enormous heart of love.

The answer to your deep need is not found by busily
going to and fro working in the name of God.

"Whoever tries to keep his life will lose it, and whoever loses his life will preserve it" (Luke 17:33).

He did not see mission's trips and giving money and saying the right things and not upsetting anybody and doing things for Him as the answer. If you are doing things for God because you think it will make Him happier with you then you are trying to save or 'keep' your own life.

The bible says you are not actually able to save your life at all
if you feel God's love for you is based upon your 'good works'.

"Whoever tries to keep his life will lose it, and whoever loses his life will preserve it" (Luke 17:33).

Surrender your heart and soul to the fellowship of God. That is all He is asking for.
Give up on any other means of salvation.
Give up on trying to be good enough.
Give up trusting in that paper you signed pledging allegiance to the founder of your group!
To trust only in Jesus Christ to save and forgive means you will be 'losing your life'.
This means, you will not be working for God to earn His love.
Salvation is a free gift for all who put their faith in Jesus Christ alone.

Intimacy with Jesus is the beginning of a life of ministry rooted in God's love.
Even if all you are doing for God is stripped from you one day
the intimate fellowship can't be taken away.

I heard of a missionary once, who was told on the foreign field where he had worked a long time that he was to do a certain thing. His head office was unmoved when he told them he was persuaded that God wanted him to do another thing entirely. They told him if he did what God was telling him to do they would take his denominational papers *and* take away his pension - which was not legal. He obeyed God. They took away his papers and broke the law by taking away the pension he had paid into for a long time. They rejected him and cast him out of the fellowship. The wonderful history of works he had done was outwardly stripped away by other church people. This dear brother and his loving wife were upheld however.
They had an intimate relationship with Jesus Christ, not with their organisation or it's leadership. Please, join with me in prayer today for this dear couple and all those within the ministry who continue faithfully to follow Jesus.

"Mary has chosen what is better, and it will not be taken away from her" (Luke 10:42b).

Dear Reader, please know that ministry comes in seasons. It is subject to change.
Sometimes the change is out of our control.
Life presents us with doors that open and close.

Friend, at a time like that, all you will have is Jesus.
But I tell you the truth today - it is enough.

That is why Jesus also told Mary, 'only one thing is needed.'

475

Dear Reader, at one time we were all lost like sheep without a shepherd.

"When Jesus landed and saw a large crowd, he had compassion on them, because they were like sheep without a shepherd. So he began teaching them many things" (Mark 6:34).

Jesus saw their need and was moved with compassion.
He immediately met their need
by teaching them.

He spoke to them.

Those that were listening availed themselves
of the very assistance they needed.

"Jesus Christ is the same yesterday and today and forever" (Hebrews 13:8).

Once you receive Jesus your Shepherd
the answer to your eternal need is to stay close to your wonderful Jesus Christ from then on.
Your need was to be forgiven of sin and transformed through the born-again experience.
Once forgiven, you abide in Him to receive His rest and care
until one day - one glorious day - you are standing with Him in eternity.

Standing with the Friend of all friends.

Once rooted and grounded in the fellowship of His love your activities will bear much fruit.
That is because you actually know the Person you are representing.
Somehow, though you are a weak and frail human being,
His love will be shed abroad from your heart.

You will love as Jesus loves!

"A new command I give you: Love one another. As I have loved you, so you must love one another.
By this all men will know that you are my disciples, if you love one another" (John 13:34-35).

"Let no debt remain outstanding, except the continuing debt to love one another for he who loves his fellowman has fulfilled the law" (Romans 13:8a).

476

"But many who saw them leaving recognized them and ran on foot from all the towns and got there ahead of them. When Jesus landed [in a small boat] and saw a large crowd, he had compassion on them, because they were like sheep without a shepherd. So he began teaching them many things" (Mark 6:33-34).

Jesus had mercy on those who ran after Him.

Once they caught up to Him the love of His heart overflowed
and He began to teach them many things.

He understood their need and He responded by speaking to them.
He did not separate them into groups and tell them to think up things and get busy!
No one was made to feel less than adequate -
with Jesus.

"The teachers of the law and the Pharisees brought in a woman caught in adultery. They made her stand before the group and said to Jesus, "Teacher, this woman was caught in the act of adultery. In the Law Moses commanded us to stone such women. Now what do you say?" They were using this question as a trap, in order to have a basis for accusing him. But Jesus bent down and started to write on the ground with his finger. When they kept on questioning him, he straightened up and said to them, "If any one of you is without sin, let him be the first to throw a stone at her." Again he stooped down and wrote on the ground. At this, those who heard began to go away one at a time, the older ones first, until only Jesus was left, with the woman still standing there. Jesus straightened up and asked her, "Woman, where are they? Has no one condemned you?" "No one, sir," she said. "Then neither do I condemn you," Jesus declared. "Go now and leave your life of sin" (John 8:3-11).
"For God did not send his Son into the world to condemn the world, but to save the world through him" (John 3:17).
"Therefore, there is now no condemnation for those who are in Christ Jesus, because through Christ Jesus the law of the Spirit of life set me free from the law of sin and death" (Romans 8:1-2).

477

A son or daughter will give anything to hear mother or father say to them, 'I love you dear one.'
'I am so proud of you.'
'How are you today sweet-heart?'

A child settles nicely when a parent is consistently interested in hearing
the opinion of their little heart and mind.

A loving parent can be counted upon
to protect their sweet little child.

Great paintings on display have
a perimeter,
a cordon,
many guards,
a security system,
alarms and cameras in place.

All of this is in case someone puts a little teeny fingerprint
upon these works of art.

How much more the child in your care?
How much more valuable is a child?
I ask you today how much more valuable is a child, and in need of being kept
from unwanted 'fingerprints' of an abuser?

I once heard it said, 'it only happened once.'
Not with our most precious paintings and artefacts.
They are not to be touched!
How is it everyone finds this so much easier to understand?

How carefully each child has to be taken care of.

478

Hearing kind words from a parent is surely better than the sound of any music ever written.

No matter what happens out there in the world
a loving parent is safe harbour,
a listening ear,
a warm meal,
a believing heart,
a laundry load or two and one day perhaps a babysitter!

A mother or father who listens to the voice of their child
has given them a gift beyond any treasure.

That child feels complete.
They are grounded against the tides of the world.
The future is within their grasp for they can get up
and keep on going when the storms
of life assail them.

A child needs a parent to love them.

Nothing says 'love' more than listening to your child.

479

There is something about our need to be loved.

No matter what we have done we still need to feel valued.

When we live without God He knows this.
He reaches out.
No wonder young and old alike ran to Jesus.

They felt valued.
He knows before you do
that you just need to be valued
no matter what you have done.

When you accept His forgiveness and enter into His care
His kind and loving words become your bread.

Those precious words of Jesus enable you to live.
Jesus Himself,
becomes your salvation.
The things He says and does become your anchor, future and safe harbour.

The bible says He is a refuge, a safe place
a strong tower.

"The name of the Lord is a strong tower; the righteous run to it and are safe" (Proverbs 18:10).

Dear Reader, you go ahead and do that!
Run to your strong tower who is the Lord Jesus Christ!
Make the movement into your safe place by going aside to be alone with Him.
Let Him surround you with His everlasting love.
Nothing else on earth compares
to the safety of the love of Jesus.
No apostle,
prophet,
pastor,
teacher,
evangelist,
head office,

doctrinal statement,
theological degree,
paycheque, overseer or the leader of a home meeting
compares to the Son of God.

"Therefore God exalted him to the highest place and gave him the name that is above every name,"
(Philippians 2:9).

480

"Then the Lord said to Moses, "I will rain down bread from heaven for you. The people are to go
out each day and gather enough for that day" (Exodus 16:4a,b).
"Then Jesus declared, "I am the bread of life. He who comes to me will never go hungry, and he
who believes in me will never be thirsty" (John 6:35).

There wasn't sufficient food in the wilderness.
God was aware of the need and sent bread from heaven.
Always enough to keep everyone alive.
He provided without fail. Each person went out to gather it for themselves.

If they collected it on the ground each morning they had enough to eat.
If they gathered a lot it was enough. If they gathered only a little,
it was also enough.

Remarkably, Jesus says He is the Bread of Life.
At the time Jesus taught this truth his listeners had no trouble associating this
with the need of their forefathers to collect and eat the manna in the wilderness.

They would never go hungry.
They were in God's care.

Jesus taught that they could be assured of their future because He is the Bread of Life.

"Then Jesus declared, "I am the bread of life. He who comes to me will never go hungry, and he
who believes in me will never be thirsty" (John 6:35).

481

Like the manna in the wilderness, each person who goes out to get what they need for the day
will be sustained.

Just as physical food sustained life in the desert,
spiritual food is essential if we are to remain
in our own path of Life.

"I have set the Lord always before me. Because he is at my right hand, I will not be shaken" (Psalm 16:8).

"You have made known to me the path of life; you will fill me with joy in your presence, with eternal pleasures at your right hand" (Psalm 16:11).

"I am the vine; you are the branches. If you remain in me and I in you, you will bear much fruit; apart from me you can do nothing" (John 15:5).

There you are Dear Reader!

Does it seem more real now when you consider the words of Jesus - 'remain in Me'?

How much more sensible it is to be a follower of Jesus based upon your relationship with Him, rather than how you present yourself to others on His behalf.
Or become an expert for Him.
There is no such thing as 'measuring up' or being 'good enough'!
It is all by grace and Jesus will call each sheep by name one day.

Matthew 25:40 " 'The King will reply, 'I tell you the truth, whatever you did for one of the least of these brothers of mine, you did for me.' "

Unconditionally you are accepted and loved
by Jesus Christ.

Say the name. Jesus Christ.

"They overcame him by the blood of the Lamb and by the word of their testimony; they did not love their lives so much as to shrink from death" (Revelation 12:11).

482

Jesus Christ is 'your' Bread of Life.

That is so very important for you to know.

As you meet with Him daily you will be filled with His love.
You will be sustained with all the love you need.
He will become a deep love in your heart.

He will help you know how best to touch the lives around you.

As you sit with Him you will watch Him work.
You will see how He desires to move upon a heart or upon a situation.
As you agree with Him it is done!
Now that is power.

He is our all-powerful God after all.

"but the righteous will live by His faith" (Habakkuk 2:4b).

There are many things you can do for God.
There are many good things you can do for your neighbours and your world.
If you first take time to collect your manna each day
then Jesus will become wisdom unto you.
Your life will be pleasing to God.

This will not always be how others feel about you.

You will be misunderstood.
Some will say you are serving the devil when it's really about them
choosing not to go and collect their own manna.
They will feel you are strange and uncouth
when you don't bow down to their idols of tradition, religion,
the fear of man
and the flesh.

None the less, you will feel loved and valued by your God
just as you should.
It will still break your heart at times
to see things as God does.

You will feel inwardly full through the wonderful fellowship
of the Holy Spirit inside of you.
Daily He will reassure you,
'everything is alright'
'everything is ok'
'all is well.'

You will have the peace that passes all understanding and be strengthened by God's personal word
each day.

483

When you wonder sometimes how much God loves you as I often have, He will tenderly endear
Himself to you saying, 'I have loved you with an everlasting love.'

If a dark shadow seems cast upon your life because you feel you have missed the mark
He is right there to say, 'I have led you every step of the way.'

Remember, this will be because you have been abiding in the Vine.

All things leading up to that occasion have unfolded
in His care,
His wisdom
and in His plan
to refine and shape you as the clay in His hand.

He is slowly and steadily becoming closer and closer
as your friend
though you pass through many trials!
Through the good times and the hard ones.
To the faithful
He will show Himself faithful.
If you have a fellowship each day with your beautiful Jesus
He will be right there always and show Himself faithful on your behalf.

Hallelujah!

"I have loved you with an everlasting love; I have drawn you with loving-kindness" (Jeremiah 31:3b).

484

When Jesus is the Bread of Life then you understand what He is thinking about issues.

He guides you in your understanding to see things as He does.
In some instances this is called discernment.

Other times He shows you in His wonderful word, the Bible, the verses that will lavish
His understanding upon you. Always, what is written in the bible will be in accord
with what the Holy Spirit puts upon your heart.
If He feels He needs to
He shows you if His Holy Spirit
is at work in the activities around you.

Sometimes people gather in the name of God
without spending time with Jesus to receive their daily bread.
Then they gather with no desire to seek for this Bread together.
They blindly wander in the wilderness without taking time to benefit from the Bread
God is willing to send them at that very moment right from Heaven.

What a tragedy to one day
look into the face of Jesus
and see an unrecognizable stranger.

For some Jesus will be a welcome sight.

For others He will be an unknown.

For some He was their food and drink.

Others will be shaken to the core to see that Jesus had walked in their midst on many occasions without being invited to participate in the prophecy, preaching, evangelising, teaching, healing, casting out of demons, the collection of money, worshiping, baptising, dancing, shouting and praying. Imagine the surprise and dread for the pastor who once boasted with confidence of his thirty years in ministry only to find out God meant it when He said 'only one thing is needed'.

"Thus, by their fruit you will recognize them. "Not everyone who says to me, 'Lord, Lord,' will enter the kingdom of heaven, but only he who does the will of my Father who is in heaven. Many will say to me on that day, 'Lord, Lord, did we not prophesy in your name, and in your name drive out demons and perform many miracles?' Then I will tell them plainly, 'I never knew you. Away from me, you evildoers!' " (Matthew 7:20-28).

People who gather in the name of God
while excluding Jesus <u>as</u> the Bread of Life,
are bereft of the leading of the Holy Spirit.
This is a group of people agreeing among themselves to do what they think God is looking for.

Dear Reader it is a heart break beyond description that these same kind and well kept people
will one day be cast into the Lake of Fire for all eternity along with the most vile,
sordid and scandalous human beings to live without regard for God or man.

485

A leader who does not seek his or her own manna is unable to bring other people to the manna.

They will be wandering about from the start of the service to the finish.

Those few in the midst who do enjoy a fellowship with Jesus are kept busy by the Holy Spirit
as He reaches out for the lost sheep - sitting in church. Praying and agreeing with the Holy Spirit
to redeem this time being squandered while they sit in church.

There are good community service organisations in most towns that meet in a similar fashion to most North American churches. They follow rules and directions without giving a thought to humbling themselves in the presence of a Sovereign God. None of their members spend any time with God during the week. They are also assured that they are good people doing good things around the world. And this is true. Community service organisations do a lot of good!
Thank God for the good work they do helping children, seniors and business leaders.
They do a lot of good in their communities along with benevolent fund raising
and donations to hospitals and medical needs.
Usually, it is much more pleasant to be involved with these local service groups.

They are genuinely pleased with those who join their gathering.

It is also the way of the cults.
Pseudo Christian groups who think
they are the only true church on the entire planet.
Along with their own unique 'revelation' they consider everyone
who is not with them to be going to hell. All you have to do to escape hell
is belong to their group.
You join, sign the papers,
give them the amount of money they require and you're in.

Can you see why it is important to spell out the consequences
of ignoring the Bread of Life
Jesus Christ?
This strongly worded passage is in the bible. It is stronger than what I have just written.

It is written to the people who go to church.

"You hypocrites! Isaiah was right when he prophesied about you: 'These people honour me with their lips, but their hearts are far from me. They worship me in vain; their teachings are but rules taught by men.' " (Matthew 15:7-9).

Hold onto your relationship with God.

Jesus is the Bread of Life and all the Christian service in the world will not equal even a second spent alone with God.

486

When you set your sights on meeting with God you will be well fed.

Just as it was in the wilderness, the Bread given to us by God is the only safe food available.

In the wilderness it would have been apparent very quickly
if someone was failing to collect their manna.
It is the same today when you are not sustained
by the Bread that comes down from heaven.

Here is Psalm 16.
It will become the beautiful account of your walk with Jesus - your Bread of Life.

Jesus is the lover of your soul.

Jesus is the God of your salvation.

"Keep me safe, O God,
for in you I take refuge.
I said to the Lord, "You are my Lord;
apart from you I have no good thing."
As for the saints who are in the land,
they are the glorious ones in whom is all my delight.
The sorrows of those will increase who run after other gods.
I will not pour out their libations of blood or take up their names on my lips.
Lord, you have assigned me my portion and my cup;
you have made my lot secure.
The boundary lines have fallen for me in pleasant places;
surely I have a delightful inheritance.
I will praise the Lord, who counsels me;
even at night my heart instructs me.
I have set the Lord always before me.
Because he is at my right hand,
I will not be shaken.
Therefore my heart is glad and my tongue rejoices;
my body also will rest secure, because you will not abandon me to the grave,
nor will you let your Holy One see decay.
You have made known to me the path of life;
you will fill me with joy in your presence,
with eternal pleasures at your right hand" (Psalm 16).

Dear Precious Reader,
it is my prayer that you have found God's love to be everything you hoped for and more.
If you are in a difficult situation,
may you find the comfort you need by taking time to be alone
with the lover of your soul.

The truth is you are not alone.

Not only is Jesus with you but you are part of a vast network of believers all over the world.

A couple of friends said this about Alex.

I met Alex in Osoyoos, B.C. Canada. He was guest speaker for the weekend at a mutual friend's church which also housed the local prayer center. With his quiet spirit along with his gentle voice it was truly apparent to all of us in the congregation that Alex was and is a man of God, filled with the Holy Spirit. As he shared the truth from the word I could hear how importantly he was being used in engaging us in the ministering of the full gospel. We saw in him an unquenchable fire. In the five years since our first meeting, Alex has personally blessed me and my brothers and sisters in the faith with loving, teaching, preaching and doing whatever God has called him to do. Alex's character is centered on showing whoever will listen and is hungry for the Bible that Jesus - Yeshua - is Lord. Feeding God's children is what my dear brother Alex does best.
God bless, Elizabeth 'Elisheva' Messina - Intercessor. WA, USA

I am very much privileged and honoured to have an opportunity to state a few lines about the author of this spiritual devotional book. On a visit of brother Alex and Kathy to India, we met and served God for a few months at a charity for boys in central India. That was 23 years ago. God established a very serious relationship in our hearts. We celebrate and rejoice in this close, vital Spirit-led friendship to this day. A car wreck, numerous surgeries - in times of hardship Alex was sustained by God with a real comfort. These years of difficulty and severe loss proved to bring a treasure trove of spiritual revelation through the faithfulness of Jesus Christ. God has now opened the door for him to share these things with us so that we can read them and be renewed in our spiritual life. I am very grateful to our God for helping brother Alex to write this spiritual devotional book. The divine insights we see in this book came from a prayerful man of God, committed to Jesus for His glory. I also praise God for his dear wife Kathy who is a part and parcel of this wonderful work with brother Alex. I really give all glory and honour to our heavenly Father and pray that this "Spiritual Devotional Book" may be a great blessing to many by intimately knowing God and examining ourselves to get right with Jesus for His honour and glory.
Yours in His plan, Sudhir and Sunanda Ingle - Pastors. Maharashtra State, Nagpur India.

You can reach Alex at: alexgaustin@hotmail.com
He is available if you would like him to be involved in your speaking engagement. Please feel free to contact Alex directly if you want to share about your walk with Jesus, or you would like to pass along your feelings about the book.

Manufactured by Amazon.ca
Bolton, ON